Europe's Stars
of '80s Dance Pop

ALSO BY JAMES ARENA
AND FROM MCFARLAND

*Stars of 21st Century Dance Pop and EDM:
33 DJs, Producers and Singers Discuss Their Careers* (2017)

Stars of '90s Dance Pop: 29 Hitmakers Discuss Their Careers (2017)

Legends of Disco: Forty Stars Discuss Their Careers (2016)

*First Ladies of Disco: 32 Stars Discuss the Era
and Their Singing Careers* (2013)

*Fright Night on Channel 9: Saturday Night Horror Films
on New York's WOR-TV, 1973–1987* (2012)

Europe's Stars of '80s Dance Pop

32 International Music Legends Discuss Their Careers

JAMES ARENA

Forewords by Mel Brooks *and* Audrey Landers

McFarland & Company, Inc., Publishers
Jefferson, North Carolina

Unless otherwise noted, all photographs are either from the author's collection or were supplied by the artists themselves.

LIBRARY OF CONGRESS CATALOGUING-IN-PUBLICATION DATA

Names: Arena, James, 1960– interviewer.
Title: Europe's stars of '80s dance pop : 32 international music legends discuss their careers / [interviews by] James Arena ; forewords by Mel Brooks and Audrey Landers.
Description: Jefferson, North Carolina : McFarland & Company, 2017. | Includes index.
Identifiers: LCCN 2017030124 | ISBN 9781476671420 (softcover : acid free paper) ∞
Subjects: LCSH: Singers—Europe—Interviews. | Sound recording executives and producers—Europe—Interviews. | Popular music—Europe—1981–1990—History and criticism. | Disco music—Europe—History and criticism.
Classification: LCC ML3488 .E9 2017 | DDC 781.648094/09047—dc23
LC record available at https://lccn.loc.gov/2017030124

BRITISH LIBRARY CATALOGUING DATA ARE AVAILABLE

ISBN (print) 978-1-4766-7142-0
ISBN (ebook) 978-1-4766-3014-4

© 2017 James Arena. All rights reserved

No part of this book may be reproduced or transmitted in any form or by any means, electronic or mechanical, including photocopying or recording, or by any information storage and retrieval system, without permission in writing from the publisher.

Front cover design by the author

Printed in the United States of America

*McFarland & Company, Inc., Publishers
Box 611, Jefferson, North Carolina 28640*
www.mcfarlandpub.com

*To my parents—the most loving people I have ever known.
Without them, I might never have discovered much
of the music discussed in this book.*

*And to the artists featured here,
whose music has made me feel truly alive for over 35 years.*

Acknowledgments

I'd like to express my gratitude to the many people who stood by me throughout the making of this book. They gave me support, guidance and truly invaluable assistance.

I thank all of the artists featured in *Europe's Stars of '80s Dance Pop*, who kindly granted me the extraordinary privilege of sharing their stories and memories. I will never forget this experience. I am very grateful to the artists from the original version of this book, who offered so much support on social media with their endorsements, photos and videos.

I am extremely grateful to Nick Bunning for the many hours he spent reviewing the words and details contained in this book.

My thanks to the honorable Mel Brooks and Audrey Landers for composing and contributing their very special introductory commentaries for this project.

Manfred Esser graciously and generously shared many of his beautiful photographs with me in an effort to help boost the historical significance of this book. I am tremendously grateful.

From Europe, I am much obliged to Mary Susan Applegate, Antoine Aureche, Ugo Cerutti, Roland Colerus, Christian de Walden, Natalie Graham, Pasquale Mammaro, Bernard Mcintosh, Christa Mikulski, Enrico Monti, Johann Perrier, Stefanie Schwarze, Dennis van Korven, Thomas M. Stein, Rebecca Stevens and Sabine Warning.

Very special thanks to Steve Coy for arranging my interview with Pete Burns and for his great support.

My great thanks to Frank Peterson and Mike Heisel for their efforts to get this project noticed in Germany.

From the U.S., I thank Elvis Bramble, Robert and Maureen Arena, Mark Kostabi and James Washington.

There were many others who took an interest in this project and offered their encouragement and assistance. If I have neglected to mention you, please forgive the oversight and know that I am deeply grateful for your contribution.

I'd like to make note that Discogs™ (discogs.com), the *Music & Media* charts I scoured decades ago (and kept copies of, thank God), and Joel Whitburn's *Billboard's Hot Dance/Disco 1974–2003* (2004, Record Research, Inc.) were most helpful as data verification resources.

Table of Contents

Acknowledgments vi
Foreword by Mel Brooks 1
Foreword by Audrey Landers 4
Preface 7

Thomas Anders, Modern Talking	9
Jo Bogaert, Technotronic	18
Pete Burns, Dead or Alive	24
Phil Creswick, Big Fun	36
Hazell Dean	42
Manfred Esser, Photographer	47
Yasmin Evans, aka Yazz	53
Claudie Fritsch, aka Desireless	64
Junior Giscombe, aka Junior	68
Jaki Graham	76
Phil Harding, PWL Mixmaster	82
Klaus Hirschburger, Songwriter	90
Tom Hooker	96
Leee John, Imagination	104
Carmelo La Bionda, Producer, Composer	110
Caroline Loeb	116
Paul Mazzolini, aka Gazebo	121
Liz Mitchell, Boney M.	128
Fab Morvan, Milli Vanilli	134
Romano Musumarra, Producer, Composer	141
Taco Ockerse, aka Taco	148
Linda Jo Rizzo	158

Jack Robinson, Songwriter   165
Fabio Roscioli, aka Ryan Paris   170
Jennifer Rush   175
Sabrina Salerno, aka Sabrina   183
Ivana Spagna, aka Spagna   192
Amii Stewart   200
Ric Tess Teiges, aka Fancy   212
Harriette Weels, MaiTai   218

Appendix: The Record Shop—Noteworthy Tracks   225

Index   231

Foreword
by Mel Brooks

What can a Jewish-American comedic genius and entertainment legend who has won a Tony, Grammy, Emmy and Oscar possibly add to his resume of stellar accomplishments? How about rapping a controversial dance song about Adolf Hitler and the Third Reich? Mel Brooks (the creator of such immortal film farces as The Producers, Blazing Saddles *and* Young Frankenstein*) successfully took on the challenge in 1983 and raised eyebrows throughout Europe when he released the skillfully written and stingingly comical single "To Be or Not to Be (The Hitler Rap)." This sharply executed vinyl history lesson was created to support his film of the same name, which starred Brooks and his wife Anne Bancroft. The song was reportedly banned in Germany, whose nearly 40-year post–World War II reconstruction phase was still underway at the time. Still, "The Hitler Rap," against all odds, managed to be a Top 20 smash in the UK, reached number 15 in Switzerland and was a Top 3 hit in Australia. From Culver City, California, Mel takes a moment to look with humor and affection at his unlikely brush with fame in the international dance-pop music arena.*

My 1983 film *To Be or Not to Be* was a remake of the 1942 movie starring Carole Lombard and Jack Benny. I won't say whose was better, but I think we did a pretty good job. I think I showed bravery right from the start of the picture by singing "Sweet Georgia Brown" in Polish. Anne took to the song and language naturally—she learned it immediately, and she had to teach me. I struggled with it, but I finally got it. We needed another song to promote the movie, and that's why I wrote the dance-pop-rap single "To Be or Not to Be (The Hitler Rap)." Since they weren't doing rap in the 1940s (the era the film was set in), the song was too hip to actually appear in the movie, so our intention was to use the track just to build publicity for it.

When I wrote "The Hitler Rap," I just followed the storyline of Göring, Himmler, Goebbels, Bormann, Hess and all the guys that concocted the administration known as the Third Reich, led by Adolf Hitler. I think I called Martin Bormann "Marty" and rhymed his name with "Nazi party." I really took it soft and easy with those guys when I think about the song. I was very intrigued by how lucky these guys in Munich got when they put their scheme all together and how—I hate to say it—brilliantly they stole the government. I was always a history buff, and I was always trying to understand why things happen politically. I'm surprised I ended up in show business and not a history teacher or assemblyman somewhere in Brooklyn.

Foreword by Mel Brooks

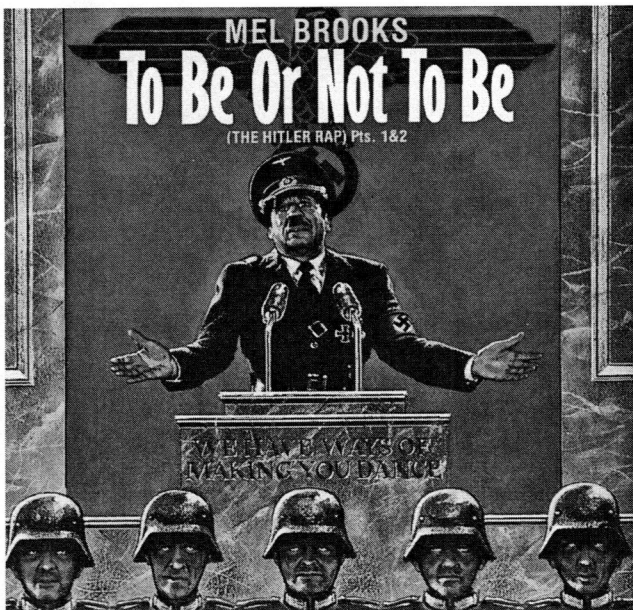 

Left: Brooks' "To Be or Not to Be (The Hitler Rap)" seven-inch record sleeve on Island Records. *Right:* The legendary film producer in the twenty-first century. In a 2006 interview with Lars-Olav Beier for Spiegel, Mel Brooks said, "by using the medium of comedy, we can try to rob Hitler of his posthumous power and myths."

Pete Wingfield, the producer and arranger of the track, worked with me a little on the lyrics, but he didn't know too much about the Third Reich, so there wasn't much he could do there. But he was a big help with the rhythm. Here I was, a man in my 50s—what did I know about rap? He was 26 and was very much involved in pop music at the time. So he coached me on how to handle the beat, the musicality, and my delivery. Having already done the rap on "It's Good to Be the King" a couple of years before, it wasn't too difficult. "The Hitler Rap" was a very similar song. Plus, I had been a drummer in a band and had a gift for tempo and timing. I think it took me one rehearsal, and I understood what the beat should be.

The man who helped make the video we did for the song was Alan Johnson, who also directed the film *To Be or Not to Be*. He choreographed the song "Springtime for Hitler" in my first movie, *The Producers,* way back in 1968. We worked very closely together to make "Springtime" a good, stand-on-its-own number in that film, as well as a satiric escapade. Alan was the perfect choice to stage "The Hitler Rap" video. He did such an amazing job. You'll notice I'm not wearing the swastika armband in the video. We knew we might have some resistance to the song in Germany and weren't sure how other countries might react if I had worn it. So we opted to leave it out and stick with less obvious references, such as the eagle symbol hanging in the background. That was definitely a choice. Alan also included the most beautiful girls imaginable in the clip and had a few touches of Nazism, S&M and weird sexual references thrown in for good measure. It ended up being a very hot number. I think it was Alan that really made that song work—I just wrote the damn thing. We ended up leaving the swastika band on the cover artwork of the seven-inch and 12-inch record single jackets. I guess we felt it might generate some attention in places outside of Germany.

Releasing a pop song as a tie-in to a movie could be useful in the marketing of a film, especially in Europe at that time. "It's Good to Be the King" may have helped the box office for *History of the World, Part I*. We did very well with the song and the movie in the U.S. and France. I can't say that "The Hitler Rap" did much to boost "To Be or Not to Be" though. They wouldn't play it on the radio or television in America. They thought the video was a little too sexy and a little too out there. I guess they also didn't want to push a song about Hitler too heavily. I suppose the single may have placed some attention on the movie in Germany (with the very limited underground airplay it received). The film did well there, considering they wouldn't let it play in the regular movie theater chains. But the Germans did have something I believe was called the cinema club, sort of an underground movie theater circuit, and there must have been a thousand of those places all throughout the country. If we made any money from the film, it was there. But they banned "The Hitler Rap" record from being played on radio or TV in the German mainstream commercial markets. I never anticipated it would be so problematic—not at all. I thought everyone would get a big kick out of it, especially in Germany. It was almost 40 years after the war and the whole Hitler thing, and I figured what the hell—there shouldn't be a problem any more. But I guess the Germans knew there were some bad things in their past, and maybe they didn't want to be reminded of it in a rap song.

That feeling may still hold true. It was only [in 2009] that my stage version of *The Producers* finally played in Berlin, but we couldn't put a swastika on the stage. They hung a banner with two pretzels on it I think. The fun of the big song from the show, "Springtime for Hitler," is the boldness of the swastikas and all of that regalia. When the Germans in the theater saw the number, you could hear a pin drop. Not a sound; no response. They didn't know how to react to "Springtime for Hitler." But yet at the end of the show, they stood and gave the production a standing ovation. Keep in mind this awkward combination of reactions took place over 65 years after the war. It was tricky, and I'm sure that this same uneasiness in German society today was even stronger at the time I came out with "The Hitler Rap" in 1983.

I had no idea until just recently that I had reached some top positions on a number of international pop charts in the '80s with "To Be or Not to Be (The Hitler Rap)." I was right up there with many of the artists in this book. I must have been so busy doing other things that I didn't pay attention. Since I don't recall knowing those statistics back then, I can only tell you that, right now, it feels *great*. And I'm happy to be one of *Europe's Stars of '80s Dance Pop*. So to all the good people who bought "The Hitler Rap" single, I thank you and say, "How could you have been so far ahead of the curve? How could you have known what a smart decision that would be?"

You are, indeed, the best of the bunch.

Foreword by Audrey Landers

Audrey Landers was a bright young American celebrity in the making in the early '80s. This curvaceous and pretty young actress was a rising star on American TV blockbuster nighttime soap opera Dallas, *as well as a talented singer and songwriter. Looking to expand her musical horizons, Audrey teamed with renowned German producer Jack White (known for his work with Laura Branigan, Pia Zadora and Engelbert Humperdinck). In 1983, under his direction, she co-wrote and sang a melodic and gently danceable song about the pain of a romantic break-up called "Manuel Goodbye." Released in major portions of Europe through Germany's Ariola Records, the track made Audrey an overnight pop star. "Manuel Goodbye" reached top positions on the Dutch, Austrian, Swiss and German pop charts. The summery, disco-fused follow-up hit, "Playa Blanca" charted even higher in some territories. Landers' tenure at Ariola lasted several years and earned the singer numerous gold and platinum records throughout Europe. The singer, anxious to record in a fresh style following her departure from White's fold, joined forces with celebrated pop producer Christian De Walden (Amanda Lear, Bonnie Bianco, Thomas Anders) in 1988, and together they created the artist's critically acclaimed album* Secrets. *Though her musical success in Europe still remains a bit of a secret in America, her many fans abroad continue to embrace her irresistible sound today.*

When I won the role of Afton Cooper in the nighttime TV drama *Dallas* in 1980, my character was a singer. I wrote all the songs that Afton sang on the show. *Dallas* was not only a huge hit series in America, but also a smash in 100 other countries, including Germany. Jack White, a German record producer, saw me on the show and recognized my musicianship as well as my potential marketability with European audiences. The '80s were in full blast and dance-pop music was popular worldwide. By now my songwriting had evolved and grown. I had studied music at Juilliard and had already written hundreds of songs. I listened and learned from the songs of the era, from ABBA to Donna Summer. My first international single release, "Manuel Goodbye," which hit store shelves late in 1983, is now considered a standard in Europe, as are many of my subsequent hits. Throughout the '80s and into the '90s, I recorded for Ariola, BMG, Bellaphon, WEA and Polydor Records and did concert tours in Europe, with my mom by my side as my manager.

During the mid-to-late 1980s, my popularity in the United States was predominantly due to the success of *Dallas* and my roles in feature films like *A Chorus Line*. However, in

Left: **Singer and actress Audrey Landers' star quality is captured during a photo shoot with Manfred Esser for the 1988 album** *Secrets* **(courtesy Manfred Esser).** *Right:* **Ms. Landers poses today with some of her gold records.**

Europe my celebrity status was amplified because of my recording career. If my face was on the cover of one publication a month in the U.S., I was on the cover of 20 magazines during the same period in Europe. My success in Germany, the Netherlands and other nations with songs like "Playa Blanca" and "Never Wanna Dance (When I'm Blue)" was fueled by the kind of fan support that only rock stars were experiencing. To my great surprise, fans were camping outside my hotel, waiting to get an autograph. No matter how tired I was, I always stopped to say hello and sign my record albums and singles for them. Sometimes I would sign for as many as two hours. My mom and bodyguards weren't pleased with me because they had to cope with crowd control. But I always asked them to give my fans and me some space. I knew that some of these people had been waiting for me all day. I would never want to disappoint them. I have always been grateful to the people of Europe who supported my recording career.

Yes, *Dallas* was popular in Germany and many other places, but my records were topping the charts and reaching gold and platinum status in many countries across the globe. I supported my records with mini tours. Unfortunately, they usually had to be short because I was still filming the television series. So, for a number of years, my schedule went something like this: I would finish filming *Dallas* in Los Angeles on a Friday. My mom and I would get on a plane and fly non-stop, arriving the next morning in Frankfurt, Paris or Amsterdam. At the airport, TV crews and the press met us. I would do interviews at the airport, then an afternoon TV show, such as *Top of the Pops,* and then do a concert at night. Sunday was more of the same, including a magazine shoot. Then we would fly back to L.A. on Sunday night (or Monday, with a little luck and schedule permitting), and I would go back to the set of *Dallas*. My mom was still running her printing company, so she would usually fly to New York and go directly to her office. When I had a filming break, my concert tours would be extended for a week or 10 days.

During our tours in Europe, Ruth and I noticed that the U.S. televison show *Knight Rider* was new to German audiences and that our friend (and its star), David Hasselhoff, was becoming popular there because of the program. David was experiencing a lull in his American career—*Knight Rider* was off the air in the U.S., and *Baywatch* had not yet been created. One day, David visited us on the set of a film my mom was producing, and she came up with the idea to introduce David to my producer, Jack White. David and Jack struck a deal, and that's how his successful German recording career got started. As many people know, it led to his huge number one hit "Looking for Freedom" in 1989.

It was a crazy whirlwind most of the time, but I loved performing in Europe. The '80s was definitely an exciting time for me as a performer and a songwriter, and I enjoyed a unique dual career in entertainment that few people can say they experienced. I wrote most of my hits in English, which was no problem for my audiences or me. The challenge was to write my songs with a hook that anyone could sing along with in any language. However, no matter what the subject matter was, I needed to *feel* the music. My European style was romantic, melodic and often very danceable, and I am proud that so many people embraced my work and responded so well to it.

To this day, whenever I perform in Europe, they always ask me to sing "Manuel Goodbye." I love the fact that a new generation is listening to my music and that it's still relevant more than 30 years after it was born. Every time I hear the song's introduction, I get butterflies in my stomach, and I can't help but smile. I would like to say thank you to anyone who has listened to and enjoyed my records. This music is absolutely a piece of my heart, and it's been an honor to be able to share it with so many people.

Finally, I warmly salute my fellow artists in this book, with whom I often shared the European music charts and stages back in those wonderful days. Our music has stood the test of time, and it's a joy for me to be back in the company of *Europe's Stars of '80s Dance Pop* once again.

Preface

Why is an American writing about European dance-pop songs of the '80s and the artists and professionals who created them? The answer is simple. These individuals and the music they cultivated mean the world to me. Despite living on the other side of the planet during this decade, I developed a deep connection with Europe and this wonderful music, as well as a tremendous respect for the people who made it. The artists contained within these pages are, in a way, citizens of all nations, and they communicated great positivity through their creative efforts. Thousands of miles away in New York, they made my life (and the lives of millions of others around the planet) more enjoyable.

Beginning around 1981, I began to discover the dance-pop sounds of Europe. Some of this hypnotic music had elements in common with the American disco style I loved in the '70s, but in many ways it possessed highly exotic differences. These overseas recordings were often saturated with unusual synthesizer and electronic sound effects, an intoxicating dance beat or a quirky, edgy blend of punk, rock and new wave rhythms. Even ballads frequently had a kind of energetic spark that set them apart. Many songs possessed a touch of classical influence, adding to their international flavor. European dance-pop had what the French might call a certain *je ne sais quoi*, and the inspired creativity found in these unconventional songs was magnificently unique and inventive. Some records simmered with a wonderfully alluring style, reflective of the region and culture from which they had originated, including Austria, Belgium, France, Germany, Italy, the Netherlands, Spain and Britain. Their melodies sounded so original and decidedly beautiful to me, I'd often gasp at how unusual they seemed upon first listen. I soon learned the names of songwriters, producers, remixers and even the photographers and record companies that were advancing these incredible productions.

The vocalists of European dance-pop mesmerized me. They intrigued my senses with their mastery of song, distinctive styles and their ability to convey passion and energy through this very physical music form. Though I was raised at a time and in a place where American mainstream entertainment suppliers generally had little interest in foreign languages or accents, I vigorously embraced the unfamiliar dialects of many of these vocalists. Whether a song was sung in French, German, Spanish, Dutch, Italian or English, it didn't matter to me. I didn't need to fully understand a track's literal meaning (though such comprehension might have further enhanced my experience); I just knew I *loved* what I was hearing.

This book project evolved from my desire to know more about the people responsible for so much of my bliss and a drive to create a memento of this era. I wanted to hear what was in the hearts and minds of these great artists at the time they participated in the creation of these wonderful records. Their impressions of the present day and their outlooks for the future were also important to me. I asked each individual a series of basic questions about his or her life and career. Documented here is what each of these fascinating artists wanted to share.

Most of these artists (and myself for that matter) consider themselves smack in the heart of "middle age" today. Some have moved past this phase and now possess an even broader view of life. Regardless of the point each of us is at in our personal journeys, I think we can all agree that humans tend to become increasingly reflective with the passage of time. We reminisce a bit more as we progress with our lives, appreciating where we've been and what we've done. But make no mistake—the artists in this book are not confined to or bound by nostalgia. Many of these vital, vibrant and dynamic individuals continue to make valuable contributions to the world (whether still involved in music or not). They will never be defined solely by the '80s. Expect the unexpected from these great people in the years to come, whatever direction they may take. Mick Jagger probably said it best in his 2001 interview with Juan Villoro—"The past is a great place, and I don't want to erase it or to regret it, but I don't want to be its prisoner either."

It should be noted that when I first self-published this book as *Stars of '80s Dance Pop—The European Edition*, the project featured interviews with 50 stars of the era. I am most grateful that McFarland saw some merit in the earlier version and decided to re-fashion and re-release it traditionally, thus ensuring this material is preserved for posterity. However, the realities of today's challenging book market and daunting production costs made it necessary to reduce the number of artists featured in this edition. This in no way lessens the importance of the contributions of the great singers and producers whose commentary was omitted. Also, please note that the country listed at the beginning of each artist's chapter refers to the location where their primary hit(s) were produced, not necessarily the artist's nationality.

When I began work on this project and throughout the many months that followed, it seemed to me that the world was besieged by an unprecedented series of man-made threats. Maybe it was the same amount of trouble that's always been plaguing our planet. However, the level struck me as being even higher than usual for our time. Truly unsettling politics, terrible crimes against humanity, constant skirmishes and outright warring, gross displays of greed and corruption, vicious racism and discrimination, stunning barbarism, insufferable indifference and intolerance—the list goes on and on. We continue to live in a world where profoundly dismaying negativity and brutal hostility threaten to divide our cultures, day in and day out. The dark events that make headlines today are still a bitter pill to swallow. By contrast, the beauty of the music discussed in these pages is an inspiration. The artists you will meet here remind me that man can always choose to uplift the souls of his brothers and sisters, rather than cause harm. The artistry celebrated in this book can provide us with the fuel that our worldwide quest for peace, love and unity desperately needs.

Music is emotion, and we all can be moved by it, regardless of our location on this island Earth. Sharing their talents, *Europe's Stars of '80s Dance Pop* brought all of us a little bit closer to each other. These artists matter because they made this world a better place in which to live, and I have been deeply touched by what they have done. I salute *all* the extraordinary music professionals who found success throughout Europe and Britain during these remarkable years, and I invite you to experience their magic once again.

Thomas Anders
Modern Talking
"You're My Heart, You're My Soul" (1984)
Germany

"Many people still come up to me and say, 'You changed my life with that song.' I always answer, 'That song changed my life as well!'" So remarks Thomas Anders, once the lead singer of the international mega-duo known as Modern Talking. He's referring to their game-changing debut hit, "You're My Heart, You're My Soul," a multi-million selling, ground-breaking chart-topper that helped make he and his partner, producer and songwriter Dieter Bohlen, worldwide stars in the '80s. The song also paved the way for Anders' mesmerizing voice to become one of the most recognizable and beloved of the era. The history of Modern Talking spanned three decades, and their impact hasn't lessened over time. Their 2014 "best of" album, *30*, quickly became a top selling download on iTunes in Germany and Russia upon its release late in the year, charting beside such contemporary acts as Taylor Swift, One Direction, Sam Smith and David Guetta. The feat clearly demonstrated that Modern Talking's appeal has remained undiminished over time.

Anders' passionate spirit was palpable in each of the group's mammoth hits. As a solo vocalist following his tenure in Modern Talking, his recordings and live performances continued to convey that warmth. Today, his concerts are frequent sell-out events throughout Europe and Russia. Extremely articulate and pleasantly disarming, Thomas is a man with a sharp memory of his astonishing career journey—one that continues to evolve, surprise and delight his legion of fans. From his home in Germany, he reflects on his exceptional career and some of what he's learned over the years.

"I grew up in a middle-class family in a village with 120 inhabitants. My parents taught me the values of life. They brought me up with respect and made me realize that you have to have respect for others. They taught me that our society is built on this respectful give-and-take," declares the artist, born in Germany in the early '60s. "I always wanted to stand on stage and sing. I gave my first public performance when I was six years old. By the time I had turned 12, I could already look back on over 200 performances. When I was 15, I was discovered at a radio casting session and signed my first record contract one year later. A few years later, I met Dieter Bohlen, who produced a single with me. I really wanted to make music and hoped to break into the charts at least once in my life—and maybe even to receive a gold record."

Thomas' youthful recording career began in earnest with a series of light, German

Left: Modern Talking's Dieter Bohlen (left) and Thomas Anders are seen during their early glory days in this 1984 RCA Records publicity shot. *Right:* Anders continues to record and attract huge concert crowds in the twenty-first century.

language singles produced in the schlager style for CBS and Hansa Records (later, a division of the Bertelsmann Music Group). "At the beginning of the '80s, I was a young man who first wanted to graduate from school," he recalls. "I knew that when I passed my A-levels, I would be able to focus completely on music. The music scene in Germany was in a state of flux at that time. The great era of German folk music, schlager, was at an end, and new music was evolving in the form of German new wave. The lyrics were becoming more ironic and bolder. Artists were changing their appearance, wearing more provocative clothing and looking less like they were part of the folk world. But every strong movement has a counter movement. In contrast to the strange sound of German new wave, more melodic songs characterized by keyboard sounds were also being created. That was the beginning of German-based Euro-pop.

"After recording a single with Dieter," Thomas continues, "we agreed that more songs would follow [such as "Endstation Sehnsucht" and "Heißkalter Engel"]. Unfortunately, these productions would not enjoy any chart success. I told Dieter that I would really like to sing a song in English. He was unsure whether a German artist singing in English could break into the market. It was October of 1984, and I was standing in the studio, recording yet another German single. After the recording was done, Dieter came to me, gave me a demo, and asked me if I could also record this song. It was 'You're My Heart, You're My Soul'!"

According to Thomas, Hansa decided to release and market the English language song as if it was the work of a duo, giving rise to the somewhat ambiguous name "Modern Talking." It was determined that a partner for Anders would be found a bit later. A sneaker and dress shoe were all that record buyers were permitted to see on the cover of the entity's first single, "You're My Heart, You're My Soul." "It didn't sell at all at the beginning," remembers Thomas. "As of early December 1984, only 6,000 singles had been sold, and internally the song was being viewed as a flop. Christmas came and went, and I rang the record company on the first day of work after the holidays to inquire as to how many records had now been sold. I actually wanted to find out how my new single, 'Es Geht Mir Gut Heut' Nacht,' was doing. 'Not well' was the answer, but 'You're My Heart, You're My Soul' had sold over 60,000 copies. This meant that the song would enter the charts three days later."

Modern Talking's debut was suddenly like a lightning bolt illuminating the night sky, and the record marked the dawn of a new era in European dance-pop. The song was a highly unusual blend of hip dance floor beats and keyboards, peppered with the synthesizer sensibilities of a '80s rhythmic ballad. Anders' dreamy vocals perfectly captured the youthful, melancholy mood of the song. The track was also released in an extended maxi-single version for the clubs. Credited to what sounded like an American producer and songwriter named Steve Benson (a pseudonym used by Dieter Bohlen), the track is often cited as the beginning of a highly melodic, high-energy dance music revolution spawned in Germany, paralleling (and often merging with) the sounds of Italy's Italo-disco movement. Eventually, the song reportedly sold over eight million copies worldwide.

"I can't describe the success of 'You're My Heart, You're My Soul' in words," Thomas says, pausing to think about the enormity of the experience. "I grew up with my family in the countryside, and all of a sudden I had a number one hit in 81 countries all over the world. That song altered my life. It was the start of an international career. [From the moment the song caught on], things started to happen really fast. There was no time to cast for a partner. Modern Talking, who didn't actually exist yet, were going to be broadcast on three TV channels, one week later. Dieter would have to partner with me on television. They were small channels, and the plan was to replace him afterwards. We went into the charts, and five weeks later, we were number one in Germany. Replacing Dieter was no longer possible."

A follow-up single, "You Can Win If You Want" (released in 1985), had an even harder, more powerful, and energized sound that easily managed to capture the summit of Germany's pop chart. Modern Talking's debut LP, simply titled *The 1st Album*, achieved platinum certification in Deutschland, where it also reached number one. Thomas observes, "My working relationship with Dieter had been pretty relaxed. Not any more, however. We were very happy with the sudden success of Modern Talking, but each of us showed it in his own way. In order to be clear about our music, I need to say that I was never involved with the production. Therefore, I was not involved with the 'sound' of Modern Talking. Dieter was always guided by successful chart productions. (That was also the case with our comeback.) In the '80s, Luis Rodriguez was the sound engineer. The formula was always as follows—Dieter would write a song, which I would sing. He would always turn up at the studio with a stack of current hits on CD. He then outlined to the sound department the style he wanted [for his songs]. Everything else was the job of the sound team. That's why lots of sound engineers parted ways with him. They couldn't handle Dieter constantly telling the media that he produced everything and that he was also getting the most money.

"I think I fit into the picture because of the uniqueness of my voice and the way I sang Dieter's songs. I interpreted his tracks in my own way. When I got demos from him, which were always terrible to be honest, I knew exactly how he felt about the song, how he heard it. My [second] wife, Claudia, once came into my study as I was listening to some new demos from Dieter [from our second tenure as Modern Talking]. The demo CD was playing, and I was sitting with the text in front of me. Claudia asked me, 'How do you recognize a melody there?' I just said, 'I know what he wants.' Perhaps that's one of the reasons for our success. I could always completely empathize with Dieter's songs and melodies. I often felt like I had the voice that he'd always wanted. It was a kind of symbiosis. He wrote the song, and I gave the song life."

The duo's fame grew bigger by the month. The *Let's Talk About Love* LP was unveiled in 1985, and Modern Talking mania began to spread even further across Europe. The only official single off the second set, "Cheri, Cheri Lady," kept the hit formula intact and was quickly chased by a third LP, *Ready for Romance,* in 1986. The singles "Atlantis Is Calling (S.O.S. for Love)" and "Brother Louie" featured more of Dieter and Thomas' well-established signature style—pounding beats, passionately sung (though somewhat unconventional) English lyrics, and energized falsetto choruses. "Brother Louie" gave the team their only Top Five British chart hit, but their ability to break through virtually any border was unparalleled. Bohlen widened his scope by producing and composing for other artists, such as C.C. Catch ("Strangers by Night"), who enjoyed notable success on the German charts with a similar sound.

"The music of Modern Talking was, basically, very simple. They were essentially kids' songs that were produced in the spirit of that particular time. Every child in kindergarten can sing along to 'Cheri, Cheri Lady.' I believe that if someone were to cover kids' songs and re-release them with the current pop sounds of today, they would almost all be hits!" Anders conjectures. "When we recorded, I sang all of the songs fast and professionally. One Modern Talking album would take me one day to record. I flew to the studio in Hamburg in the morning and was on the late flight home. The song 'Atlantis Is Calling' was done in one take. One time through and it was a wrap. At first, Dieter was always really proud [of my ability] and said it was unbelievable how great I could sing. Later, he would tell me how I was getting too much money for so little work. I offered to help him with the production, but he refused (as then he would have had to share the profits with me)."

For this unstoppable team, touring and performing for gargantuan sell-out crowds soon became the norm. A smile returns to the artist's face. "The first Modern Talking tours were pretty normal," he observes. "At first, nobody knew us. I received my first gold record in Paris. It was surreal. We were sitting with a half–French record company in a gourmet restaurant and received our gold certification. We didn't have time to arrange a press conference, as our schedule was full, but my dream was more than fulfilled. Not only did I have one gold record, I soon had several. As of today, the number of gold and platinum records stands at over the 430 mark!

"My biggest solo concert was in Santiago de Chile in front of an audience of 85,000. It was unbelievable. I came on stage in the stadium, and I couldn't hear my band any more because the applause was so loud. They played the intro to my song for several minutes before I found the point to come in. It was amazing. The biggest Modern Talking concert was in Budapest in front of 250,000 people. It really makes no difference whether it's 85,000 or 250,000—your mind stops comprehending the size of the crowd at this point. Your eyes can tell the difference between 5,000 and 30,000, but more than 30,000 and you can't really judge it any more. Is it now 30,000 or 50,000? Who cares—there are a hell of a lot of people out there," he beams.

However, there was still one major music market that seemed to be immune to Modern Talking fever—the United States. The duo's sound never made a dent in America, though their hits received DJ play in many of the underground clubs catering to the European music of the period. Anders says he had mixed emotions about the group's lack of presence in the U.S. "You always want to make it into the Top 10 of the *Billboard* charts," he admits. "The Americans created the entertainment business, but unfortunately they act like it. They make the rules, and we have to follow them. It would have been extremely difficult for us had we tried to promote ourselves in the U.S., with so many other countries on our schedule. We were offered the chance to do a three-month promo tour through the U.S. the second time around with Modern Talking. However, it would have meant turning our backs on our main market and putting our faith in an uncertain future. Besides that, Dieter's song texts were so simple that even the most undemanding of townsfolk in the country would have probably felt unchallenged. I'm not sure America would have taken the music seriously." Modern Talking made a few references to American culture during the second phase of their evolution, typified by the single "Last Exit to Brooklyn" and the album *America* in 2001.

Despite the pressures that came with being at the top of the record business and the efforts necessary to maintain such a position, Thomas says he never let the strain affect him. "Success spurs you on, and it makes stress bearable," he asserts. "I never felt any pressure. It wasn't my job to take care of the sounds or worry about trends. I had to sell the band—on stage, on TV and in pictures. Dieter and I both had completely separate realms. There was more tension as to whether the new single or album would make the Top Five again. Our success grew from single to single. Neither the record label nor we as artists had any idea just how successful Modern Talking would become.

"I remember a manager at our record label came up to me after 'You're My Heart, You're My Soul' and said, 'Enjoy it Thomas. It'll be the last number one of your life.'" The singer laughs at the executive's prediction. "After that, we had four more number one hits and six number one albums in Germany. Modern Talking had *the* sound and was one of the most successful acts in the world!" Successful is an understatement. The group released a new hit LP almost every six months, including *In the Middle of Nowhere* (1986), *Romantic Warriors* (1987) and *In the Garden of Venus* (1987). *Venus* featured the duo's final commercial single of the period, "In 100 Years," an allegory of a doomed and loveless future society. By then, Thomas discloses, he had become fatigued with his situation in Modern Talking.

"After the grueling period from 1985–87, I felt a sense of freedom when, at the end of '87, Modern Talking came to an end," he admits. "As for Dieter, unfortunately he had a character flaw in that as he realized he was earning enough money for himself, he trampled over all his partners. He doesn't understand responsibility or loyalty. As soon as somebody waved a cheque, they became his best friend. What a shame. We are two completely different people with different attitudes towards life. Yin and Yang personified.

"He formed a new band [Blue System] behind my back and made deals with event organizers. We had agreed on taking a break after the album *In the Garden of Venus*. After three years, we really had no more left to give. We decided that we would get back together sometime during the course of 1988 and talk about a new album. After our meeting, I flew to New York and Los Angeles for a holiday, and Dieter informed the big German newspapers that Modern Talking was finished. In the end, I was fine with it. I was just tired—exhausted from three years of promotion throughout Europe. Sometimes it was three countries in one day, along with thousands of photos and interviews. I missed my friends the most. Dinner with my family often had to be planned six weeks in advance and often was cancelled just a few days before because we had to do a new TV show.

"After splitting with Modern Talking, I received a multi-million offer from another German record label. But I said no. I relocated to Los Angeles to get away from the negative German headlines and enjoy a more carefree life in L.A. I spent almost three years there. Here and there, I gave international concerts, from Cape Town to Hong Kong, Singapore, Santiago de Chile, Moscow, Bangkok and more. I traveled around Russia for six and a half weeks one spring and gave 38 concerts. There were lots of wonderful moments.

"With a new decade about to begin," Anders continues, "I was sitting at home in front of my English fireplace and asked myself whether that was it for me. I was 28 and could look back at a great career, but what was ahead? It became clear to me that life isn't defined and shaped by chart success. Rather, it is built with friends (I can tell you that I have incredible friends), family and warmth of the heart. As long as you possess these things, nothing bad can happen to you."

By the close of the decade, Thomas decided to return to recording, releasing music that reflected a new and sophisticated sound, such as the gently upbeat single "Love of My Own." "Around 1989, I had started working with a friend of mine, Peter Ries, in Frankfurt, and we began to write songs. The first song I co-wrote was 'I Can Never Let You Go,' which was recorded immediately by Engelbert Humperdinck for his album *In Liebe*. That made me unbelievably proud. I've had countless twists and turns on my journey, but one thing that is especially noteworthy was my first solo album, *Different* (1989). Gus Dudgeon produced it [with Peter Reis, aka Marc Cassandra], and I recorded it at Alan Parsons' studio. I wanted to show the world that I could sing more than just 'Cheri, Cheri Lady.' From a vocals point of view, the Modern Talking songs were never challenging. Now I had the vision of building my own career with my own voice."

Though many of his releases were well-received and successful endeavors, sales figures were less impressive when compared to Modern Talking. However, the artist says he has always felt comparison of the works serves little purpose. "Competing against the (by then) 60 million records sold by Modern Talking and what I was able to do as a solo artist was and is impossible," insists Anders. "I had my good chart positions, but they couldn't be compared to Modern Talking. It showed, once again, that the songs of our group were simple melodies, produced in a contemporary way. The songs I recorded for my solo albums were much more complex. They simply weren't suited to the masses. I was frustrated that the fans didn't accept my music like they had with Modern Talking. But I did take one piece of wisdom with me—'The worm has to taste good to the fish, not the fisherman!'"

In 1998, a rather extraordinary and unexpected event took place. Modern Talking officially reunited, launching what became a spectacular comeback for the group that would extend into the 21st century. Anders is the first to admit it's a strange story. "I had been having contact again with Dieter since 1993," he recalls. "One day, he gave me a call at home, and we spoke for over an hour. It was an amusing, funny and very open conversation.

We agreed to meet sometime for dinner. A few months later, I was near Hamburg, and so we went out for a meal together. It was relaxed, and we parted company amicably. In the years that followed, we kept in touch regularly, but we realized that it wasn't the right time at all for a reunion.

"In November of 1997, I was enjoying a holiday with my wife in Los Angeles. I received an unexpected call from our Modern Talking lawyer. He was in L.A. and wanted to meet. Two days later, we met in the bar of the Hilton Hotel in Beverly Hills. He delivered me an offer for a Modern Talking reunion. I was unsure. Why would it be successful so many years after the end? The lawyer explained the marketing campaign of the record label (once again Hansa) to me and emphasized that a television company and event organizers thought that a reunion would be a great idea. Well, I asked for time to think about it. I had a few restless days and sleepless nights, but in the end I said—*yes!*"

Thomas notes that he believes himself to have been a wiser man at this juncture, and he intended to protect his interests. "I was no longer the same Thomas Anders from the '80s; I had grown up. I had my own ideas about business and drove a hard bargain. The record company didn't want to agree to my high demand for advance payment of royalties, as there was no promise of success. They made me a counter offer, which consisted of a high percentage share. I accepted. After over 60 million records sold during this phase, it was the correct decision. Another very important factor that helped me come to my final decision was that Dieter told me he had changed."

Beginning with 1998's *Back for Good* set, six albums were produced, culminating with the *Universe* LP in 2003. After launching this highly successful comeback, which included a series of energized remakes of their original hits, some medleys and original dance-floor shakers like the singles "You Are Not Alone," "Sexy Sexy Lover" and "Win the Race," Modern Talking once again ranked high on the charts. Many of their top tracks incorporated the rap vocals of Eric Singleton, a stylistic curve ball that perplexed some fans. "The idea was Dieter's," says the artist. "He thought Modern Talking needed an element of rap. It was the right idea. Our '80s songs needed freshening up. The sound was different, and it generated a somewhat different listening sensation. I found it great. It was a harmonious symbiosis."

"TV Makes the Superstar," released in 2003, was the final single of the duo's second phase, bringing to an end Modern Talking's remarkable reinvention. Thomas divulges, "I had felt for a while that Dieter no longer had that drive like he'd had with our earlier efforts. He told me that he just couldn't come up with those great melodies any more and that the competition was getting stronger all the time. He got more insecure. I remember a time in Vienna when we were both sitting in our dressing room before our show. He told me that he was going to be a jury member on a casting show (*Deutschland sucht den Superstar*) and that he wasn't sure if the show would be a hit. It was the German version of the U.S.'s *America's Got Talent!* As it turned out, the show was a sensation in Germany, and Dieter wasn't interested in Modern Talking any more. The show was also his inspiration for the 'TV Makes the Superstar' single, a number two hit in Germany."

Dieter Bohlen penned a book in 2003 about his experience in the music industry, not long after the group's second break-up. This work came under heavy fire because of Bohlen's reportedly harsh slams against those he worked with, Anders included. Thomas takes a dim view of the work, saying, "This book clearly showed that Dieter Bohlen was devoid of empathy and style. It wasn't just that the book was unnecessary; it was that most of the stories were also incorrect and were derived from his imagination. Obviously, there are rules for self-marketing in the entertainment industry. You have to be bigger in order to stand out from the crowd, but there have to be boundaries. I had to sue Dieter, as it wasn't just that he had made false accusations, he had brought my honor into question. I won the case 100 percent, and he had to pay damages. But I'm not someone who frets or gets bitter," contends Anders. "I live my life according to the principle—a problem overcome only makes you stronger!"

While Dieter continued record producing and began working with young rising vocalists, Thomas also moved forward with his career. He returned to Bertelsmann to record more up-tempo singles, including "Independent Girl" and "Tonight Is the Night" from the *This Time* album, as well as the popular promotional track "Just Dream." In 2009, Anders was back in the spotlight as a guest vocalist on a highly anticipated duet with another major '80s Euro-star. Sandra had scored numerous international dance hits ("Maria Magdalena," "Innocent Love" and "Everlasting Love," just to name a few) at the same time Modern Talking had been finding favor in the '80s. The two teamed up for "The Night Is Still Young," a sexy, Latin-tinged dance-pop number that caused a stir in Germany and was a Top 50 hit there. "As is so often the case," describes Anders, "things happen by chance. Sandra lives on Ibiza, and I've had a house on the island for a number of years. We bumped into each other one day on the beach, and she told me she was recording a new album. Suddenly, we had the idea that I should record a song with her for the album. The song had already been written, and two days later I was singing it. Sometimes life can be so simple."

Anders' most recent albums, including *Songs Forever* (2006), *Strong* (2010) and *Christmas for You* (2012), have explored refreshingly new musical territory for the artist and have met with critical acclaim throughout Europe and Russia. A recent duet with singer Kamaliya, "No Ordinary Love," was a major international dance smash. Anders also recently teamed with the composer of Nena's classic "99 Luftballons," Jörn Uwe Fahrenkrog-Petersen. Calling themselves Anders/Fahrenkrog, they hit the German Top 40 with the single "Gigolo." "We met in the lounge at Frankfurt International Airport. He was on his way to Los Angeles, and I was flying to Moscow. We decided that we wanted to make music together and arranged an appointment for a few weeks later. It was a wonderful collaboration. I love working with other musicians as long as the chemistry between us is right. Even as a solo artist, you can always pursue new musical ventures and paths," says Thomas. Not long ago, Anders contributed vocals to an exotic electronic dance single hit called "We Are One," featuring American/Iranian recording star Omid. Meanwhile, Sony Germany released promotional remixes of "Brother Louie" and "You're My Heart, You're My Soul" from the successful Modern Talking *30* album in October of 2014, which performed extremely well on club surveys. The singer released the solo set *History* in 2016, performing updated versions Modern Talking hits and a few new tracks, including the single "Lunatic."

Anders prides himself on having moved consciously forward with determination throughout his journey and recognizes the positivity of this drive as a key factor in his success. "I am very thankful for my life and my career," he asserts. "My motivation is the love of my job. I was lucky to be able to turn my passion into my career. There's nothing more interesting for me than to be creative every day—to have new ideas and to be able to shape your own life each day. I perform lots of shows, and I enjoy recording new songs, sometimes for the Russian market and sometimes for the rest of the world. Whether it's recording a

Christmas album or doing a duet with a Persian artist like Omid, life is quite wonderful as it is!

"When I'm together with friends and we talk about old stories," he continues, "I realize how much I've experienced. It is already enough for more than one lifetime. Obviously, I am who I am because of my past and my career. A person's character doesn't change, but the opportunities that present themselves in life give you direction. Fortunately, no one's life is made up purely of positive experiences. That would be awful. As people, we only learn through our mistakes and problems. But it's important how one deals with the problems. My secret is undoubtedly my unshakeable positive outlook. You can always make the best out of a bad situation. If you fall, you have to get up and try again. And I never lose sight of the beautiful things in life. When the first buds appear, when the flowers bloom for the first time, a smile from a stranger—there are millions of little things.

"I never look back with regrets, only with pride," the artist smiles. "I was a successful part of the '80s musical world, and I gave lots of people a lot of joy. I am very grateful for this. 'You're My Heart, You're My Soul' is always a highlight at all the shows I have given over the years. I stand on the stage and look at thousands of people and sing this song. Every face I see tells its own story. Every single person has his or her own personal memory of this great song. I still have a long way to go. I've still got so many ideas in my head that there's little room to think about when it will all be over. But as I move forward, I hope that my family and friends will think of me as someone who always wants to make life better for others."

Jo Bogaert

Technotronic

"Pump Up the Jam" (1989)
Belgium

From the very first seconds that vinyl copies of "Pump Up the Jam" hit DJ's turntables, club-goers knew they were in for a wild ride. With its simple, almost malevolent opening bass and synth chords, hypnotically drawing dancers to the floor, Technotronic's debut single prompted a stampede. It still rallies fans to get their groove on over 25 years later. This trend-setting creation of producer Jo "Thomas De Quincey" Bogaert, first released in 1989, was a mammoth international hit that literally marked the end of an era. But more importantly, the artist clarifies, it signaled the beginning of a new direction in the dance-pop genre. Still residing in Belgium, the chart-topping hitmaker enjoys his privacy in the twenty-first century and rarely gives interviews. But on this particular day, he doesn't mind making an exception to discuss his innovative accomplishments and to look closer at the beat that is Technotronic.

"There is a bio about me that circulates on the Internet which has some wrong information," Bogaert insists. "So this is a good moment to set the record straight. I am Belgian, from the Dutch speaking part of the country (the other part is French speaking). I always lived here, and I *never* relocated from the U.S., as some information alleges. I was born in 1956, and I came from a middle class background. As a boy, '60s pop grabbed me (The Who, Small Faces, the Stones, etc.), but it was not until the triple *Woodstock* LP came out that I found my real home in music. Hendrix was the revelation, but at first, Ten Years After made the stronger impression on this 14-year-old in 1970. My first electric guitar was modeled after Alvin Lee's Gibson ES-335—though mine was an Ibanez. My second was a Strat. So Hendrix won after all. (He died some six or seven months after I first discovered his music. I remember the terrible shock when I read it in the newspaper.) From that time, 1970 until about 1984, I played in local bands. I evolved from blues-rock to progressive to new wave.

"At the end of 1983, the Yamaha DX7 synthesizer came out. I was fed up playing in bands, so I got me one of those synths and also a midi-sequencer and a drum machine. Soon after, I also got hold of an eight-track tape recorder. I began making ambient-like, minimalistic music, mainly for art projects, installations, theater, performances and exhibitions. So, from a rocking guitarist I became an electronic musician. In 1985, I started an independent record label and made a couple of electronic dance tracks with a British singer,

Left: **A rarely seen photo of the extended Technotronic family featuring (left to right) model Felly, Jo Bogaert, Ya Kid K (Manuela Kamosi, baseball cap) and MC Eric (below).** *Right:* **Bogaert today (photography by Hilde Gilbos and courtesy Jo Bogaert).**

Eileen Jacas. The music was a combination of new wave-synth, a disco beat and soul-pop vocals. I must have sensed there was something in the air, for a year later it was the start of what was called the 'new beat' craze.

"Let me explain this new beat phenomenon," he continues. "In the early '80s, there were two kinds of clubs. There were discothèques, where disco music ruled (ABBA, Bee Gees, etc.), and the new wave clubs, where another kind of dance music was played. 'Love Song' by Simple Minds from 1981 is a good example of the music they spun. You know, Fad Gadget, Depeche Mode—that style. By the mid-'80s, some of the disco clubs started to shift to the new wave style. One of these trendsetting nightspots in Belgium was the AB Club in Antwerp, where the DJ played some rather obscure tracks, like b-sides from synth-bands. When the tempo of the song was too fast, he slowed it down drastically. For instance, the mythical track 'Flesh' by A Split-Second was originally a 45 rpm twelve-inch single, but he played it at 33 rpm.

"So a new sound began with DJs playing obscure tracks as an alternative to mainstream disco. A DJ called 'T.C.' initiated me into this, and he gave me some advice on a track I was making at the time. He suggested I build up the instrumental very, very slowly and to bring the tempo down to 105 beats-per-minute. It became the first 'new beat' hit: 'Hiroshima' by Nux Nemo. It had a bit of an oriental flavor. I wouldn't give it that name if I were releasing it today, though. It charted for a whole 12 weeks. After that, everyone who could handle a synthesizer woke up, I believe. New beat records started to pour out like a flood. A style was born: electronic, quite slow, and more or less spoken vocals. Very machine-like, this music.

"Originally, it was underground music," Jo observes. "The night-clubbers started to wear the typical black and white new beat style clothing of the period. They also danced in the new beat manner. It spread like a storm. As a result, this small country of Belgium drew international attention. International music magazines, MTV, record companies—they were all interested in what was happening here. After some three years, new beat became mainstream, and it disappeared soon after. Mind you, the style vanished, but the club scene remained very strong."

As the '80s drew to a close, Bogaert was looking for a new course in which to chart his knack for musical expression. "By 1989, it was the end of the new beat era," he remembers, "and I wanted to move to something else. Kevin Saunderson's Inner City track 'Big Fun' was an eye-opener. I heard it on a Detroit techno compilation. Among all these instrumental dance tracks, there was this vocal track with the soulful Paris Grey. That is when I realized that underground techno *could* have pop appeal by adding a full vocal. I started looking for someone to do a rap on an instrumental track I had created. I mentioned it to a guy who ran a record store in Antwerp. In his spare time he managed a hip-hop band with this talented female rapper named Ya Kid K [Manuela Kamosi]. He introduced us. She was a teenager at the time. I explained to her what I wanted, and a week later she came to my studio. Half an hour later, I had all the vocals I needed. She was amazingly efficient and fast. The track didn't have quite the structure that I wanted though, so I did some serious editing and molded it into a song—you know verses, refrain and the bridge.

"The guitarist of King Crimson, Robert Fripp, used a tape-loop system that was introduced to him in 1973 by Brian Eno. Fripp used it for solo performances and called it 'Frippertronics.' That sounded cool. I applied the suffix of the genre I was doing: 'techno' to 'tronic.' The result was 'Technotronic,' the name I gave to the project. (I didn't know about the similar-sounding Mantronix name already out there at the time, and the group Electronic came after us.)"

Released in the fall of 1989, first by Bogaert himself and then by arrangement with ARS Productions for international distribution, Technotronic's "Pump Up the Jam" detonated with unexpected force on the dance floor. Utterly compelling, the song's urgent beat and smoothly melodic, yet street-credible rap proved irresistible. The track eventually topped the charts in Belgium and Spain and narrowly missed the peak position in Germany, Austria and the United Kingdom. Perhaps most impressive was the song's blockbuster reception in the United States, where, via SBK/EMI Records, it vaulted to the number two position on the pop chart. It was a number one American dance chart hit and stayed on *Billboard*'s club survey for 17 weeks.

"The song is sometimes classified as new beat," Jo observes, "but I didn't feel like I was still doing that style at the time. I feel I was definitely somewhere else when I made the track. I always obsessed over bass drums and bass sounds. You know, the wrong bass drum sound can kill a track. Being a bass head, I wanted the kick and the bass to stand out, making it sound powerful. I succeeded in coming up with a recognizable colour. But the big difference was the vocal. Here was a rap that was like a sing-along and a chorus with a great hook—the 'make-my-day' reference, delivered by an excellent voice. Someone later coined the name 'hip-house,' but to me it was really techno."

On single jackets, "Pump Up the Jam" was officially credited to "Technotronic featuring Felly." Felly was, in reality, an attractive fashion model hired to promote the project. During this period of scrutiny over artist credentials (a front page issue with the Milli Vanilli debacle), the Technotronic project took some heat of its own for its so-called misrepresentation.

Explains Bogaert, "Here is the story. When 'Pump Up the Jam' was considered to have hit potential, the record company that I had teamed up with wanted to do a video and photographs with vocalist Ya Kid K. I passed the message on to her manager, but I don't know if everything was communicated properly. He told me she didn't feel like promoting the track, wanting to concentrate on her hip-hop band. That is when the record company decided to have Felly promote it. I emphasize the fact that this was *not* my idea. It didn't feel right to me.

"I think of Black Box," he adds. "They were smarter. They had learned their lesson from our project and Milli Vanilli. Let me explain. Black Box used an acapella from a Dan Hartman-produced track sung by Loleatta Holloway as their vocal source [for the single "Ride on Time"]. (By the way, I later met Dan, and we had plans to collaborate, but unfortunately he died before we could realize them.) When 'Ride' became a hit and they needed to promote the record, they hired—just like Technotronic—a model. To my knowledge, this model said in every interview that she was not the real singer, but rather just the face for Black Box. The public accepted this. Unfortunately, the record company presented Felly as if she was the real singer. I think that was a mistake, like it was in the case of Milli Vanilli. We changed this with the second single, 'Get Up! (Before the Night Is Over).'"

Despite the controversy, Bogaert feels his experience working with the ARS organization was a positive one. "My friend Marc Adam and I had our own label, Clip Records," he says. "One of our distributors was ARS, who also had their own label, ARS Records, that exported the 'Pump Up the Jam' 12-inch single worldwide. When they became aware of the song's hit potential, we teamed up with them for Technotronic. The relationship was not without tension, but looking back, they did a good job getting it released all over the world. Stewart Copeland once commented on the fame of The Police, saying that nobody is ready for success. Well, we weren't for sure. I would need an entire book to explain that side of the story. All of us—artists, business people and the lawyers who operated out of Belgium—were inexperienced as far as the worldwide situation was concerned. It was a fascinating experience. A lot of ups and downs. It cured me of any naivety forever but without becoming cynical.

"This kind of producer's project was unknown territory for the promotion guys and the media at the time," he admits. "Since I did not like the spotlight, I had felt comfortable staying incognito in the new beat days. But with 'Pump Up the Jam' being such a big hit, I had to step out of the dark. But to this present day, I don't enjoy that aspect of the business. Of course, now it is very common—this mix of producers, DJs and sampled voices—even the invisibility of artists is accepted (e.g. Burial). But at the time, we all thought that the public would only accept a proper band. And as far as the song goes, well, there is no recipe for a hit. But clearly the vocal is the secret—and the sound. 'Pump Up the Jam' and Technotronic enabled me to become a professional producer and musician. Ya Kid K also made music-making her profession."

A series of follow-up singles kept Technotronic front and center throughout Europe and the U.S. "Get Up! (Before the Night Is Over)" was written by Bogaert and Manuela Kamosi and properly placed the rapper and vocalist in the spotlight. Following a similar musical formula, the song was a massive hit in 1990, landing just shy of the number one spot in the UK. It was a Top 10 smash in America. "This Beat Is Technotronic" and the neo-psychedelic "Rockin' Over the Beat" (with remix versions by Shep Pettibone and New Order's Bernard Sumner) were enthusiastically received jams. A hit megamix single also scored top positions in several countries. The *Pump Up the Jam* album, whose master tapes were flown by Concorde jet to New York for speedy release in the U.S. (in the care of SBK Records' Nancy Brennan, the artist confirms), was also a tremendous success.

"Though released late in 1989, the 'Pump Up the Jam' single really only became a worldwide hit in 1990," Bogaert clarifies. "So it built up gradually over several months from being a club hit to radio and then TV. In the meantime, I put down some new tracks, and I focused my sound on the clubs. But sometimes I would do single edits in case some of the tracks crossed over to radio. When we hit the *Billboard* Hot 100 chart, I was asked to deliver an album, and I was able to deliver one in about three weeks time. So I didn't feel that much pressure to put the LP together, apart from that which I always put on myself."

Technotronic quickly became an in-demand act, prompting a huge international tour. Says Jo, "Technotronic toured as a 'live-to-tape' band, so Ya Kid K and MC Eric (the male rapper heard on 'This Beat Is Technotronic') did live vocals over recorded music. There was also a DJ on stage (like in hip-hop) and a couple of dancers. Since I don't like touring and I didn't see the point of setting up my studio on stage, I wasn't part of the live act. I went to see them in New York though, where we were opening for Madonna. Forty thousand people going wild over our song—wow. After the show, I tried to go backstage, but I wasn't allowed in—the record company had forgotten to arrange a backstage pass for me. Brings you down to earth again!" he smiles.

Bogaert's music attracted additional lucrative commercial benefits when the Technotronic single "Move This" was used as the backdrop for a well-known U.S. television ad for Revlon cosmetics. The exposure helped send the 1992 single into the American Top 10 and no doubt contributed to the sale of a few thousand crates of lipstick and eyeliner. The *Trip on This—The Remixes* LP, the *Body to Body* album and a 1993 greatest hits set kept the party going. Technotronic's final album, *Recall*, was released in 1995. A few more singles by the group were unveiled in the years that followed, with "The Mariachi" (featuring Ya Kid K) and "Runaway Blues" concluding a long and prosperous run at the dawn of the twenty-first century.

Today, Bogaert spends time as an avid non-fiction reader, writer and painter. He's leading "a simple life," as he puts it. He also continues to produce music when the spirit moves him. On the occasions where thoughts of his experience with Technotronic pass through his mind, he prefers to think of "Pump Up the Jam" as the start of an era, rather than the end of one. "Not that 'Pump Up the Jam' was the cause, but after that hit," he opines, "there was a continuous flow of inventive, beautiful electronic music coming out in the new decade—the underground, that is. New blood, new sounds, new structures, experiments. Also, music technology took an enormous flight. It's interesting what happened—eventually a music studio could be reduced to a laptop if necessary. On the other hand, those same advancements and the dawn of digital distribution of audio ended up destroying the old business model."

In the process of creating a new and sensational dance-pop sound with Technotronic at the twilight of the '80s, Jo Bogaert paved the way for a new generation of artists to explore progressive and exciting avenues of dance floor creativity. "Pump Up the Jam" and his enduring legacy of arresting hits did Belgium proud. Smiling, the artist says he'd be very happy if history simply views his contributions "…as a nice colour!"

Pete Burns
Dead or Alive
"You Spin Me Round (Like a Record)" (1984)
UK

"I hated the name Dead or Alive, but it was a brand name, and it really ended up being Pete Burns that everyone knew," asserts the star vocalist himself. The 55-year-old Englishman's observation is spot on. Burns was one of the most unique and iconic figures to emerge from the dance music scene of the mid–'80s. His eclectic image, maverick attitude and uncensored persona earned him copious amounts of paparazzi attention, as well as a plethora of accolades and criticisms. A relatively short time after the first hits of Dead or Alive broke across the European continent, Asia, Britain and America, the masses did, indeed, know the name of the group's front man. And they still do today.

Dead or Alive evolved from Burns' gradual rise through the ranks of the British punk and new wave scene. The incarnation of the band most widely recognized included Steve Coy (drummer), Wayne Hussey (guitarist), Mike Percy (bassist) and Timothy Lever (keyboards/saxophone). Pete Burns, serving as its avant-garde, powerful lead vocalist, orchestrated the transformation of the group from unknowns to chart-topping superstars. It began with their first major hit, 1984's "That's the Way (I Like It)," but the success of their razor-sharp reinvention of the K.C. and The Sunshine Band disco classic was just a warm up. Pete's punky, darkly androgynous, goth-styled appearance, flair for decidedly original showmanship and intoxicating vocal delivery became the very definition of all that was edgy and revolutionary about the period. More groundbreaking international dance hits followed, most notably the monumental smash "You Spin Me Round (Like a Record)," a scorching tour de force that charted exciting new high-energy musical territory. It was a song that had major artists from across Europe clamoring to duplicate the sound in the hope of duplicating the commercial success of Burns and his band mates.

In the years that followed, the accomplishments of Dead or Alive and the musical talents of the group's innovator were often eclipsed by Burns' own larger than life personality. In the twenty-first century, tabloid television exposés and gossip rag probes into his personal life, not to mention his aberrant appearances on programs like the UK's *Celebrity Big Brother*, further fanned the flames of curiosity that surrounded him. Adding to the drama, the artist says a lip enhancement procedure a few years back (part of an ongoing quest to attain a look that he believed would eventually result in a truer representation of his identity) had disastrous consequences. As a result of the ordeal and the unfinished medical procedures

Pete Burns' avant-garde style and powerful voice became the signature of the group Dead or Alive, one of Britain's most influential bands of the era. The image on the left was used as the cover of the band's 2010 *That's the Way I Like It: The Best Of* album (photography by Peter Brown). *Right:* Burns as he appeared early in 2003 (photography by James & James, courtesy Pete Burns and Dead or Alive, with thanks to Epic/Sony BMG Europe).

the artist says were necessary to repair the damage, Burns' ever-changing facial appearance continued to bring him sensationalistic attention. Meanwhile, he sedulously committed himself to the process of regaining his health and deciding on what would come next.

At the time of this interview, Pete said it hads been a long time since he agreed to speak with anyone about his career. He made a rare exception given of the nature of this project. There wasn't a moment that he hesitated to say exactly how he felt about any given topic. His manner throughout the conversation was consistently calm. Though he warned he might drift off onto tangents, he rarely did. On those occasions where multiple memories of his vast experience actually managed to tangle with each other, he always quickly came back to the subject at hand. Throughout this interview, he seemed to be treating it as something of a cathartic exercise.

"I choose *not* to do interviews now because of my principles," he stated resolutely. "I was paid rather highly for trashy interviews, and I am asked trashy questions all the time. I always came out feeling bad about it and decided about two years ago that I was going to put a full stop to the trash interviews and wouldn't do them any more—not for any amount of money. I'd rather do without the financial benefit than continue promoting that kind of thing. Our talk is a bit different."

Burns briefly recalled his younger days and his mother, Eva. "My childhood ambition was to become a doctor. I was an incredible painter and cartoonist when I was young, but they weren't exactly the qualifications necessary to enter a college and study medicine. My mother was a Nazi concentration camp survivor. She escaped and worked for the Russian Secret Police at one point. Her father owned a film studio and directed some of Dietrich's silent films. She had me when she was 51 years old, which was very unusual in 1959. And I'm not from Liverpool. I'm from a small village called Port Sunlight. I wasn't put in school until I was seven years old because my mother thought it was more important to let me have freedom of expression (much against my father's will) than to know when the Battle of Hastings took place or who Henry VIII married. She was very troubled, especially when she found out her father had been murdered (after having disappeared).

"About 1974 or '75, I worked as a hair stylist in a salon and my appearance was so extreme (I was already buying clothes from places like Vivienne Westwood's 'Let It Rock' and wearing blue foundation and things like that), as was Lynne [Corlett], my ex-wife, that they had to employ extra security at the mall where the salon was located to handle the crowds. We had to stop dressing that way, Lynne and I, and wear uniforms after the crowd broke the glass of the front window of the shop. I was very talented at hair dressing and coloring. But eventually we were fired.

"I found myself with nothing to do and had about £250. Lynne and I rented a small room and started buying army surplus clothes, customizing and dying them, and kind of making punk copies of the styles of the time (it was 1976, '77). We would sell them from our room. An older guy named Jeff Davis, who owned a big record store called Probe, bought a lot of our stuff and asked us to move into the back of his store."

In a 2006 interview with Fiona Cummins for Britain's *Mirror*, Lynne (wed to Burns in 1978) revealed that Pete had begun a fling with his future boyfriend, Michael Simpson, even before their marriage had (amicably) ended. Lynne said she was aware of their relationship during her marriage to Pete but expressed no resentment for it. Lynne remained loyal to Burns, and the singer confirmed they continue to be soul mates. "She is sacred to me," Pete said.

In their early days together, the couple pressed through the challenges of their offbeat appearances and lifestyle. "Lynne and I were not allowed into any gay clubs because of how we looked," Burns recalled. "We'd wear razor blades for earrings and women were not allowed in gay clubs at that time. So we started hanging out at a club called Eric's, and I opened a small shop in the back of the place. I always liked the American bands, and I was sort of adopted by many of them, the musicians, when they played there. I was treated like a V.I.P. and never had to be in the audience. I was either to the side of the stage or backstage, which was quite amazing for someone who was just 16 years old. The owner of the club, who had started to bring over bands like Blondie, Kraftwerk and Johnny Thunders and the Heartbreakers, suddenly told me I was barred from the club until I formed a band and started to sing. We thought he was joking. But he actually set me up with a band of musicians called The Mystery Girls, and my first gig was supporting a group called Sham 69. My audience was really shocked when they first saw me. It was really throwing a cat among the pigeons.

"After working with The Mystery Girls (my appearance caused some problems, and it didn't mean that much to me, so that ended), I started to get noticed by the music newspapers. They wanted to interview me and print a picture, but I didn't have a band, so I made up one called 'Rainbows Over Nagasaki.' It kind of all started to snowball. I had no band and no songs, but was asked to perform. So I pulled together a gravedigger, a strict

Mormon, a basic bass player, and a friend who taught himself to play a keyboard. We became the band called 'Nightmares in Wax.' The band name came out of my friendship with the American punk rock band The Cramps, who I did quite a few support gigs with, and they were absolutely wonderful. Our group disbanded after one single, 'Black Leather.'

"To be truthful, I wasn't ambitious about being a singer. It was just too much fucking hassle with the musicians and stuff because they were very egotistical. I'm sorry, but in my bands, there was no democracy. It was my way or the fucking highway. It was stressful. It's not that I'm opposed to stress; it was just like I would say, 'Oh this is too hard. It's not worth it.' I wasn't running around thinking I should get in a band, have a hit record and I'd be a rich person.

"I did pull together another group of musicians, though, because I had another gig still to do. I had this book about James Dean and other celebrities called *Those Who Died Young*. I thought that should be the name of the band. When we arrived at the session, the ex-gravedigger guitarist, Avery Mitchell was his name, said there was no way he was going to play in a band called 'Those Who Died Young.' He said we needed to be called 'Dead or Alive,' or he wasn't doing the session. So, okay, it didn't matter to me as long as we had the money for the session. Well, guess what? We got more and more sessions. I started recording and getting paid for it. I started getting checks, and I started to feel like I won the lottery."

Released in 1984, the Dead or Alive's first album, *Sophisticated Boom Boom,* on Epic Records, began the group's journey into commercially accessible synth-dance music. The album cracked the Top 30 in Britain and their rousing, hammering version of the disco nugget "That's the Way (I Like It)," flirted with the Top 20. Clubs in America sent the track into the Top 30 of the disco/dance chart. "Zeus B. Held, who did the album with us, was the greatest producer I ever worked with. He was the most unbelievable person to work with. I mean, it may not be the best production, but he and I worked so well together, and he totally understood what I was after. I liked certain elements of disco, others I couldn't bear. Certain disco records were breathtaking, like Donna Summer's 'MacArthur Park Suite.' Unbelievable. I used to love that kind of disco. I loved the music's ability to lift people up. Things like Cher's 'Take Me Home.' I never heard a disco record that offended me, but if I thought it was shit, I was done with it," Pete said.

The album initiated Burns' uneasy relationship with the corporate side of making commercially popular music. "I never allowed—and this never did me any favors—it was a bad attitude, but it was my way of working—I would never allow the record company people to come in on the recording of my music. That was a strict contractual term. No A&R people. Nobody from the company was allowed into the studio until the full completion of the album. That didn't make [the executives] feel very pleased. When they'd hear it later, they'd always come back and say things like, 'Hmmm … the bass sound needs altering,' or something like that. And you know what we used to do? We'd give it back to them, saying we fixed it, and it's okay now. They didn't even notice that nothing was changed, but they had to feel like they were involved.

"The other thing they'd always say to me was, 'Where's the ballad? Where's the ballad? Where's the ballad?' I never had a desire to do a ballad—I only wanted to do music that made people happy."

Though considered by many to be phenomenally distinctive in a vast sea of interchangeable pop music singers, Burns says he was never able to appreciate the unique quality of his baritone voice. "I hate the sound of my voice," he confessed. "I've only liked it on one thing—an acoustic show I did with an Australian gentleman named Jonathan Coleman. We did an acoustic medley (just a piano) from the album *Fan the Flame*. I saw it recently on the Internet, and I thought, okay, that *is* fucking good. I thought my voice sounded really good.

"I have power and perfect pitch, but you see, I have many singers I like, and they are usually female. I am sure you have heard of Sylvester (although, if you can believe it, many people have *not* in this country, even in the gay community—they don't know who Divine is either). I was quite astounded when I saw Sylvester on *Top of the Pops*. He appeared as a man singing; he put a fan across his face, and then he's kind of an androgyny. I was like, 'Wow!' Even in the punk clubs here in the UK, Sylvester's music would be played, and he filled the floors, which was quite amazing. I fully expected when I stood in front of a microphone, that a voice like his would come out of me. That was my spirit voice, the voice that I wanted. That was the voice I wanted to come out of me. Personally, my choice, I wish I had a different kind of voice, but I have to settle with what I have."

Dead or Alive's next project proved to be a groundbreaking innovation, but its evolution and eventual success required patience. "I was very motivated by *Pink Flamingos*, Divine's first movie that I saw very early on (where he eats the dog shit)," Pete remembers. "I never laughed so hard and was never shocked so much in my life. The next thing I knew, a record by Divine appeared called 'Native Love (Step by Step),' produced by Bobby O [Orlando]. When we signed our record deal with CBS for the next album, we were in negotiations for production with Bobby O. Bobby was being very, very difficult, and the plan died in the end. A while back, we had also considered working with Sylvester's producer, Patrick Cowley [1950–1982], but the record label had opposed [using] him.

"I was happy signing with Sony, and it was very nice to have a multi-album deal with them. But I wish the deal had come earlier. But CBS was only interested in us because they wanted a second Culture Club. But hey, I'm sorry, I was the one with that kind of style long before Boy George, when you look at my indie singles, the posters of me, and just look at the history. But statements like this always get me into arguments, and my mistake is that I respond; I bite back.

"We were young and naïve in the '80s. We didn't get media training. That was always the problem with my interviews—I told the absolute truth. Today, I believe people are media-trained now with what to talk about and how to do it. I always reserved the right to change my mind at any given moment. You make a decision like, 'I fucking hate that pair of shoes more than anything in the world.' Then you decide you really love them. That's the way my mind works. Maybe it's schizophrenia. It's pretty much impossible to be that way in our society, and it was totally impossible in the corporate music industry.

"Anyway, I digress. I kept a clock-radio alarm beside my bed back then (I don't have clocks any more). When it would go off, the radio came on, and the record that was being played the most at the time was 'Whatever I Do (Wherever I Go)' by Hazell Dean. I noticed the production and the cowbells and the sounds on it. Then Divine's 'You Think You're a Man' came out, and I did research into who the producers were. So we went and had a meeting with our record company and said the producers of those hits were the ones we wanted to use. Essentially, that was Pete Waterman."

Dead or Alive aligned forces with Waterman, whose fledging British production house included partners Mike Stock and Matt Aitken. The result was the album *Youthquake*, released in the spring of 1985, a number one hit in Britain and a Top 20 smash in the U.S. From the set came an unforgettable single, "You Spin Me Round (Like a Record)," a wild romp through high-energy dance music that not only gave Burns and his band mates a number one in the UK, Canada and Switzerland, it became a monster success in Germany, Italy, Austria, America and numerous other countries. It dramatically increased demand for the expertise of the Stock Aitken Waterman crew, and it became *the* sound to emulate by artists on both sides of the Atlantic. The record made international stars out of Dead or Alive. However, the single took over four months to top the British chart, and Pete insists that not everyone was initially enthusiastic about the track.

"The label kept telling us 'Spin' was not a hit. And then eventually it *did* become a hit through the gay clubs. It turned into a *huge* hit. Then it spread into the straight world. I know that Neil Tennant of the Pet Shop Boys used to write for a music paper as a journalist at one time, and he gave 'Spin' the most damning review you have ever read. I remember the label told me the maximum it could be number one for was two weeks, if I was lucky, because [their next artist] was coming out with a single, and he'd have to go to number one. That's how the corporate industry worked, and I had disgust for it."

The Stock Aitken Waterman team was reportedly quite firm about adhering to their production methods and concepts, which Burns said was a major source of friction. "We would butt heads so fucking badly; it was unbelievable. That's why we eventually walked away from them. For instance, there was a lyric from 'Something in My House' [from the follow-up album, *Mad, Bad and Dangerous to Know*] where I make a reference to a 'wicked queen.' The actual producer, Mike Stock, stopped me and said I couldn't use that term because it would mean the record is about gay people. I was like, 'Fuck this; it's going on!' They actually wiped the original vocal, but then Pete Waterman came back and said, "Let him do it the way he wants to.' There you go.

"I got really sick working with them during the making of the *Mad, Bad* album. I got really, really sick. We worked on that album from 10 in the morning till eight at night, and every evening when I arrived home, my wife had to have bath towels heated red hot in the tumble drier ready for me. I'd be trembling, and my body temperature would be so low with the stress. I thought it was really too much."

Mad, Bad and Dangerous to Know was released by Epic early in 1987, and though it spawned a number of successful singles, response to the set in Britain was a bit more tepid this time. Though it struggled to hit the UK's Top 40, the pulsating dance single "Brand New Lover" cracked the U.S. Top 15 and was tremendously popular in Japan. "The label decided they would put that album out, and that was all that's gonna happen," said Burns. "They did no pre-ads for it, and they didn't press the quantity that was required for 'Brand New Lover.' That was how they were able to tell you that you had a flop. They've done it to countless bands; it was a commonplace thing, in America too. On the first week of release, the song entered the chart here at 31 or 32 I think, which was considered low. When the American record company got involved, some kind of misprint came out that said the record had come in straight at number two in the UK. The American company must have panicked and rush-released it, and as a result, it did extremely well in the U.S. The album won me songwriting awards in America and in Britain.

"One thing that came out of that period was that we changed something huge in the music industry. It was under a confidentiality contract with Sony back then, but I don't give a fuck about it any more because we're not with them any more. But back then, artists didn't receive any royalties whatsoever on 12-inch record sales. These records were seen as promotional tools. Yet something like 72 percent of our sales for 'You Spin Me Round' were from the 12-inch mixes. It was Top 10 in so many countries and took 17 weeks to reach the number one position in the UK. The people who did the chart thing kept holding it back because they couldn't believe how many 12-inch singles it was selling. The song received very little airplay, and when radio did play it, they'd never say the name of our band. We had every door shut in our face. So if you think about the journey this song had, it is really quite incredible and unusual. But nobody handed me a gift with this record; I did it all myself.

"It depends what you think a lot of money is, but I think we lost a lot [as a result of our arrangement with the label]. In my estimation, we lost maybe three quarters of a million pounds in royalties. We didn't get anywhere near that. We told [the record company] we were taking them to court for non-payment of royalties and that we were going to leave the label. Our lawyers were about to file a legal suit in court, but the record company did not want to lose us and agreed to pay us a settlement and royalties on our 12-inch record sales. There was no way any judge was going to look at 72 percent of our sales coming from 12-inch singles and agree with the label that it was acceptable to call them 'promotional tools.' It made no sense. After we received the settlement, I just basically let it out wherever I could because I thought [the label's protocol in regard to 12-inch singles] was wrong. Gradually, other people on the label like Paul Young, Alison Moyet, Sade and others started getting royalties on 12-inch records. They don't know that I made that happen, but I did."

Towards the end of the decade, Dead or Alive released the album *Nude*, produced by the singer and drummer Steve Coy. The cover featured Burns alluringly posed—smooth, lean and very minimally clad. Pete says Epic was extremely reluctant to market the set. "The label really didn't want it to happen because of the cover of the album. At that time, the marketing people would take the record around by car to all the shops, and because they found the cover so offensive, they wouldn't take it around. But in Japan, the record went through the fucking roof. We were awarded a Japanese 'Grand Prix' Award for Best International Album of 1989 in the 'Pop' or 'Popular' category.

"My mother had gotten sick at that time. My father told me the news. I decided I was going to take care of her. She had been given six weeks to live with terminal lung cancer. She wouldn't have chemotherapy, which they said might help stop the spread. My entire—it was more than a year that I cared for her, as it turned out—my entire year was spent searching for alternative medicine, healers, Chinese herbal medicine, pulse-electro therapy, acupuncture—things that were considered witchcraft in those days. I even went to the Queen's doctor with an open checkbook and asked him to cure her. He gave me some tablets. I asked him if they would cure her. He said that it was a tranquilizer—and that I was gonna need them. I never took them. She lived 11 months on painkillers and passed away in her sleep. I felt like a failure because I had hoped for a cure. She was a medical miracle, though, to have lived 11 months. Six weeks was the maximum for someone with a tumor that size. She was 72 years old.

"At the same time all this had started, my manager and my record label, without telling me, had somehow made an agreement to place me on the Madonna *Who's That Girl* tour.

I was never consulted and didn't even know about the tour. Not at all. I played the message on my answering machine. 'We've got you on the Madonna tour. Big surprise!' I thought, oh my God, talk about a mix of shit and sugar. You know what I mean? I sat down and took a breather and phoned my manager back and told them about my mother and that I couldn't do the tour. Their terms were terrible too—Madonna's people were tough. We couldn't perform on the actual stage, but would have to be on something like a ledge. We would perform something like two hours before she went on, so literally nobody would have even seen us. It turned out UB40 did the tour, lots of gigs were canceled, and their group went bankrupt and split up at the end of the tour. I had no regrets about choosing my mother over this tour. It wasn't fun, but it was something I *had* to do in a karmic sense.

"When I declined, the manager left a message that said my mother would be screaming, bald and crawling around the ward screaming for them to overdose and kill her, just like my career will be if I didn't do this tour," Pete claimed. "I said, 'That's it!' I terminated my management contract. Unbelievable!"

The rise of Pete Burns and Dead or Alive ran parallel to the rapidly emerging AIDS crisis that befell the world during the '80s. Pete remembers the impact of the pandemic. "Very early on in the crisis, some really close friends and acquaintances started dropping like fucking flies. It wasn't a pretty death, and I was at their bedside through their deaths. At one point, the main AIDS ward in Britain then was—oh I don't know, I think it was St. Mary's something. I can't remember. The poor kids there, their esophaguses were being burned by the medicine AZT and other things they were giving them at the time. So they couldn't eat food. I did some research, and I was able to get a huge supply of fresh, organic Aloe vera flown in. I took it into the wards, and the kids started improving. They could actually start eating meals in bed. Well, I was banned from the ward when the hospital found out.

"Thinking of that crisis, the grief got to me so much. I remember in the early '90s I was brought over to the Limelight in New York by that horrible Michael Alig [co-founder of the Club Kids group, who pleaded guilty to manslaughter in 1996]—they bought me for a fucking fortune. When I arrived at the door for the sound check, Michael wouldn't let me in—I was blond and didn't come with my band; I had planned to do a different kind of show with Alvin Ailey dancers and a female vocalist. [Once I got inside], there were these tacky glitter letters that said 'Dead or Alive.' I said no way, and I just wouldn't do it. So I walked out. I continued with the rest of the tour.

"I felt I had to do something myself because I had an issue with the administration costs of the AIDS organizations that were in Chelsea, New York. I was staying at an Ian Schrager hotel, and my room had a huge glass wall. I could see down to the street level where there were homeless people with signs like 'Ex-Vietnam Vet with AIDS,' 'Homeless with AIDS, please help.' There I was, livin' it up, and I couldn't take it. So I decided to take all the gig fees that I was paid before I would go on stage, in cash, and I went with my assistant and donated those fees to certain people that I felt needed the help. So, to give you an example, one fan met me after a gig and said that his boyfriend was my biggest fan, and he was at home dying of this disease. I took the limo to his place, sang for his boyfriend in his living room with a backing tape and gave them about $25,000 to help them pay for some of their medical expenses.

"I'm not a saint, but that's what I did. I don't expect any credit, but I do my bit—

quietly. This is how I give back. But I do think it's time I kinda spoke out about it because I do keep it quiet. I seem to receive attention for some of the things I don't do. For example, I didn't do Live Aid because I didn't believe the record companies were donating all the money, if you know what I mean. It wasn't as charitable as it seems. They knew they'd make millions but didn't donate all the royalties. They donated a certain portion, but they didn't donate it all, and that, to me, just seemed really wrong."

Around the same period, Dead or Alive's previous success in Japan prompted the release of an album exclusive to that country called *Fan the Flame (Part 1),* issued in 1990. It failed to have significant impact, however, and the band fell out of the spotlight. Burns later teamed with Glam for the high-energy cult hit single "Sex Drive" in 1994 (which was remixed in 2014), and back with Dead or Alive, unleashed the album *Nukleopatra* the following year. The group's compilation set, *Fragile,* a collection of remixes, came out in 2000. Sony released a greatest hits collection in 2003 called *Evolution: The Hits,* but Burns said he didn't have fond memories of the event. "By the time Sony decided to release *Evolution,*" he recalled, "I had gradually changed my appearance over the years. As a result, they believed I was only marketable to the gay community, so they decided to only put up posts in just the one major gay area of Britain (which is in Manchester). They only placed ads in those free gay handout magazines. That was the extent of their full promotion. Then they had the nerve to ask me to go on a world tour for the album, and I was like, 'You are fucking kidding!' I just wasn't going to do it. I think that's when I really felt I should disappear."

In 2009, Burns released the electronic dance jam single "Never Marry an Icon." Three years later, the singer performed at *Hit Factory Live,* a concert presented by Pete Waterman at London's O2 Stadium, which also featured Hazell Dean, Rick Astley, Jason Donovan and others from the peak days of the Stock Aitken Waterman empire. "When I played the big Stock Aitken Waterman reunion gig," says the singer, "we brought the house down, even though we were relatively in the middle of the bill. It inspired Pete to get back into the music business. They approached me about recording and writing with them. Stupidly, without any contractual agreement, I went along with it. I said I just needed a keyboard player. Pete Waterman said he wanted me to sound like Trent Reznor of Nine Inch Nails and that should be the new direction for me. I basically had one day every two weeks to write and completely mix a track, and he was going to try and sell it to another record label. It was impossible to do it.

"Yes, I *do* want to do another record, but it may not be for another 10 years. I decided after I recorded 'Never Marry an Icon,' until I come up with a better idea, I'm not going to do it. I'm sick of 'it's fine,' 'it's good as it is.' I hate the word 'fine.' No, it's got to be the *best* I can possibly do. I hope I achieve that before I leave this mortal coil and reign in hell—rather than serve in heaven," Pete said, laughing at his dramatic delivery.

Throughout all of these extraordinary experiences, Burns conceded that the fame he achieved had been a mixed bag. "I would actually have preferred not to have such big success here in England," he said, "because it was on my front doorstep. It put an incredible strain on me. To be that famous and on the cover of all the glossy teen magazines—and you're a household name—and I got genuine stalkers and psychos, and I wouldn't use bodyguards—it was hard. I wouldn't drive around in limos, and so I walked everywhere. I refused to give up things like that, or sitting in a café or walking around in the daytime. So it was really hard.

"Why do you think Madonna is constantly on tour, when she really should have given up her heels and hung it up by now? Because she's so fucking famous, she can't even move. There is a life with fame, but it's not a real life. It's behind guarded windows and blacked out screens and private planes. It's like this weird thing with famous people. It's like a sickness where they know each other, like in a little club, and I've found most of them to be self-obsessed, shallow and absolutely vile. Except a few people, like Deborah Harry—lovely. But the others—God no. I'm talking about the big league of fame.

"But if I had to do it all over again, I wouldn't have chosen *not* to be in music because— I mean—I was able to help my friends, like take them on holidays and help pay their rent and take people to nice restaurants that they'd never have been able to set foot in. I think I wouldn't have had a number one record right away, though—I think it came too soon. After number one, where can you go but down?

"I do think I've made some reasonable records. But at the time, I thought these were often things that just needed to get done; I didn't need to listen to a record again or be involved with it. I'm there for every second of the recording and all the work to create the song, but that's it. I've never ever written my lyrics down, I just ad-libbed. And it never took me more than one take to record a song.

"I'm very grateful for it. I'm very grateful for 'Spin Me.' What I'm going to say is contradictory, but you'll have to try and make sense of it. I didn't realize that when you have success with something, I didn't realize that you were going to be expected to repeat the same formula over and over, again and again. I thought in the artistic world, art was about expression. Corporate art is actually about repetition. It's still happening—the remixes that always come out, etcetera, etcetera. It's a legendary record. I'm grateful to have had 'Spin.' Of course I get bored singing it every night. I've said this before—I'm 55 years old for Christ's sake. It's like being forced to wear your grade school uniform when you're 25 years old."

In recent years, Burns has been a media favorite, mostly because of his almost unrecognizable appearance, the result of cosmetic procedures that he began to explore in the mid-'80s. "I was one of the first to be open about what I've done in terms of cosmetic surgery. Why lie?" he asked quite pointedly. "I had my nose done the week before 'Spin' came out, and it cost £700 and was done by someone in Liverpool. The nose basically collapsed on one side, and I was basically purple. So I had to wear an eye patch to disguise the nose job disaster until it healed and could be redone. Then later on, during the '90s, I decided I would have my lips augmented. I had seen Barbara Hershey in *Beaches* and wanted that kind of collagen augmentation. I had no desire to look like [transgender performance artist] Amanda Lepore, by the way—she looks great, but I didn't want to look like that."

Burns described receiving a cosmetic procedure involving lip-filler some years ago, which he said was improperly administered by a London doctor. It marked the beginning of a grueling ordeal for the singer. "I did a gig with Scissor Sisters on the radio, and the next morning I woke up—with no exaggeration—my partner found me on the floor, writhing in pain and my lower lip had swelled up larger—and I mean this—than when a person has a disc inserted in it. It was bigger than my face—the lower lip. There was yellow stuff pouring out of holes in it. I called my doctor and my partner explained the situation. The doctor saw me in the waiting room and hid me in a back room. He removed over a liter and a half of fluid. Holes started to appear in my cheek and neck. I started to get discharges from my eyes, and I developed kidney stones and stones in my liver. It ripped its way right through my body," he said in a tone that clearly reflected his exhaustion.

The case with his doctor was settled out of court, but Pete's tribulations endured. "The pictures of my reconstruction, which people have offered good money for, have to be turned down because they can't print them. They said they were too distressing. Yet they *can* show pictures of someone being beheaded, you know what I mean? But that's not my problem. What I'm trying to say is, the majority of the surgeries I've had have been serious reconstruction surgeries. I've had many top surgeons, but I've just been unlucky. I had to go to so many other surgeons because I certainly couldn't trust the one who did the lip originally. There came a point where they felt both my lips would have to be amputated. We searched the world, and a man named Paolo, who was a fan, worked for a cancer reconstruction surgeon in Italy. I couldn't fly there, so the surgeon flew over to me with Paolo and a wonderful friend of mine from Italy named Marina. He said it would take a lot of operations [to repair the damage]—it was going to be my road to Calvary. He estimated the time to be three to six months.

"Two whole years later, I was still living in a remote place in Italy, having general anesthesia twice a week, on intravenous anti-viral drugs, steroid injections and anti-rejection drugs. It was an unbelievable experience. The media didn't want to know what the problem was. I'd tell them what happened, and they'd just make up the problem.

"Yes, I had a facelift about six years ago. Who hasn't had one that can fucking afford one? Yes, I had my jaw line augmented with a safe filler. Yes, my lips have to be augmented—it's going to be a lifelong procedure. [My doctor] couldn't get all of the [old] filler out. So every so often there will be a new eruption, and the only way to deal with it and keep the moisture in the lip tissue is to fill them to quite a large size. I have to use almost three times the usual amount of filler because of my condition, and it gives me, well, quite big lips. I now have to also cope with the health issues that have resulted from all of this.

"The cosmetic surgery thing was not a matter of vanity. It was a matter of sanity. I *had* to look the way I envisioned myself. I saw this face I wanted when I was a child, from my earliest age. I was very aware that I didn't recognize myself when I looked in the mirror. There was nothing wrong with the way I looked—there was nothing wrong with *me*. It's just like my voice—it was not the voice I expected to come out of my mouth. What I confronted in the mirror and on magazine covers—it was not the face that I expected to see. I didn't recognize myself.

"I look at my situation, and I say it's okay. If I were to die tomorrow, I've had a relatively good life. Yeah, it's had obstacles. But there are children being killed every day. So it's okay what I've gone through. I firmly believe in reincarnation, but the next time I'm sliding down the birth canal, I'll be saying, 'Honey, I'm staying in here, and I'm *not* coming out.'"

Though these were obviously difficult days for Burns, who emphasized his disdain for the aging process, he seemed able to separate the natural (though uncomfortable) experience of human maturation from his current health issues. But that didn't soften his opinion about the march of time. "Aging is the greatest act of terrorism ever reaped on humankind I'm afraid," Pete said adamantly.

There is a pause for a few moments before he continues. "We cope, but it's downhill all the way. Well, you know shit happens. I've tried to lead a healthy life. I never touched a street drug ever. Never in my life. Oh, wait, I did try a drug called MDMA [widely known as "ecstasy"]—in the '80s, during the house music days at a club. It just brought on massive depression, like I was kicked in the head. I was depressed for the next three weeks—no thanks. So there you go—I lived a healthy lifestyle. I exercised myself rigid right through the '80s. But after a while, I realized I'd really rather—*read*. I realized I wasn't exercising my brain. I was building this exterior, but I wasn't nourishing my brain. I was drinking protein drinks, watching carbs. This wasn't life. What's it for? What's it about?

"How do I feel about aging? Listen, believe me—I have a tattooed ass, right? It's covered in tattoos. I don't know what I was thinking. I never thought about the possibility that one day my ass will end up around my ankles. You know what was once a tattoo of roses will eventually look like I sat on a village of Smurfs. I'm sure under Cher's miracle body stocking she wears, I'm sure it's not too pretty a sight. She looks amazing; I adore her. I'm not criticizing her, but—you know—aging sucks.

"I have no control over the health side of my life. Que sera, que sera. As for people who may perceive me as having great strength because of it, well, I have a very limited group of friends left. They are all old friends, and they see me in a flood of tears and at very weak moments. I'm not afraid to express my emotions about things. But I do it in private. I suppose it is a contradiction. I have had people say to me on Facebook or Twitter that I was so strong for some of the things I've been through. But it was all just something I had to do. I have to be who I am."

Pete Burns' spectacular history, merely hinted at here, was less about pop stardom than it was about the courage to pursue freedom of expression, a value instilled in the artist early on by his mother. Undeniably, one of the most valuable contributions the artist made to pop culture (though often eclipsed by the performer's eccentricities and unconventional appearance) was his effort to bring people a sense of joy and empowerment through music. He succeeded in this endeavor on his own terms, proudly evidenced by his trendsetting work in Dead or Alive. In recent years, he was loved and admired by a great many; others found him, let's say, an oddity. It had been that way for most of his life. But to Pete, it seemed all quite irrelevant.

"I'm really not interested in what people think of me, especially the negativity," he saids firmly. "As a living human being, I've refused to pay any attention to it. They don't pay my rent; they don't put fucking food on my table. So what people think of me doesn't matter. If you don't hear that stuff, the bad stuff, it doesn't hurt. I've personally never given myself a good review anyway. With the music, I've said before that you're buying the record, not me. Thank you for buying the record, but you haven't bought *me*. Some people in life try to take ownership of you and get very hateful. It's beyond description.

"Being a human being is a fucking pain in the ass at times. I'd much rather be a cat."

Pete Burns died of cardiac arrest on October 23, 2016.

Phil Creswick

Big Fun
"Blame It on the Boogie" (1989)
UK

Phil Creswick has the distinction of having been a key vocalist in one of England's most dynamic boy bands of the '80s, Big Fun. Fresh off his stint in the popular dance music ensemble known as Seventh Avenue, Creswick and his group mates (Jason John, a.k.a Jason Herbert, and Mark Gillespie) were taken under the wing of Britain's unstoppable Stock Aitken Waterman production team. In a short time, they became an absolute sensation. The trio scored numerous chart-toppers in their native England with a distinctive brand of breezy, infectiously catchy and high-energy dance-pop singles, such as "Blame It on the Boogie" and "Can't Shake the Feeling." Their popularity rapidly expanded to Germany, Ireland, France and Spain (among many other nations), and their hits helped further define the PWL production sound.

As a young, good-looking gay man, Creswick claims his producers tucked away his sexual identity while he shared the media spotlight and charts with fellow red-hot compatriots Rick Astley and Kylie Minogue (just for starters). Phil's experience in the British music industry in the final years of the decade was filled with equal doses of extraordinary excitement and the bitter realities of the era's social and business challenges. He welcomes the opportunity to share his '80s adventures and speaks candidly from his London home about the duality of his tenure as a pop star.

"I always wanted to be a singer, even from the days when I was very young," says Phil. "I knew I had a good voice because I'd get a lot of solos in the youth choir. When I got a bit older and my voice broke, it didn't really change all that much. I quickly discovered I loved performing and decided I would go to London and become famous. Around 1988, I answered a personal ad in *Gay Times*. It said something like 'famous record producer looking for boy friday.' I met up with producer Ian Levine's personal assistant, who looked me over and made sure I was okay. I then met with Mr. Levine himself, and that was the beginning of our connection."

Ian and partner Fiachra Trench (who had scored a monster hit with Evelyn Thomas' "High Energy" earlier in the decade) were having success at the time with an all-male group called Seventh Avenue. The outfit had been making the disco rounds with various members since 1979. By the mid-'80s, Seventh Avenue had racked up several major dance hits, including "Ending Up on a High" and "Love's Gone Mad."

"I knew Ian's formula with Seventh Avenue," recalls Phil, "and I waited and waited until the time was right to ask him if I could audition for a new line-up of the group he was forming. Jason was already in the band when I finally became part of it. I found the concept of this group very funny and very cheeky, and that started my professional career. I can best describe Ian as funny, annoying and a perfectionist to the point of it being painful. He was quite interesting to work with because he had a very determined way of recording. There are a few horror stories that could be told about when he came down hard on us during the recording of a record. Then, after we thought the recording was finally all finished, he'd say it *still* wasn't quite right. He was a nice guy, really, and you can't knock someone for being a perfectionist, but it was challenging at times," Creswick admits.

"One of the members of Seventh Avenue dropped out (I think he got bored with all the traveling throughout the UK), and another was sort of pushed out because our thinking was he wasn't really contributing anything. We were something like 19 years old, and you just want to get to the top, you know? So you boot someone out like that. It's awful, really, and I do regret some of my actions, but you can't go back in time. We replaced him with a young man I had met in a gay bar, actually, Mark Gillespie. Mark really had a beautiful voice. After that, Seventh Avenue had a very big hit in Japan with 'The Love I Lost,' and we went there to promote it.

"While there, we met Kylie Minogue. We also met Pete Waterman. Our manager, a very good man named Bill Grainger, was a big fan of Pete's and PWL. We got to have a bite to eat with Pete and told him that we wanted to do something new. Bill later said to us, 'Stick with me boys; I'll see what I can do to make it happen.' He worked his magic with Pete. Pete loved us, and that's when we decided to join PWL. Ian Levine wasn't too thrilled with that news, obviously. All hell broke loose. He phoned us up and was screaming at us. It was quite a call. But we knew we would be in good hands with PWL," says the artist.

Using the name Seventh Avenue wasn't even a remote possibility since the boys had jumped ship, so Phil, Jason and Mark established a new group name, Big Fun. The singer says the moniker was derived from the title of a popular Inner City song. They also felt it was a cool slang term that had been circulating at the time and something that might catch on. "We're having 'big fun' or whatever," Phil laughs. He says their deal with the UK division of Jive Records came about (at least in part) after Jason had a conversation in a Covent Garden sauna with a lawyer who was associated with the label. The boys first released a modestly successful underground acid house track called "Living for Your Love" (produced by Marshall Jefferson).

From there, Big Fun joined forces with the "PWL Empire," as this golden-touch production team was justifiably described at the time. PWL's leaders were producers Mike Stock, Matt Aitken and Pete Waterman—and the gentlemen were, to say the very least, dominating the British and European charts. Their disco-fied pop sound was in high demand, and artists and groups like Kylie, Samantha Fox, Bananarama and Dead Or Alive had seen their careers skyrocket once the trio's Midas touch had been applied.

"The time was right in the '80s in England for the Stock Aitken Waterman sound," believes Phil. "We came off that old school disco sound of the '70s, and I think people were hungry for something more adventurous. So music producers ended up creating this electro-pop-dance sound that was just very new. Depeche Mode, Kraftwerk, Erasure, Human League—groups like that had really helped launch a new electronica sound, and many of their hits were very danceable. I've worked with Vince Clarke of Erasure, and he was like a god. He would work for hours and days on one sound until it was perfect. I think the Stock Aitken Waterman team took elements of that sound and added a kind of disco style to it—it was really incredible what they came up with.

"I was a massive fan of what was going on at PWL, and the music being created by Stock Aitken Waterman. I loved their sound; it was very clean and fresh, and it was unlike anything we had ever heard before in the UK. We weren't sure as a group what kind of a direction we wanted to go in after Seventh Avenue, and we didn't feel like the house music angle was right for us. We knew we had this pretty boy image and pop thing going on, so we opted to go with PWL. I kind of twisted the arms of the other guys to agree to go with them. But we were all in agreement that PWL created really good pop-disco songs, and we thought our sound would ultimately be a fit with them.

"Their production style was something everyone was able to get into. You knew if one of their songs was playing in a club, you could almost drop a curtain down the middle of the dance floor, and it would be gay guys on one side dancing to it and straight kids jamming on the other. Their music appealed to everyone and broke down so many barriers—it was embraced by young and old, gay and straight."

Creswick vividly recalls his experience working in the London studio confines of PWL's creative center. "The studios and offices were really phenomenal," he says, his enthusiasm clearly evident. "They were really lovely guys to work with when we started there. We were walking into an incredibly successful epicenter where nearly everything that came out of the place was a hit at the time. Walking into PWL, there'd be a big chart propped up in the lobby, and it would show on any given week that number one was Kylie, number two was Jason Donovan, number three was Sonia, number eight was Big Fun—and it was absolutely phenomenal to see the impact this production team was having on the industry. We would say to each other, 'Wow. *We are actually a part of the PWL empire!*' I can't begin to tell you how it felt to see our names on the recording studio list and see that Kylie would be coming in later that day, or Rick Astley was scheduled for tomorrow. It was just so bizarre and thrilling really.

"As exciting as it was, however, it wasn't always easy going. Mike Stock was a bit of a tyrant to work with, and I remember Mark leaving the studio in tears because Mike had been shouting at him. Mark hadn't gotten something right. Mind you, it wasn't necessarily an easy process to record songs with them. You'd go into the studio, but they wouldn't play the song from start to finish to familiarize you with it. You'd hear bits and pieces, like the chorus or the bridge. They'd record a song in sections—you'd start with the chorus, then go back to the first verse, then all the bridges. And you wouldn't really know what the whole song sounded like or what the song was really about. You couldn't really get a feeling for the song. The songs we sang were mostly written for us, and we definitely had a connection to them, but it was really quite bizarre the way it all came together. A week later, you'd finally hear the song from start to finish, and I have to say it was always really incredible. We would record a lot of our tracks in a week, and the singles were picked out from the final versions."

Big Fun, combining tight, high-pitched vocal harmonies, irresistibly catchy melodies and youthful, sexy looks, had a remarkable run of hits. Fresh out of the gate in 1989, they reached number four in the UK with a bubbly, energized remake of The Jacksons' disco nugget, "Blame It on the Boogie," which was a Top Five hit in Spain and a monster throughout Europe. "Can't Shake the Feeling" nearly duplicated the feat, and in 1990, "Handful of Promises" made a sizeable impact in numerous territories.

"I understand why people called it a factory and why some of the stars didn't like it," concedes Phil. "In some ways, they were sort of manufacturing your product. But at the same time, they weren't because they were always really guiding you. They tailored the songs to our group's sound, like 'Handful of Promises,' and it came out quite cool actually. Even the material the three of us wrote for ourselves was produced at PWL with a very specific feel for us. It's true, however, that over time the songs started to sound just like each other. They had a formula that worked for quite a while, but they may have stuck with it too long. And unfortunately, we never had any of the tracks *we* wrote released as singles."

For a time, the boys' star power seemed invincible, and Creswick recalls many extraordinary moments that left an impression on him. Says the artist, "I think the very first *Top of the Pops* we did in 1989 really stands out for me. We were standing in the area where the audience would dance for a run-through, and also on the show was Liza Minnelli and the Pet Shop Boys. She was singing 'Losing My Mind.' Jimmy Somerville was there too, and we were like, 'Oh my God, check us out—we're on *Top of the Pops* with these incredible performers!' We couldn't quite believe what we were seeing, and I remember thinking this was going to be the start of something really big for us. Once you were on that show, you had really hit the big time.

"I also remember we had done a radio show interview, and after about an hour on the air, we finished and were getting ready to leave. We couldn't get out of the station because there were hundreds of screaming girls gathered outside. We were literally trapped in there until they could get a police escort for us to leave the place. It was actually quite frightening. I also recall going to a concert in Spain, and we were driving past a whole block of buildings plastered with Big Fun posters, one after another. It was an amazing feeling to know we were beginning to become popular in other countries besides our own. We did TV shows there, and they just loved our stuff. It was *very* cool to see three of our songs hit the Top 10 in Spain," he says, a touch of astonishment still in his voice.

Creswick alleges that he and his group mates were advised by their marketers to keep matters of sexual preferences private, fearing the impact such revelations might have on their mass popularity. "Mark (our lead singer) and I were boyfriends at the time, and the producers knew [about our relationship]," he says. "They would not allow us to be out in any way. When we'd be staying in a hotel, we'd always have separate rooms. But Mark and I would end up staying in each other's rooms overnight to get some time together and go back to our own rooms in the morning. Nobody ever noticed. But it was very difficult to have a relationship, and we did end up finally breaking up.

"It's funny. I had the courage to come out as being a gay man early in my life, and it felt like I had to go back in the closet when we became Big Fun. There were days I felt really bold, and I thought I was going to tell everybody. That would be it. Then there'd be other days where I'd think twice about it. I mean, I always thought, 'How could they *not* know we are gay?' I mean, look at our hair back then!" He laughs. "I know that our fans knew we were gay, and clearly they didn't care.

"I also knew I was HIV positive at the time I was signed to the label, but they didn't know it, and neither did my manager," Phil discloses. "Eventually, I had to tell my manager because the label had asked us to all go for a blood test, thanks to the panic that was surrounding HIV and AIDS at the time. It was considered a death sentence back then, and I knew a lot of my friends were dying. I guess the label wanted to make sure that we weren't going to die any time soon. I panicked, but my manager told me not to worry about it and that he would deal with it. He told the label I wasn't going to do any blood test, and they finally backed down. It was quite frightening for me at the time because I was afraid this whole thing we had going would fall apart because of my status.

"Luckily, I got through it, and I remain really healthy to this day. It's kind of a relief that people know about it now because it *is* a part of my life and my story. I dealt with it back then, and life went on. Sometimes I think I should have come out with it when we were having all that success. I think it would have helped other people who had contracted it—and the public—if they had seen a celebrity with it. Jason and Mark didn't think it would be a good idea, and so I didn't tell anybody—just my family and close friends. But looking back now, I think it would have been a good thing to do."

Big Fun's debut album, *A Pocketful of Dreams*, was released in 1990 and was a Top 10 smash in England. Germany and other countries favored it as well, but despite its commercial impact, the set ended up being the group's first and last full length LP. "The young lady who signed us to PWL was very upset when she found out they had dropped us. It is my understanding that they made so much money with the first album by us, that they didn't think they could do it again or that they felt they had exhausted what they could do with us. And so they dumped us. Either way, we didn't understand it at all—we had worked really hard. We were flying high after the success of the album, and we expected the next one to be even bigger. To be told you've been dumped when you are *still* popular didn't make any sense, and it was a very difficult pill to swallow. We always got along with everyone. There were no arguments with anyone, and there seemed to be no reason at all why they would do that. It was difficult for us to move forward after that. We recorded a few more tracks. Some were good and some weren't. But when people became aware we weren't produced under the Stock Aitken Waterman banner any more, they were no longer interested in us."

Creswick says he left the industry and eventually became an interior designer and painter. He reports that John became an artist manager, later working with former Spice Girl Geri Halliwell, and that Mark went on to work for a film production company. "I came out of that era worse off financially than when I started," Phil admits. "Part of the reason for that was I was young, naïve, making a lot of money, and didn't realize how much I was spending. I think we thought it would all last forever. But you know what? So what. I don't regret it. Life went on, and I did fine. I have no regrets about how I handled that part of my life. And as for being dropped so abruptly by PWL, eventually you move on because you don't want to end up being bitter about it.

"For a long time, I was kind of angry with the label," he continues. "They charged us [a large sum] to record our album—a lot of money back then—a lot of money even now. The songs all had the same loops, the same drums—I don't believe it was that big of a production for PWL or the guys from Jive Records and Zomba Publishing. Record companies back then had a point system, a percentage given to the artist based on what a release makes after you pay back expenditures. So those airplane flights, hotels, everything you eat—that all gets paid back to the label before an artist makes any money. We were supposed to get 12 points of whatever was left.

"Come Christmas, we did a big promotional tour, and the record company took another 1.5 points off our 12 points for that. PWL took another 6 points off our 12 points for the honor of just recording with them. Then another 1.5 points were taken for a TV campaign. In the end, we were left with about one point each. There was no way in hell we could ever recoup. And that's why I was angry with them—I felt they totally screwed us. We didn't know; we thought we had this great deal. It seemed to be going all right, but it didn't quite work out so well in the end. I think if we had gotten to do a second album, we would have reached an even higher level. They would have made serious money, and maybe we would have, too.

"We worked so hard and put in really long hours to get those records to the level that they attained," Phil says, the frustration in his voice clearly evident. "I'm telling you; we worked our asses off for them. I didn't even want to talk about it after it was all over. I thought, 'Okay, I tried the music business; it's not good. I'm not going to do it any more.' But life is short, and I didn't want to go through the rest of my life holding a grudge. I must admit, in the time that came after that, I grew to love being anonymous.

"I love what I'm doing today, and it keeps me very busy," the artist says contentedly. "My friends and family keep me sane. I'm lucky to have them; they've been with me for many years. The Big Fun thing was a wonderful part of my life, but it's these personal connections that have really kept me going and that mean the most to me. I confess I do miss performing, but I wouldn't want to be famous again. I like leading a less conspicuous life, and I enjoy who I am now. I have more fun today than I had in my 20s, believe it or not. It's funny how life changes. I've never been happier than I am right now. I live my life like every day is my last. And as for Big Fun, well, I just want people to remember us with a smile. That's it!"

Hazell Dean

"Whatever I Do (Wherever I Go)" (1984)
UK

"Most kids dream of being a pop star—I have lived my dream. *I am the queen of Hi-NRG!*" declares singer Hazell Dean. There's nothing arrogant about her proclamation, and few would challenge it. The singer has an enviable place in the history of European dance-pop of the '80s. For starters, Hazell was one of the first artists to bring high-energy dance music to the Top 10 of the British pop charts, beginning with her 1984 smash "Searchin' (I Gotta Find a Man)." A few months later, "Whatever I Do (Wherever I Go)" sent the singer even further up the survey and gave the rising Stock Aitken Waterman production team their first UK Top Five crossover success. Dean, whose voice was often praised for its power and emotion, enjoyed a string of pulsating, pumped up smashes during the era, many of which are widely considered classics of the genre today. Truly a regal contributor to Britain and Europe's greatest hits list, Hazell takes a look back at her distinguished accomplishments with noticeable pride.

"I am the youngest of three from a very close knit Essex family," the singer says from her home in London. "I discovered my love for music at school after taking guitar lessons. I always struggled academically (which I now know was because of dyslexia). Suddenly, I was good at something, and this gave me massive confidence. Everything changed once I learned to play guitar."

Hazell began singing professionally in the 1960s and says she always had the drive to be a great entertainer. She released a number of pop singles in the mid–'70s, including the upbeat "Got You Where I Want You" and the ballad "Who Was That Lady (I Saw You With)." Despite the proliferation of disco records making waves at the time, dance music wasn't yet on her radar. "I always wanted to be a successful recording artist. No compromise, and I knew I would achieve that through sheer determination and hard work. In those days, I never entertained the idea of being a dance music artist, to be honest. I enjoyed some of the disco music from back in the '70s, but it was not my first love, and I didn't recognize the sound as being anything special. However, after hearing Gloria Gaynor's 'Never Can Say Goodbye,' my opinion of the genre changed. It made me realize that disco wasn't just fluff and that this style of music could accommodate a big voice like Gloria's. So, I firmly blame Miss Gaynor for the path my career eventually took," she says with a smile.

Dean's official dance music debut came early in 1983 with a single she penned for the fledgling Proto record label called "Jealous Love." The track was produced by Willi Morrison and Ian Guenther and made a modest dent on the UK pop charts. Sometime later, the zippy

Left: **An EMI Records UK publicity shot of singer Hazell Dean issued in 1988, the year her European smash hit "Who's Leaving Who" topped the chart (photography by Lawrence Lawry).** *Right:* **The singer as she appears today.**

electronic disco cut was paired with an unlikely dance remake of Barbra Streisand's "Evergreen," and the 12-inch single mixes soared to the Top 10 of *Billboard*'s U.S. dance chart. "I had no hesitation at all about covering Streisand's 'Evergreen,' as I chose the song myself," confirms the singer. "It was Ian Anthony Stephens who recorded the track for me originally to use for shows I was doing in America. The tracks went down so well, and I gave them 100 percent, which the audience picked up on. I worked very hard on this release."

As auspicious a debut as "Jealous Love" and "Evergreen" were, they paled in comparison to her monster hit "Searchin' (I Gotta Find a Man)," first released in 1983 and written by Ian Anthony Stephens. "Ian tracked me down because of my success on the Northern Soul scene. My then manager, Meg Van Kuyk, and I had found Proto Records and [its head] Barry Evangeli through networking—it was as simple as that. Ian already had the track recorded, and needed to add a voice like mine. We recorded at Scorpio Studios on Euston Road in [Camden] London. Ian was very good—totally in tune with what was happening at that time. His tracks were never 'cluttered,' and we had fun making the record.

"'Searchin' was successful upon its initial launch in Europe in 1983. However, it was re-released in 1984 after I had entered the 'A Song for Europe' contest. Proto and I decided that if I didn't win the competition (and thankfully I didn't) we would re-release 'Searchin',' which is exactly what we did. There was already demand for the single via the gay clubs, and through hard work and a massive amount of personal appearances, it started to chart and grow." "Searchin'" was a major success in the UK, and it had significant impact throughout Europe. America strongly embraced the track as well. Thanks to its availability through the California indie label TSR, it reached number eight on the U.S. dance chart, where songs sung by females that exalted the qualities of males (think "It's Raining Men" by The Weather Girls and "So Many Men, So Little Time" by Miquel Brown) were in high fashion. "Life became a lot busier and very hectic," the singer says. "I was working non-stop, which is exactly what I wanted and expected to happen. I traveled constantly and had, in general, a fabulous time."

Proto Records enlisted the talents of Mike Stock, Matt Aitken and Pete Waterman (better known by their last names or simply as SAW), a production ensemble that was building a sizable name in the UK, Pete Waterman had formed a partnership of sorts with Evangeli, and the pair enjoyed tremendous success with drag icon Divine's frantic smash dance hit "You Think You're a Man." Divine's monster success had set a new standard in high-energy music. The SAW team helmed Dean's next single, and the results were tremendous. "Whatever I Do (Wherever I Go)" earned the singer a number four placing on the British pop chart, securing the positions of the vocalist and her production comrades as superstars of the period.

"I had a great time!" Dean says of her days with the famous production team. "I was very high on the charts with 'Searchin'' and by fluke met Pete Waterman when he was visiting Proto Records one day. He asked me what I had in mind for a follow-up. He suggested I meet Matt and Mike, who played me the Divine track 'You Think You're a Man'—I *loved* it. We recorded 'Whatever I Do' very quickly after they sent me a demo. I loved the verses but not the chorus, so I asked them to re-write it. Within a couple of days, they had written the chorus you know today. I did the first vocal when I was really tired. Pete asked me to sing it again, which I did, and the second vocal was the one that was actually used. Also, here's something not everybody knows—I didn't sing it in a vocal booth. I sang it in a corridor to get the sound they wanted. That was the start of the relationship and our success."

Hazell followed her smash with "No Fool (For Love)" and an LP, *Heart First*, which didn't quite meet the chart expectations of her producers. Still, the SAW team's work at PWL Studios in London continued to gain more recognition, and the trio's clout expanded worldwide as artists like Dead or Alive sought their expertise. Dean became well aware of the unit's media branding as a so-called "hit factory," pumping out dance-pop music at a breakneck pace. "Sometimes I wish things had evolved in a different way, and I didn't always agree with their choice of singles for me," the singer reflects. "However, if you chose to work with them, you knew the way they worked. If you knew Pete and his aspirations, you would know it was his dream to have a British Motown. I actually loved the term 'Hit Factory' that was used to describe the place because that's exactly what it was—'The Sound of a Bright Young Britain.' Was the term justified? Of course it was—they *were* churning out hits. But my experience was never negative. I can honestly say it was all a great time that I am grateful for, and it is a wonderful part of my life history—why would I be negative? I have great memories, and I am still friends with Pete Waterman and his team."

In the late '80s, Dean left the independent label circuit and signed with EMI, a highly prestigious record company at the time. The move seemed to revitalize her productions with the SAW team (whose names and accomplishments were, by then, often collectively and rightfully referred to as the PWL Empire and The Hit Factory). "I *loved* working with EMI," she beams. "What's not to like? It was EMI—huge at the time. I was very happy. By then, 'The Hit Factory' was in full swing, and again our production process was very simple (just the way I liked it). The boys would send me the tracks; I would learn the lyrics, then come in and record the vocal in my own style. I never had a bad experience recording with them, ever. Once the session was over, we'd go to the pub and discuss the track—and that was that. Done. I know people would like to hear horror stories, but there aren't any. I never had a negative experience with Matt, Mike or Pete (or any of the other members of their extended team)."

Though initial releases through EMI such as "They Say It's Gonna Rain" and "Always Doesn't Mean Forever" were extremely well-crafted dance productions with the signature sound of the SAW team and Dean's powerful delivery, they garnered only moderate attention in the pop market. Hazell was still a major force in the clubs, however, where the tracks had tremendous support. With EMI's promotional muscle fully behind her, the next single hit the bull's eye. "Who's Leaving Who," a clever, melodic and highly danceable pop song penned by Jack White and Mark Spiro (who had scored attention-getting hits with Laura Branigan), returned the artist to the upper echelons of the British pop chart in 1988, peaking at the number four spot. It was another broad and massive success, charting throughout Europe and earning high positions in Germany, Austria and Switzerland.

A few more high-energy hit singles followed ("Maybe [We Should Call It a Day]," "Turn It into Love," and "Better Off Without You" among the highlights), but eventually Dean parted company with the Stock Aitken Waterman team. Though she was less in the spotlight in the days that followed, she continued to record in the '90s, causing a stir on the dance floor with an album of ABBA covers (*The Winner Takes It All* in 1996) and a riveting cover of Bon Jovi's anthem, "Living on a Prayer" in 1999. In the summer of 2015, Hazell released the album *Nightlife* and the *Re: Extended* set in 2017.

Dean has also enjoyed a strong gay following over the years. The community has cheered her career onward since her first days in club land, a period that also marked the dawn of the devastating AIDS epidemic. "There's been a mutual loyalty over the years," observes Dean. "The gay audience has stuck by me throughout, and I have been an equal constant. The gay audience appreciates a good voice. My audience isn't exclusively gay, but I guess it's a very high proportion—and for that I am very grateful. I lost friends; we all lost friends to AIDS," she says, gently sighing. "It was shocking to see strong, beautiful people ravaged by this terrible disease. I have people close to me who are HIV positive, but thankfully now it's not the death sentence it once was. We understand more about the disease and I hope have more compassion about it today."

She reflects on some significant moments in her career. "There are two shows I did that really stand out for me. One was my first appearance at the club 'Heaven' in London. Everything changed with that show. I could hear the audience chanting my name—*and I liked it*. A few years ago, I did the *Hit Factory Live* show at the London O2 Arena in 2012—everything had come full circle. To perform in an arena of that size is always special, but to perform in an arena in your 'home town' is amazing. I cannot describe the feeling of walking onto that stage—it was spectacular. It was packed. I had friends and family there, plus, of course, my PWL peers. I came off stage and walked straight into Pete Waterman's arms. It was magical, and it was emotional. I don't think I will ever experience anything like that again," the artist says breathlessly.

Hazell feels comfortable in her skin today. "Life is too short for 'what if's' and regret. My life is what it is. There have been ups and downs, but as Gloria would say, I will survive, and I am very happy," the singer smiles, easing back in her chair. "As I said earlier, I have done what most people only dream of. My family, friends and my home are all things that keep me grounded today. I am not rock 'n' roll. I rarely drink, have never been involved with drugs, and I don't do the party circuit. I work and I enjoy myself. That's it. When I go into the studio nowadays, I only record what I like. Nobody tells me what to do. I choose what I like; I record it in my style, and I am lucky enough to work with remixers who appreciate my voice. And when you are good at what you do, your audience will stick with you.

"I'd like the people who matter to me—my daughter, sister, nieces and nephews, my partner, mum and friends—to remember me as a good person," she states. And she also has one final decree—"Oh, and I would like to be remembered as having one of the best female dance-pop voices to come out of Great Britain. *The Undisputed Queen of Hi-NRG!*"

Manfred Esser
Photographer

Artists: Modern Talking, Milli Vanilli, Samantha Fox, et al.
Germany

Once upon a time, people used to hold music in their hands. What a glorious feeling it was. Thanks to their captivatingly illustrated paper and cardboard sleeves, exploring the details of an LP, 12-inch maxi-single or seven-inch record was an opportunity to feel the essence of the artist, learn about the production and appreciate the music in a very personal way—beyond just the audio experience. Record jackets were able to evoke a mood and a powerful connection between music consumers and the sounds contained on their vinyl, while at the same time helping to brand and market an artist from a commercial angle. This physical and visual element played a vital role in the '80s dance-pop music experience, even as the industry converted to compact discs. Paramount to the creation of these extraordinary canvases of pop culture art was the all-important jacket photograph, the impact of which could often help determine a record's success in the marketplace.

Manfred Esser and his partner Helge Strauss were among the most trusted and popular photographic artisans of the decade in Germany, and their works graced the covers of many of the biggest selling recordings of the day. Their striking promotional portraits of artists such as Modern Talking, Jennifer Rush, Milli Vanilli, Bad Boys Blue, Taco and countless others remain quintessential images that have been burned into the memories of many fans. Esser continues to be one of the country's premier professional photographers, and while on holiday in Italy, he recalls his unique experience as one of the era's most accomplished visual artisans.

"I took my first photo at the age of six," Manfred says. "To this day, I can still recall every detail of the experience. I used a so-called box camera, which was nearly impossible to adjust. My grandfather was there, sitting in a camping chair, and we were in the middle of a forest."

As a young adult, Esser teamed with fellow photography enthusiast Helge Strauss. "The dynamic between Helge Strauss and myself was based on friendship," he remembers. "We always enjoyed the process of planning and carrying out projects and concepts together. We would invariably agree on which direction to take and what we thought the photos should look like." The duo became known as Esser & Strauss, and they worked together in the German advertising industry for several years before entering the entertainment market. "A friend asked us if we would be interested in shooting an album cover. That first cover was for a band called Underdog. The project was offered to EMI Records in Cologne. The

Left: Milli Vanilli's Fab Morvan (left) and Rob Pilatus (center, holding paper) discuss their session with photographer Manfred Esser (right) and his associates. *Right:* Manfred Esser today (courtesy Manfred Esser).

label was so impressed with the photo session that they had us come to Cologne for a meeting. After that, we landed some more jobs in the music industry, and that's basically how the story started."

From there, Esser & Strauss built an impeccable reputation for photographing music groups and singers at their best. Their work began appearing on dozens of album and single jackets. Says the photographer, "When we began working with record companies and artists, we were used to the advertising industry presenting us with their layouts and concepts so that we could plan the shoot. It was completely different in the music business. There were no layouts. It was very rare for a record label to have a solid idea for the take. We planned 99 percent of the photo sessions ourselves. We created the entire look. That included hair, make-up, location and the perception for the visual identity of the project.

"It's not easy to describe a typical photo shoot back then. There was no such thing as a typical photo shoot. And it remains that way today. You see, each shoot is as individual as the artist and all of the details related to them. Take, for example, a studio session. The artist arrives in the early morning, or maybe even the night before the shoot, and is brought to a nearby hotel. On the day of the shoot, after the entire team has been introduced, we usually sit down for a cup of coffee in order to get to know each other, if that's not already the case. Of course we've done our research and know everything there is to hear and read about the artist. We're well-prepared and know a lot about the person. We then present our ideas to the artist, explaining just when and what they should expect. Then we pick out the outfits together that we have selected for the different sets and concepts we have arranged. After that, the artist gets make-up and hair taken care of. Finally, we start the photo session and go through all of the planned ideas, one after another."

Several elements related to the artist and his or her music were integral to the photographer's blueprint for each project. "The music style was always vital for the look we sought—probably the most important fact of all. If the image created was a perfect fit, then a record-buyer was usually able to deduce what the music sounded like by just looking at the jacket. When shooting, I was never too concerned with what countries a record would ultimately be distributed in, unless the release was planned for a country with certain religious restrictions, where maybe only specific clothing is allowed. More important than the country was the definition of the target audience that the product was meant for.

"The most important factor in a good photo is light—understanding the concept of lighting makes for a real master," Esser asserts. "You can give your all to capture a great picture, but if the lighting isn't perfect, you lose. The light decides the outcome. The artist's age can influence the overall planning from the very beginning. It defines the target group, the clothes and perhaps even the lighting itself, which would then be softer or harsher, accordingly. Photo editing plays a huge role, which of course simplifies matters. At the same time, editing also encompasses a certain tendency to exaggerate, which can potentially leave the artist almost unrecognizable.

"I'd say the second biggest secret for a good photo shoot is the trust that an artist must have in the team he or she is working with. Everything combined—including the briefing—has to give the artist the feeling of being unique and that the project is very exclusive. That's exactly how we work to this very day. That's how we approach every project, always with the same caring diligence, the same passion, and the same outstanding goal."

Once a photo session was completed, Esser estimates that out of, say, 100 photos, about an average of 10 were considered "usable." "But that depends on a variety of factors," he admits. "Some people are extremely talented in front of the camera; others just struggle. It's always been important to us that the artist is content with our work. That's the reason why we call ourselves team workers. We ask the artist to let us know if they want anything—any special requests during the shoot that will make them more comfortable and allow them to be more at ease. Back in the '80s, it wasn't yet possible to have a look together at a monitor to see how the work was coming along. It was essential for us to take a few Polaroids now and then to show the client what kind of changes were taking place. It was vital to have an atmosphere that created a bond of trust—and that always worked out well with us. The artists had complete faith in us and were never afraid that we'd mess up the session where they wouldn't look good or have unflattering pictures.

"With the photography completed, the follow-up work was just as important. We had developed some special procedures in the lab for that time, which made our photos unique. They included special techniques for developing the slides and the negatives, as well as the techniques we used for the production of the prints.

"In the early '80s," Esser adds, "some of the major record companies had art departments that would create the actual record jackets. It was rare, but there were a few. If an artist was considered a high priority, then we all met in a conference room at the label headquarters to discuss his or her look. The companies were healthy and rolling in the money in those days. As soon as everybody agreed on the direction, we either flew out to Ibiza or put up a big set in the studio. The cover of the record—the photos—always had the second most important position to the music. It was like that in the '80s, and it's still like that today. That favored picture wasn't only on the cover; it was also used for the entire campaign with the press, touring posters, autograph cards, etc. To this day though, bad cover designs, the final look of the album or single created by others, are a problem. More often than not, when my team and I want to present our work, we show the actual photos and not the final album covers."

Manfred says he only performed contract work during the '80s. "The price for our services was a set fee and had to be paid, regardless of the success of the project. That had its pros and cons, but it probably gave the same results as any other method at the end of the day," he confirms. "Thinking back, I can't say any one photo or one individual session stands out for me from those days. There are too many artists and shoots to choose from. If I were to go to the archives and start researching, I would discover a treasure trove of wonderful photos. Often, the best take from a shoot isn't the one you see on the cover of a record. But I can say the commercial success of a production probably did have something to do with the photos. It was important for a newcomer to stand out and for an established artist to present something special and fresh with their photos. I've worked with some artists just once and others repeatedly. Knowing someone well makes it somewhat easier. On the other hand, I used and photographed a lot of themes throughout the years. There were some music genres and artists that allowed for a lot of creativity. Others didn't, and that could be difficult, especially if the musical product they were releasing tended to sound the same each time, and the artist wasn't open to change," he observes.

The extensive list of artists who posed in front of Manfred's camera during the '80s reads like a who's who of Europe's most famous dance-pop stars. The photographer describes his experience with several notables.

"Jennifer Rush was an amazing vocalist," he says with great enthusiasm. "So many sold-out concerts. She was an absolute sensation. I'm not even sure how many sessions we did together. I do recall our very first session, when her career was about to take off. Her [self-titled 1984 debut] album cover (where she is wearing a jeans jacket) is a Jenny that we never saw again. Ultimately, she looked very natural and down-to-earth, a young musician who seemed like she was oblivious to the intensity of the music business. I was actually surprised when the record company chose that set of pictures for her album cover. Our first session also generated some very sophisticated photos. For example, look at the single cover for 'The Power of Love'—the dark background, front lighting, sequined dress, hair, makeup. [*Author's note: refer to Jennifer Rush's chapter to view an alternate photograph from this session.*] It was the big ballad singer look, just as we saw her on stage later on. I also photographed Francesco Napoli for his *Balla* LP and a few singles in 1987 and 1988. I truly enjoyed working together with this lively and animated Italian. It was always quite a pleasure to meet up with him in the studio. We always had an amazing time together. And then there was Dieter Bohlen. He immediately made sure everybody knew that there was a life after Modern Talking with his Blue System project. I did photography for his *Body Heat* album in 1988 and singles like 'Under My Skin' and 'Silent Water.' He was an unbelievable artist, equipped with a sixth sense and an unusual talent for being able to write one hit after another. I spent a lot of time with him. It wasn't always pleasant, but it was often very interesting and inspiring, for sure.

"When Frank Farian first called the studio to book the gentlemen from Milli Vanilli, nobody knew what was going to happen with this group. The music always arrives at the studio before the artist does so that we can catch the mood and be inspired. I remember the song 'Girl You Know It's True' blew us away. Mago Reim, our amazing stylist and makeup artist (with whom I did most of the photos and productions in the '80s and with whom I still work today), brought the outfits and jewelry from Paris. Rob and Fab looked amazing. The photo was a perfect fit with the unique sound of their record. The photo on the back of the maxi-single was taken here, directly on the main street in front of our studio. The guys were really shy and reserved at the first session. When we saw each other a year later for a new shoot, they were number one around the world and were completely different. I know it wasn't easy for them dealing with that kind of fame."

Well into the '90s, Esser continued to work with legendary artists whose careers had initially been launched in the previous decade. "Fancy is a unique artist, and I worked with him on the 'When Guardian Angels Cry' single cover in 1990, which is an especially wonderful portrait. It was done using a special technique, the basis of which was a very harsh black and white print which was then tinted to a blue-brown hue by hand in a very particular process. I also had a session with Samantha Fox, shooting for her 1997 album *21st Century Fox*. I guess you could say she was the British forerunner of Pamela Anderson. That was a really unusual day. Samantha could barely be contained. She was in more of a party mood than a photo mood. Still, we managed to get some excellent takes. It was quite thrilling to be able to do the comeback photos for Modern Talking and their *Back for Good* album in 1998. We developed a wonderful concept for the project, together with Mago. Black and white, white and black, as a marketing idea. It looked great and worked well. I always admired the calm composure that Thomas had when standing next to Dieter. I'm sure that wasn't always easy.

"These are just a few small excerpts from a much bigger story. There were, of course, hundreds of other artists and hundreds of photo sessions with wonderful people and amazing things that happened. Many of the records that our photography appeared on were very successful hits. And frankly, for my own career, it was important to work with artists that were selling a lot of records and CDs. But my philosophy has always been that every shoot should run as if it was the most important one ever. Each artist deserves special treatment on the day of his shoot. Everything must be taken seriously, and my team and I must always give it our best. The music industry was and is a tough business, and if you deliver poor photos, they'll drop you with the blink of an eye."

Around 1995, Esser and Strauss dissolved their partnership. "We had a great time together," Manfred assures. "Personal developments led to our parting ways, and it was difficult for both of us. For me, there was no doubt that I would continue working as I had, but I also wanted to develop artistically." Both photographers embarked on successful solo careers in photography that still flourish today, with Esser creating modern-day portraits of such German vocal luminaries as Kristina Bach, Olaf Berger, G.G. Anderson, Claudia Jung, Michael Wendler and Andrea Berg, among others. He also helms the productions of major music videos and is an accomplished photographer of industry and architecture. Many of his latest works are on view at manfredesser.de.

The continued demand for Esser's extraordinary talents has ensured his longevity in the business. "I'm very pleased and a bit proud about that," he remarks. "I guess it's rather special and maybe even unique that I have prospered in this industry as long as I have. In the prologue of my organization's new brochure, which was especially made for agencies and major companies, I talk about production 'safety' and that I've seen everything there is to see in this profession. Any client that books me not only gets a part of my creativity, but also a big part of what I call 'safety.' In other words, it's something like a guaranteed result—you know your money is well invested. Besides all of my experiences, I also have an insatiable hunger for the new. Not one hour goes by where I don't take at least one new picture on my iPhone. My wife is a psychologist. She thinks that I'm crazy—in a positive way—because I can't leave out a single sunset. I can't sit still. I watch each one and take my shot. I am always running around taking my pictures," he laughs.

The art of photography has progressed a great deal since the '80s, and Manfred has kept pace with the technological advancements that have rapidly developed, especially over the past few years. "Digital technology reached the level of quality where we stopped working with film about two years ago," he says. "I've never been that interested in film material or which camera to use. I rather liked working with the weaknesses of a material or even provoking them, i.e. by intentionally developing film in an incorrect way or using the wrong exposure in order to find that one special look—that was my goal. It's also about making the material grainier, extremer, harsher or whatever is possible. Exposing a normal slide was simply too banal for me. Nowadays, a lot of people think that if they have Photoshop on their computer, they automatically know how to use it. I feel that the overall niveau in photography has dropped. Clients expect to see the photos on their desks even before the shoot is over, which leads to less fun and more stress during the production.

"The change in music distribution through MP3 formats has been dramatic as well. Being able to hold an LP in your hands from your favorite artist was surely a pleasure—especially for people of my generation. It's become increasingly difficult to tell stories on such small digital formats. But all in all, the need for good photography remains the same. Nobody looks at lousy, boring or unspectacular pictures on the Internet," he smiles.

In many ways, Esser's photographs of Europe's stars of '80s dance-pop are as much a part of the legacy of this era as the music. "It would be great if people were able to recognize the respect and appreciation I had for each of the artists I photographed," he says softly. "I hope they can feel all the emotions that went into each of those photos. If they sense that and talked about it when they looked at those records, it would be wonderful. I'm thankful that I was able to experience those wonderful times and to have been an element of that history. It makes me all the more happy to still be here and to be a part of the trigger that makes music play in people's minds."

Yasmin Evans
aka Yazz
"The Only Way Is Up" (1988)
UK

"We all need to be rescued. We all need to be saved. And music can do that for you—for a while," says Yasmin Evans today. The singer, better known as Yazz, conveyed her point quite clearly in 1988 with her hit single "The Only Way Is Up." Music buyers responded strongly to her message, recorded under her alternate moniker, Yazz and the Plastic Population, by sending the track to the top of the charts. Relentlessly upbeat and optimistic, it became the most popular single in Europe of its day, outpacing those of even Phil Collins and Milli Vanilli, according to a September '88 *Music & Media* Hot 100 chart. Just two months later, Yazz was back near the chart summit again with the call to "Stand Up for Your Love Rights." The smooth and powerfully voiced singer became a major dance-pop star in Britain and throughout the world. However, most fans were blissfully unaware of the formidable pressures that fame was creating for the performer behind the scenes. By the mid–'90s, the singer says she found her faith, was rescued, and made a decision to accept a spiritual calling to lend her voice to Christian music. She left the flashing strobe lights and the unceasing demands of the pop world behind and says she has never regretted it. While on tour in Spain with her special brand of contemporary faith-inspiring music, the vocalist offers some detailed insights into her journey from dance icon to servant of God.

"I have always had the sense that my birth came straight into the cradle of music," claims Yazz, whose nickname goes back to her childhood. "I cannot remember *not* having the sound of music in my ears in some way or another. My father was Jamaican and my mother English, and our home was rich in color, rhythm and plenty of soul food. I was born into the UK of the '60s—the first generation of mixed race children. This was God's pleasure and His choice. However, I would later experience first hand the hard realities of racial abuse (that would lead to the meaningful messages I needed to express in songs). I grew up in a small basement flat in the suburbs of London Town, surrounded by tall poplar trees and every nationality as my neighbors. I was blessed to have a father that enjoyed his music and introduced me to the world's finest composers at an early age.

"I remember the day a very sacred piece of furniture arrived in our home—the 'gram' (record player console), the iPod of the day, but about the size of a small sofa. A light brown stereogram made by Decca, it had two front door panels—one side held the drinks cabinet

"Your chart position, not your track content, takes over—as hard as you try not to let it," says singer Yazz. *Left:* The pressure she describes was well hidden in a cheerful promotional photo supplied in the '80s by Elektra Records, U.S. *Right:* The singer as she appears today.

and the other a record player. There it was that I would fall in love with music and vinyl. A small seed was sown for my future. I remember my father sitting me down before the 'gram and introducing me to Dionne Warwick, Miles Davis, Nat King Cole, Ella, Dusty Springfield, The Dragonaires, Aretha and of course the darling of our home, the venerable Bob Marley. These were my inspirations. 'Listen to this, daughter,' he would say, 'these songs are written by two of the world's foremost writers.' I was listening to Burt Bacharach and Hal David songs sung by Dionne and Petula Clark. A good intro to music, don't you think? Much later on, I found myself in the wondrous Royal Albert Hall singing (with great amazement) for Burt Bacharach and Hal David's Lifetime Achievement Award show. What a circle of life!

"I can recall from my youth watching the explosion of Motown in America—The Jackson 5 show, Diana Ross and the Supremes. For me, it was the first time I was seeing mixed races and colored performers excelling and possibly earning a healthy living. I remember feeling so inspired by them and just the hint of a thought beginning to rise up in me that, hey, maybe I could do that too. In the UK back then, racial discrimination was a bad wound with no real medication for its healing having been found. To watch and see others like myself, in all colors and with frizzy hair, being admired and having a level of integrity was inspiring. They were my first music role models. Identity is such a major part of growing up, and I struggled to find my place because of my mixed race background. Of course there were racial issues in the States too, but in America I could see that there were doors open for mixed race people if you had the talent and courage to go for it!" the artist observes.

By age 17, Evans says she was buying 12-inch vinyl singles and albums galore. "I listened to a variety of sounds, from reggae to funk, to New Romantics, to soft rock. Prince, The O'Jays, Average White Band, Light of the World, Chaka, Earth, Wind and Fire, Maze, Duran Duran, The Commodores, Funkadelic, Clapton, Joy Division, The Pointer Sisters, Stevie Wonder, Michael Jackson, S'Express—the sounds coming out of the States and Europe were incredible. My female muses were Diana Ross, Carole King, Karen Carpenter, Roberta Flack and Donna Summer. I loved the female sound, especially those with long, soft-held tones that floated across the productions. In the beginning, I think I was trying to imitate that sound, but I would eventually grow up more and develop my own tones."

Yazz joined her first band at the age of 18, playing keyboards (in a way which she humorously describes as "appalling"). Once she was relegated to backing vocals, Evans found she was no longer the square peg facing a round hole. "I took singing lessons and began writing songs with a vengeance," she remembers. "By 19, I had my first record deal in a band called The Biz. (So twee.) We put out a track called 'Falling,' and it quite literally did exactly that. But we were in the door. Later, the band folded, and I decided to go solo. I needed good management, and around that time there was a band called Wham! bubbling on the charts. I thought these boys looked good and looked like they were going to go all the way, and I wondered who was managing them. I made an appointment to see their management team and played them some rough material (*very* rough). One of the managers, Jazz Summers, took a liking to it and decided to take me on as an artist-in-development. God was at work, yet I never even knew Him at that point."

Jazz Summers eventually became Yazz's husband, and he proved to be an important source of influence and motivation in her music career, according to the artist. "He is a very charismatic natured individual with great resolve and conviction when he believes in something. Our relationship, although troubled, was, in part, how Big Life Records, the banner under which my first hits were released, was built. I admired many of his qualities and despaired of others—and am sure he felt the same about me. I remain resolved to say thank you to him for all his input in my music career at the time."

As she honed her sound, Yazz says the classic disco vibe of the '70s was a major source of inspiration. "Giorgio Moroder, the 'father of disco,' had devastated dance floors and was the thief of my heart. When Donna Summer sang his tracks, I was captivated. He knew how to drive a song and twist and turn you inside out. He had crossed the sea to the UK and dominated the dance charts there as well. Eventually, with the fast advancement in music technology, DJs were soon able to make, mix and create music from home studio set-ups (as 'house' music would signify)."

In 1988, the door to commercial success was flung open with the release of a breakthrough single called "Doctorin' the House," a project developed by the production team known as Coldcut (Jonathan More and Matt Black). The track featured vocals by Yasmin, who was credited as "Yazz and the Plastic Population" and on some pressings as "Yazz and the Plastic People." "My manager decided to sign with two DJs called 'Coldcut,'" the singer recollects. "I remember him telling me about them one night over supper and how excited he was about the new innovative music and beats they were experimenting with. I remember saying, totally filled with pride at that moment, that I wasn't really looking to work with those kind of writers and wanted to continue with what I was doing as a solo vocalist. Oh dear, we artists are such insecure people, aren't we?" she sighs, shaking her head.

"Anyway, Jazz insisted that he felt they had something and that I had something they needed. I knew how to write a song, and they didn't. But they had the skills for the trending beats and a certain something that was unique. He felt we would gel together. I agreed to meet them and spent the entire day in their home working on music. I thought I had walked into a mini Moog factory. They were everywhere. I *loved* it. One track they played for me included cuts and vocals sampled from other tracks. A brilliant bass line drove it. The beats-per-minute were 120 with a four-on-the-floor groove, but they had no chorus or real song structure. So I started tampering around with a few lines, and as they weren't traditional musicians or players, I only had a few chords to play around with. The track 'Doctorin' the House' was born that afternoon.

"We had no idea of its potential and how it would be a door opener in its genre—we were just loving the creativity we infused into this track. We recorded the track in a day I seem to remember, and we cut a video incredibly cheaply—maybe around £6,000. I knew a fantastic dance mime actor friend who agreed to participate in the vid and perform over some of the vocal cuts in the song—he was so fantastic. Jonathan and Matt seemed pleased with the track and did all the production and mixing. They are two of the sweetest people—very humble and down-to-earth, really. I just adored what they did. I respected what they did and how they were steadfast in remaining in their genre zone."

"Doctorin' the House," which featured snippets of movie and television show dialogue, was launched via a modest grassroots promotional effort by the label. It turned out to be Coldcut's biggest commercial hit ever, reaching the Top 10 in England. Among the many other countries that favored the track were Germany, Ireland and the Netherlands, and the song was a Top Three hit on *Billboard*'s U.S. dance chart. "We literally put the stamps on the record sleeves to post them out everywhere—that's how small an outfit we were!" Yazz exclaims. "By then, I was married to Jazz. He had started an indie label called Big Life, and we had very little money, but some support from the bigger guns like Polydor Records. These were very exciting times. Again, because we were not famous yet, we saw life through excited eyes and the joy of just the whole creative process and its potential. We didn't think (and weren't motivated) the way big record companies were, and I think that had a positive effect upon the whole process of making music and putting out records. It just boosted the enjoyment factor. The only pressure came from ourselves as we were driven to make the best out of little. But there was no worry about creating a hit. I think that shapes an artist differently, as opposed to having to be the best instantly. It really felt like it wasn't about hits (although that was possibly very naive of me, and I am sure the accountants would bury me for saying that). But I am being honest, for, as with many things in life, the journey is the joy, and the arrival can be most disappointing!

"Slowly, I would learn about the other side of the industry I was in," she continues, "and to a certain extent, I think I did not want to look at what I was seeing. I think for a while I preferred to remain in 'an age of innocence' in a way. I looked the other way when I heard about 'deals' being done to achieve potentially higher chart positions, preferring instead to believe that ultimately the masses decide the outcome of a record's success. Even now, I still do believe to some extent that this is the case. Of course, I respect that marketing a record means a lot of different things and is a powerful tool. But at the end of the day, I believe that music, whether sold on vinyl or digitally, holds emotion. That's what leaps out at ya' from the radio or TV, YouTube or your iPod. People know plastic and contrived music, and they know what's real and genuine, whichever way it's wrapped—because the heart is (or ought to be) in the matter."

The artist says she is often asked about the origins of "Plastic Population," the moniker attached to her name for a short time. "I ought to jazz up the story a bit, but the truth is quite simple," she concedes. "The name came about whilst we were in the studio recording 'Doctorin'.' We had gotten a few guide vocal tracks down and were working on the final lead vocal. It was about four in the morning, and we were all exhausted. To be frank, we had reached that 'tired ears' syndrome that's consistent with working way over time and not being able to discriminate about any sounds any more. Spending an hour or two searching for the right high-hat sound tells you you've pretty much lost the plot and need a break. Anyway, we had finally finished and sat there chatting and wondering what on earth we were gonna name the group, band or whatever we were becoming. Coldcut came up with Yazz and the Plastic Population almost as a kind of tongue-in-cheek idea. Plastic was the vinyl, and the Population was the record buying public—*voila!* I thought it was a way for me to have the freedom to be a solo artist or come and go as an invited artist—probably took no more than a few minutes. I wonder how many other band names are born that way."

The artist's solo debut single, "The Only Way Is Up" (originally a modest 1980 hit sung by soul vocalist Otis Clay), took the singer to the next level—and then some. Produced by More and Black, the song was released under the moniker Yazz And The Plastic Population in the summer of 1988. Almost overnight, the irresistibly uplifting anthem became a huge club, radio and sales hit, locking up Britain's peak chart position for weeks and earning top spots on the pop and dance surveys of almost every European territory. She settles back to describe the origins of her breakthrough anthem. "The actual birth of that track was due to the efforts of a serious DJ, Dr. Bob Jones, who hosted a solid soul music program on Kiss-FM radio in London. Coldcut also had a show on the same station, and they were good friends. Many writers were sending over track ideas for our forthcoming album, and Bob sent over Mr. Clay's track. He said, 'You gotta do this Yazz; it's a great northern soul hit song, and I think you can take it to the general public!'

"Otis Clay's version was completely different in style. He is a fantastic soul singer, and his take on the track was possibly half the tempo of ours. It was gorgeous, but I didn't think I could sing it in a soulful style, and I might ruin it. The producers insisted we go in and demo the track in my key and play around with a house groove. Well, it was a monster. The incessant driving bass line played on a Moog was infectious, and coupled with the house beat and a 'grab ya' monster horn riff at the intro, it captured you immediately. Then it got dressed up with a very high, floaty vocal. It seemed to just take you up right from the start. I was extremely nervous and unaccustomed to vocal recording in studios, so I belted out each take way too hard and learned after a few takes, gasping for air—this is *not* how you do it!" she laughs. "I had no studio coaching, so I just learnt as I went along, but somehow we got some takes and dropped in overdubs where we thought they were needed.

I think we did the backing vocals first, which would become a trademark for me. I tend to do all my backing vocals now with my daughter (I'm a *biiiiiig* fan of harmonies). I like to have a solid chorus in place to lean on and play off, and I think that all began with the production of that first album.

"The boys brought in some good musicians for the track, but they mostly did all of it themselves," she adds. "I contributed some middle section ideas with the whispering and long notes in and out of choruses or breakdown sections. That kind of became another Yazz trademark, which I was flattered to hear other singers imitate after this song's release. Because we were so tired running from studio to studio and just working flat out on tracks for so many hours, I think we just kinda thought it was an okay track with a good feel—a good vibe and an uplifting, driven chorus. I never imagined its potential at the time. In fact, I remember when we took it to our manager and played it for him, we were all surprised by the look on his face. He called in his favorite record promoter at that time and sat him down to hear it. By the end of the session, they were out of their seats jumping around. They told us this track was going to be a Top 10 hit. I think the boys and I just sort of laughed—non-believers."

Evans needed a hip image to go with her music and notes that before any tracks were released, she made some enhancements to her appearance. "I did some modeling in Europe, which was very helpful to me later in my career. I had learned all about lighting, studios, cameras, presence, performance and carrying one's self. All of those qualities were a great assistance to me later on. I decided to cut off all the long, fuzzy, fireball-like, unruly and rebellious hair I had!" she laughs. "I remember walking into a Vidal Sassoon salon in London's West End. I was shown to a seat and a cool girl came over and asked me what I had in mind. I told her to cut it all off and dye it blond. I think she thought Christmas had come early. That very same lady, some 15 years later, was to lead me to find Jesus Christ and helped save my life from ending."

With her cutting-edge look now set and "The Only Way Is Up" burning up the charts, Yazz had arrived. The track was instantly embraced worldwide for its ability to empower. The song was a dynamic listening and dance floor experience, stirringly delivered through uplifting lyrics, an energized arrangement and the artist's scintillating vocal delivery. "It was just one of those songs that can reach down into wherever you are and pull you up," Yasmin observes. "I think it just hit home with so many people because most people are either in, going into, or coming out of some kind of difficulty. There are some similarities between 'The Only Way' and Gloria Gaynor's 'I Will Survive,' except that the 'Survive' theory is based upon you having the power to lift yourself up. 'The Only Way' was written with a partnership idea in mind, and I believe that to be the truer philosophy. I did think that we got the lyric and music arrangement for the dynamics of the song right in many ways, and we also had a social factor working on our side upon its release. Firstly, the lyrical content reflected where most of the UK was—in a very bad recession, and people had been hit very hard. Many were broken down and wondering what on earth they were going to do, literally. So naturally the song leant into their circumstances, offering a sense of hope to hold on and that things will get better. There is a lyric in the song about moving somewhere else and still carrying on. So many people love that line."

She lingers on the song's many charms. "The chorus of 'The Only Way Is Up' really slammed!" Yazz says with great enthusiasm. "It was so uplifting, and the boys placing a big stab sound after that title line was sung made it even more confirmed. I wanted to have male vocalists on the backing in the bridge section instead of just female vocals so that it would have potentially a stronger crossover appeal. I loved those vocals. Once you had reached the first chorus, you were in. The second verse talked again about living tough and the strength of having someone alongside you and that a brighter day was coming. We purposefully built the dynamics of the music arrangement all around the lyrics—just the bass line and some keys in the verses, then the strings and vocals built on the bridge. Then that slamming chorus again. A good and nicely arranged dance-pop track I thought," she laughs in satisfaction.

However, pop stardom came with a high price, the singer admits, and the demands of fame quickly took their toll. "Success in the music industry is a powerful, emotive road to be on; that's for sure," Evans says in retrospect. "The nature of the beast of success is that it wants to be maintained, nurtured and kept going. It's simply not happy to have one hit; there have to be more. It is like a drug, and the monster machine of the music industry knows and likes to go into overdrive to get what it wants. It was perilous to reach number one on your just your second release. I couldn't believe it—the pressure was so intense early on. You are number one pretty much all over Europe and other continents, and it felt like it happened too quickly—*way too quickly*. Everybody is suddenly your friend, and everybody wants you. You cling onto what you know to be real and hold on for the ride. I was hopeless at it. I loved being a part of a team, a combo, and would quite happily have been in a band that played small local venues and made just enough to earn a living.

"Sadly, when the success hit me I found the level of pressure overwhelming and found people's scrutinizing of me agonizing. With no tools to handle things, you simply dive into your own strength and ideas about how to cope. I had no faith at that time, so therefore had no foundation outside of myself to walk this journey with. I was just unable to cope with life—and most definitely fame. I speak personally here. I don't believe we were created so that we would be worshipped and adored. Today, it is my belief that we were created to reflect another's fame and glory—our maker, our God, and to live creatively in adoration in a personal relationship with Him. Therefore, it's in our DNA to be in relationship with God. When we find ourselves separated from that relationship, I think as humans we tend to place our attention and adoration onto other things in like manner. Maybe it's placed on our children, money, lust, footballers, drink, movie stars, etc., etc. The list is endless."

There is frustration in her voice as Yasmin describes the lifestyle and personal changes that came with her monumental success. "I felt I had to be prettier and became self-conscious," she admits. "I struggled with attention, competition and then past insecurities started rearing their ugly heads. I just wanted to retreat quietly into the studio and not promote the records. I loved music. I hated fame. Don't get me wrong—I felt fortunate to be traveling the world and meeting like-minded artists, but at the same time I found myself becoming so damn insecure because of the pressure to secure another hit. Subconsciously, you find yourself believing that your value or weight as a person is judged upon performance. I became driven by my chart performance—in fact, a slave to it eventually. Your chart position, not your track content, takes over—as hard as you try not to let it. Competition seeps in, and instead of there being enough room for all, you are constantly told that you have to maintain your position at the top."

Oddly, "The Only Way Is Up" failed to make a sizeable dent on the U.S. pop charts (though it spent two weeks in the number two spot on the *Billboard* dance survey). However, Yazz believes working primarily within the borders of Europe and Britain was probably for the best. "The times that I did go over to the States for work found me in plush record company offices with men in expensive suits all trying to figure out into which damn category they were going to be able to fit this girl!" the singer grins. "Again, the question of being successful worldwide was high on the list of my label's priorities. The U.S. seemed to be the 'be all and end all' for them, but of course their motivation was always rooted in money. Fortunately for me, I did not hold those thoughts and was content to remain in Europe working. I really mean it when I say 'fortunately' because I think I would not have coped with the U.S. at all. God at work?"

Yazz, leaving "The Plastic Population" portion of her name behind, teamed with the production team The Beatmasters for her next single, "Stand Up for Your Love Rights," which followed hot on the heels of her previous megahit. By November of 1988, the single was lodged in the Top Five of *Music & Media*'s pan–European hit chart. The track was featured, along with "The Only Way Is Up," on the artist's debut album, *Wanted*, which made it to number three in Britain.

She reveals, "Surprisingly, 'Stand Up' was not written with a gender or sexual orientation agenda in mind at all, as so many people believed. The Beatmasters were introduced to me by my manager and had been working alongside some hot UK artists, including P.P. Arnold, The Cookie Crew and Betty Boo. They were asked to work on the track with me, and we would see how it flowed. I liked Amanda Glanfield and Richard Walmsley (members of The Beatmasters) and the way they approached music. They knew that the current groove was important, but I felt they cared about connecting the lyrics and groove. I loved the horn intro they added, continuing the theme of 'The Only Way Is Up.' The lyrical content was inspired by a friend I had known for a long time, who managed to overcome her fear and get out of a physically abusive marriage. Another writer had some input in the song, but it was always sung with her in mind. Of course, many social groups identified with the lyrics and embraced the song as an anthem for their causes. So, for example, the gay community embraced 'Love Rights' in its quest for social equality. In truth, I did not know how to handle some of the actions and reactions of fans and followers. To my mind, part of the beauty of music is that it crosses all barriers, colors, classes and creeds, but I found that others wanted me to have agendas with my music. More and more they wanted me to side with their ideals, social agendas, etc."

This was also a period where the dark side of club culture and vices tied to the world of nightlife were often in the spotlight. Yazz's sizeable dance hits, such as "Where Has All the Love Gone?," were an active part of the soundtrack of that scene. "What I did not like at all and regret to this day was the drug culture that attached itself to the club music genre," the artist asserts. "House music, garage, disco, acid house and jungle, etc.—with them came fashionable drugs and the probability for abuse. I struggled consistently knowing that remixes of my music were being played out in that drug arena. I did not take drugs, but I did begin to drink alcohol more and more," she says without hesitation. "By the end of the first tour, I found that I would be drinking more than I had ever had before. I don't know if I was an 'alcoholic,' but I knew I felt it was a way to help me through the pressure I was placing on myself. If I had to attend an event outside of personal performances or interviews and such, I just could not go without having had a drink. I was too insecure and nervous.

Behind that smile I projected was someone struggling with a poor self-esteem and some past issues, and I was giving the power to a glass of this or that to fix it."

Yasmin repositions herself in her chair and leans in. "Being 'number one' means so much to so many people," she says earnestly. "I found for some it meant they thought you were sexier, funnier, more intelligent, richer or whatever. That builds high levels of expectancy—a horrendous challenge for anyone to bear. You can cover up many things behind a fake smile plastered on your face, but deep inside you know that you are really seeking out genuine truth in your life. Listen to me now, because this is important—having that desire for truth is *never* to be despised or rejected or neglected. I believe that thought has been placed within all of us from before time, prepared by the sovereignty of God. Why? Because He desires you to find the truth. And once found, you learn that the truth will, indeed, set you free! Fame is a label placed upon people who have decided on what they determine success really means. Generally, you have to reach a level of performance and recognition for the label to stick. I think by the end of promoting 'Stand Up,' I was in trouble with the whole expectation level of that label. The balance began to shift, if you know what I mean. The pressure for making more out of each product was constantly building. I sought refuge in the dance studios and recording studios. I became obsessed with work, perfection and achievement. I didn't do the parties and appearances, etc. I didn't want to wear the see-through negligee styles that might have pushed me up a chart position or two.

"On this subject, I feel I must digress for a moment to say I am saddened to see how sexually motivated female recording artists have become now. It's not just because of a gender bias, but simply because I believe beauty and showing as much as you can does not sustain you. Sadly, I think these artists don't realize they are role models for children, perhaps even their own child."

Despite the formidable troubles she experienced, a number of distinctly positive life events stand out for the singer, such as the birth of her only child. From the challenging peak of her fame, she can recall several moments that still make her smile. "The moment you hold your first record sleeve in your hand is always a big event," she says. "I remember sitting around a table in a studio kitchen listening to the UK national chart radio show and hearing the DJ finally say, '*...and here's the song that has leapt out of nowhere and gone straight to the number one top spot—Yazz and 'The Only Way Is Up!'*" You also never forget the times when you see the faces of people as they tell you that they really love your music—that it means something to them personally. Like when a mother on the street told me that her son was in prison and that 'The Only Way' saved him from taking his life. And I recall winning a place at the table for the Women in Achievement yearly event and sitting next to Glenda Jackson and Diane Abbott. There are so many things like that which are memories I treasure."

Yasmin also remembers the professional challenges of the time, as she honed her live performance skills. "Getting out on stage presented interesting tasks as a dance-pop artist," she confesses. "Much of my music was synth and sequence-based. Drummers found it hard to be able to play all the parts, so we learned to trigger off sections on certain drum pads, etc., which worked the more performances we did. But, of course, there were some hilarious drum triggering moments with beats going off accidentally all over the place and at the wrong times. Thankfully, I had a very professional band and drummer, an amazing person and artist to work with and so patient. Singing live started off as a difficult thing for me, and I struggled with getting a good ear balance in my monitors. It took me time to develop that skill. Funny, now I enjoy it more than studio vocalizing!"

Evans' dance-pop career began to slow down in the early '90s. The hit "Treat Me Good," an update of the disco nugget "Never Can Say Goodbye," and a duet with Aswad called "How Long" were well-received at various points during the new decade, but much was changing for the artist on a personal level. With an exhale the singer says, "By then I was struggling in my profession as an artist and as a wife. My marriage had failed, and it was public knowledge, and I felt deeply ashamed. Intensely. I could not fix anything any more. All my own efforts were failing. I was beginning to reach the place called conviction. I was beginning to recognize that I couldn't cope with the strain of having to record another hit album. I was just about to become a mother of the most precious gift in the whole world, but I felt like a failure as a wife. Doors were closing, and the title of that track 'Treat Me Good' spoke volumes. I think it was like a cry for help in a way. I like the fact that my songs speak about real lives. I remember thinking that it was so important that I remained true to myself and write or sing songs that meant something to me."

Following a visit to church at the suggestion of her hairstylist and friend from years back, Yazz began a new phase in her life and a quest for a closer connection with God. She says she became a Christian after a long journey searching through many religions. "I would say my music career has been a lifelong journey that reached a magnificent crossroads some years back," the artist observes. "One way was surely leading to oblivion, dissatisfaction and death. The other was also a little scary because it was completely unknown to me, and yet I knew it was the only road to take. So I took it. And guess what—I never looked back. As roads go, the Christian avenue is like many roads. It twists and turns and has bumps and upward bends, but you do not walk that road alone. Ever. You learn where that road is leading you. You need not fear on that road. You meet extraordinary people on that road. You are inspired on that road—creatively, experientially. There is music on that road that you've never heard before. There are angels and demons too. But you are *never* alone. Because I took that path, my music is on another level compared to everything I have ever thought about or written before. That road has taught me that all I write has eternal consequences. This path shapes you because you have been given a gift to help rescue others. That changes how you write and what you want to write. How you sing. How you perform. What drives and motivates you. This road matures you. It is a path that leads you to freedom in your life," she says.

Moving firmly forward with her inspired goals, Yazz successfully released the Christian album *Running Back to You* in 2008 and the *This Is Love* set in 2011. She continues to tour throughout Europe and performs at prisons, schools and inspirational and charity events, such as the World AIDS Day Concert in Switzerland.

The artist readily admits she now places comparatively little importance on her dance-pop legacy."I simply didn't play the game very well. Now I know that success for an artist is not defined by recognition and never ought to be. It is personal. *Very* personal. Today, I know that I am loved with an unconditional love that is not defined by my achievements or performance, but rather on the plan God has for me. I did not have that kind of wisdom in those early years, so I looked to others for help. People all fail you because we are all flawed from birth. I thank God now that I finally came to look for help outside of myself and from others. I cannot tell you the happiness I feel when I remember that I finally let go and began to look up to find out who holds the source of all help, hope, peace and salvation. I don't really think it's necessary that I be remembered for anything,. But if I am, perhaps it will be for being a fairly good mum, friend and daughter—and as an arrow that eventually pointed to heaven!"

Claudie Fritsch
aka Desireless

"Voyage, Voyage" (1986)
France

Born on Christmas Day, the stars aligned rather well for Claudie Fritsch. She is better known as Desireless, an expressive French chanteuse who stretched the boundaries of gender identification with her stylishly androgynous look. She also displayed a remarkable ability to cross multiple international borders with the irresistible '80s dance classic, "Voyage, Voyage." The song is reported to have sold over five million copies, and it became an undisputed hallmark of European dance music of the era. Desireless delighted, perplexed and fascinated fans of her silky intonations and avant-garde, upbeat music. Her songs spoke of love, pain and the freedom to choose one's own destination—an idea she has most certainly embraced in her own life. She is a woman of few words today, at least in this particular conversation, but she puts great thought into all of her statements, and her viewpoints are clear and concise. Claudie is cheerful, and yet she seems perhaps just a bit reticent to reminisce about those remarkable days some 30 years ago. Still, her carefree, irresistible charm shines through—a quality that still sparks intrigue, admiration and affection for this highly unique and talented performer.

Claudie's professional life began in the fashion world, but she dislikes referring to her journey as a "career." Her protest is reflective of what appears to be a fondness for independence from the confines of categorization, possibly bolstered by her studies in Buddhism over the years. She recalls, "Years after taking lessons in fashion design at the Berçot Studio in Paris, I was a stylist from 1973–1980. I would design new collections every six months—changing colors and dreams of many forms. I liked it very much." The artist says she designed many of the costumes she wore as Desireless and continues to do so in the present.

While fashion design provided great personal satisfaction for the artist, Claudie discovered a means of creative expression that was even sweeter. "In 1980, a few musician friends asked me to come and sing with them. I realized that singing provided me with great pleasure and very quickly, without any transition, music became my passion and priority. It remains my passion to this very day."

The singer forged a musical partnership with Jean-Michel Rivat, a French lyricist and producer who had enjoyed great success in the '60s and '70s with such celebrated artists as Nana Mouskouri, Joe Dassin, Sylvie Vartan, France Gall, Patrick Juvet and other notables.

Left: **Desireless performs in trendsetting attire during a late '80s show.** *Right:* **The artist as she appears today (photograph by Benjamin Brolet, courtesy Antoine Aureche).**

"I met Jean-Michel thanks to a friend and fellow musician, a bass player with whom I played. It was our hope to give him a demo of our work and sign a contract with him," she says. The plan worked—at least for Claudie, who assumed the stage name Desireless (intended to mean precisely the word's definition—without desire, according to the singer). "Jean-Michel was a multi-faceted character," she recalls. "He was a very good songwriter, an intelligent composer and a redoubtable businessman. We worked together for six years, and I learned a great deal from him."

After signing in 1986 with CBS Records in France, the duo could not have asked for a more sensational debut. Written by Rivat and Dominique Dubois, produced by Rivat and recorded at Studio Aguesseau, Desireless's premiere recording "Voyage, Voyage" took Europe by storm. The dance single reached the number two position on the French charts, but claimed the top spot in Germany, Austria, Belgium, Denmark, Norway, Spain, Yugoslavia and as far away as Thailand. Ironically, the song itself seemed to revel in a poetic crisscrossing of world geographical references. The infectious beat and universally understood theme of travel and freedom projected by the song overwhelmed any potential speed bumps created by a recording made in the French language. Claudie's lilting vocals were the perfect complement to the electric beat.

Over the course of its nearly two-year active life, the song was remixed by Britain's famed PWL mixmasters, Pete Hammond and Pete Waterman, to further enhance its appeal in the clubs. The so-called "Britmix" helped make the track a sizeable hit in the UK, where artists like Kylie Minogue, Hazell Dean and Rick Astley were the reigning pop stars. Desireless is unable to provide any information about the genesis of "Voyage, Voyage," saying that she became involved with the song only at the time of the recording. "Jean-Michel and I spent a crazy amount of time in the studio making this song," she remembers. "Again, I have to say I learned a lot, and one of my qualities was that I was a good listener. I think the appeal of the song was that it allowed everyone to see what he or she wanted—to go forward or back—to choose one's vehicle and one's destination. I think with its title, it was predestined to appeal to many people. I didn't think very much [about the future of this song]. But Jean-Michel was a very good producer, so perhaps I assumed [it would be a hit]."

Part of Desireless's stunningly successful debut may be attributed to her unusual look and aloof personality, a persona that favored a gender-neutral aura at the time. Though often sexually non-specific, her eclectic costuming, punkish hairstyle and impenetrable personality had many a fan initially assuming Desireless might possibly be a young gay male. Such labels seem unimportant to Claudie. Claims the singer, "I am an androgyne—Yin and Yang. I never wanted to create an image. I just wanted to be myself. It's so easy and effective, no?" In a 2011 interview posted online by the entertainment hub Envrak.fr, the artist claimed to have no interest in being a man. Desireless was quoted as humorously insisting (loosely translated), "I have no balls or cock, but I can do everything like [a man]."

Despite the sudden glare of the spotlight and the novelty of pop chart success, she says her journey was unencumbered by fame. "[Success] did not change my life. I just took the plane a little more often. I drank a bit of champagne; I paid a little more in taxes," she says with amusement. When asked if there was a moment where she felt she had crossed into the world of pop stardom, she simply laughs off the question.

By 1988, the momentum of "Voyage, Voyage" had eased, and the time was right for a follow-up. A riveting lament to the futility and hopelessness of war, "John" was the powerful track chosen as her next commercial single. Rhythmically, it progressed with an intoxicating dance beat that was in some ways more infectious than its predecessor. Remixed by Les Adams, the production surged with a high-energy rhythm as Desireless's soothing, yet determined vocals hypnotized listeners. Says the singer, "I love the song 'John,' even more than 'Voyage, Voyage.' Ninety-nine percent of my fans also prefer the song. Unfortunately, the subject of this piece remains present." "John" reached the Top Five and was a huge hit in France, while making a significant impact in Germany and on the UK club charts.

The following year saw the long-awaited release of the Desireless debut album, entitled *François*. "François is the name of my companion all these years. He is the dad of my daughter, Lili. I loved the work we did in the studio for this album, from the sound of the kick drum, to the vocals and the final mix—I simply loved it," she says with fresh enthusiasm. The set featured Claudie's previous hits, as well as riveting dance cuts like "Les Commencements." The eclectic dance single, "Qui Sommes-nous" (which, like most of the Desireless catalog, was deep in spiritual references), was lifted from the set and extended for the clubs. The track received its most enthusiastic response from Germany.

The breezy, more melancholy single "Elle est Comme les Étoiles" followed in 1990, and with this final release, the artist left the confines of CBS. "I think there was too much pressure," she says without elaborating, but with a smile on her face. "That's why I left Sony and broke my contract with Jean-Michel after the release of the album. I regret nothing. The best thing about my success with these songs was my connection with the public. These songs have instilled an emotional and intimate link between us. It's magic!"

Claudie's daughter Lili was born in 1990. Though Desireless was less in the spotlight in the years that followed, she continued to explore her musical creativity. Most recently, Desireless teamed with Alec Mansion in 2011 for the well-received EP *L'expérience Humaine* (featuring the irresistible track "Tes Voyages Me Voyagent," which might be viewed as an evolution of "Voyage, Voyage") and in 2012, the album *XP2*. Continuing to express herself in inventive ways, the artist collaborated with Operation Of The Sun's accomplished innovator Antoine Aureche to release a critically acclaimed album called *L'Oeuf du Dragon* in 2012/2013, which mixed retro-beats and synth-pop for a surprising overall mood of serenity and introspection. The pair released a new Desireless set in mid–2014 called *Noun*.

"Since 1996, I have been on stage with different musicians in France and abroad," the artist states. "In fact, I have never stopped making music. I simply haven't been exposed in the media as often. Today, I continue 'my little snowman path,' just singing and being happy. I enjoy being in touch with people on the Internet. I think I'm still a popular artist, and I love that. Many people have supported me over the years, gay and straight. However, I am absolutely not nostalgic about the '80s, and my password is 'live in the present.' I advise everyone to read the books of Eckhart Tolle [spiritual author of *The Power of Now* and *A New Earth*].

"The '80s are the past for me. But from those years I have kept a little magic key, which allows me to open the hearts of people. I still represent and sing the song 'Voyage, Voyage' today, and I certainly will until my death. But I need to do many other things in order to live and be happy," the artist says firmly. When asked how she'd like the world to remember her after all is said and done, the prodigious artist smiles once more and, with a wink, says, "This is not my problem!"

Junior Giscombe
aka Junior
"Mama Used to Say" (1982)
UK

The international smash single "Mama Used to Say" was as much a dance floor hit in 1981 as it was, perhaps unknowingly to most listeners, a testament to the philosophy of being true to one's self. Sung by an artist named Junior (also known as Norman Giscombe, Jr., and Junior Giscombe), the young vocalist enjoyed the distinction of being one of the first British R&B singer-songwriters to find substantial success in the United States. His records have topped the charts of Europe and South America as well. However, despite his fame and the unyielding pressures of a demanding recording industry, he insists he has never allowed anyone to prefabricate his dreams. Over 30 years after his stellar debut on the charts, Junior remains determined to trust his instincts and to pursue integrity in all aspects of his life. From a quiet room in his London home, the artist settles back and talks about navigating his own path as a '80s dance-pop star.

"I first got my feelings for music when I'd go to church as a little boy," Giscombe says, his British accent and bright smile setting an inviting tone to our conversation. "I don't remember a time where we didn't have some form of music in our home. I think watching the energy, the spark, the joy and the way that music moved people really got to me early on. My parents were very flexible about religion (and life in general), and when my brothers and sisters and I got older and started thinking differently, they allowed us to make our own choices and to find ourselves. For me, I knew I didn't want to do the nine-to-five. I knew that fact as young as 12 or 13. That was out of the question for me. I didn't see where 50 years of doing the same thing was going to work for me. I chose soccer as my sport in school and went on to play for South London. I was a trainee for a pro team, but I didn't care for the way you were treated. I thought you could be your own man, but in this sport, you were trained how to think, and I didn't want that.

"So, I knew I was good with music, and I decided to put a band together with some friends. We got some gigs at pubs and such and were pretty good at it. Around 1980, a friend of mine named Junior Douglas was putting a song together and asked me if I'd help write the lyrics and melody. It was fun, and we put out a song called 'Get Up and Dance.' It was recorded at the end of the disco era and had that kind of Chic sound. I didn't expect anything to come of it, but it was the learning experience I wanted. [The record was released in France] using the artist name of Norman Giscombe, Jr., and it became a huge success.

Left: **A publicity photo issued by Mercury Records in the U.S. appropriately suggests that Junior hit a home run in 1982 with the single "Mama Used to Say."** *Right:* **The singer continues to perform today.**

I didn't even know it had been a hit until I went to the country years later with the success of my international hit, 'Mama Used to Say.' People started shouting for me to play 'Get Up and Dance,' somehow knowing that it was me on that record. Somehow, the French people put two and two together."

Following a stint as a backup singer with the successful British R&B dance group Linx, Giscombe was signed as a solo singer with Mercury Records. "There was a A&R guy from the label I got signed with named Roger Ames, whom I was working with. I asked him if he knew about an artist named Prince. I told him that his sound was the kind of music I wanted to make. I wanted to do an album that didn't have a hundred different arrangers and producers. I wanted something closer knit, something different—like Prince. He said the label was open to the idea, but they wanted me to work with Bob Carter (who had also been with Linx). I had no problem with that as long as it was just the two of us. He liked the one-name idea, so we decided to drop the Norman Giscombe name and just go with Junior.

"Believe it or not," he laughs, "I had a side gig at this point in time—making handmade shoes. I would design them for the Royal Family. It was brilliant because I had learned a trade, in case music didn't work out. I didn't stay in it for that long, however, because my music career really kicked in. I was 23, going on 24, and chatting with my mom one night. We got to talking about how different I was from my friends. I liked going to the theatre, and my friends liked hanging in the hood. But it didn't stop us from all being friends or being who we were. (Our friendships have remained intact, 40-odd years down the line!)

My mother was talking about being an individual, yet being part of the human community. I had started to write a new song and some of our discussion and her advice had found its way into my lyrics. At one point I played the basic melody demo for my mom, and she said, 'Junior, this song is going to work for you. Everyone around the world—they love the word "mama." Remember that!' I laughed about it and finished the song. Bob and I worked on the track some more and finished the arrangement. And that's how 'Mama Used to Say' came about."

As it turned out, Junior's mother was right. His 1982 debut single, a punchy jam that bridged infectious dance rhythms with insightful lyrics, proved to be perfect fodder for the hit-hungry international pop charts that summer. A Top 40 success in America, the song climbed to Britain's Top 10 and earned the singer/songwriter the best newcomer award from the industry music bible, *Billboard* magazine. "I didn't see the song as being dance music at the time. Bob and I saw it as our own blend of R&B. I was trying to do more than record a song that would make people jump up and down. I wanted to touch them in other ways. That was the joy of being an artist.

"When I first got to America with the song, I had no idea radio was segregated. Radio in the UK was limited (in that you had pirate radio and the regular radio), but you'd always hear different styles of music. In the U.S., it was much different. There'd be a head of 'black' A&R and the one who handled 'white' A&R. The black one would have to prove his record was good enough for the white guy to take it on board. My A&R man actually felt my version of the song was a bit too rock-oriented, 'too white' as he put it. There was definitely a color thing going on. I wasn't used to color being such a prevalent consideration. Segregation was very evident. The U.S. label made it quite clear they weren't going to push 'Mama Used to Say' in the beginning because it was an English record and a black record. The record company didn't break Junior in America; the record broke me.

"The single sold, I don't know, something like 50,000 to 100,000 copies a day at one point in places like Chicago. The sales were phenomenal," Junior claims proudly. "One reason the record did break so big was because of the remix version we did with Tee Scott. I was reluctant at first because 'Mama' was going to be one of the first records where the label would try to release a remix. Why experiment on mine? But then I got curious to see what someone else would do with it. I loved it. I loved the original version with the rock-R&B sound. But Tee Scott captured the sound that would work for a specific market, an evolution of the original. And, in turn, it made people want to hear the original version. Tee opened the door by getting into the groove of the track. He was a remixer for Frankie Crocker, a DJ on New York station WBLS. I was told if Frankie played the record, I'd be able to leave my job, and we'd be set—it would explode. I didn't know anything about any of that, so I just laughed. Well, Frankie played it on a Sunday night, and by Wednesday, there wasn't a station in New York, black or white, that wasn't playing it. Everybody followed. We didn't have a DJ in England with that kind of influence."

The triumph of "Mama Used to Say" led to the release the same year of Junior's debut album *Ji*, produced by Bob Carter. The up-tempo, funk-tinged singles "Too Late" and "I Can't Help It" kept the artist on the charts and in the spotlight. The experience of being a new star was profound, according to the singer. "When you initially have the kind of success where people in so many different countries are loving your song, it's beyond the dream," he readily admits. "You can walk into your record company, and they put their arm around you and say, 'Oh, you've sold 100,000 copies today.' I'm trying to fathom 100,000 people who worked really hard that day who go into a shop and spend their money on my record. There's no city in the UK where we were going to sell that many copies. Maybe 5,000 in Manchester or Liverpool, and then, eventually, it adds up to a total of 100,000. But to have the record sell 100,000 in so many different cities in the U.S. (and then Europe and Asia) was mind-blowing. I went from playing pub gigs where there were three or four people to venues where there were 10 or 15,000 people—it was amazing.

"You were treated like a star, and it was a complete mind trip. I met Luther, Stevie, Aretha—and everybody took me under their wing. I remember doing a television show with Rick James, and he fixed my tie backstage. He asked me how I was going to sing my song, and I showed him. He said, 'No, no, no. The women aren't going to like that. Don't do that thing with your hand'—you know, things like that. I was so fortunate. That record put me in a place where I met some wonderful people and was given some great advice. I can still call many of these people my friends to this very day. I used to buy their records—it's wild. I'm a fan. I still am. They must have thought I was ridiculous. I remember my palms sweating like crazy when I was about to meet Stevie Wonder. He said, 'You don't have to be so nervous.' All of these things happened just by making one record."

Carter produced Giscombe's second album, 1983's *Inside Lookin' Out*. The single "Communication Breakdown," a brassy dance-popper, continued to incorporate the popular British beat style but failed to attain the chart heights of his formidable debut. The set was reflective, says the artist, of life in the music industry fast lane. "I didn't handle the aftermath of my initial success very well, to be honest with you. I found it very difficult. The heat was on to have another hit—which wasn't bad; I could deal with that. But now the record company was saying the songs weren't good enough. Instead of needing 10 songs, they wanted 30 so they could choose 15, record those and then cut that group down to 10. Remember, my whole thing was I didn't like being pushed into that 'you have to do this' mentality. So I started to rebel—*badly*.

"During '83 and '84, the record company and I were really at odds with each other. Bob had taken sides with the label, so I was feeling like I was really on my own. The whole thing about the songs not being good enough was really bothering me. They trusted me with my first album and never even heard the songs that we did in advance. Everything was great with it, and we sold millions of copies. You'd think they would have thought just maybe I knew what I was doing. Nothing was broken, so what were they trying to fix? The pressure was all coming from the business side, and it was hampering my creative side. I had nobody I could talk to. I started feeling nothing I was ever going to do would ever be good enough. I was trying to create songs to please a guy who was probably a failed musician who sat behind a desk instead of being true to myself. I realized my success triggered *their* success and began to understand people's egos."

Junior recorded more LPs and released several singles as the decade progressed, but the collections were less than major commercial successes for the label. "I was working non-stop for the first five years after 'Mama Used to Say,'" he remembers. "I finally said to hell with this, 'I'm off!' I went on vacation and was out-of-touch for about three days when they finally found me. And then they were on me again. 'We need you to go to Germany, to Italy,' etc., etc. I could see I was being pimped. I wasn't making music for people; I was making it for a corporation. I wasn't down with any of that.

"I did a song in 1985 for the movie *Beverly Hills Cop* called 'Do You Really (Want My Love).' It became a part of one of the biggest selling soundtracks of all-time. I was proud of that work; it was music I wanted to do. So yes, I knew I needed to record songs that were successful, and I needed to make money. But I needed the freedom to be able to make music that I could take pride in. That's me. I made a good amount of money from my records, which definitely gave me more freedom to make that decision, but I think I would have done it anyway. I couldn't live with making music that didn't mean something to me. Eventually, I left the label."

Around 1987, Giscombe cut a new deal with MCA Records. Pairing with Brit singer Kim Wilde (who had blasted up the U.S. and European charts with a remake of The Supremes' nugget, "You Keep Me Hangin' On" and later with "You Came"), he released the high-energy "Another Step (Closer to You)," which was a Top 10 smash in England. It was also Junior's biggest European hit.

Says the singer, "Kim and I go back a long way. She had 'Kids in America' about a year before I had my hit with 'Mama.' I was recording bits and pieces of my first album at the same studio she used, so I used to see her and her brother there. We got on really well. She rang me up one day and said she wanted to do a duet with me. At the time, Michael McDonald and Patti Labelle had done well with 'On My Own,' and she wanted to do something like that. I said no—I didn't want to do *anything* like that. I suggested to her that if we were going to do a duet, it had to be something that was *us*—English with an edge. Not American. I said, 'To hell with the black and white thing; let's make something colorless so that it just drops!' We got together, and I kind of rearranged what she had written and adjusted the melody, and that became 'Another Step.' And people never went near that color issue with us, which was brilliant. Kim and I used to laugh about the whole color thing, which was still very much an eyebrow raiser in those days.

"That record was number one all over South America. I remember we flew down there, and when we arrived, people threw pebbles on the ground at our feet getting off the plane. It meant they thought of us as a kind of royalty. By the time we got to the hotel, the biggest news on the TV was the two of us arriving in French Guyana. It was a wild, wild scenario—you know what I'm saying?"

When the record was released in America, Junior believes his label was uncertain of how to market it. Unconcerned, he simply enjoyed the attention the single received elsewhere.

"Kim and I thought, okay, we'll just have to wait and see if anything happens in the U.S. But in Europe, it just blew up. So we traveled all over Europe with that song. What I love about it is that it fused a synthetic music style with energy and pop-sounding voices. A lot of people at the label in the UK were very skeptical about the record and said, 'Oh, that will never work.' I told them, 'Wait till it gets on radio, man. You'll get it.' They changed their minds. Once again, record companies just tend to sell a record; they don't feel what people sometimes feel about the music. Instead of dismissing everything, it would have been great if they just took a moment to listen to the music. So often they just pooh-poohed a song without even hearing it."

By the mid-'80s, a three-man production force known by their collective last names as Stock Aitken Waterman (Kylie Minogue, Rick Astley, Jason Donovan, Dead or Alive) was dominating the dance-pop charts of the UK, as well as a big chunk of the European and U.S. markets. Many artists were anxious to release new material that incorporated their sound, but not necessarily Giscombe.

"The group Maze had done an instrumental record called 'Twilight,' and my record company was telling me how that sound was selling and that I should do something like it. They were also mentioning Stock Aitken Waterman a lot. They were telling me about the success that those producers were having, and they said the guys wanted to work with me. I wasn't that interested in doing it, but I tried to keep an open mind (as I wanted others to do with my music). So I said I would meet with them.

"I went down to the studio and met all the gentlemen, who were all very nice people. They would play samples for me and ask me what I thought of the music. I wasn't feeling anything they were playing and suggested maybe we should start by writing something together. They told me that the way they worked, they write the song, and I would just come on top. It was all very polite. About five hours go by, and we still haven't come up with anything. Then Pete came in, and don't you know he's carrying a copy of 'Twilight' and tells Stock that we should make a record that sounded like it. That was it for me!" Junior laughs.

"I left the studio, went home and never went back. My label, the Stock Aitken Waterman guys—everybody was vexed about it. I wasn't. If you're telling me I have to make a record I have no feeling for, which they could have given to anybody, just so I can get some kind of airplay somewhere or to satisfy some A&R guy's desire to work with them—forget it. This would have been at my expense, and yet they were telling me this would be a good thing for me. I wasn't interested in that kind of approach."

The singer experienced other challenges in the music business during this era besides battles over artistic freedom. Drug abuse was rampant according to the artist. "Where I came from in South London wasn't too far from a place they call Brixton. Brixton was like the hood. Drugs were prevalent—heroin, coke, the whole lot. It was just part of the environment. When I got into the music industry, I had no idea how much was being used. When I went on tour with Linx, I never saw so much cocaine out there in my life. I'd seen a lot of things in my day, but the use was staggering to me. An artist or group could actually order x-amount of cocaine, and the record company would turn around, buy it, and make it available. When I first came to America for 'Mama' and was driven around in a limousine from the airport, the limo driver lowered the divider window and said, 'Mr. Junior, we have on your left barbiturates, cocaine. On the right there's heroin, LSD, brandy and champagne.' It was an amazing time for drugs. You could do a whole tour and not be paid any money and just get drugs. I had a great guitarist at one point, but he couldn't play without doing a line. I couldn't cope with that after a while—it was just draining.

"In America, everybody seemed to be on some kind of a drug. I know it sounds far-fetched, but I really couldn't find anybody who was completely drug free. I remember doing a telethon against drug abuse. And once the TV camera was off, pretty much everyone in the room was taking a hit of something. It was incredible to me. I did some drinking and smoking as a kid (outside of my parents' home), but I wasn't prepared for this. It was bizarre. I'd meet these stars, these individuals who had these amazing careers and great lives, as portrayed by the media. Then you'd find out how insecure, shallow and desperate they were. And often, drugs were behind their problems."

No less impactful was the AIDS pandemic of the '80s. Junior's voice reveals his frustration with the course this crisis took in its early years. "The AIDS epidemic hit me more in America than in England. I remember a lot of people contracting the disease in '84 and '85. Again, it was something that changed your mindset because you were told all these stupid things, like 'don't sit on a toilet seat that someone with HIV might have used.' Or 'don't use utensils they might have eaten with.' I had two close friends who contracted AIDS, and I watched them die. I remember pharmaceutical companies had drugs that might have helped people, but they were so expensive, nobody could afford them. What was the sense of having a drug and nobody having access to it—unless you had a lot of money? It was abhorrent to me—that period when it all began. And then to see the targeting of a particular section of society—to me, it was lowest of the low. To say it was a gay disease was such bullshit, to be honest.

"In England, the scare mongering that was going on ('you don't really need to have a gay friend,' 'if you caught it, you must be gay or bisexual'—things like that) was so over-the-top. Most of my information about the disease came from America, because the UK was getting everything wrong. And it was creating a very anti-gay mood in England. Now we all know that HIV is not a death sentence, and there are better treatments today. In the twenty-first century, there is less fear. But at that time, it was just terrible, and I think a lot of the authorities, pharmaceutical companies and doctors who orchestrated the dissemination of information, and the way the crisis was handled, have a lot to answer for." Junior exhales and sits back in his chair.

Giscombe maintained a more subdued recording profile in the '90s and beyond, but continued writing for and producing numerous artists, including Amii Stewart, Warren G., Cam'ron, Heavy D and Brand Nubians. Throughout his journey, Giscombe says he's always tried to maintain a sense of positivity in life. He's had more than his share of uphill climbs, which have tested his determination. "I think tragedy has actually kept me positive," he observes. "I know that sounds odd. I lost my mom, my dad and some brothers all within a period of about five years—one after another. Everybody around me that was really close to me had passed. I felt like I was on my own—I wasn't, but it felt like that.

"Then in 1998, I had a car accident and broke my back in two places. I was told I would be paralyzed. Two orderlies from the hospital would come to my room every night and ask me if I wanted to go out for a smoke (I know that wasn't healthy, but I needed it). They would literally carry me outside every night until I was finally able to walk with them on my own. These things changed my thinking and made me look at life beyond the things we are usually running after.

"My partner (who has passed)—she had multiple sclerosis, and my daughter does as well. Having to deal with my daughter's condition and knowing there still isn't really a treatment out there to fully stop it and realizing, over time, she is likely to lose the use of different parts of her body—it is a very humbling experience. So, where I'm at as a man today—I look at my life the way I did when I was very young. I want to use my mind to move forward, as opposed to following what other people think is best for me. That philosophy has always served me well, and it still does."

Looking back at his history with "Mama Used to Say," the artist says, "I didn't really acknowledge the impact of the song until almost a decade after it had come out and been a hit. I would hear the song come on so many times over the years that I would turn off the radio when I heard it. I didn't realize the effect of my music. All I could think was they were overplaying it. I remember I was in my car waiting for the light to change by a train station, and the song came on again. I didn't turn it off this time. I listened to it, and I suddenly realized I had written something that was going to stay around. I always wanted to write a song that would last 20, 30, 40 years from now. When I'm dead and gone, you could still hear it played. And I realized I've done that. I made a song that made people want to get up and dance, but one that had lyrical content with substance. I touched people with my music, and that's what I hope to do for a long time to come."

Junior's daughter, Jenique Louise Giscombe, passed in the spring of 2017.

Jaki Graham
"Round and Around" (1985)
UK

Being a Guinness World Record holder as the first black British female solo artist to have six consecutive Top 10/Top 20 hits in the UK clearly indicates there is something very special about Jaki Graham. Her unpretentious, earnest vocal style was an ideal match for the soulful compositions of her producer and primary songwriter, Derek Bramble, for much of the mid-to-late '80s. Graham's hopelessly addictive, R&B-fused dance tracks, such as "Round and Around," "Set Me Free," "Breaking Away" and "Step Right Up," provided a refreshing diversion from the high-energy confections that saturated the period. She continues to deliver her very genuine approach to music today, and her audiences love it. Still living in the Midlands of England, where her family established roots decades ago, Jaki enthusiastically speaks with humility and candor about being a premier '80s star.

Graham was born of Jamaican parents in the Birmingham borough of the UK. "My mum, dad and grandmother came over here in the late '50s seeking more opportunities and a better life I imagine," says the singer, with a warm English accent. "My dad died when I was quite young; I was just 10 years old. My grandmother raised me during my early years and brought me up really. I loved Motown music, The Jackson 5 and The Osmonds. I remember as a kid seeing these artists on TV, and I'd be using my hairbrush as a microphone, and I'd be singing their songs. I think that's when music started clicking with me. I had two uncles, one of whom was into jazz, and the other was into soul and R&B. I was exposed to Aretha, Al Green and artists like that. My grandmother was always listening to reggae. So I always had these musical influences around me as I was growing up. By the time I was in secondary school, I was singing in little competitions, and I think my talent started to really manifest itself. To be truthful, I felt like I was given the gift of a voice.

"My hubby, Tony Ormsby, who was later my road manager, got me into my very first band. We went to school together when we were in Birmingham, and we've been together since we were 14 or 15 years old," recalls the singer, who married at the age of 19. "Tony and I have been husband and wife for 38 years. He's always been there with me. When I started to have hits in the '80s, people thought I was an overnight success. But I wasn't. I'd already been gigging, paying my dues, acting as a roadie and performing with bands for a good 10 years or so. I started off as a vocalist in my own band called Ferrari. I'd hold down a job during the day, and at night we'd perform at clubs, pubs and universities—all throughout the UK. I was thrilled to be in a band and getting the little level of attention I was receiving. Some girlfriends and I would also do some backing vocals.

Left: **Jaki Graham seems to reach into her very soul as she belts one of her many hits during a performance in the '80s.** *Right:* **Jaki in the twenty-first century (courtesy Natalie Graham).**

"I did a vocal session in Birmingham for an instrumental jazz funk band. I did some vocals as a front person for them, and the EMI record label that was showing some interest in them happened to notice me too. That's primarily how my solo career came about. I also provided guest background vocals on a couple of UB40 songs (one of which was a cover of Jimmy Cliff's 'Many Rivers to Cross') at the same time that I had signed with EMI, which also helped raise my profile a bit. I had always been part of a band or a unit. It was my husband Tony who encouraged me to give the solo career a go, but once I was thrust into the public eye, I felt a bit lost."

The artist's debut album, *Heaven Knows*, was released in 1985 and was a sizeable hit that cracked the British Top 50. The set was packed with funk-tinged soul-pop singles like "Could It Be I'm Falling in Love" (a Top Five hit with former Linx vocalist David Grant) and the catchy, synth-pop dance track "Round and Around," another Top 10 success. The singles also gave the artist her first modest hits on the U.S. R&B charts.

Recalls Graham, "When I came on the scene in the mid–'80s and I'd say in interviews that I was from Birmingham, they all thought I was American and thought I meant Birmingham, Alabama. I always had to say, 'No darling, Birmingham, the Midlands, England.' I didn't even have an American accent, yet they just assumed I was American because of the style of music I did. American music was something we all grew up with in the UK, and we wanted to emulate it. It's funny because I met a lot of American singers, producers and record company people during this time, and I came to realize how much they admired British soul and wanted to emulate *our* sound.

"I think I can attribute a lot of my success to the foresight and songwriting skills of Derek Bramble. He had been a member of Heatwave at one point. He was working with Shalamar and artists and musicians who had that kind of funk-pop-soul sound. He was very into that kind of dance style. He approached me with these great songs, which we recorded as demos, and thanks to those, I got the deal with EMI. It was a production deal, so I was initially signed to Derek's production company, which was signed to the label. Derek came up with all those great songs on my first album, and my voice really suited them. I wasn't a technical person, so I never got involved in most of the studio work Derek did. I didn't have a clue about that end of it or how he came up with those ideas. There was a learning curve for us though, really. Our sound evolved as we went along. We wanted to capture the American sound with a little twist, you know? So we sort of created our own soul-dance style, and my vocal interpretation of what he'd write just happened to hit the mark.

"But EMI Records in the UK had so much trouble understanding our brand," she insists. "They didn't know how to promote our music; they didn't really *get* me. They didn't understand what we were doing, the black-soul-dance music thing, and I was finding myself in competition with other artists on their roster like [the new wave group] Sigue Sigue Sputnik ["Love Missile F1–11"], which they were putting all their energy and money into. So there I was, still managing to have some big hits, without the record company really behind me. 'What's the Name of Your Game' off my first album started circulating on pirate radio stations and Radio One in the UK. That was a big, big help to us. They embraced what Derek and I were doing, and they seemed to really love it. The record company would drag their heels, and they just figured my records would do their thing in the clubs or whatever.

"The first week of release of the 'Round and Around' single, it got picked up very quickly on radio. The next thing I knew, I was on *Top of the Pops*. The show had this segment called 'The Breakers,' which were sort of 'bubbling under the Top 40' songs. We had debuted on the pop chart pretty high, like in the mid–40s. Sure enough, we started climbing, and I found myself on the show. The show's producers were always watching the sales figures of the songs of any artists they were planning to feature. Back then, to be in the Top 40 you had to sell *a lot*—tens, if not hundreds of thousands of copies. So being on the chart back then spoke volumes."

Jaki says she felt frustration over her label's seemingly indifferent attitude toward the momentum she was gathering. "I suppose under a bit of duress, the label finally agreed with my management that we needed a video for 'Round and Around.' I remember at first they wanted the video to be about a minute and a half long. Their logic was that if the song doesn't continue to climb the chart, they haven't wasted too much money. EMI was so concentrated on Sigue Sigue Sputnik, and they thought that group, who I think only had two major hits, was going to be the next big thing. They understood that band's sound, and that's all the label could concentrate on. But British soul was definitely not on their radar.

"Well, my record flew anyway, didn't it? EMI were like headless chickens and didn't know what had happened when it reached the top part of the chart. That scenario was really repeated through all the hits that I had.

"I remember I had a single out during the Christmas period. It was Top 20 on the radio, and the album already had multiple hits on it by that point. Still, EMI would not promote the LP on TV or do the marketing necessary to keep the project on top. I went to a gig with the group Maze in London at the Hammersmith Odeon, and I met some of the top people from the American counterpart of my label. When they figured out who I was, they said, 'You know Jaki, we really love your album, but the UK just won't give us the money to do what we wanted to do in the U.S. It would really fly in the States if we were given a budget to promote it.' That really did it for me. I wasn't even aware that the Americans even knew about me."

Graham's "Could It Be I'm Falling in Love" and "Round and Around" managed to make just a gentle dent in the U.S. soul charts (where the singer was often compared to Evelyn "Champagne" King), but her popularity in her native England and countries like New Zealand, Switzerland and Sweden continued to grow.

"I think my management and Derek experienced the pressure of having to strive for more hits," the artist observes. "I was really oblivious to all that. I just wanted to go out and do my thing. I just wanted to make good records that I could vocally reproduce in a live setting. I was more concerned with my performance ability rather than sales figures. But I must admit I felt a bit nervous every time a new single or album would come out. I always felt like I was starting all over again. So the anxiety as to whether it would work or not was always with me, but I tried not to pay too much attention to it. I was fully aware that I could be just a one, two or three-hit wonder.

"As an artist, I just wanted people to like the songs, whereas management was really focused on chart positions. I really tried never to take that extra pressure on board," Jaki insists. The artist released the album *Breaking Away* in 1986, again produced by Derek Bramble. The set scored major hits on UK radio and international dance floors with the LP's title track and "Set Me Free" (which reached Britain's Top 10 and the same level on the U.S. dance chart). The jubilant dance jam "Step Right Up" proved to be yet another hit for the accomplished singer.

"Tony had taken me to the British office of EMI," she recalls, "and he asked the executives why they had such a problem with me as an artist. He said to them, 'I'll give you £10 for every photo there is of Jaki on the walls of this place.' As you would go up the stairs of EMI, there were all these pictures of their stars and even one-hit wonders. There was an A&R guy who looked after us, and he had a little picture of me up in his office—that was the only one. I had made all these hits for them, and I was nowhere to be seen. I had always wanted to just enjoy doing the music, and I didn't really understand how the industry worked. I was a bit oblivious to it all back then. I figured we were doing well and charting, so I didn't consider things like perhaps some degree of racism possibly being a factor or anything like that.

"Now I realize with the industry that in those days I was just a commodity, a number, and I didn't really matter to them. You would have thought that if I were helping the record company do so well, they would have been more invested and focused on me. It just didn't seem to work like that. But they sure were into gambling on Brother Beyond and Climie Fisher. I just couldn't compete with artists like that. If I had a single scheduled to come out when one of their other key acts had something being released, especially American artists, I'd get pushed back. But you know what? I'm okay with it now. My songs got out, radio picked up on them and they were big hits. The public wanted them—and that's what counts."

Despite the lack of corporate support Graham describes, there was no shortage of demand for her talents beyond the confines of her label's headquarters. With so many balls in play, the artist says she didn't always get to focus on the spotlight. "I was having this music career, and I was also a mom. I was traveling with my child, and we did it all as a family. I came into the industry thinking I would probably be in it for five minutes. I was enjoying what was happening, but I wasn't absorbing it—do you understand? I probably should have, but there were just so many things going on. My family kept me grounded and because my attention was often on them, I wasn't as likely to get caught up in the glamour or excitement.

"I do remember they used to call me a diva, and I liked that word at the time. I know now, if you think about the meaning of that word, I wasn't really a diva. You experienced all this adoration going on, but you also had to rush offstage to the dressing room, sometimes going from one event to another. There was just no time to pay attention to the cheering of the fans and things like that. When I think of the big venues and TV shows I did, I love the memories I have. But I have to say, I also remember the traveling and being on airplanes all the time, which was difficult and sometimes tiring. I had never been out of the UK before, but when my career took off, I was being flown *everywhere*. First class, I must admit. I wasn't used to that at all. I used to worry that when they gave me a little bottle of champagne, I might be getting a bill for it.

"I was doing some promotional touring in the south of France, where a record of mine was doing very well. Suddenly, I needed to be on a live TV show in Northern England. They got me a Lear jet to fly me to that show and then flew me back to finish the tour in France. I was in an airplane that only had four leather seats, a stewardess and the pilot. I was in awe. It was an incredible experience, although the cost of things like that—they tell me—has never been recouped. As a result, I never made any money directly from the albums I did."

As the era progressed, Graham performed background vocals for luminaries like Kim Wilde and teamed with singer Michael McDonald for his *On My Own* tour in the UK. The artist remembers that McDonald reportedly called her "one of the best singers Britain ever produced." With the decade winding down, she released one more LP for EMI. *From Now On* hit store shelves in 1989, and its funky electronic title track returned the singer to the British and American charts.

As wild as the '80s have often been described, Jaki says she kept her feet firmly on the ground through all of it. "I think my husband Tony shielded me from most of the drugs and things like that, which were so prevalent during the era. I'm sure it was all around, but I wasn't exposed to it, and it didn't impact my career or me. I do remember being at a party and somebody asked me if I wanted coke. I said, 'Oh yes, I am dying for some.' Unfortunately, they meant cocaine, and I meant the drink," she laughs. "But all throughout those days it was a family situation for me to be perfectly honest. That was the priority. I wanted some degree of fame, and I wanted my daughter Natalie to see the music industry but not be affected in a bad way by it. My family and I continued to live in the Midlands. (Natalie, along with my husband, manages me today, and I have a son Ryan, who is also in the music business.)

The artist continued to record well into the '90s, highlighted by the top-selling *Real Life* album. Her single "Ain't Nobody" was an international hit and remained at the number one spot on *Billboard*'s dance chart in the U.S. for five weeks. The song was a hit as far away as Japan, where it reached gold status. In 2009, Graham performed a *Gershwin & Soul* concert with the BBC Big Band for the UK's Radio Two network.

"I knew most people knew me for my hits in the '80s," she concedes, "but I always wanted to do something like that—something that might have very broad appeal. I quite liked some of the Gershwin material, and I realized my dad had often whistled some of these melodies to me as a child. I took an opportunity to perform this kind of music live, which was very nerve wracking. I did the show at the Birmingham Town Hall. The audience that came that night was comprised of big band fans that didn't necessarily know who I was. I was nervous as hell, but loved it. The feedback I got afterward was amazing. It was just as I suspected—many didn't know me, but they told me they were going to explore my music and find out more about what I've done. I eventually recorded an album of this music in 2012 called *For Sentimental Reasons*, which I looked at as kind of homage to my dad."

Though completely cognizant of middle age, Jaki says she isn't letting it slow her down. "I always wanted to grow old gracefully and to hang onto my voice," she admits. "I don't know how long I will be able to do that, but so far it's all been brilliant. I think about aging sometimes. I think I ought to calm down a bit in my shows, or maybe I shouldn't wear my skirt so short. My daughter tells me I am still carrying it off just fine. She may be biased, but at the shows I still get that validation. The males still show you they like you, and they're cool with you, and the females tell me I haven't changed a bit. A woman said to me, 'My God, your pins (legs) are something else!' You have to listen to your female fans, and when they endorse you, you know you're okay. If you aren't looking right, the women are going to tell you. That's a blessing for me that I have their approval because—*the women will tell you*! I think a lot of it also has to do with how you approach your audience. I am always nervous before I go onstage, and the older I get the more nervous I am. I suppose I worry about people's expectations. I want to do the best I can—better than what they may remember about me.

"I think of the love fans showed me back in [the '80s], and I can appreciate it even more today," she says softly. "Even now, fans greet me with such warmth. And that's all I can ask—that people remember me fondly. I love seeing a new generation enjoying my work. And I love that my voice today still gives people joy. I never take for granted that people know my history. I always perform as if this might be the first time the audience is hearing me. But when I discover they *do* know about what I've contributed to pop music, I think how blessed I am, darling. I am a part of a lot of people's personal history. The music will outlive all of us. Pass it on, and enjoy it!"

Phil Harding
PWL Mixmaster
Artists: Dead or Alive, Kylie Minogue, Bananarama, Rick Astley, et al.
UK

Though much media attention has been deservedly bestowed upon the vocalists of Europe's top dance-pop hits of the '80s, the production professionals supporting these projects have sometimes been relegated to the shadows. These engineers and remixers were wizards of electronic technology and expert at multitasking. They worked diligently (and often ingeniously) behind the scenes to enhance and refashion the sound of original recordings that were placed in their care. Many of the songs they revamped became magnificent commercial and artistic successes, reaching much broader audiences than ever thought possible. Their original productions boldly explored exciting new and uncharted musical territory and sold millions of records. One of the most prolific and successful of these pioneers was Britain's Phil Harding. As an integral member of producers Mike Stock, Matt Aitken and Pete Waterman's elite technical force at PWL Studios, Harding mixed, remixed and produced some of the biggest hits by the greatest performers of the era.

The list of luminaries who benefited from Phil's visionary style and transformative applications, forged together with partner Ian Curnow, reads like a dance music who's who—Dead or Alive, Samantha Fox, Bananarama, Erasure, Kylie Minogue, Rick Astley, Sabrina, Big Fun, Divine, Diana Ross, Sinitta, Sybil, Billy Ocean, Jason Donovan, Donna Summer, The Three Degrees, Climie Fisher, Debbie Harry, Pepsi & Shirlie and ABC, to name but a few. He also had a hand in designing the unforgettable alternative-industrial dance sounds of acts like Depeche Mode and Nitzer Ebb. Phil's career extended well into the '90s, and he continues to produce hip and exciting music in the twenty-first century. From his home in Suffolk, England, Harding, an eloquent, highly knowledgeable and decidedly agreeable man, offers his impressions of the extraordinary experiences he enjoyed as Europe's premiere mixmaster.

"I started piano lessons at the age of 14 and began playing in some small groups," Phil remembers. "When I was a bit older, I asked my career officer at school if there was any way he could help me get into the music industry. I got sent to the usual places for interviews, but then he made an appointment for me at an audio/electronics company in West London. They didn't think I had the technical background to work for them, but they had

Left: (Left to right) Pete Waterman, Ian Curnow and Phil Harding discuss their next PWL project back in 1989. *Right:* Waterman as he appears today.

heard the studio located behind them was looking for a new assistant. It was called the Marquee Studios, and I got an interview with them. Within 24 hours I was given the job. That was a lucky break for me back in 1973. When I first started working there, there was a ton of rock and pop music being made. But by 1974 and 1975, we were doing a number of disco sessions as well.

"I'll be honest; I was more into rock music at the time. But I was very quickly drawn into the disco-pop sound. In part, it was because one of the studio managers was a DJ at one of the big London clubs. We used to get free guest passes for the club, and I started hearing more of the disco sound. So I began to veer away from the rock scene and moved into dance-pop. Punk got in the mix for a time as well. But by the time I was engineering in the late '70s, I was working on a number of disco records, including some from France and Germany." Among Harding's early credits was the engineering of *Knock on Wood*, the massively successful disco album debut of singer Amii Stewart. The title track reached number one in the U.S. and was a worldwide smash in 1979.

"Ian Curnow came from the same town as I, basically, and we got to know each other," says Harding. "We started writing song material together and eventually connected with the publishers and producers behind the Bay City Rollers, Bill Martin and Phil Coulter. They were getting involved in a lot of dance records, and they looked at us as young people that they could sort of groom to be 'the new them.' We knew of Pete Waterman even in those days, as he was a DJ and was working at a London record label at the time. It seems like all of us were on our paths to creating records ourselves. The first time I met Pete, he was promoting a record for Bill Martin and wearing a red leather bomber jacket with red trousers and outrageous boots. He was a larger than life character, even then.

"I must have been barely 20 or 21 when I was introduced by Pete to this idea of taking a three to four minute pop song and creating a six-minute extended version. [Because of the] need the record companies had at the time to develop extended versions, I was able to develop my skills to find the sections of a song that would accomplish that goal. I learned where you can get, say, eight bars of a section of the song onto the two-track tape, introduce some other instruments and build up what would become a six or seven-minute 12-inch version."

Working at Marquee Studios, Harding teamed with producers Stock Aitken Waterman (SAW), who used the facility to launch their PWL (Pete Waterman Limited) production brand. "The blueprint I'd learned to create these extended dance mixes ended up being the formula we'd use at PWL right through the '80s. You'd extend the intro of a seven-inch record for one or two minutes. In the middle, you'd probably have a breakdown on the 12-inch version that would be double or triple the length of the seven-inch version, get back into the song for a bit, maybe add another verse or bridge, and then extend the ending. This would give the DJ a chance to mix out from that point. Pete Waterman was very much a big driver of this formula, and pretty quickly it was the format we'd all conformed to," he recollects.

"Generally, we'd start off recording with just the three or four minute original version of the song. The thing that was vital was we had to know what the SMPTE code (Society of Motion Picture and Television Engineers timecode) and the B.P.M. (beats per minute) of the song were. Once the LinnDrum machine arrived in the '80s, the machine would be driven off the 'SMPTE' code that you would record onto tape. Before you would work on any music or audio, you would strike a piece of two-inch analog tape with the SMPTE code and make sure that it was able to drive all your machinery (most of it made in Germany)—sequencers and drum machines. Once you have a solid code working, then all this equipment could be synched to create the song recording."

Stock Aitken Waterman began enjoying their first commercial success in the early '80s with Hazell Dean, who had been starting dance floor fires with robust concoctions like "Whatever I Do (Wherever I Go)" and "No Fool (For Love)." Likewise, bigger than life drag sensation Divine scored a monster hit with the high-energy powerhouse "You Think You're a Man," which vaulted to the upper regions of the UK and Australia's pop charts in 1984. Capturing the gay market was the goal in those days, and they achieved it. "I would say, and I think Pete Waterman would agree, the success of Stock Aitken Waterman was totally built on the gay scene and making records for the gay clubs," Harding claims. "That was what Pete deliberately set out to do with Divine, Hazell Dean and then Dead or Alive. With Divine and Hazell, he was almost working in a partnership with Barry Evangeli (who owned and ran Proto Records). Barry had initially said to Pete that although the gay scene may have seemed small, he thought that if they made music specifically for the gay club world and added a commercial edge to the records, they could break onto the pop charts. And that's what happened. Pete was very clear about his intentions to target the gay community, and he made that known to everyone on his team."

The breakthrough for Harding, Curnow and the SAW ensemble was their stupendous mix of the avant-garde new wave band Dead or Alive's 1985 smash hit "You Spin Me Round

(Like a Record)," sung by vocalist Pete Burns. The song gave the production team their first number one hit in Britain. The track was ferociously paced and deliriously high-energy in style, falling just shy of the Top 10 in the U.S. "Once we had success with Dead or Alive's 'You Spin Me Round,' which made it to the top in numerous territories," observes Harding, "it set a benchmark for us. When Pete Burns' label [Epic Records] originally came to us at the Marquee Studios (we were still there at the time), they said Pete was adamant about wanting a record that sounded like the ones he saw people going crazy to in the Liverpool clubs, such as Divine's 'You Think You're a Man.'"

The success of the SAW productions attracted the attention of another pop-new wave ensemble in 1986. The girl group Bananarama was interested in covering the Shocking Blue nugget "Venus" and approached the SAW team with the idea. "Most of the time, artists and record companies came to us for what would later be termed 'the PWL sound,'" Phil observes, "which could range from high-energy to soul, house to straight-ahead pop. They would have to specify what they were looking for. In the early days when we first worked with Bananarama, they were already a successful group. They had already had hit singles and a couple of albums. They were a good example of a group who were not initially thought of as a dance act. Pete Tong of London Records came to SAW with the idea for the group to do a cover of 'Venus.' As is often the case with an act that is already established, you wonder exactly what it is that they want. Do they want a simple dance-pop cover or do they want it sound like something we'd done before?

"Pete had this rule in the studio that said everyone, including the artists, should stop working by 10 p.m. and come to the pub around the corner for a round. In those days, British pubs used to close at 11pm. Siobhan Fahey, a vocalist from Bananarama, came down, and so would Rick Astley. Afterward, we returned to the studio. We had done this pop radio type of version for Bananarama, and Siobhan popped her head around the corner and said, 'We didn't really want it to sound like a pop record. We wanted it to sound like the Dead or Alive record.' Matt Aitken and I looked at each other and said, 'Why didn't you tell us this before?'" he laughs heartily. "The version we'd already done sounded *nothing* like Dead or Alive. We knew we could do it though. And with that technical process I described, working to a SMPTE and B.P.M., SAW very quickly got the Dead or Alive drum samples out, reprogrammed the bass pattern, and transformed the song. It ended up being a huge hit and their first big record in America."

"Venus," with a newly pumped up beat and scalding energy, broke Bananarama worldwide and gave the group a number one smash in the U.S. The song also topped the charts (or came mighty close) in Switzerland, the UK, Germany, France, Belgium and Australia. The group collaborated with SAW for numerous other hits, including "Love in the First Degree" and "I Heard a Rumour." With this mammoth success, PWL was officially formed, and Phil Harding became their chief engineer and remixer. Unsurprisingly, the plates of Harding and Curnow became very, very full. "Stock, Aitken, and Waterman were so busy writing and producing," explains Harding, "that the majority of remixing was handled by myself and Ian. I can cite hundreds of examples, from the Pet Shop Boys to Jermaine Stewart, where the record label executives felt the quickest route to that PWL sound was to let Ian and I do a remix. We had all the sounds, so it didn't matter that much if the credits read Stock Aitken Waterman or us. Pete had dubbed me the 'mixmaster,' and Ian and I were among the biggest remixers in the UK at that time.

"Once records like Bananarama's 'Venus' made it in America, I made an effort to head to New York for the New Music Seminar that was held there annually. It must have been 1985 or '86 and after I met some of the U.S. record label people that we started getting a lot of remix offers from America. We soon were hitting the *Billboard* dance and pop charts on a regular basis. Once house music started coming into vogue, a format in which we had done extremely well with Mel & Kim, that sound seemed to be in demand for a good three or four years." Harding's 1987 remix of "Jack Le Freak," a reinvention of the Chic "Le Freak" classic produced by Nile Rodgers and Bernard Edwards, became one of the cornerstone house music recordings of the period.

"As remixes became more popular, our work became increasingly complex. Sometimes it would come down to just keeping the artists' voices and recreating the entire backing track from scratch," remembers Phil. "It's common now, but it was a new concept back then. This became, in our eyes, more like production work, as opposed to just remixing. Increasingly, the record companies would ask us to mix a radio version as well as a club version. As that level of work rose, we began to receive credit for what was called 'additional production and remix.' As soon as that term came into the business, we wanted more than just the remixing fee. That's when we started requiring a royalty, a cut from the sales, as well. That kicked in around the mid-to-late '80s, and we certainly must have been among the first remix and production teams to start pushing for that. It became a standard. So suddenly you went from charging, say, £1,000 for a remix to £1,000 plus a royalty. If your version became a big seller, your income started to increase substantially. I've had records where I earned as little as half a percent as a royalty rate (like on the first two Basia albums), and I'm sure the label thought that was nothing—hardly worth even negotiating. But each of those albums sold a million in the U.S. So it was a very important step forward for me."

Harding says the sound of PWL continued to evolve in different musical directions. "After that initial starting point of PWL," he remembers, "the whole soul and R&B sound got very big, and we worked with a group called Brilliant, which featured Youth from Killing Joke and Jimmy Cauty (who went on to be in The KLF). We did a different kind of nu-soul sound with them (such as the single 'Love Is War' in 1986), and one of the background vocalists was Princess. Mike and Matt were a bit driven to pursue that soul and R&B sound. Pete would do a weekend radio show in the north of England, where he lived and worked at a record shop up there in the afternoons. By Monday, when he came back to the studio, he'd know what was selling, what the DJs were playing, and what was happening in America. He caught on to a sound that he thought might work well for Princess. Her record 'Say I'm Your Number One' came from that thinking, and it worked out nicely. This really was the beginning of our expansion, if you will. We had the Hi-NRG club sound and then a slower tempo R&B sound."

Though the team seemed to be invincible, their work didn't always find favor with all of the artists that passed through their portal. "I can't say it happened often, but there were artists who rejected our mixes once in a while, and SAW rejected projects submitted by artists and labels as well. That probably happened more towards the end of the '80s and into the early '90s. I recall we had a mix rejected by Marc Almond and also by Erasure (even though we did a lot of work with them in the past). Most artists were quite pleased with the results, but it wasn't impossible for us to experience rejection."

Some critics of the period held the view that PWL was a mill, churning out hits at a breakneck pace. It's a notion the remixer looks at with some degree of amusement. "It's true; one of the reasons we got nicknamed 'The Hit Factory,'" Harding asserts, "was, yes, because so much music came out of us. Ian Curnow must have joined us a few months after we kicked off the new studio in the south of London. We went from having one studio at Marquee to five in the same building. Pete had set out to create the UK version of Motown. So his aim was to go way beyond the four or five people we had working in our old studio, to having several studios going at once, a publishing company, a management company, more buildings and maybe a staff of 50 or 60. As Ian and I progressed as a team and were getting more and more productions to work on, it became vital to have people other than me start remixing records. Hence, the arrival of Pete Hammond and then Dave Ford. So the factory staff was getting bigger.

"Pete wanted them to mix the Stock and Aitken stuff and to come in during what was essentially the night shift. The boys finished at 10 pm, and Hammond and Ford would come in after them and start mixing. So then, when Mike and Matt came back in the morning, tracks would be mixed and ready to listen to. Mike, Matt and Pete might make a few adjustments, but then Pete Hammond and Dave Ford would go home and sleep. So that contributed to the notion that we were a factory, not solely the number of hits we were churning out, as some people like to think. Funnily enough, unlike some factories, we never really worked weekends, unless it was urgent. That was another early edict of Pete's. Pete and Mike had families and wanted to preserve that structure.

"The studio was, at the time, in a very undeveloped area of London," he describes. "Early on, the building next door was turned into three flats. Pete bought one of them and was literally living almost above the new studios. It reached the point in the late '80s where Pete would tell the guys working at night (or possibly on the weekend for a high priority project), 'I don't care what hour it is. I'm only upstairs, and if you need me to hear a mix or make a decision, phone me, wake me and I'll come down.' Such was Pete's dedication. Eventually, we got the second and third studios built. The first was called 'The Borough,' and the second was called 'The Bunker' (which was my studio). Below The Bunker (in what was basically a small basement) was Ian's studio, a compact set-up with a small vocal booth. While Pete's apartment was being built upstairs, he used to sleep in that booth—with a dog. Even when all that work was going on in the studio. We would come in every morning, the dog would stink, and Pete would take a shower upstairs and start his workday," Harding laughs.

"Certainly, at the time, Rick Astley and Kylie Minogue (and some of the others) were very much looked at as being the puppets of Stock Aitken Waterman," Phil admits. "That was what the media largely accused them of being in the '80s. That affected them quite badly (I think Kylie has gotten over all that since then). They didn't want to be seen that way. But in all fairness, there was another way to look at it. Considering the amount of work that SAW put into them, these producers could easily have been the front men. It could easily have been 'Stock Aitken Waterman *featuring* Kylie Minogue.' Really, the artist got all of the credit. I'm not discounting the wonderful job they did singing and promoting their hits, but there *was* this very hard-working creative team behind them, wasn't there? I think it could just have easily occurred in the '70s. It could have been Giorgio Moroder *featuring* Donna Summer, couldn't it?

"But, that said, by the time Kylie was involved with PWL around 1987, PWL had really gone pop. I don't recall even being involved in her first album. The music was very commercial at that point and not very clubby. I remember going to the Dance Music Club Conference in London, which was sort of the equivalent of the New Music seminar in New York, and Tilly Rutherford (PWL Records' Label Manager and also Producer-Manager for the teams at PWL, but not SAW directly) was on a panel being questioned by a few DJs. They were asking him why PWL had gone so commercial, like with the records by Kylie. We still had a lot of the clubs on our side and were producing some club-friendly material with the Mel & Kim tracks, Rick Astley and others. That is, until Kylie broke. Tilly turned around and said, 'Well, we don't need the clubs any more. We've gone global with Kylie, and it's a massive success.' Of course that went over like a ton of lead bricks. I loved Tilly as a person, but Ian and I looked at each other and said, *'What did he bloody say that for?'* After that, it spread around to all the clubs and DJs that PWL didn't care about them any more."

Harding describes the backlash that mired PWL by the decade's end. "By Kylie's second album, Pete realized we *had* to get the clubs back on our side. We couldn't just keep going with sugary pop and no dance versions. I believe I was first drafted in for the single 'Hand On Your Heart,' off Kylie's *Enjoy Yourself* album in 1989. He wanted to kick off the album with not necessarily the most commercial single but rather the most danceable. I barely thought about how the track would sound on the radio; I just thought 'club.' We really went back to how we worked in the past, doing a very danceable 12-inch first and then cut the radio version from it. Later, we came out with Kylie's 'Step Back in Time' (1990), which was very club-oriented. Again, it was a very deliberate move to get PWL back in the clubs. Pete started putting effects into the mixes and intros and samples that had nothing to do with the song so that people wouldn't recognize it as a PWL record. However, apart from a few people that stuck with us, PWL never really got the clubs back on board."

Harding and Curnow opened their own production house in the '90s and enjoyed continued pop success working with youthful, all-male ensembles, such as Boyzone and East 17, as well as other buoyant dance projects of the day. The duo parted company around 2000.

After taking a break from the industry, Phil slowly began to return to his production and remix roots. "It's been interesting what motivates me and sparks my creativity today," he says. "After the boy band stuff I did in the '90s, I realized I'd spent the better part of the last 20 years doing nothing but manufactured, programmed pop. I had a real hankering to work with live musicians, which I hadn't done for years. So I spent the last 10 or 12 years doing that, but not at a particularly high level.

"I got a call from Lamont Dozier, of the Motown Holland-Dozier-Holland team, and he asked me to mix a Cliff Richard album he had produced in Los Angeles. It was probably the biggest project I had worked on in many years. It was hard work, but I was surprised by how much I enjoyed it. That motivated me to get back into mixing again a bit more seriously. I realized I still have something to offer in the mix process. I was asked to do a remix for Tina Charles in 2013, the song 'Always and Forever' by Carl Cox and Steen Ulrich. It evolved into writing and producing some new tracks for her, with a bit of a retro '80s sound. I'm enjoying being back in it." In 2014, Harding remixed Holly Johnson's then latest hit "In and Out of Love."

Phil says he's more relaxed these days and enjoys maintaining a grounded sense of wellbeing. "Somewhere in the middle of the past 14 years, I went back to being a vegetarian," says the production maestro. "I got into the raw food diet and became very motivated spiritually. That's kept me very positive-minded. I don't have to work too hard if I don't want to, which is a real blessing, and I suppose you could say I kind of semi-retired at the age of 50. I've very much taken the attitude of working on only that which I want to. I've been very inspired by the new lyricists I have met in the process of doing some projects, including my own singer-songwriter acoustic album in 2008 called *The Story of Beginners*. I sort of discovered the acoustic guitar playing with my church music group, and that's what triggered this whole new side of me. I've also gotten involved with education quite a bit. I'm actually the chairman of a company called JAMES, Joint Audio Media Education Services, and we try to form a link between the studio side of music and entertainment companies and what's going on at universities. I do a lot of lecturing and recently began work on my PhD."

In 2010, Harding published *PWL from the Factory Floor* (Cherry Red). Now in its second edition, it's a 600-page behind-the-scenes look at the PWL studio during its '80s heyday. "I hope I came across in my book as someone who was happy to have been a part of the PWL team. One of the reasons I wrote the book was because Pete Waterman's autobiography and Mike Stock's book—and across the years, they've been in various disputes—came across as a little bitter in their views from the top. My thought was that pop culture needed to have a different view of this time and experience. Being that I was with the team almost from day one, I felt I was in a good position to do that.

"I'd like to be remembered as someone who contributed a lot to pop culture history," he says with pride. "I do find when I talk to students today about dance music, so much is taken for granted. It's very difficult (as someone who's come through those technological developments) for me to convey the excitement of being on the cusp of new technology, making use of those innovations, and getting the music out there—and then watching it become a hit.

"With downloads today, nobody knows who played on a song or who produced it. They never learn about who did all this important work. I think one of the reasons vinyl has made a small comeback is because people want to know more about these credits. I'd love to see all the creative people that were in the studios building these hits get the credit for what they did.

"If I could be remembered as a non-egotistical, creative technologist," he laughs, "that would be fantastic. PWL stands as a great example of the creativity that production and remix teams put into those records of the '80s—the songs that everybody still loves. I am very happy and proud to have been a part of that era."

Klaus Hirschburger

Songwriter

Artists: Hubert Kah, Sandra, et. al.
Member of Hubert Kah
Germany

"Many people feel [the music we made] in the '80s was something that transcended them, that gave them hope. I think our music showed them it could also be fun. This is what hit records were all about," says Klaus Hirschburger. He's a songwriter, musician and a former member of the prodigious German electronic dance band Hubert Kah. In addition, he was one of the key players who helped develop the hit sound of the international dance-pop icon Sandra. As co-writer of such evocative hits as Hubert Kah's darkly sumptuous "Limousine" and Sandra's expressive powerhouses "Innocent Love" and "Little Girl," Hirschburger has a long and distinguished resume. Looking exceptionally youthful in middle age (and decidedly learned as he sits wearing dark framed glasses in the study of his Berlin home), he skitters through some of the highlights of his '80s career, which he believes were all blithely rooted in spontaneity. It's a word he often uses to describe those extraordinary days.

Klaus, by his own admission, is not a public person today. "Not at all!" he emphasizes. "I *used* to be a pop star, but then decided to concentrate just on writing. I don't do interviews often because nobody usually gives a shit about writers," he laughs. "I'm not even sure how much I remember from those days because there was so much going on, and we were so busy.

"Germany was a country in waiting in the early '80s, I guess you could say. There were heavy metal artists here and many British groups like Depeche Mode working with our musicians in Dusseldorf. Then our new wave productions started exploding, and this really put Germany on the map. My story started off the same as everyone else's. I came from a small German city, and I spent a lot of time making music and writing poems when I was young. I wanted to express myself, and music was the best way to do it. Our town was small, and we all found each other—Hubert Kemmler (vocals, keyboards), Markus Löhr (guitars, keyboards), and myself on bass. That was our group—Hubert Kah. We were the best band in the area, and we had a good reputation from the age of 12 onward. We really started off as youngsters and had our first hit when we were just 18. It all came very naturally to us."

Left: The 1985 12-inch single jacket from German artist Sandra's hit single "Little Girl," whose lyrics were written by Klaus Hirshburger. (Sandra photography by Dieter Eikelpoth/Ink Studios/Virgin Records GmbH). *Right:* Hirschburger today.

As a German synth-pop band, Hubert Kah enjoyed their first commercial success with quirky new wave styled hits like 1982's "Sternenhimmel." Another early single, the frantic "Rosemarie," peaked at number six on the Swiss chart and number five in Austria. Kemmler's offbeat costuming and the group's tight sound helped momentum to build through 1984. That's when the band connected with producer Michael Cretu (Inker & Hamilton, Münchener Freiheit, Cretu & Thiers and later Enigma). Once their bond was established, the team began developing an edgy English-language dance-rock-electronic sound. Bolstered by the meticulous Cretu's intoxicating melodies, as well as production and arrangements by Swiss musician and producer Armand Volker, Hubert Kah made tremendous strides forward in popularity.

"Germany was not so big I guess because it was by chance that we first met Michael Cretu, who was making his music right next door to us in Frankfurt," explains Klaus. "It was all about the melody, the vocal and the groove. There was something kind of cold, gothic and melancholic about the music we made together, and that's what many people liked about us in the '80s. I think we knew from the start we were all going to be writing a lot of music. And writing songs in English was not a problem for me. I traveled throughout the U.S. by rail at one point of my life, which I think helped me greatly to understand the language. In the '90s and '00s, I wrote a lot of German language material, and it wasn't as easy for me. When it comes to German music, it's lyrics first, and creating a song is more complicated. I've always liked to write with spontaneity, and I simply want my songs to reach people."

By 1986, Hubert Kah hit their stride, and their appeal reached as far away as America and Japan. "We were on tour for maybe two or three years by that time," the artist recalls. "Our main market was Japan and parts of Europe, and our manager was Australian. So I guess you could say we were a whole international mess in those days. The dance hits we had were extraordinarily successful in America, especially New York and Los Angeles. We never crossed over to the pop charts there, but we didn't care. We made enough money, and we were very happy with how things were going in the U.S., Europe and Japan. It was quite a feat for us to have our records on the same charts with British electronica like The Eurythmics, Thompson Twins and artists like that.

"We decided to do an album of short stories, which ended up being called *Tensongs*. It took us a long time to make the album—almost two years, in fact, before it came out in 1986. But after all that work, we realized we didn't have a track on the set that would be a good single. 'We are fucked without a single!' I remember us saying. We thought about the track 'That Girl,' but it was about someone who died and picking her body up at the morgue, so that wouldn't work.

The whole album was kind of dark. We'd been to London seeing Siouxsie and the Banshees and bands like that. Maybe that set the tone. So we ended up going to Frankfurt to create another song that we could use as a single, and Hubert and I had an idea about a limousine. It worked, and we incorporated a classical approach in the melody (I grew up with classical music). 'Limousine' was done very spontaneously, and we composed it in Markus' apartment in about 20 minutes."

The single "Limousine," which chugged across dance floors with the power and mystique of a fuel-injected Orient Express, was part Hi-NRG, part new wave and part pop bliss, complete with shattering glass sound effects. The track was a Top 30 hit in Switzerland and a solid club and radio hit throughout Germany and the continent. It was also a hit in edgier American clubs with a taste for imports. MCA/Curb Records in the U.S. took a liking to the band, releasing "Limousine" and another single by the group, "Military Drums," in 1987 (and included both on the group's *Best of Dance Hits* LP in 1990). The latter song, with its snare drum-fused electronic power, became one of the band's most popular hits, reaching the Top 10 on the American dance chart.

"'Military Drums' is one of the songs that really follows me. Seriously, [this song was written] in about 10 minutes in Ibiza feeling very jet lagged. We added trumpets, recorded it in about five hours and launched it as a single. I liked the song, and I enjoy thinking about it," says Hirschburger. More singles followed, notably the brilliantly lush and expansive "So Many People" (1989) and the perky "It's Me, Cathy (Follow My Heart)" in 1990, but Hubert Kah's days were numbered. In addition to some health problems that reportedly developed with lead singer Hubert Kemmler, Hirschburger says it was simply time to move on.

"The break-up of the band was, in some ways, like the break-up of a marriage. [The decline] started in 1986. There were no bad feelings between us, but sometimes you just have to move in a new direction. I moved to New York for a while, writing books, music for movies and writing my own songs. Markus went on to be a famous musical composer, and he still takes care of back catalog and legal matters today. For example, there's an album out now called *The Very Best of Hubert Kah* (part of the *So80s* series), curated by the production team of Blank & Jones. He's up on all that. Hubert is still writing songs and doing quite well as a live performer I understand. I met him two or three times over the last 20 years or so. Maybe he will end up writing and performing more world hits. Who knows?"

Hirschburger's career extended significantly beyond his experience with Hubert Kah. Along with other members of their team, he and Michael Cretu were responsible for fashioning some of the biggest hits of Sandra (Lauer), one of the era's best-known and most influential vocalists from Germany. Sandra, the former lead singer of a trio known as Arabesque and Cretu's wife at the time, scored a stunning list of solo hits on the Virgin label during the decade, including her triumphant 1985 breakthrough "(I'll Never Be) Maria Magdalena" (which reportedly topped the charts in 21 countries). Subsequent blockbusters included "Heaven Can Wait," "Innocent Love," "Everlasting Love," "We'll Be Together" and "I Need Love." Sandra's impact was profoundly felt throughout Europe, and she became one of the region's most revered dance-pop performers. With Cretu and other writers, Hirschburger helped compose much of Sandra's musical repertoire well into the '90s, many songs of which are artistically regarded as among the most sophisticated productions of the period.

"Michael Cretu was one of the nicest guys I've ever known," Klaus says most genuinely. "It was just so easy working together. We'd meet in the south of Germany, and we'd say, 'Okay, we have to write a hit for Sandra and Virgin Records.' Virgin was a company comprised of about maybe six people in Munich who controlled almost the whole European music business. We were like a family, and I liked it. The music we made was in our blood. We knew how to create this music, and we knew what singles would be hits. The process was very easy—the music was created first. In regard to lyrics, Michael would always say to me, 'You have to take your time and find your inspiration.' I'd always think, 'Fuck it—I can get that done by tomorrow!' I could do it *that* fast—I didn't need to make finding inspiration complicated. It was like plucking daisies. I'd get my inspiration from reading books, watching movies, swimming, climbing mountains, listening to rock music or Mediterranean folk music. But there'd come a point where I'd say I was going to write a song—right now— and I would do it. That's how I composed many of Sandra's songs. I'd write some lyrics, and I'd go through our approval process. Then we'd finish the recording, and that was it.

"Sandra was the perfect singer, and I liked her very much," he adds. "We haven't spoken in over 10 years, but I know she is still very successfully touring today, just like Thomas Anders of Modern Talking and other major stars of the era. Our team was like a family, and we all worked together through every minute of the creation of her debut album, *The Long Play,* in 1985. And it was the same way for her subsequent albums that were made well into the next decade. We always discussed the whole project together—every aspect of it. We realized that the lyrics to the songs on her debut set weren't that important, or rather didn't need to be complicated, because Sandra didn't have a good command of the English language. But we made it work, and in the end, it was fun."

Sandra's international record sales figures were a dream come true for Virgin. Thanks to equally vigorous club demand, priority tracks from her first set, such as the top-selling "In the Heat of the Night," were often extended on 12-inch singles. "It was absurd to us because in one or two weeks of *The Long Play*'s release, I think she had sold over a million records throughout Europe," Klaus states. "It was a wonderful feeling for all of us. We started touring and established an international contract, and it was crazy. We started focusing on the next singles because we all knew Virgin was going to torture us for more. But I can tell you the label was one of the best record companies ever. Everyone has an opinion about songs and lyrics in the business, whether it's a label executive, a producer or the wife of an engineer—they're all just a pain in the ass," he laughs. "But Virgin at that time was not like that at all. I think Richard Branson realized he had a handful of great people running his label in Germany. We had the best time with them, and they did a great job working with us."

Over the remainder of the decade and into the '90s, Hirschburger says the team never strayed from the creative blueprint they carefully established for Sandra. "I spent so much time out of Germany, living, working and recording in Ibiza with Sandra and Cretu (where the couple lived). It was kind of strange because the people there were from all over—France, Hungary, Romania. I'd present ideas to her and Michael, and she would say whether she liked it or not. We had all kinds of concepts, like the songs 'Son of a Time Machine' or 'Johnny Wanna Live,' which was a tribute to animal rights. Again, we always tried to keep things spontaneous, and we'd discuss whether the song was right for her—technically and personally. And if Sandra didn't care for something, there were no hard feelings."

Klaus says that he and his fellow artisans didn't worry too much about the pressure of being successful. "'Little Girl' [Sandra's third single from *The Long Play* album] is one of my favorite Sandra songs. It was written while I was on a trip in Venice with a girlfriend, and you can hear in the lyrics that it was a very spontaneous song. I came back with the idea; everyone liked it and it worked. It turned out to be one of Sandra's biggest radio hits. It's a good example of staying cool. You learned to relax. When the pressure gets hotter, you needed to be a little bit softer. There were plenty of people shouting, 'We need something big!' We'd just say, 'Yep, we're gonna do it.' But we'd say it calmly," he smiles.

"We did things differently from the way many artists work now. Today, many artists don't ever meet or talk with the songwriters. Sometimes it's just about marketing—and I have no problem with that. But in the case of Sandra, we didn't approach the songs as software or just singles. We did *albums*, sitting together. Our best-selling album, as far as I remember, was *Paintings in Yellow* in 1990. That project was really a journey. I came back from New York, and we wrote it in Paris, Barcelona and Ibiza, giving the album a real Mediterranean flair. The single 'Hiroshima' did well, but the album really went through the ceiling," he says proudly. The set was Sandra's highest charting album ever in Germany.

"The '90s weren't that great," he opines. "Germany stood for techno at the time, as far as I could tell. Techno was kind of about 'stealing' to me—take a verse, take a chorus, take part of the groove—the music used all the elements that had already been around. There's nothing we can really say was new about it. By that time, I was more into being a father and mountaineering, film work and other avenues of expression."

Though he appreciates what he and his unique team created in the '80s, he says he doesn't often find himself waxing nostalgic about it. "Every generation says their music was the best—the '60s, the '70s, the '80s. You know what? Fuck it. It's always going to be the same thing," he laughs. "To be honest, I don't listen to my music from the '80s too much. But it's fun when I do hear those songs, especially when you see the gold or platinum record on the wall. I don't usually listen to a song we did and think of ways I could have done it differently or better. The first album by Hubert Kah, *Meine Höhepunkte*, was recorded in two days. We had some mistakes on two or three tracks, but we couldn't record it again because the tape was too expensive. But I like this album very much just as it is because we were so spontaneous with it, and it was so much fun to make. Sometimes it's the memory of making it that I enjoy the most about these recordings. And I always think, if the song still touches you today, it can't be that bad."

Klaus reflects for a moment on the crossroads he sees many of his fellow '80s dance-pop stars facing. "The problem is we can't reinvent that period—you can't do those years over again. Some of these artists and producers from the '80s tell me they feel they missed the bus. People producing so-called new material come to me and say they need good songs done in the '80s style, made with 'the German approach' or 'the continental approach.' Well, you really can't simply go back in time like that.

"For an artist trying to reinvent themselves or staging a comeback today, it comes down to whether or not you have something new to say. I think it's a problem for some. I think they have to ask themselves whether they really *do* in fact have something to say. I think it's better to try and shape a new future, rather than recreate the past. Maybe they just need the money or want the public appearance. And I can appreciate wanting that—listen, I love pop stars. I really do—I love them just for *being* pop stars. I've been that way my whole life.

"I remember going crazy to see an upcoming Italian singer named Madonna at the Limelight in New York City. What an experience! It was around 1985, and the club was a converted church. I was crazy about pop stars even then. But my thought today is, you have to reinvent music—and that's the good thing about it. You *can* reinvent it, day by day. It's all about the songs. And I love hits. I'm not afraid of hits. So, you focus on those three minutes and pack it all in there—everything you want to say."

Hirschburger is a busy man today, still an in-demand lyricist, composer, producer and background singer. Amidst such a demanding schedule, the artist has come to embrace some simple philosophies. "They say time is a healer," he observes. "I think the mountains are the healer. You don't need cocaine and alcohol. To be honest, you just need to keep moving forward in life. You need to enjoy the things you are doing. If you are not enjoying them, you have to get away from them. And you need to surround yourself with people you can trust and love. Keep the pressure off and move on. Believe in your intuition and be open to what your subconscious tells you. It's very simple—there's nothing else I can say.

As for his dance-pop legacy? "To be honest," he smiles, "I would just like people to say my music was fun. We were young, it was fun and it was not a lie. Music and words—they are unbeatable!"

Tom Hooker
"Looking for Love" (1986)
Italy

Tom Hooker was one of Italy's most accomplished singers and songwriters at a time when the country's bumper crop of dance music was in hot demand throughout Europe. Enjoying great personal success as a solo artist in the '80s (with such hits as "Looking for Love" and "Atlantis"), Hooker also contributed to the record chart achievements enjoyed by another tremendously popular artist of the time named Den Harrow ("Future Brain," "Don't Break My Heart," "Catch the Fox [Caccia alla Volpe]," and others). Tom has been widely acknowledged as the vocalist and co-writer of many of Den Harrow's biggest hits, but this recognition didn't come until decades after the songs were chart successes.

The artist has no misgivings about the era and all that happened. Nor does he mind discussing it. But these days, he prefers to focus on his highly successful career as a photographer (for which he is better known as Thomas Barbey). From his home in Las Vegas, Nevada, Tom takes a look at his journey from dance-pop star to visual artisan.

"I was born in the U.S., but my family moved to Europe when I was six months old," says Hooker. "After piano, guitar and violin lessons, I started playing the drums at 10. I was more into music than anything else. In Switzerland, where I grew up, you become either an attorney or a banker. Being that Switzerland was such a small country, the music business was practically non-existent. I left the University of Geneva after one semester and turned pro as a musician with gigs and studio recordings by the age of 18. After working professionally as a drummer for years, I joined a vocal quartet. Later, I recorded a song I wrote and sang—on my own—in a studio with a friend in Geneva. It was called 'Flip Over,' and a record company in Milan, Italy, picked up the track. That's why I moved there in 1980.

"My ambition at 20 was to have money for nothing and chicks for free, to paraphrase the Dire Straits song. I never had a nine to five job in my life. I don't even know what it's like. Much later on in life, I sometimes fantasized about having one, but it never happened. With my first record, I appeared on *Discoring*, which was a TV show in Italy like *Top of the Pops* in the UK. From then on, with a record company behind me and two girl dancers and me on roller skates, I did shows in clubs all over Italy from 1980 to 1983. I made more money than most people my age. I had an agent and did over 40 shows a year.

"I had done the Festival of San Remo in February of 1981. It was a big deal in Italy, especially in the South, where they also had an event called Feste di Piazza. The taxpayers' money would fund a yearly summer show in nearly every little town in the south of Italy, and the agents would organize the line-ups of artists on the roster. It was free for the public,

Left: **Handsome and gifted singer and songwriter Tom Hooker found himself caught in a tug of war between his solo career and that of Italo-disco sensation Den Harrow.** *Right*: **Hooker is a well-regarded photographer today.**

so nobody would complain if the show was bad," Tom laughs. "With the beggars can't be choosers motto, the audiences would just clap for anybody who came from the north to entertain them. The good thing was, we were all professionals and made a living playing music. I was very content and happy with my job. I was having fun and getting paid for it."

Hooker examines the emergence of the Italo-disco music genre at the time. "I think a lot of its success had to do with the record companies at that time. It seemed like Severo Lombardoni (founder of Italy's Discomagic label) was releasing five to 10 disco mixes every day. Every once in a while, he'd hit the jackpot. It was a numbers game. Today, Italo fans like everything that was released back then. I can say that in those days, this was not the case with the general public. I sometimes feel today that the fans like a record because it's extremely rare and believe it is precious because of that. If a record is extremely rare, that means it didn't do well, plain and simple—and therefore wasn't considered any good. The roles have been reversed over time. We were looking only at record sales in those days, and a record became officially good when it sold a lot of copies.

"After saying this, it is clear that there was an energy in the '80s at every level in Italy. There was an economic boom with the private radio stations and TV stations. The small TV and radio stations could promote an artist and their song. An average disco mix would sell a minimum of 10,000 copies, and that was a decent sum of money. There have always been talented musicians, but in this period, they were rewarded. The Italo sound became popular because of this opportunity. The Italians were trying to do Anglo-Saxon music but couldn't help but sound different because of the melodic culture that was ingrained in them. The electronic sound was also cheaper and more affordable to record than hiring musicians to play every instrument, like the Anglo-Saxon bands. This is why the Italo sound is very electronic, as opposed to the music of rock bands like U2 or the Stones. The Italo-disco market thrived because of these numbers. All the DJs would buy the disco mixes after only listening to the first 10 seconds of the song. A lot of terrible records would sell because the initial groove started off right. I remember checking this out at the Bazaar di Pippo in Milan. They would buy 50 mixes at a time, and the clubs would pay the bill. The DJs didn't have to buy them. They bought a lot of mixes because they wanted to make sure no hit would slip by them."

By the mid–'80s, Tom gained momentum as a singer-songwriter in this prosperous Italian music lanscape. "After doing TV shows and always having a record company promoting me, most people in the business started to know of me or about me. I didn't have much competition as an English lyricist in Italy because everybody just spoke Italian!" he smiles. "I met [producer and arranger] Miki Chieregato in 1985 through my record company at the time, as I recall. I was with Merak Music, and Miki was with Baby Records. He wanted to work with me, and it was possible because [of a connection to] Roberto Gasparini of Merak Music (Valerie Dore, Alba, Novecento), who was in good standing with Freddy Naggiar, the head of Baby Records. Gasparini, who had me under contract, could have prohibited me from working with them, but he didn't."

Hooker's path soon crossed with that of a popular Italo-disco star named Den Harrow. The story of Den Harrow, one of the most well known dance-pop acts to emerge from Italy in the early to mid–'80s, has been a source of controversy for years. Fronted by a good-looking young man named Stefano Zandri, the Den Harrow project scored numerous top hits in Italy, France, Germany, Switzerland and Sweden. A few years back, Hooker stated that he was the actual vocalist behind many of the act's biggest hits.

Despite the media brouhahas that disclosures like this always seem to churn up, the practice of lip-synching and ghost-singing was not all that uncommon in Europe at the time. Still, the Harrow-Hooker revelation generated a good deal of chat room conversation and a few tussles among interested parties on outlets like Facebook and Twitter. Tom offers his recollection of the creation of Den Harrow's records of the period. "We tried numerous times in the studio to make [Zandri's] vocals work, but to no avail," he asserts. "Today, everything can be found on the web—the truth comes out. Only in an interview [a few years ago] did he finally admit that he didn't sing the songs. However, he said that they were sung by a 'corista,' which translates to a 'choir vocalist,' without mentioning my name. Anyway, I am more amused by all this than most people think. [My involvement] began back in 1985. Chieregato and [production partner and musician] Roberto Turatti were looking for a new singer for their Den Harrow project. I think Freddy Naggiar wanted a singer who was fluent in English for the German and Scandinavian market because Silvio Pozzoli [also known as Silver Pozzoli of the hit "Around My Dream"], although very talented as a singer, was not proficient in the language. Silvio sang the Den Harrow single 'Mad Desire' after Chuck Rolando sang some previous Den Harrow songs. Chuck had to quit because he was under exclusive contract with Durium in a group called Passengers. I agreed to sing for the Den Harrow project if I could write the lyrics and would get a royalty of three percent on sales. The music of almost every song was written by Chieregato, and I wrote the lyrics."

He says that part of the overall production process involved Turatti presenting the record demos to Freddy Naggiar in an effort to convince him that the songs could be a hit. "At the time, we thought this was important because if Freddy didn't like a song, it would be trashed. Freddy was very opinionated. If he didn't like something, there was no chance of publishing it. After the initial demo approval by Freddy, a song could become a hit because of a certain edit, a cut, or a mix, and it would go from being horrible to fantastic, just like that. I was always amused by this fact. I never really understood how people could be so convinced a song was or wasn't a hit before it was released. It's always been a mystery to me. If it were so easy, anybody could do it—repeatedly. Why do people have a 'run' of hits, and then it suddenly stops? I thought they knew how to write a hit—or did they? The only way to know if a song is a hit is after its release."

Hooker describes the evolutionary details of the single "Future Brain," the record that began his connection with the Den Harrow project. "We had stayed in the studio every day until five in the morning," he recalls. "I loved the creative process in the studio. I never wrote any music because it would have been totally out of place for me. That was Miki's job. I was more into funky music anyway, and I didn't have the Italo-spirit that Miki had. I was well aware that my musical culture was different. I liked to work with different genres, and Italo was different to me. The trend at the time was very electronic and musicianship with funky guitarists and bass players was going out of style. All the instruments were triggered by a Midi signal in the computer. Miki would sing the melody, and I had to write the words to go with that exact melody.

"They told me the song had to be called 'Future Brain.' I had to make sense of it and write lyrics to that exact song title. They were very convinced about emotions and sensations when songwriting. I just wanted the lyrics to make sense, which is not characteristic of Italo-disco. I struggled a lot with the fact that nobody understood English and didn't understand the importance of making sense. Some songwriters don't make any sense, that's true, but it's intentional. Like Seal's songs, for example. They don't make any sense, but he has a style and logic in his lyrics. In Italo, you could feel that they didn't know what the hell they were doing when writing lyrics. Freddy, who spoke several languages, understood me. In his office, we would switch from French, to Italian, to English all the time. Over time, he respected me as a lyricist and signed me under an exclusive publishing contract. I was probably one of the only English lyricists who received a cash advance in Italy at that time.

"'Future Brain' did very well and was a summer hit. I had come out with 'Real Men' on the Merak label around the same time, with no video. Merak Music was a very small company compared to Baby Records. I did no promotion and no TV shows, compared to Den Harrow, who did the *Festivalbar* competition that summer. I only went to *Festivalbar* as a spectator, but I was able to be backstage. I remember Den Harrow's agent telling me how great he was on stage, and he made a comment to the likes of, 'You are nothing compared to him.' It was such an absurd statement. I could understand such a statement by a fan, but not a professional who knew that he wasn't the singer.

"I wasn't offended or hurt by his comments, but instead I was amazed at how easily impressed people get when you are successful. People start thinking you are god-like when you have a bit of success. Everything you do becomes 'amazing.' Even if you can't dance, you suddenly 'move well.' If you can't sing, you 'project well,' etc. If your song is a hit, you become sexy, attractive, extremely good-looking, etc. However, when your song doesn't get onto the charts, you are back to being the guy who's doing something wrong, and you are just another human being."

Tom eventually recorded a dance single under his own name for Baby Records, "Looking for Love," released in 1986. Hip, savvy lyrics, a powerful electronic arrangement and Hooker's irresistible vocals sent the song to the top of the Italian club surveys and right up the pop charts. The track did well across Europe and was a sizeable underground import hit in the U.S. "At the time it was released, I viewed myself as being already successful, even though I wasn't as famous as Den Harrow was in France and Germany. The difference was that I had previously been signed to very small labels. I was able to reach a new level by working with Baby, one of the best record companies in Italy. 'Looking for Love' had a video shot on film by David Rose in London, just like all the Den Harrow videos. Was the song a hit on its own? Or was it all the promotion around the song? I will never know.

"To this day, I think that the success of that song was mostly due to [music producer] Claudio Cecchetto, who happened to like the song, and it made it to number one on *Deejay Television*. Cecchetto had a very big influence on the music scene at that time with his radio station and TV show. I don't know if it's a coincidence, but after the video came out, I became 'sexy as hell,' and everything I did was suddenly fantastic. I had this wonderful voice—I was good-looking—blah, blah, blah. I was the same person as before, but I changed for everybody else. I didn't have to convince girls to go out with me any more; they were begging me to go out with me," he laughs.

At the height of all this activity, Hooker worked on other projects as well. "I also sang the demos for every Eddy Huntington track and wrote all the lyrics for his songs. In the chorus of his hit 'U.S.S.R.,' my voice is louder than his in the mix. (Much later, I also did other projects under the name David Harleyson, and these records sold very well in Thailand,)" he adds. Tom also mentions the success enjoyed by Paul Lekakis, who hit it big in 1987 with the high-energy dance monster "Boom Boom (Let's Go Back to My Room)." "I wrote the lyrics and sang the demo for it. Again, my voice is louder than his in the chorus. Paul was very successful in the U.S. with it, but he dumped us for an American record company. We had a follow-up single ready for him that would have been great, but we gave it to Eddy Huntington instead. That song was 'Meet My Friend (Called Dick).' It would have been perfect for Lekakis, who, unfortunately, was a one hit wonder in America. To this day, I believe that if he had stayed with us, he would have had at least one more hit. Paul was very good-looking and was also gay. That helped him do very well in the gay clubs. Had he released 'Meet My Friend,' I think he would have done very well. Paul was hot and sexy, and Eddy was more like a fun, happy-go-lucky guy. Eddy Huntington was perfect for 'U.S.S.R.,' but his high-pitched voice and his image weren't right for 'Meet My Friend.'"

Meanwhile, according to the singer, the imbalances of the Harrow-Hooker situation became increasingly significant. "With 'Future Brain' being a hit, Freddy wanted an album. So we did it,' Tom recalls. "The name Den Harrow was a brand with a face attached to it. Mr. Zandri was the face, not me. His videos were splendidly shot in London, again by David Rose. 'Looking for Love' did better in Italy than Den Harrow's summer release 'Charleston' in 1986. My song was a huge summer hit, and 'Charleston' was the third release off his album that came out the previous winter. But suddenly, Freddy got cold feet about me. The train had already taken off with Den Harrow in France and Germany, and there was a fear that Tom Hooker would ruin the project.

"There was another problem. People don't realize that creating a brand and putting all the CDs in the stores took time. You can have a hit, but if the CD isn't available, you won't sell. It's all about timing and planning. The truth was that Freddy never released a Tom Hooker album in the fall of 1986, after the very obvious success of 'Looking for Love' during the summer. There wasn't an album to sell when I was hot on the market—you cannot buy what isn't available. Most people never consider this, but it happens. My next single was 'Help Me,' released in the fall. Instead of a video with David Rose, we did a cheap video in Milan just to have something. Still no album.

"Instead, Franco Donato of Italy's FullTime Records took some old demos from 1982 and remixed them and tried to make it look like a new album by Tom Hooker. He tried to take advantage of the fact that I was hot at the time; Freddy did not. The track 'Only One' was remixed, and they tried to make it sound like 'Looking for Love,' but they really had no clue how to make a dance record. I cringed when I heard it. Freddy never sued them and never even tried to block them. His main focus was pushing Den Harrow in Germany and France because the money was coming in. Italy wasn't where the money was. My name was tarnished, but at least I was still making a ton of money doing shows, thanks to 'Looking for Love.' Girls were fainting at my live shows, and they all wanted a piece of me," he smiles.

"I always did the gigs for the money and to respect the contract (and not for the applause) because I was a professional. Sure, it was fun doing it at times, but sometimes it was a drag. You had to show up at a resort in the mountains during a snowstorm when you had a cold. You still had to pretend you were having fun, singing in a smelly, smoky club in front of guys who hated you because the girls thought you were the sexiest man on earth. In these instances, you are doing it for the money they paid you. But I will say that I always felt very honored and blessed that they would pay me so much to sing and to be there. The most enjoyable part was usually after the show. The people would invite me to restaurants and have me taste delicious Italian cooking and many times wouldn't let me pay for it. It's like they were honored to invite me. I must say the Italians are very warm and friendly."

As Hooker juggled the many balls in play at this point in his career, he began to further evaluate his position in the Den Harrow project. "I was also the lead vocalist on every song of Den Harrow's that was a hit from the first two albums [*Overpower* and *Day by Day*]. I asked to do the single 'Don't Break My Heart' as Tom Hooker, after 'Looking for Love' had been a hit, but Freddy told me it was out of the question. (I just had a feeling 'Don't Break My Heart' was going to be a hit.) This refusal to give me that song was one of the reasons I didn't want to sing for Den Harrow any more. I understood the conflict of interests. My promotion for Tom Hooker was stalled to let the Den Harrow project fly because it had already taken off. I wrote all the lyrics on the third Den Harrow album (*Lies*, using the name T.H. Beecher) and sang all the demos, but I was done. Turatti and Chieregato tried to convince me to keep on singing for [the project], but it was a losing battle. The lead vocals were then re-sung by Anthony James, but it didn't do as well. By then, the concept had begun to run its course (or maybe somebody noticed the voice change, but I wouldn't count on that.)" Den Harrow's *Lies* album largely marked the end of the act's presence in the European pop mainstream. Several independent dance market productions and a number of greatest hits collections featuring the Den Harrow moniker have been released over the years since.

Throughout the latter part of the '80s, Hooker, ruggedly handsome and well built, enjoyed the perks of stardom. However, Hooker says it was a personal sidestep that ultimately prompted him to explore the social benefits that came with fame. "My longtime girlfriend cheated on me in February of '86," he is quick to recall, "and we broke up after six and a half years. I took it pretty badly, but the timing was perfect for me to be single. At that time, I didn't know that 'Looking for Love' was going to be a hit. By summertime, I could have had practically any girl I wanted. I was on TV a lot, and that certainly helped. The combination of being single and bruised by my ex's cheating made me quite cynical about having serious relationships, and I really went for it. I dated *many* women. I was going out every night and dating models until I got tired of it.

"Eventually I turned back into a normal, one-on-one kind of guy. It did take some time, though. I am essentially a faithful person and very happy with my marriage today. I don't need to bounce around from one woman to another. It's not my cup of tea. Those were fun times when I was young and experimenting, but I somehow don't miss them at all.

"I admit I was not careful at all in those days, and I thought AIDS could happen only to other people—not me. I had affairs with way too many women to remember. However, I did take an AIDS test in 1992 when I met my wife at the end of it all, and it turned out negative. We are still together today. As far as drugs and alcohol are concerned, I never was into that. I would get free drinks in clubs but would stop at one drink. I never tried cocaine, but I had girlfriends that did, and many people around me snorted the stuff as well. I just thought that people on coke acted stupid, and I didn't want to imitate that. I was fortunate that the people I worked with were not into it either. In my experience, musicians seemed to be all sober and married. The fashion industry is where all the drugs were. It seemed to me that the music industry was mostly straight, and we were into work with not much interest in messing around.

"I observed that people attached too much importance to exterior appearances," Hooker continues. "I used to think it was very important, and then I realized that it wasn't after being married to someone I really love and no longer being in show business. My wife happens to be very beautiful in my eyes, but even if she weren't to others, I would still love her deeply. I realized after dating the most beautiful girls in Milan, it's a drug to look at a woman's appearance. There will always be a girl who is more beautiful than your wife somewhere—but she's not the one you love. Therefore, it's completely irrelevant and unimportant. It's just the cover over a box that could be filled with worms."

Hooker eventually decided to return to America in the early '90s, where he was absolutely unknown. "Every record company was signing either grunge acts or female singers. I sang in some coffee shops for a while but realized it was absurd for me to be doing this after having sung in front of huge crowds in Italy. I lived off my savings for a couple years because nothing was really happening (before I became a photographer). But after one exhibition, my career as an artist took off pretty fast. Most important for me was the fact that the money was coming back in. I dropped music to focus on my new career, and my income grew progressively to the point where I am very comfortable today. It is a sad truth that money *does* facilitate the creative and artistic process. When there is no money, you doubt yourself and place your focus on the insecurity, instead of creating.

"The record industry today is limited to making profits on live shows," he insists. "When someone has a hit, they immediately go out on tour. [A while back], U2's new album was available for free on iTunes. If you can get a new album by U2 for free, why should you have to pay for smaller productions? U2 realized that there is no money in digital sales. Therefore, they gave the people some new music that they could sing along with at their next concert. That's where the money is—live performances. The ticket prices have gone up 100 percent in 20 years, and the price of listening or owning music has gone down 100 percent."

Though the singer-songwriter has a distinguished resume in European dance-pop of the '80s, he admits he rarely reflects upon it. "I feel that it is behind me," Tom asserts. "I tend to look ahead and not backwards. The amusing thing is that I happened to change my legal name when I moved to the U.S. and got married to my wife (who didn't want to become Mrs. Hooker because of the typical meaning of that name)," he laughs. "In 1994, I changed my name to Thomas Barbey, which was from my mother's side. I somehow got lucky again and became an artist in a different medium at the right time. I say the right time for two reasons. First, digital downloads have destroyed the music business for a lot of musicians, and second, I am too old for the music business now. I have signed many autographs for fans as Tom Hooker, and I've also signed many autographs as Thomas Barbey. It's a different name and a different medium.

"Somehow, even though the music career was a lot of fun, I have the feeling that a century from now, if anybody still remembers me, it will be as Thomas Barbey. Not Tom Hooker. I am quite sure of that because I am already in the permanent collections of four museums as a photographer, and I'm not sure my music will be as well-preserved." He smiles. "And let's not forget—I'm not dead, yet."

Leee John

Imagination

"Just an Illusion" (1982)
UK

"'Just an Illusion' let you get away from it all, and there was a real sexiness to it," proudly surmises singer and composer Leee John, formerly of the group Imagination. Deceptively soft and dreamy in texture, the track boiled with a funky under-groove that was heady with sensual rhythms. This intoxicating creation, along with "Body Talk," "Flashback, "Music and Lights" and a host of other infectious hits helped make John and his group mates international superstars in the early '80s. Their unique brand of British funk, soul and dance was an inspired standout of a decade that thrived on innovative sounds and explorations of new musical territory. Leee led Imagination through its over 10-year journey, a trek that saw the ensemble reach the top of the charts in numerous countries. From his home in London, the artist recounts the personal passage he has taken from one life stage to another.

"I was born in London and brought up on the Beatles and the early Motown sounds," says the singer, his voice possessing a youthful quality. "We only had two channels, BBC1 and ITV, but I watched a lot of the early TV programs like *Ready Steady Go!*, and I kind of latched on to them. I also listened to reggae and ska. My father and mother split, and I got carted off to America and lived in New York with my dad. This was an explosion for me in terms of media because now I was exposed to multiple TV channels and color. It was around 1968–69 when I started seeing Sly and The Family Stone, The Jackson 5, Janis Joplin and The Carpenters. It was an exciting time in the United States, especially for a black kid. It seemed like *everything* was black—you had the blaxploitation movies like *Shaft*, Diana Ross doing *Lady Sings the Blues*, Eddie Kendricks' songs were hits—so many things happening. I was introduced to all this great black music and found I really loved harmony and melodies with strings and horns.

"I was kind of skinny and shy, but somehow I got pushed to go on a singing audition for a company called Worldwide Records, who signed a lot of young artists. They signed me, and I recorded something for them, but my father feared this would take me away from my schoolwork. He kind of pulled me out from it. My mom also wanted me to come back to the UK, and there was a sort of a family tug of war going on. So I had a very short career in America!" he laughs. "I came back to London, which seemed really barren and dull in comparison to the States to me. I was 15, and a friend of mine, Russell, who was like my brother, reunited with me, and we formed a duo—we were like The Jackson 2.

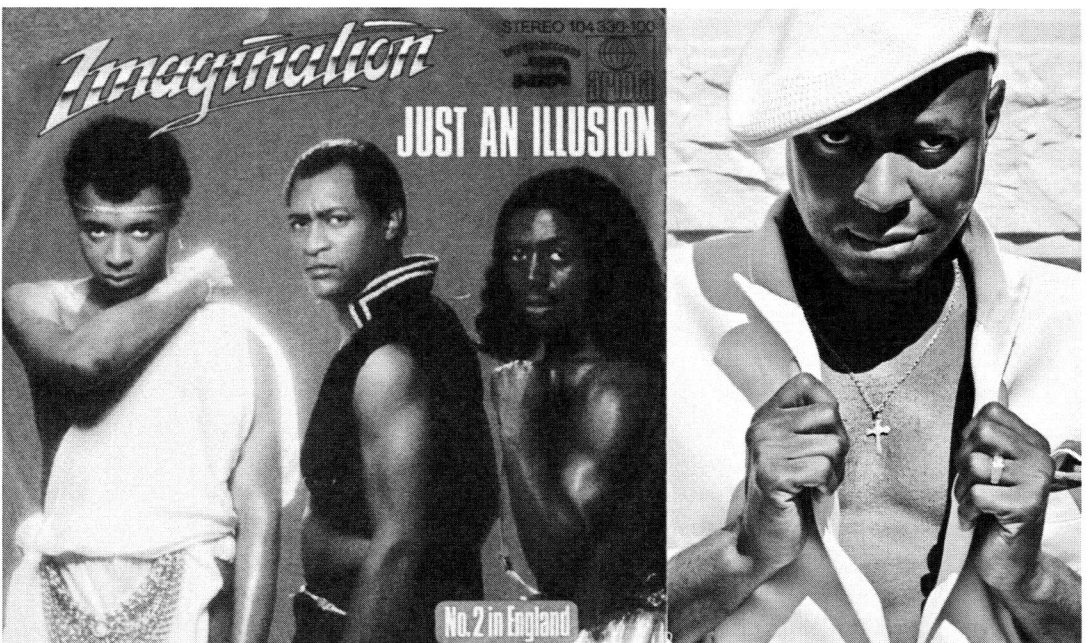

Left: **Unusual costuming was a trademark of Imagination, as seen on the cover art of their 1982 hit "Just an Illusion," pictured here in its German 7-inch single version (Ariola Records).** *Right:* **Former Imagination lead singer Leee John today.**

"We decided to just walk into EMI Records, and we met a guy named Roy Fisher, who was a manager and happened to be in the reception area at the time. Quite good timing on our part. He had just signed David Bowie's backing band from the early '70s, The Spiders from Mars. He was also working with a group called Gonzalez (who later went on to have the disco hit 'Haven't Stopped Dancing Yet'). We were really bold, and we went up to him and told him we were singers. We tried to be very adult about it, and we sang for him right there at the reception desk. Well, he signed us up. We recorded a track with Roy called 'Get Up,' which featured Lou Reed's backup singers and the musicians from Gonzalez. We were still going to school. But after the school day was over, we wore our velvet jackets and snakeskin shoes—we were always showing off. It was really incredible for us to have a recording contract at such a young age. Unfortunately, the record wasn't successful, and we didn't go anywhere with it. But it was a wonderful learning experience."

Leee was determined to honing his skills. "In 1981, [I was] introduced to Tony Swain, who was one of their producers at the time. He liked my songwriting and asked me if I could write some lyrics for a piece of music he had on a cassette. It was a very rough track, but I remember I took the tape home, and that very night at my mother's kitchen table, I wrote the lyrics to the song 'Body Talk.'

"We called in my friend Ashley Ingram, who was a bass player I had started working with. Drummer Errol Kennedy [of the group Central Line] was brought in after the 'Body Talk' single had been recorded. And that's how we became a trio. I think we had it in our heads to try and emulate The Police, who also had three members. Most groups in those days were much larger. If we had formed a big group and went out on the road, I knew we'd only make tuppence. I said no way to that idea. It was a three-way split. Even though everyone didn't write the song 'Body Talk,' I gave percentages to everyone. Everyone was given equal credit on our first album. I felt we came from nothing, and if we could achieve something with our records, we could reach higher platforms. I wanted us to all be in it together. 'Body Talk' turned out to be our very first hit record, and we became know as Imagination (a name inspired by John Lennon)."

Imagination's smooth and sexy debut single was a slow shuffler that fell somewhere in the middle of the period's ever-broadening spectrum of dance and funk music. A surprising smash in the UK, it reached the number four position on the nation's pop chart and nearly cracked the Top 10 in the Netherlands. The album of the same name, produced by Steve Jolley and Tony Swain, was certified gold in Britain and stayed on the charts for nearly a year. "Morgan took 'Body Talk' to all the clubs and really pushed it," remembers Leee. "It was one of the slowest records of the year, anywhere. It was a very different kind of sound. I loved bass and piano, and I wanted a lot of emphasis on those. I had a lot of input on the song and was very proud of it. Our group became part of this whole Brit-Funk experience, with groups and artists like Central Line, Hi-Tension, Linx and David Grant, Level 42, Five Star and Jaki Graham.

"I believe 'Body Talk' only got as high as number 44 on the pop charts at the very beginning," he remembers. "Then a band dropped out of the *Top of the Pops* show, which was one of the biggest TV shows in all of England. To be on it was everyone's dream. I can't remember which group it was that dropped out, but we were pushed in by a stroke of luck. We had to be ready on very short notice, so we had to start thinking about what kind of costumes to wear. We wanted to be very different from the normal groups, who were always in suits. We wanted to be really out there, like Funkadelic or Parliament. Some critics ended up saying our outfits were very camp, but that's only because they found out we were British. If we had been an American group, they would have said, 'Oh wow, that's so cool!' At any rate, you never saw a black English group on TV, and there was a lot of pressure to live up to that. It was only in the mid–'70s that black men had even been allowed into nightclubs.

"The song just went up and up from there, and it was amazing!" John says with infectious enthusiasm, as if it all just happened recently. "The *Body Talk* album was a hit in so many countries. Each song on it was a major hit in some part of the world. It was like our very own *Off the Wall*. But I didn't let it go to my head. I was always about the work—as long as I was working, I was cool. I knew and studied how black artists in the music industry got treated, and I knew careers could be very short-lived. I had a very realistic vision of it in my head, and I knew right from the start that Imagination would never last forever."

The album yielded two more hits in Britain, the seductive, groove-laden "In and Out of Love" and the upbeat "Flashback." The track "Burnin' Up" caught the attention of the DJs in the U.S., and the track was a Top 10 hit on *Billboard*'s club chart. John's energized, falsetto vocals, some edgy costuming and sensuous rhythms quickly became Imagination's signature. The ensemble soon went to work on a follow-up album, 1982's *In the Heat of the Night* (again produced by Jolley and Swain), which surpassed everyone's expectations. The set's lead single, "Just an Illusion," put Imagination over the top. With its slow burn and scintillating undercurrent, the track was an international smash, reaching the number two position on the UK pop charts and vaulting to the Top 10 in Germany and the Netherlands. The song was a huge club hit in the United States, with DJs spinning the track continually throughout the summer season. "We went to America and appeared at The Paradise Garage in New York with DJ and remixer Larry Levan, just after recording our second LP," John recalls. "He wanted to do an original mix of our newest track, 'Just an Illusion,' which was starting to get played as an import record by Frankie Crocker, the ultimate radio DJ there. We had barely heard the record ourselves at this point, but it was starting to build. It was a very exciting time, but an awful lot of work. We had to travel to a lot of countries, visit a lot of radio stations and do a lot of promotion work so that people could see us. This was a bit before MTV had really caught on. So we had to really sell ourselves to build a fan base."

Imagination's grass roots efforts did, indeed, build a sizeable fan base, and their distinctive sound soon warranted a third LP. *Night Dubbing* (1983) was a collection of hits from the first two albums served up in dub-version dance remixes. The *Scandalous* album, known as *New Dimension* in the U.S., also followed in 1983, maintaining the group's lofty position as a gold selling, chart-topping act. Says the singer, "On one of our first tours, we appeared at the Dominion Theatre in London. We did eight shows in seven sold-out nights. That was an achievement, and we received awards for it. We were one of the first black British bands to ever do that. We became one of the super groups of Europe.

"We were working so much and the demands on me to write the songs, sing them, arrange them and still be somewhat normal with my mates was difficult. I suppose there was always the temptation to indulge in something to relieve the pressure, but we were never into drugs.

We had our wild times, but we were very grounded. We liked the champagne and did get drunk sometimes, but that was it. There were so many people coking it up. Pot-smokers and such surrounded us, but I never did any of that. I was too concerned with my instrument—which was my throat, my voice. I knew I had to maintain myself for my audience. Every artist goes through times where they indulge in something at one point or another. We're not superhuman. I was lucky to have grounded people around me, but ultimately it was up to me as an individual to actually stay focused. I knew people were looking up to me. In the '80s, you were in this horse race with the record company driving on you to get another hit, and there was a lot of pressure. That's why many artists turned to their vices. The labels didn't actually know what a hit was until a song *was* a hit. It was always, 'We need another 'Just an Illusion!'' I just would have to stop, pull myself together, and come back to it again. But I didn't need drugs to do that.

"I can tell you some very magic moments for me, too," he eagerly says. "Luther Vandross was playing at a theater where we were also performing, and he came backstage to say hello. There was a little party afterward, and he sang 'Just an Illusion' *to me*. I'm sitting there thinking, 'Wow!' Another great memory was going to perform in Los Angeles on *Soul Train*, and Marvin Gaye was a guest. It was around the time of his 'Sexual Healing' hit. He told Don Cornelius to watch us because we were going to blow up big. If you see the clip, you can hear Don say, 'This is the group that has Marvin Gaye's stamp of approval.' I went to his dressing room to thank Marvin and asked him why an old album track of his sung with Diana Ross, 'I'll Keep My Light in My Window,' was never released as a single. In London, in 1977, we used to dance to it. He couldn't remember what song it was and told me to sing it. So here I am singing to Marvin Gaye. Can you imagine?

"Another moment was with Freddie Mercury. He loved my tones and sounds. He wanted to know how I achieved them. He invited us to his house, and we were up in his music room. He was playing all this funky music, very different from his Queen material. Then he played me this amazing track he did with Michael Jackson. I was like, 'Why don't you release this?' He said it didn't sound quite right. It turned out to be the song 'State of Shock,' which Mick Jagger later sang. When I told everyone Freddie had done this track with Michael, nobody believed me. I've had so many more incredible moments like these!"

The remainder of the '80s saw a measured decline in Imagination's staying power on the charts. A greatest hits package in 1989 returned the group to the top of the UK surveys, but original material from the period fared somewhat less favorably. They continued to tour to enthusiastic crowds, but Leee admits his feeling for the group had been changing. "By the end of the '80s," he observes, "I was moving out of my home and planning what I knew would be 'the last party.' I sensed things were going to end for Imagination soon. You could just see what was happening. I think, for me, I hit the fork in the road around 1985 when we got an offer to play Sun City in Africa," continues the artist. "When the offer came in, I didn't know that much about the political situation there, but we were being presented with an awful lot of money to go perform. Other UK artists had gone there, but many had not. I was learning about Artists Against Apartheid and heard Harry Belafonte speak about it, and he inspired me greatly. I became a part of the movement, and Sun City blacklisted me. So that closed the chapter on the group going there. Some of the group members were a little annoyed because of the huge amount of money involved. To be honest, this sort of caused a shift in me with how I felt about the group. I don't think they were aware of how I was feeling, but I was changing inside.

"Around 1986–87, Errol decided to leave. He had an argument with our manager Brian Longley; I didn't agree with Errol, and neither did Ashley. So he left the group, and we brought in a good friend of mine from the band Loose Ends, Peter Royer. Our manager was killed in a car accident in 1991, and it was very, very hard on us. You could just feel all these things breaking us down. Ashley had started doing production work with the artist Des'ree, and the writing was on the wall. He and I weren't communicating as well as before, and I was frustrated by how much work was falling on me with our manager gone. I suggested Ashley continue forward with his production work, and I would continue separately with the group. I brought in Nat Augustin from the group Light of the World. He was a part of our *The Fascination of the Physical* LP, and we continued to tour as Imagination for a while longer.

"I worked on projects with other artists like Arthur Baker, Club 69 and Tata Vega. I kind of went underground and started doing a lot more hardcore dance material. I was introduced to David Morales, who handled our track 'Instinctual,' which was extremely big for Imagination and went to number one on the U.S. club charts. By 1992, I wanted to reorganize myself and decided it was time to move past Imagination."

As Leee sought to discover a new balance in the '90s, he began a new phase in his personal journey. As a solo singer, he scored hits with a number of dance singles and also explored jazz music. Along with Junior Giscombe, Omar, Don-e and Noel McCoy, he formed an ensemble known as The British Collective in 2014. In 2017, a new Imagination album (featuring Leee John) called *Retropia* was released.

Leee is very upbeat and confident these days, nearly as busy as he was at the peak of Imagination's fame. "I have a philosophy I believe in very strongly which keeps me moving forward," he says of his present day outlook. "Let every moment count. I also believe you have to keep on learning. You can never stop. Even if what you learn about is from the past, you can still discover new stuff. When I travel to a show today, I tend to go a day early so I can breathe in the atmosphere of the place I'm going to. I want to learn about the area and get a sense of what the people are about so when I go on stage, I'm part of them. I think you also must enjoy whatever you are doing. You have to put 1,000 percent into whatever you do. You can't be afraid to make mistakes either. They are a part of what is supposed to be. This is how I feel about life today. Also, I've noticed as one gets older, you become more of a teacher. So I guess I like to impart my wisdom a bit more these days. I'm surprised at all the rubbish I know," he laughs.

Reflecting on the appeal of his group and their iconic music, Leee takes an extended pause before offering a theory. "It's hard to say why so many people in so many countries identified with our music," he conjectures. "We had a simplicity, and we kept our sound very 'urban UK.' Most of our records had a street vibe—we came from a very homegrown audience. We were never part of the U.S. disco scene or anything like that. We never ever dreamed our songs would cross over the way they did. We had an Afro-Caribbean flavor with the essence of jazz. I think our music had certain frequencies that people heard that kind of stayed in their minds. I think it was the combination of the bass, piano, the kick and the vocal harmonies—and I think there was what I call 'the escape factor.' In our live shows, we kind of re-enacted that sense of fantasy and escape. Our sound was definitely not American—even though many Americans think we were from the U.S. 'No, I'm from North London mate!' I'd always say.

"As they say, 'I wouldn't change my life if I had to live it all over!' I'm still surprised when I hear people tell me they loved 'Just an Illusion' or the other tracks I've done. I get little butterflies in my stomach when I hear them say that. It makes me feel very good. But I never want to go into that place where I'm dramatically bellowing, 'I'd like you to all remember how marvelous I was back then, darling!' I'm still trying to make a contribution."

Carmelo La Bionda
Producer, Composer
Artists: La Bionda, Righeira, et al.
Italy

The accomplishments of Carmelo and Michelangelo La Bionda have earned the brothers the title of "music royalty" in their native Italy. They were responsible for creating several major international hits during the disco frenzy of the '70s (under the monikers of D.D. Sound and La Bionda), and they emerged in the '80s as hugely successful producers and songwriters. Among their most popular efforts in the latter decade's dance-pop arena were a series of hit records made with the edgy Italian duo known as Righeira. As a result, in the minds of many, the La Bionda brothers were absolutely integral to the launch of the Italo-disco sound. Today, they continue to perform, are composers of film and television scores, and manage a popular hi-tech recording studio in Milan utilized by the likes of Depeche Mode, Rihanna, Laura Pausini and many other notables.

"My brother and I were born in Sicily. I was born in 1949 and Michelangelo in 1952," says Carmelo. "We moved to Milano in 1954. Our mother was a housewife, and our father worked for the National Electricity Company. There wasn't much money in the family, but the radio was on all day. We only had the Italian Government Radio channels in those days. I have to say, they didn't play much of the music that my brother and I liked—rock 'n' roll. Fortunately, the jukebox in the bar down the street played Elvis, Little Richard, Fats Domino and many other American stars. Luckily, we found a way to hide under a table there when we were kids, and we listened to these marvelous and tasty records.

"Our father could play some chords on the guitar. He was a great fan of Neapolitan music, and that helped us to develop a sense of melody. Later, in 1963, we fell in love with The Beatles, and that totally changed our lives. We became the biggest Beatles fans, and that gave us the will to go and buy a guitar (a very cheap one, of course) and start learning the chords of those wonderful British songs. As we did not have money to pay for some lessons, we got to learn a lot from the street players in our neighborhood. After a few months, we tried to put together a band.

"We started being in the business as songwriters, singers and producers," La Bionda continues. "Being brothers and possessing nearly the same tastes in music, we spent much time together writing and producing. I was usually the one who got the songs started, and he'd join in with additional parts or suggest changes in chords and things like that. Sometimes he would start the process, and I'd join in. Michelangelo has a natural sense for what can eventually be a marketable song. I plunge into songs with tremendous enthusiasm, and I fall in love easily with all the parts of the work. Fortunately, Michelangelo is tougher, which is, again, good for marketing. He is also a good publisher and knows much of the music business. I'm more of a 'crazy boy' and put all of myself into writing, programming and trying to have a vision. I love scouting for artists, and I much prefer to work with female voices.

"I'm also very keen on technology, studio equipment and synthesizers. The Prophet-5 was our main synth in the disco days. But our collection included synths by Oberheim, the ARP Odyssey, Minimoog and many others. We found out that we really liked the possibility of controlling every side of our activities. In Italy at that time, it was difficult to find a good producer and musicians who shared our interest in British and American music. We loved strong rhythm patterns and attractive bass lines. That's why we soon moved to London and then to Munich, where we lived for six years."

Early on, the brothers recorded two albums as "Fratelli La Bionda" (La Bionda Brothers) using an acoustic approach—"very Crosby, Stills, Nash, & Young," as Carmelo describes their sound. The projects led to work at the legendary Apple Studios in London with The Beatles' sound engineer Phil McDonald and pianist Nicky Hopkins. However, it was the emergence of the disco movement in the '70s that shifted the brothers' careers into high gear.

"After our experience in London," recalls La Bionda, "we decided to move to Munich, bringing with us a lady who was very famous on the British music scene, but as a model—Amanda Lear. We met Amanda in London through a mutual friend who believed she had potential as a rock star, even though her voice was very deep and unusual. She was basically a model for fashion photographers, but also posed for the legendary painter Salvador Dalí, who was her close friend. She was also very familiar with the rock star scene, having been featured on the cover of a Roxy Music album.

"She desperately wanted to sing, and at the time we met her, she was going to perform as the opening act on a David Bowie tour called 'Star.' Unfortunately, it was cancelled before it ever got started. The opening song she was going to sing was written by two famous English writers and had already been recorded, also called 'Star,' but it was never released.

"Our mutual friend was interested in experimenting with something different for Amanda, so we became her producers. In 1975, we recorded a Leiber & Stoller song with her, the famous 'Trouble,' originally performed by Elvis Presley. We tried to give it sort of a disco feeling in the arrangement, and we backed the single with a new song called 'Lethal Leading Lady,' written by my brother and me, using Amanda's lyrics. The record was released in Germany (by Ariola) and in France and Italy (through Polydor). Later, we recorded a song ('Diamond Thief'), written by a British guy, which was more pop-rock, but we did not get much out of it.

"She agreed to move to Munich with us, where the disco scene was getting very big with Giorgio Moroder, who was producing a new international act named Donna Summer. There was a guy in the A&R department at Ariola who was really in love with Amanda. He was basically the only really enthusiastic person in the company in regard to her. So because of him, we got a deal in which Ariola was going to sign Amanda, who would be under our supervision and management. They wanted a German gentleman (Anthony Monn) to be the producer of Amanda's first album (*I Am a Photograph*).

"As it turned out, Amanda's debut album was a tremendous success, due, in part, to her ambiguous reputation and the fact that, indeed, she was very good on stage and in interviews. I believe she had it exactly in her mind how to be a rock star (now a disco star), having always been so close to the big names. Her success developed quickly in Italy, France, Spain and so on, but not in England. TV appearances really helped her to gain fame. The music success was mostly limited to her first and second albums due to the fact that she couldn't really go too far with her musical concepts."

While nurturing Lear's early music career, Carmelo says that he and his brother wanted to get into the disco scene themselves. They created and performed as D.D. Sound (Disco Delivery Sound), which also included a collective of studio musicians. "We thought it was better not use our Italian name to get into the international music market," La Bionda recalls. "With the help of very talented international musicians in Munich, D.D. Sound became popular in Italy and in some European countries. Our style was still more pop than disco, but the combination of our pop with the so-called 'Munich Sound' was different and gave us a precise identity. Our album *1-2-3-4 Gimme Some More* had a sort of a bubble-gum sound, but it was arranged in that Munich disco style."

Though D.D. Sound released several albums throughout the golden age of disco, the brothers decided there was room enough for a second entity. "Since we realized that D.D. Sound had worked quite well on the scene and in the market, we decided we could start to use our real name, La Bionda. The D.D. Sound group was gonna continue 'cause we didn't want to lose a winning name in the market. However, at the same time, we had a surplus of songs. We realized some were more pop-oriented. We decided to keep those songs for D.D. Sound productions, and the rest were gonna be released as 'La Bionda.'"

The upbeat "One for You, One for Me," recorded in Munich, was a substantial worldwide hit for La Bionda in 1978. The song reached the mid-regions of the British pop chart, a significant accomplishment for an Italian act. "I remember in the early days of this production, we were waiting for our arranger, Charly Ricanek, to pick up a cassette with two songs on it, just piano and voice, so that he could begin writing the arrangements for our first self-titled La Bionda album. For a few days, we sat at the piano and started putting down some lines of a couple of songs that we had in mind, 'One for You, One for Me' and 'There for Me.' 'One for You' was a mix of various styles—a kind of Leon Russell piano, bluesy arpeggio, doubled with a synth sound and an electronic synthesizer bass. It was very up-tempo with a Latin feeling. Very powerful in sound and very simple to remember because of the easy riff. It wasn't a pure disco production, but it sounded very sexy and right for the discothèques. The sound was unusual, and we think this was why people got hooked on it. We were actually very surprised to see the song hit the charts of the UK and other countries.

"We've been on the charts of most European countries, particularly in Germany, France and Spain, but also in smaller nations. We enjoyed lots of appearances on big TV shows, including *Der Musikladen*, a top music show in Germany that helped a lot with pushing our hits. At that time, we would meet other big stars on the show like Blondie and Dan Hartman (and we became good friends with many of them)."

Carmelo says he and his brother loved to be producers and relished any opportunity to break free of standard ideas and sounds. "We needed to be free to approach things our way. Our pop-electronic song 'I Wanna Be Your Lover' from 1980 was a great example of our spirit and what could happen when we would look for new sounds and styles. As a result, we did not have too much time to perform in those days because we wanted to spend so much time in the studio. In 1983, we stopped producing our own projects in favor of working with other artists."

The La Bionda brothers soon became innovators of the newly emerging Italo-disco sound coming out of Italy in the early '80s. "Many musicians took from us the idea that finally you could successfully record songs in English, and the dance genre was an excellent form of music in which to do it. The new electronic facilities that were developing were a big help to independent producers like us. With these studios, almost everyone could cut songs, even with a small budget. I believe the sound of sequencers contributed to the explosive growth of Italo-disco productions. Strings were disappearing, and the bass lines were programmed with sort of a funky movement. But they were played automatically. For example, when we recorded the Righeira album, we were going that way, but with a little Latin touch in the production."

Righeira was a duo from Turin, a northern city in Italy famous for Fiat cars. The group was formed in 1981 by members Stefano Rota and Stefano Righi, and thanks to the La Bionda composition "Vamos a la Playa," they became an international sensation in 1983. The summery dance song was a hit in Great Britain and a chart buster in Italy, Germany, Spain and numerous other countries. An equally compelling and energized follow-up, "No Tengo Dinero," released later that year, was another major international hit.

Remembers Carmelo, "Righeira were musically influenced by the new electronic trends and at the same time, by Italian '60s summer songs. They were also wearing crazy but fashionable outfits in those days. My brother and I had decided to move into producing music TV shows with a modern theme, based in graphics and hip fashions. Something new for the sleepy Italian TV situation," he laughs. "Those were the years when Armani and Versace were becoming big stars of fashion all over the world. Someone introduced Righeira to us as singers, but we thought they might be good hosts for the show we were planning because of their look and attitude. But they were pressing to get some recordings done, so instead we sat down and wrote some stuff together. Fortunately, things went a different way from our original plan because our recordings with them became worldwide hits.

"Our first creation was 'Vamos a la Playa' ('Let's Go to the Beach'). The song had a real summer feeling in its title, but hidden in its lyrics was the true meaning of the song. The theme of the song was a call to go to the beach, a nuclear bomb has exploded and the radiation will tan us. It took six months to have a finished and convincing final master. We recorded it first in Milano and then in Munich, which, in 1983, was in West Germany. We largely used analog synths but also tested a brand new sampling machine ('The Fairlight'). We wrote the lyrics in Spanish, but the song is really anything but a Latin song. It was more in the style of new wave, I would say. We kept the up-tempo feeling we loved that makes people dance easily. Working with Righeira was really fun, as much as we could keep their exuberance under control.

"We couldn't believe that 'Vamos a la Playa' was becoming such a huge international hit," Carmelo says with a touch of excitement. "In Italy it is considered the most popular summer song (with a social statement). The Spanish language sounded nice because it was an unusual combination with electronic pop. The follow up single, 'No Tengo Dinero,' was also an international hit and still in Spanish. Funnily enough, there were producers in Spain who got the inspiration from these hits to start making similar music. We soon recorded an album with the duo to be ready for Christmas. The sound of the production was very electronic, but still powerful. I can still hear the songs in the clubs today and not feel any difference between their hits and today's high-powered dance productions."

Righeira enjoyed more hits in Italy with "L'estate Sta Finendo' and "Italians a Go-Go" under the guidance of the La Bionda brothers, but the party began to wind down. "By 1985, we had done quite a few records with Righeira. We wanted to record another album, but we decided to quit the adventure because we thought that the two singers had in mind to produce themselves. I think as a team we were losing some of the energy and groove we had at the very beginning. We did not force them to do another album with us. In hindsight, I think it was a mistake that they didn't continue to work with us. Righeira moved from Milan to a city not far from Venice and started recording with new programmers and tried to be their own producers.

"I think my brother and I knew exactly what was necessary to make their songs hits. It was always a lot of long work in the studio, changing and fine-tuning various aspects of their songs. They needed gimmicks and a very special sound. We would spend days and days and a lot of money to find very good musicians that would help to make their songs become hits. Righeira started doing more live shows based more on the original early material we made with them. They still work quite a lot today with live gigs. We have been talking about creating a recording comeback for them, but somehow it still hasn't happened."

Though major labels in America picked up the music of the La Bionda brothers (notably Righeira), their sound never fully caught on beyond the U.S. club scene. "It is always a dream to be on the U.S. charts," Carmelo admits. "However, it was not really very easy to enter them. I always believed it could happen if you had something appealing to offer that doesn't appear to sound like it is trying to be an American production. After Righeira, we were involved on the business side of Falco's 'Rock Me Amadeus,' which we pushed hard in the United States. It was signed to A&M Records and went to number one on the charts there."

As the '80s progressed, Carmelo and Michelangelo began composing more music and songs for movies, TV and publicity projects. "We were very successful internationally because we started working with these 'Miami cop' productions with the famous Italian 'spaghetti western' actors Bud Spencer and Terence Hill. One of these productions was successful in American theaters and on TV and featured Terence Hill and Ernest Borgnine. Other films we worked on were mainly for Italy but with top Italian actors. One of them featured Giancarlo Giannini (of *Swept Away*). All together, we worked on more than twenty movies."

The artist observes the pros and cons of the music business, then and now. "Being in the business back in those days obviously meant working with the majors, but even small labels could help with the success of a project. I think that the atmosphere was much more relaxed and friendly in the '70s and '80s—professional, but friendly and nice—for the most part. Nowadays, everything looks more surgical. You tend to find this cold atmosphere when you visit a record company today. The feeling you get at major labels today isn't much different than the atmosphere of a bank!

"I'd say life in the music business was much easier then, as opposed to now," Carmelo concedes. "Now it is almost impossible to connect with major entertainment and record companies. It was easy to have good relationships with people in the business in the '70s and '80s, even though sometimes they might become arrogant. However, I will say there was a downside back then. I think that many artists, particularly in the Italo-disco arena, were ripped off because they simply did not know much about their rights, particularly regarding publishing, etc. Many of these artists were dealing with small labels, and maybe sometimes their contracts were not very—let's say—clear. I would say that many of these artists were mostly used."

Today, the La Bionda brothers spend a great deal of time in their oft-praised Logic Studios, which has served a wide variety of contemporary music stars. "In 1985," says the artist, "after having spent six years in Munich and having gathered good experience at studios in London, Los Angeles and many other cities, we decided to build a big complex of studios that would include recording facilities, audio-video post production, mastering, a cutting room and so on. We could offer almost anything. It's become one of the biggest such studios offering these services in the world. Many international artists have used our studios, including Depeche Mode (who recorded their *Violator* album with us, with the hit 'Personal Jesus'), Robert Palmer, Paul Young, Sting, Ray Charles, Hugh Padgham and many others. And obviously, almost any big Italian artist you can name has worked here," he says proudly.

"We've always been very enthusiastic about music and our work in the business. But we've never let the negativity that exists in the business keep us from having good relationships with the artists we have worked with over the years. I think that if you don't enjoy making music and don't treat it as a part of real life (and the qualities of life we value), you become a sad or cold person. My brother and I will do 'nice and friendly' until we've got no more energy left to do it. Emotions will always come first with us. I hope we will always be remembered as two nice guys with a vision for mixing fantasy, music styles and cultures and for having a great deal of passion for making hits—and always with a strong, human approach!"

Caroline Loeb
"C'est la ouate" (1987)
France

Caroline Loeb's creativity has always been multi-dimensional. Today, she is an actress, theater director, author and radio host, in addition to being a popular singer. Her distinctive voice can convey all manner of emotions. Back in 1987, the petite and stylish young go-getter was the toast of France with her hugely popular single "C'est la ouate." The unusual composition was a quirky, avant-garde dance-pop tune whose remarkably uncomplicated construction was nothing short of hypnotic. The song's portrait of a lazy young woman on a jaded, dreamy love quest was actually an over-achiever, commercially and artistically. It bounded up the pop charts in numerous countries and became an evergreen that many singers have covered over the years. From the City of Light, Ms. Loeb shares her memories of the enormous success she enjoyed during this period of her career, the chaotic challenges that accompanied her remarkable achievement, and her journey to modern day creative fulfillment.

Caroline spent her early childhood in New York, a memory she describes as still vivid and enchanting. "I was brought up there from the time I was four years old until I was six," says the artist. "We were in one of the Eldorado towers on Central Park West. Central Park was our garden. My childhood was very much like the TV show *Mad Men*. My father had an art gallery on Madison Avenue, and my mother was very elegant. Life was poetic and fun. New York still has an incredibly strong attraction for me. My only regret is that we left. I would have loved to live my entire life in 'The Big Apple!'

"My family left New York and moved to Paris after my grandfather's death. His name was Pierre Loeb, a very important art dealer in the '30s and '40s and founder of Galerie Pierre. He was a friend of Picasso, Miró, Balthus and Giacometti. I started going to Paris nightclubs at a very young age. I was 16 when I started to dance every night at the Club 7, owned by Fabrice Emaer, who later opened the Palace, the French version of Studio 54. For about 10 years, I was a hard night-clubber. That was the time when I met Pierre Grillet and Philippe Chany, with whom I created my hit 'C'est la ouate.' In the '80s, we were all crazy night birds. Dancing in clubs was our main activity. I remember very well how Guy Cuevas, Philippe Krootchey and Henry Flesh, the DJ stars of the time, played disco mixed with salsa, Eartha Kitt and new wave all night long. We were absolutely *mad* about dancing!" she smiles.

Exploring her potential as a singer and songwriter in 1982, Loeb had the opportunity to record her first album, *Piranana*, which fit well into the edgy new wave style that was

Left: **The jacket for Caroline Loeb's breakthrough hit single "C'est la ouate."** *Right:* **Ms. Loeb as photographed by Olivier Denis in 2015. Her book** *Mes Années 80 de A à Z* **was published the same year.**

in vogue at the decade's dawn. "I owe a lot to Michael Zilkha, who discovered the songs I had been writing," says Caroline. "I really started to sing because I loved writing lyrics. Then he introduced me to Ronnie Rogers [songwriter of "Deputy of Love" by Don Armando's 2nd Avenue Rhumba Band] who worked with August Darnell and Kid Creole. Ronnie is the one who composed almost all of the music of my first album that we cut at Electric Lady, the studio Jimi Hendrix had opened. At the time, we were all high on cocaine, and I remember well the night we mixed the last song of the album, 'Narcissique.' We were so fucked up we thought we heard Hendrix's ghost on the tracks. Yet today it is my favorite song on that album. I have mixed feelings about the set. I was pretty lost at that time and am still pretty embarrassed about my singing," she laughs. "Since then, thank God, I have improved a lot. The album wasn't a big success.

"This period in the '80s, before AIDS, was fun and has become, in my memory, a bit like a fantasy. It was a time when everyone seemed more carefree; there was a lot of money, and sex was wild and free. But I suppose that's only partly true. The drug situation caused us to lose a lot of great artists and musicians on the way. One often forgets it was also the 'no future' period, the punk era. And that wasn't such a fun party!"

For the next few years, Loeb concentrated on acting for television and writing more song lyrics. Recalls the singer, "One morning, Pierre Grillet came to my flat with a couple of phrases, like 'J'opte pour le soft dit-elle, Et toutes les photos d'elle sont des photos couches,' and the words that would later be used in the 'C'est la ouate' chorus. I chose some of them, added my own words, and a couple of weeks later, the song was born with Philippe Chany's music.

"I met Philippe when I was working with Jean-Baptiste Mondino as a photo stylist. He thought we should work together, so I brought Chany a dozen songs I'd written. He chose one, which I had previously called 'Paresseuse.' When I listened to the music he created, I noticed this 'c'est-la-ouate' gimmick. I told him I thought it was fun, like an African sound. He turned it into a hook, changed the title of the song, and there it was. Then he tried to get us a contract for nearly six months. No one wanted it until Philippe Constantin of Barclay Records (who had launched Rita Mitsouko) fell in love with the song.

"The funny thing is that I had been a night bird for some years, and I had my own look and visual style. But when we signed to Barclay, they decided to have a publicity agency give me a makeover. They talked about me as if I had to become a brand. They discussed it for hours, and it cost them a fortune to finally decide on my hairdo for the record cover. It was pretty absurd, because when the record came out and became an instant hit (thanks to a friend who started playing it on the FUN Radio network), I dressed in my own style. I never needed those guys. After all, I had been a photo stylist myself. It was totally absurd. They just had too much money to spend. And they thought I was going to become a product. I was—*an artist*."

Selling reportedly over 450,000 copies in France, "C'est la ouate" joined an expanding, but still relatively elite, group of French dance-pop songs that found favor beyond the country's borders. The methodically paced electronic dance track was a marvel of minimalism and a club and radio monster that reached number five in France, number three in Spain, and went straight to the top of the charts in Italy. The enchanting melody scored a Top 10 position in Germany and reportedly did the same as far away as Argentina. An inventive video (directed by the talented Philippe Gautier, who placed the singer's flair for high fashion in the spotlight) and the release of an additional remix version kept the song in heavy rotation for several months. In the video, Caroline says she chose to feature the three men that she felt had made the "C'est la ouate" phenomenon happen—Pierre Grillet, Philippe Chany and Stéphane Martini.

"For me," admits Caroline, "this song is like a little miracle. We made it with the money of one of my dearest friends at the time, Stéphane Martini, who sent me the money after a phone call from Paris to Milano. He could barely hear the demo, but my enthusiasm convinced him. I never felt there was a particular message in the song. It was more like a mood reflecting this laid back feeling that came about in the '80s. The funny thing was that the lyrics (at least some of the parts I wrote) were rather depressing. It was really a song about a girl who has a lot of lovers and is pretty desperate. That's what I was like at the time—on a daily hangover. But the music was so fresh and the gimmick so special, everyone thought it was just fun and sexy."

According to Loeb, the unprecedented success of the track came as a surprise to all involved. "Of course, I thought it was going to be a success," she explains, "just like every time I did something. But I had no idea this song would go around the world and still be played almost 30 years later. It was crazy, and it *still* is. It seems to me what people loved about it is that it was so different, so mysterious. With that minimalistic musical arrangement and lyrics that no one really understood, everyone could make up his own meaning for the song.

"I was lucky to be part of a group of very few French singers who were loved in other countries. I believe this was thanks to an Italian gentleman who was in France and heard the song on the radio. He went back to Italy and convinced the Italian Polygram label to release it. One guy who has an idea and stands up for it always writes history. It was certainly true in the '80s. Otherwise, the whole commercial music system would be based on American or English supremacy.

"I was a huge Madonna fan, so it was amazing that Seymour Stein, co-founder of Sire Records in the U.S. and a V.P. at Warner, would be interested in my song for distribution in America. We did a wonderful English version with another friend of mine, Serge Grunberg, and called it 'And So What,' but it was only the French version that caught on worldwide. The English version played in some elite clubs in San Francisco and a couple of times on BBC Radio one in England, but it was never a huge hit in America or the UK."

With success arriving on such a grand scale from virtually every other global direction, the singer says life suddenly got—*crazy*. "People were nuts about that song," she remembers. "It was in Italy where it was the wildest. At TV shows, the audience would scream and pull their hair. I felt as if I was all four Beatles for a couple of years. My absolute favorite moment was in Siena during a performance on a huge Italian TV show. I performed with the audience singing along throughout the whole song. There were about 10,000 of them out there in that gorgeous city in Tuscany. It was magical."

There was a flipside to the coin, Loeb admits. "The period that followed our breakout success was a nightmare. So many people [in our circle] were fucked up from morning to night—and I wasn't much better. Drug abuse hurt everyone. And not only artists were doing drugs. In the record companies, the boss, public relations people—everyone seemed to be hooked. It was pretty bad. The drug abuse of some of the guys who were important in show business ruined some artists' careers because they were so busy getting stoned instead of working with the singers. Then AIDS arrived and killed so many great artists and suddenly death became very present. Before AIDS appeared, we were just going from one party to another."

Loeb says her relationship with Chany became severely strained. "In my own personal circumstances, I tried to free myself from Philippe. But, unfortunately, I didn't do it early enough. It cost me 20 years and almost killed me as an artist. It was really difficult.

"The album that followed the single, *Loeb C.D.* [also called *C'est la ouate* in some territories], remains a very painful memory. With the huge success of 'C'est la ouate,' everyone around the song became a megalomaniac. Every day when I got out of the studio while making that album, I cried for hours. It was a horrible experience. The album should/could have been much better had the egos been kept under control," she conjectures, the memory seemingly still fresh for the singer.

A follow-up single off the set, the agreeable "A quoi tu penses?," generated interest in Italy and Germany, but additional releases from the album like "Le Téléfon" failed to keep the momentum going. Caroline says her falling out with Chany hurt her deeply, and she was engulfed in a negative spiral. "Bad choices were made for the singles that followed," she remembers. "I didn't have any more confidence or self-esteem. During my period of success in dance-pop music, I had lost all vision of myself. For many, I had *become* my hit. As far as how the music industry treated me as a female at that time, well, let's say show business isn't any less misogynistic than the rest of the world. And since there was so much money to be made on you, they treated female singers pretty much like 'Class A' hookers. If you were a female singer, you could be treated very badly (even if you were a songwriter, too). Show business people decided I was finished—and that was that. I thought I was strong enough to overcome all that, but it took me longer to get over it than I had imagined it would. It is really when I started directing other singers and actors in 1993 that I began to feel happy again as an artist. Writing started my whole music adventure—since, as I said earlier, I began singing because I wrote songs. But it is when I directed shows for other artists that I discovered where I really stood. It was a very strong, very powerful feeling to be the director. I loved working with the lights and the singer/actors," she says with enthusiasm.

Abandoning pop music, Loeb immersed herself in theater and the performing arts. "In 1993, I directed *Michel Hermon Chante Piaf*, my first musical show at the Théâtre des Bouffes du Nord, one of the most beautiful theaters in Paris. We actually brought that work to New York, as well as another of our shows called *Dietrich Hotel*, a tribute to Marlene. I directed quite a few shows, including my play *Shirley* with the last true French theater diva, Judith Magre, who won a Molière (the French Tony award) in 2000 for her performance. That was a very strong moment in my life. People loved the play. Even Yves Saint Laurent came to see it twice, and we got amazing reviews."

In 2007, Caroline finally returned to pop music, releasing the critically lauded album *Crime Parfait* (followed by an expanded edition in 2009). "I had never stopped writing songs," she clarifies, "at first with my old buddy Pierre Grillet, then with other friends or on my own. I recorded demos, sent them to the record companies and met producers, but I was unable to make the right connection. It took me a long time to realize the music business had buried me alive, and the only way out for me would be to be my own producer."

"The truth is I have never stopped working. I am always looking for new ideas, and I'm always interested in meeting people I believe may be good to collaborate with. I love launching new shows and new songs. The paradox is that back in the '80s, I experienced this incredible hit song, and I was on TV and the radio all the time. I did nothing but interviews (which was a lot of fun). Yet I have never worked so much and so well as during these last 20 years. And every year that comes along is a better one," she beams.

Says the chanteuse, "I hope I will be remembered not only for 'C'est la ouate,' but as a woman and an artist who fought to be different and struggled to be as sincere as possible with her work and her life. As a Dorothy Parker fan, I loved her epitaphs, and I think I have found mine. Perhaps everyone thinks it will be 'c'est plus la ouate.' I think 'a giant step for me; a small one for mankind' is much better. At least, it makes me laugh!"

Paul Mazzolini
aka Gazebo
"I Like Chopin" (1983)
Italy

"I remember when the single 'Masterpiece' came out, and I was so proud," says Paul Mazzolini, known best throughout Europe by his stage name Gazebo. "'Wow, I have my own record!' I thought. And that was my satisfaction—the achievement of creating a record. I didn't worry about whether anyone would like it or buy it or if would hit the charts. I only thought, 'This is *my* record!' I put it on a record player, and I listened to it, and I loved it. My approach to life has always been as simple as that."

Had he done nothing else, the singer and songwriter of "Masterpiece," one of the very first songs to typify the Italo-disco sound in 1982, might well have been regarded as one of the great pioneers of European dance-pop of the era. But Paul surpassed that milestone when he delivered the gargantuan classic "I Like Chopin" the following year, which reportedly has sold over eight million copies. Mazzolini remains among the most celebrated of Europe's musical innovators from the '80s. From his home in Rome, the artist—still handsome, soft-spoken and decidedly relaxed with his remarkable history—candidly discusses his multi-decade journey in popular Italian music and the priorities that have kept him grounded.

"I was born in Lebanon, and my father was a diplomat from Italy," Mazzolini recounts. "He was shifted around quite a bit, so I was placed in various English or international schools. So that's how I learned the English language. When I was 10 or so, I started playing guitar while attending a school in Denmark. I was discovering Simon & Garfunkel and Bob Dylan, and the guitar was my first introduction to music. I remember there was a German girl in my class, you know—a pretty blonde girl—and I tried to impress her with my guitar playing. It didn't work," he laughs, "but my interest in the instrument remained, and I continued to learn songs. Eventually I started writing my own stuff. In the '70s, I started studying it a bit more seriously and became a big fan of progressive music that blended jazz and classical. I started taking more lessons in that vein. I was really interested in groups like Yes and Genesis.

"As I got a bit older, I started my first bands. By the end of the '70s, I moved to London, and that's where music was changing a lot. Punk had come and gone, and the first electronic instruments were starting to emerge. From this scene, bands like Ultravox and Human League began. They were being referred to as 'new wave' bands and artists, and I was very much into it. There was a lot of energy in the music, but at the same time, it had that classical background. It was an intelligent use of synthesizers, good harmonies and melodies.

"When I returned to Rome in 1981, I reconnected with my fellow musician friends like Pierluigi Giombini, who became my producer," he continues. "He had started doing a form of Italian disco music, sort of a derivation of the American disco sound—like Chic and groups like that. We started blending our mutual experiences—on the one side, the dance thing, and the other, the new wave/electronic approach. That's where my first

Left: **Handsome and charismatically voiced, Gazebo (Paul Mazzolini) also composed the lyrics to many of his worldwide hits in the '80s.** *Right:* **Mazzolini today.**

song, 'Masterpiece,' came from. 'Masterpiece' had this perfect blend of a simple dance beat, minor chords that were very romantic, synthesizers and thoughtful lyrics. I really tried to give the song meaning with my words because I never really liked generic lyrics that simply sound like they fit just so people could dance to it. Even if it was a dance track, if you could put something poetic and a bit deeper in there, people could dance *and* think *and* feel hooked. That comes from my progressive music background. I loved the lyrics of Peter Gabriel and artists like that.

"My producer had a melody that became the foundation of 'Masterpiece,'" Paul continues. "He had the verse, but no chorus. I knew we needed an explosive chorus, and that's how we'd work together to create songs like this. When I wrote the lyrics to 'Masterpiece,' I was thinking of Gloria Swanson and *Sunset Boulevard*. The whole song is about an actress who doesn't accept the idea of aging and her 'masterpiece' was to have a big party in her Hollywood villa and commit suicide in front of her guests. It would be her ultimate performance. In the film, it's William Holden telling the story, but in 'Masterpiece,' I am in the role of a gigolo telling the tale.

"'Masterpiece' was released in May of 1982—it's hard to believe the song is 35 years old already. We recorded it on a 16-track machine, and two of those tracks were broken. So it was basically a 14-track machine. The song was really just a small experiment. No major label wanted to release it, so we got a wholesaler to release the song on a white label 12-inch vinyl single. In a week's time, it blew up. The club DJs loved it right away. Our wholesaler agreement led to a commercial 12-inch single, and then Baby Records' [founder] Freddy Naggiar showed an interest in it. Baby was a very small but dynamic label with Freddy giving the orders to a team of about 10 powerful ladies executing his directives. It was amazing because he was working against the major companies who had hundreds of people on staff.

"When we decided to try and release the song, we knew that Italian DJs and the radio people were very provincial. In other words, there was a prejudice among them that an Italian production, especially sung in English, was probably going to sound cheap and like B-material. A-stuff was American and British—that was the cool music, and that was the attitude at the time. We were afraid they wouldn't give the song a chance if they saw an Italian artist's name on it. We decided to pick a stage name that would allow us to bypass that problem. I thought of that word 'gazebo,' which I took from the lyrics, and [the co-producer of 'Masterpiece,' Paul Micioni] said, 'Oh yeah, that sounds perfect!' So the white label ended up reading 'Gazebo—Masterpiece.' The DJs didn't realize it was an Italian production, and this was the key to our success. We were not the only ones in the business who had to use this ploy. Ironically, in the years that followed, Italy became *the* source for great dance music, and many German productions were made in such a way as to sound like Italian records."

"Masterpiece" narrowly missed hitting the top spot on the Italian pop charts, and its impact was felt strongly on the Swiss and German surveys. Paul credits the gay community for helping to generate initial interest in his stellar debut. "'Masterpiece' got to be number one on the gay dance charts in England and stayed on their chart for almost an entire year," he says. "I think the people of the gay community were the first to really respond to the song, and I think they connected to the poetic aspects of the track. You had to be sensitive to get the subtleties of songs like 'Masterpiece,' and I was very proud that gay men and women related to it. I remember that the first club in Rome to play the song was called Easy Going, which was like a small, gay Studio 54. It was in a basement, but everybody knew about this club. The DJ there, Marco Trani [1960–2013], was one of the first to break the song. He invited me to go to the club and hear him play it. I went, and the funny thing was he'd play the song at a slower speed. There were tons of beautiful models there (they wouldn't get bothered when they went to the gay clubs) and tons of guys freaking out to the song, which sounded a bit like it was playing in slow motion. I was overwhelmed by the experience. I owe so much to the gay community. Without them, I'm not sure my career would have taken off the way it did."

Mazzolini helped create another song that thoroughly enchanted Europe, though it didn't fall under the Gazebo umbrella. Says the artist, "I had a great exchange of inputs with my producer [Giombini] during those days. We started working with a label called Discomagic run by Severo Lombardoni and gave him a track called 'Dolce Vita.' 'Dolce Vita' has a bit of a history. I had the idea for the lyrics of 'Dolce Vita' based on the films of Fellini and the Italian movie classics. He liked the idea of that concept, and from that, he created the bass line that the song became famous for. At some point the song was taken to Freddy in Milan, but he didn't like 'Dolce Vita' at all.

"We thought it was a pity to not use the song," he continues. "I was sorry our version wasn't going to get out there, but why not let another artist try? Giombini felt Ryan Paris was tall and good-looking, the girls would love him, and he supposedly spoke perfect English—so he was our man. We went to the studio, and he was good-looking, but I can't say his English was exactly perfect. I helped Ryan with his pronunciation. But the amazing thing about the whole production was that it was sung, recorded and mixed in maybe a day and a half. It was done so quickly. I remember the track was sold to Discomagic within one day. That song became this label's first major hit. It marked the label's transformation from just a wholesaler to a wholesaler/record company, specializing in Italian dance product."

Paris' version went on to become a mammoth hit across Europe. But soon the spotlight fell back on Gazebo. "At the end of the demo tape we made for my first album was a track with a piano, a small drum machine and the vocals on top, which was 'I Like Chopin,'" Paul remembers. "It was lovely, but I wasn't thinking of it as a dance track. I thought of it more as maybe a crossover ballad type of thing. I thought it was very melodic—maybe even too melodic. Freddy, however, fell in love with it. He said we must go to the studio and develop the song further. We started working on it, and Giombini kind of fashioned it as an orchestral ballad. Naggiar hated that version, and he gave us a record by producer Bobby Orlando, who was working with the Pet Shop Boys and The Flirts at that time, to give us an idea of what he wanted. We figured out what he was really looking for was that electronic sequencer sound. But we thought that would be cheesy and mechanical. Instead, there was a delay on our mixer, and it gave the song this unique sound. We thought, 'That's it. We've got it.' We finished the track. Freddy loved it, and Baby released it."

"I Like Chopin" was a triumph for Mazzolini. Soft and elegant, the song managed to fit within the beat-conscious parameters of Italo-disco and became a monster hit. Its eloquent, almost perplexing lyrics, fused with the singer's hypnotic voice in a haunting melody, resulted in a track that was greeted with tremendous favor in Germany, Austria, Spain and Switzerland, where the song reached pop chart summits. Numerous other countries embraced the single (even as far away as Japan), and several artists, anxious to benefit from Gazebo's momentum, recorded cover versions. In Italy, Gazebo's "Chopin" earned high marks for being one of the biggest songs of the entire year. His successful *Gazebo* album was released, which also featured the popular track "Lunatic."

Paul recalls the interesting dynamics of the year's summer season, in which he and Ryan Paris virtually ruled Europe. "I remember when 'I Like Chopin' was first becoming a hit in Italy. It was up there on the chart in May or June of 1983. 'Vamos a la Playa' by Righeira and 'Chopin' were the two biggest hits of that summer. 'Dolce Vita' was a big hit in Spain. The German people would usually go on summer holiday in Italy, and the British would go to Spain. By September, 'I Like Chopin' went to number one in Germany because they all came back from holiday and wanted the record. The same thing happened in the UK, where all the English wanted 'Dolce Vita.' 'I Like Chopin' didn't make it in England, however. It was released very poorly there, and they didn't promote it properly. I don't think it even hit their pop chart. Meanwhile, 'Chopin' was a huge hit in Germany and scored better there than even 'Dolce Vita.' Each song covered different territories, it seemed, and both appealed to a huge cross-section of people.

"It was an amazing feeling, this massive success," he adds. "I put so much heart into this song, but we didn't think everybody would understand it. So when I saw what a big hit it was, I was completely thrilled. It was number one in so many countries, and I started getting awards like the top European chart act award by *Music Week*, an important English music publication. We were doing better than Culture Club and The Police—and you can't really explain or describe that kind of intensity. Although we did a video for the song, it was before music videos had really become established, and so therefore it was actually hard to reach the level of success we achieved. You had to physically go from country to country to do TV and radio promotion." The video for "I Like Chopin" was directed by

David Rose and was shot in 16mm in the UK. Various Internet postings of the video and track have received millions of hits.

The songwriter and singer says that while the international impact of "I Like Chopin" was extremely gratifying, its success could not have been predicted. "You can't really worry about where a song might be a hit," he insists. "When you write it, you just try to make it the best you can—as beautifully as possible. With my lyrics on 'Chopin,' they were very cryptic—it wasn't like a typical vertical story. At the time, I was also attending a university and studying literature. I was very much into eighteenth century French literature. My idea was to give an impressionist's view of my thoughts—so my lyrics didn't always make sense in terms of good English phrasing. I wanted people to have artists like Renoir in mind when they heard the song, but of course that's too much to expect for a pop hit, especially a dance song. I just tried to go a little deeper and make people go behind the face value of the song. The musical part of the song is also quite articulate and complex. There's a lot going on that you don't catch unless you hear it several times. Even in the video, we left our meaning a bit ambiguous. That was our whole goal—something more than just a simple pop song."

Inevitably, expectations were high for Mazzolini's next endeavor. "I was promoting the first album for almost two years," the artist says. "It was amazing, but at the same time it didn't allow me to work on the tracks for a new follow-up album the way I wanted to. I also couldn't do as many live concerts as I wanted to. The success I was having was keeping me a bit out of the world in a way. Baby Records wanted a new album—*fast*. It ended up being *Telephone Mama*. Pierluigi started working on it with a bit more of that 'big producer' kind of attitude. I was in the studio working on it one day, and then I'd be out for a week promoting the first album somewhere else.

"I did like the lyrics I ended up creating for the set. I had my own idea of writing material by this point. I had to fight a bit for that—I got one song I wrote and composed on the first album. But I wanted to contribute more of my own material to my projects. I liked some of the songs on *Telephone Mama*, but because we had done so well with 'I Like Chopin,' I felt we should have rested a bit before tackling a new album. I didn't think we needed to rush out a new set right away. I wanted to think about the songs and maybe work with others on the production—maybe Trevor Horn or somebody with a different style. By 1984, there were millions of songs out in the Italian disco style we had forged. I felt we had to get out of our little Roman fish bowl. Rome was not Milan. Milan was very much high speed, and Rome was much slower. I tried to talk to Naggiar, but he felt my producer and I were still a good team, and he didn't want to change the formula.

"*Telephone Mama* came out, and it was basically a flop," he concedes. "The single did very well in Italy [where it reached the Top 10], but people didn't understand it in other countries. Most of the soft and romantic style we had before was replaced with a harsher sound. The 'Telephone Mama' song was about a Russian spy, and all the songs on the set were linked together. I tried to go with the whole concept thing, but it just didn't work. Around this time, I had to serve in the army. I had postponed it with my schooling at the university. Service was mandatory, and so I had to go. I have to say, I felt abandoned when I did that. Naggiar was working on new acts. I think he felt I was always talking about our projects too much in terms of art and quality. So, while I was away, he developed a new production team, hired a model to be the front man for another project concept he was working on, and hired a singer to make those recordings—someone who wouldn't ask too many questions, argue or make suggestions." [*Author note: Mr. Mazzolini is probably referring to the Den Harrow project gaining popularity at the time.*]

Upon his return from the military, the *Univision* LP was made in 1986 and marked Gazebo's final project working with Baby Records and Giombini. Despite Mazzolini's insightful lyrics and strong vocals, the album had difficulty finding an audience.

"When I came back from the service, I reconnected with my producer, and we came up with a few good songs for the album like 'Sun Goes Down on Milky Way' and 'Trotsky Burger.' But afterward, I insisted that I wanted to work on some of my own compositions too—and that's where the friction started. It was just a lot of arguments all the time, and it wasn't fostering creativity any more. With the money I had earned, I bought a home (where I still live today) and built a recording studio in it. I learned how to be an arranger and a producer. For my first album on my own, *The Rainbow Tales* (1988), I called Denis Haines, a lovely person from the UK, who had been a keyboard player with Gary Numan [of the hit "Cars"]. I loved the songs we did for that project, like 'God Bless the Moonshade' and 'Tycoon.' All of the sudden, I discovered the joy of making music again with someone who would smile at you and just be nice again. Honestly, it was paradise.

"When I realized I could do things on my own, working with pleasant people—even if the songs weren't quite as popular or as commercially successful as my previous work—I was happy," Paul admits. "And I never went back to the old way of doing things. I think it just made sense to do my music on my own."

Gazebo continued to hone his craft, releasing more albums and singles through the remainder of the '80s and '90s and into the twenty-first century. His projects were often critically lauded and vigorously supported by his sizeable and loyal fan base. In 1997, the artist formed his own record label, Softworks. He released singles that were immensely popular on the underground circuit, including "Tears for Galileo" in 2006 and the infectious dance hit "Ladies!" in 2007, a highly astute commentary on the times. In 2011, the artist unveiled the electronic dance single "Queen of Burlesque" and the album *Reset* in 2015, which featured the single "Blindness."

Paul says he is comfortable with the road he has taken, the highs and lows of commercial success, and the inevitable changes that have come with life. "I know it's hard to believe," he offers, "but I never really felt I *had* to have a million-selling song or album. I never thought that way. If I had, I wouldn't have done, for example, the *Telephone Mama* LP. We knew that LP was a risk and totally different from the sound we had created with 'I Like Chopin.' Everyone was doing our original sound, and we didn't want to copy ourselves on that album. It was a gamble. Our idea of going in a new direction was courageous and correct, but we made the mistake of going down the wrong path too quickly. And it worsened because of ego problems and conflicts.

"I am a very easy person. When I was a teenager, I used to go around with a guitar and a rug sack and sleep in the train stations and go to the rock festivals. I have always thought what was beautiful in life was *life itself*—not the luxuries and money. I put all my money in the bank at the height of my success because I had no idea what to do with it. I can say this—money makes your bed softer, you're gonna drink a better wine and you're gonna drive a better car. I always liked fast cars, so I admit I treated myself to a Porsche. But I never got to drive it because I was working all the time. It sat in the garage. In the end, none of that was important. I really came to realize that when I had my children in the late '80s. I knew then that *this* was what life was all about—loving family, friends, moving things forward. The rest is bullshit.

"When I did *The Syndrone* LP in 2008, I did what I wanted to do. It was made almost 17 years after the last album I had done. I didn't worry about what the market was like or how things had changed. That is my approach to life and my work. Releasing music today is like living on a different planet. The fact that there really aren't any more physical sales— no CD and vinyl for the most part—is very weird. For those of us who grew up buying records, looking at the jacket, reading the liner notes, and putting the vinyl on the turntable, today's digital world is sometimes very unsatisfying. But for young people, they were born with iPods and MP3 files. I think they are missing out on something—the magic and affection you can feel for a physical record.

"Many of my fans will keep those records I put out in the '80s for the rest of their lives. Those records belong to their youth, and they are a part of their lives. The music is going to bring you memories, but the object itself adds another dimension. I feel sorry for the young guys. They are missing that. And I know people may argue this, but the music today, generally, is very artificial, over-sampled, computer-based and overly compressed—which is something I *hate*. It has no dynamics. In order to make the music loud enough for today's technology, they reprocess the music to add power to it. It kills the low parts, the small details of the music. Music is made of sound, but it's also made of silence, and all that is lost. With technology, singers are also so perfectly in tune now—on their recordings—not when they have to sing live!" he laughs.

The artist continues to look ahead, contemplating his next creative move. He observes, "My children are gone now, and the nest is empty. So it's just me and the studio in my house. I find plenty of motivation there. I go inside it, and I go into my own little musical world. I always have a new goal—like doing a new album. I don't know if 10, 100 or a 1,000 people will buy it, but I want to do it. It's always about moving forward—taking steps in your life. You don't want to look back at your life and say you haven't done anything since the '80s. That would be terrible.

"When I do shows today," Paul concludes, "I try to look in the faces of the fans. They all sing with me, especially on 'I Like Chopin.' I can see they are moved and that the song means so much to them. It's like it belongs to them. That's the great legacy of songs like this—when you have a successful hit, the song then belongs to the people, not the writers."

Liz Mitchell

Boney M.

"Boney M. Megamix" (1988)
UK

"My personal feeling for music, obviously, is *love*. It does good things for me, and I hope the music we did as Boney M. has done good things for those who have heard it," humbly offers Liz Mitchell. She need not worry. As the lead vocalist of one of Europe's most beloved pop groups and the voice behind the megahits "Rivers of Babylon," "Mary's Boy Child," "Brown Girl in the Ring," "Sunny" and many more, Liz brought joy to countless millions across the globe. From her start with producer Frank Farian's ensemble in 1976 until their break-up late in the 1980s, Mitchell's distinctive and spirited vocal quality, rooted in her Jamaican heritage and forged with a powerful sense of faith, became synonymous with the Boney M. sound. An integral player in the formation's sometimes complicated history, she has continued to perform the group's music right through to the present day. From her home in England, the venerable singer warmly remembers her illustrious career in one of dance-pop music's most revered major league acts.

"I grew up in Jamaica until the age of 12," she remembers. "We listened to gospel music and reggae music—they had so many different names for that style of music at that time. When I came to England as a young girl, I was, of course, influenced by the popular music that I heard played on the radio. I listened to a lot of the music coming out of America that was being played on British radio. Many wonderful artists influenced me, but at that age, I didn't know I was going to have a career in music. That idea wasn't in my head yet.

"Later, after attending technical college and working as a secretary, I came to Germany in the '70s and auditioned for a leading role in the Berlin musical *Hair*, understudying the role once held by Donna Summer in the cast. From there, I became part of a gospel choir called The Les Humphries Singers. I met producer Frank Farian, and when he discovered I was a member of The Les Humphries Singers, who were a very famous group in Germany at that time, he became very interested in me. He suggested I try working with him for a year. On the night of the show (when he and his wife saw me perform) when he first spoke with me, I felt that he liked my image. He gave me a compliment and said that I was very 'clean looking,'" Liz laughs. "I didn't understand that comment at the time, but I believe now he meant that he was appreciating my background from the church and such. He invited me to his studio, and I sang 'Sunny.' He and his team liked the way I delivered it, and they decided to go ahead with the first Boney M. album."

Left: A 1980 publicity photo captures the exotic energy of Boney M. as they perform one of their many dance-pop chart hits on a television soundstage. Left to right are Liz Mitchell, Maizie Williams, Bobby Farrell and Marcia Barrett. *Right:* Liz Mitchell poses today.

Visionary producer, songwriter and vocalist Frank Farian launched Boney M. in 1976 (with Liz, Marcia Barrett, Maizie Williams and Bobby Farrell as its official core line-up) on Germany's Hansa International label. This announcement came following the release of a single credited to Boney M. called "Do You Do You Wanna Bump," which contained only Farian's vocals. Boney M.'s debut album, *Take the Heat Off Me,* was commercially stagnant for a time until two of the set's disco-charged tracks eventually caught Europe's attention in a very big way. "Daddy Cool" and "Sunny," featuring powerful vocal work by Mitchell and some scintillating bass lines, topped the charts in Germany and several other countries. They also reached the Top 10 in the lucrative British market. "Ma Baker" and "Belfast" were major successes in 1977. In the years that followed, Boney M. racked up numerous hits that made them seemingly permanent residents of the international pop and disco charts.

In 1978, the ensemble reached a milestone with the double A-side single "Rivers of Babylon/Brown Girl in the Ring," which, like so many of the group's hits, featured Mitchell's distinctive Caribbean-flavored vocal charm at the forefront. It became one of the biggest selling singles of all time in Britain, reaching number one throughout Europe and scoring a Top 30 position on the U.S. pop chart. The song "Mary's Boy Child" nearly duplicated the feat. Fiery dance tracks like "Rasputin" and "Hooray! Hooray! It's a Holi-Holiday" solidified Boney M.'s standing as one of the most important international pop groups of the decade and Farian as a master producer and composer.

"It wasn't difficult to go in the studio and get the sound right," Mitchell recalls. "I guess the debut Boney M. album was the most challenging because that was the album where my personality and Frank's ideas had to come together for the first time. Marcia was with me, and I think the toughest part of the whole process was deciding who would be the lead singer on various tracks. She wanted to be 'found' as a singer, just as every artist does. Frank allowed us both to literally sing all the songs as lead vocalists, and then he and his team chose the ones that sounded closest to what he envisioned. My vocals were determined to be the best match. It was a fair process. Frank had brought Bobby into the studio to try to sing 'Ma Baker.' I think his problem was pitch, and they realized he was not going to be able to do it. It ended up that it was me, Marcia and Frank that handled Boney M. vocally.

"Frank was the ultimate producer—he really knew what he was doing," Liz adds without hesitation. "He recognized my abilities as a singer. He allowed me to express myself the way I could best do that as an artist, and he appreciated me for who I was and what I could do. I think that was the vocal presence I brought to the music. I believe very much in God, and I didn't sing any of those songs without my bible next to me. I know that sounds whacked to a lot of people. But for me, it was confirmation that the word and the spirit were with me, and I went in with that belief. I think my belief came through in my voice, even though I have a unique sound. I think I was able to convey spiritual warmth that helped a lot of people over the years. So Frank allowed the direction I wanted to take to resonate. He allowed me to project my God, rather than criticize me for it. As a producer, he could have been negative towards that because he was not a follower. But he didn't interfere with the way I was. Never a negative word about where I took my strength.

"I found my faith when I was younger during a period of severe difficulties. I hadn't been able to find myself, and my mother told me to try very hard to search for God. When I tried to communicate with God, I found He really was answering me. You know, everything we want in life is not always good for us, so the answers we get may not match what we seek. We have to remember that. I think faith gave me the courage later in life that I did not have when I was young. And I think it's that courage that gives you the ability to choose what is good for you and what is not. I learned in my faith walk that I'd be no good to anyone unless I was good to myself."

The singer admits the racy images seen on Boney M. album jackets, the spicy costuming of its members, and the free-spirited atmosphere of the clubs in which they performed were elements of her experience that initially posed a few issues. "I did take my bible in the clubs with me," Mitchell recalls. "I think people thought I was crazy, yeah. But I felt comfortable knowing God was with me wherever I went. I struggled with some of the photographs we took, but I think back on that now, and I think many of them turned out to be very artistic rather than vulgar. Even the photographers didn't want to offend my values, beliefs or my family. So in the end, even though the pictures might be viewed as raunchy, they actually were very clean."

Mitchell reflects on her professional relationship with her producer. "When I first started working with Frank—I've said it before, and I'll say it again—I thought he was a very kind human being. I'm a very sensitive person, and I would not have been able to work with him if he was aggressive or insensitive. He observed me very carefully and worked with me very well. I think he worked well with most of the artists who made music with him. I think that the area that some people found uncomfortable with him was his need to also be an artist. He did put himself [as a vocalist] on most of the records he made with many of his artists. I think his voice is there somewhere on the records of just about everyone he produced. I don't know—that may have been viewed as intrusive by not allowing the artists to shine properly. I think that may have been one area of difficulty.

"I think another area people might have noticed, and I actually did, was that where the business was concerned, there wasn't enough care taken for the artist. All of us who worked with Boney M. didn't have personal managers. His office did everything. Truly, I think his office was managing Frank Farian, and Frank was managing us—you know, Boney

M. and all his other groups. I don't think Frank had the people [on the business side] who cared enough, and in turn, that reflected on him," Liz opines.

While the group basked in the love of millions, Boney M. also experienced their share of public controversy. When it was widely reported that group members Bobby Farrell and Maizie Williams hadn't contributed vocals to the group's hit recordings, the practice of lip-synching came into the spotlight and was labeled by some as deceptive. Farian encountered the same situation years later, though on a much grander scale with his mega-group Milli Vanilli. "When I met Frank early on, he wasn't presenting himself as a man who wanted to produce an artist," Liz explains. "He wanted to be an artist too. After all, he was the artist singing on the 'Do You Do You Wanna Bump' single. I understood right then that he would be on the records. But I didn't realize then that he wasn't going to actually perform [on stage]. That was the trick—where things became complicated. He wanted to sing and be on these records, but he never wanted to perform. So somebody had to mimic his voice. This was a problem for some groups who didn't know what to do with his voice on the track when they had to perform their songs. On Boney M.'s records, Bobby Farrell was literally hired to mime Frank's voice—that was his job. I don't know why Frank didn't want to perform. That was never clear to me. But in the interviews I've seen where he discussed it, it seems as if he did not feel his image was right for being out on stage.

"The problem that happened with Bobby and Maizie was one of the things that wasn't good for Boney M., or even for me," observes Liz. "The fact that Bobby and Maizie were miming pushed all the good work that I did to the side and created shocking conversation. This controversy became the topic of conversation, rather than the fact that 'Rivers of Babylon' and 'Brown Girl in the Ring' were two of the biggest selling records of all time. And these records had nothing to do with Frank's voice—his voice was not on them. It's not like his voice was on *all* of our records. People starting focusing on the negative, instead of looking at the real power of Boney M., which was the fact that we had sold millions of records."

The Farrell-Williams controversy (which was further exacerbated by Bobby's eventual departure from the ensemble) triggered a great deal of gossip about Boney M. as the '80s began, and the era marked a significant reversal of fortune for the group, says Mitchell. Boney M.'s albums, such as *Boonoonoonoos* in 1981 and *10,000 Lightyears* in 1984, fared somewhat modestly in comparison to their previous efforts. However, the group scored a number of top pop hits (though largely confined to Germany and nearby countries) as the decade progressed, including a remake of Tony Esposito's dance gem "Kalimba de Luna" and the euphoric "Happy Song" (a Spagna composition that momentarily returned Farrell's name to the fold, at least on record jackets). The group also had some modest success with their version of the Stevie Wonder evergreen, "My Chérie Amour." Another track, "Young, Free and Single" (once again featuring Farrell's name on the record jacket), was issued as a single without much fanfare, as their hits of the period were gathered together for the 1985 album *Eye Dance*. The set did not have major commercial impact, and Farian was reported to have become fatigued with the Boney M. project.

"Pop music in general took a turn in Europe at this point as punk and new wave emerged beginning in the early '80s," Liz says. "We had to decide whether to blend or not to blend. This was a difficult period for Frank, because arguments between he and Bobby had taken their toll. Bobby was no longer a part of the group—he was gone by 1982 and replaced by Reggie Tsiboe. Though Reggie had vocal ability, he didn't have the same charisma as Bobby. Our market had been greatly reduced. Frank found it difficult to work with Reggie, and so he backed off the group by 1986.

"Prior to the *10,000 Lightyears* and *Eye Dance* albums, our music traveled the whole world. But when Reggie came, people did not recognize him as Boney M. The singles we did in the mid–'80s were a success mostly with diehard fans, but we didn't cross over to all the countries in which we had charted in the past. I remember a DJ on the radio saying 'Who is this?' after playing one of our new songs, and the general consensus was that Boney M. didn't sound the way it should. We were missing that 'Daddy Cool' sound. I guess Frank was hearing the same critiques, and I think he might have been disappointed by what was happening.

"I think we had the German market at that point because the record company could force promotion there. But in countries where they couldn't see us as easily, like Russia and places where they didn't have as much access to television, if they couldn't hear that traditional Boney M. sound, they wouldn't accept the record. Frank was the one who decided we wouldn't do any more recording. He felt we were at the stage where if we came out with another record, it was going to sell even less. We didn't leave the scene entirely, however. By 1987, Bobby, Marcia and Maizie wanted to get back to work, and we started performing together again as Boney M. again for a while."

In 1988, Boney M. resurfaced on the charts with a hugely popular megamix culled together by Pete Hammond and Alan Coulthard, working in conjunction with Britain's PWL Studios. The track was a great success and paved the way for the *Greatest Hits of All Times—Remix '88* album. Liz was invited by Farian and Simon Cowell to participate in 1992's "Boney M. Mega Mix," yet another updated medley that saw significant pop chart action in the UK. ("At that point, I told them it would always have to be 'Boney M. featuring Liz Mitchell,' and they agreed," notes the singer.) Throughout the '90s, Boney M. was an on-again-off-again project that spawned periodic singles like "Papa Chico" (another Tony Esposito track remake) in 1994. Members of the group were able to spin off their own touring versions of Boney M., and Boney M. featuring Liz Mitchell has been one of the most successful. Mitchell released solo albums as well, including the set *No One Will Force You*, which featured several tracks written by the artist.

"Destiny has a way of placing us in life, so I have never been one to argue with God," Mitchell assures. "The road that He gave to me was to be a part of Boney M. I've always said that Bobby, Marcia, Maizie and myself were four pillars. My pillar was imbedded very deeply in the soil, and I'm still standing and still working. That's how I look at it. I never worried about having a solo career when I was with Boney M. If God had wanted that for me, he would have made a path for me. I have made solo records since those days, and they have all been dedicated to my faith. The people who should receive those recordings in their lives have, and those that still need to will discover them. I'm very happy with the journey I've taken, and I'm still standing," she says smiling.

"The fans have always been integral to the success of Boney M.," she offers, thinking about the group's huge following. "It was the most amazing thing to observe. No matter what nationality our fans were, even in the most reserved of countries or those that were out of the way—wherever we went, my husband and I were always stunned to see their reaction. You'd hear them sing 'Brown Girl in the Ring,' and it would be amazing. People who love the music of Boney M. across the world have the same response. It must be one source of energy that everyone is connecting to.

"There were so many places we played and performances that were just simply wonderful. If I began to list them, you'd see how overwhelming it was. Like performing for the Queen of England. That was exceptional, and the evening was incredible. Then we were in Russia, and we were the first Western European group ever to go there in 1978. President Brezhnev sent a plane to London to pick us up. They were amazing people, and the Russians remember that performance even to this day. We went to the Middle East, which was a delicate place at that time, but we were well-received and warmly welcomed. We had to walk around in the black robes during the day, but at night on stage we wore our crazy costumes, and the people were just so appreciative of our music. South America—the same. Everywhere we've been, the shows and audiences and love have all been amazing."

On a less positive note, Mitchell believes the issue of race discrimination may have crept into the dynamics of her career in Boney M., at least on some occasions. "Well, I have to admit that there were times where especially Marcia and I felt we were ignored," she says. "For instance, I often wonder if we had not been women of color when the Bobby and Maizie situation started, might we have been heard more and had a chance to explain our roles and feelings about the situation—to be who we really were? It's hard to say for sure [that the reason we were not heard was] because we were women of color. The question was never with the audience. The audiences were always 100 percent supportive. Our problems always came with those who were making the behind-the-scenes decisions. In making those decisions, I believe a lot of them may have been made with the memory that we were black, rather than just women and artists who worked hard."

Bobby Farrell passed away unexpectedly on a December morning in 2010 in his hotel room, following a performance in Russia. "I was actually quite devastated when Bobby died," sighs Liz. "It was quite sudden. I guess in the back of my mind I always thought we would get together again at some celebration, party or something. I felt so hurt by his death—as if I was robbed. It was very painful to go through his passing. I wish we had been able to get the healing we all deserved from the difficult days we experienced in Boney M. But there was no psychologist around to help us back then. We all ended up having to deal with our problems ourselves. It wasn't a normal thing that Bobby and all of us went through. We were just normal people, young and loving music. We were catapulted into fame, and success can be quite detrimental, even though it should be a good thing. I suppose the people in Frank Farian's management office were young too, and I suppose they didn't know what we needed. So they were of no help to us."

Liz sums up life today by saying simply, "I'm doing pretty good!" For certain, she isn't spending much time dwelling on the negative aspects of aging. "I still enjoy performing today and doing Boney M. songs. It is helping to keep the music I am responsible for alive. So when I perform today, it's Liz Mitchell, and people know that. And they know I carry the music of Boney M. with me.

"There are so many things I'd like people to think about when they think of Boney M. and myself," she says most genuinely. "I know that the most important thing in life is your legacy—your name. If you live right, then people can only have positive things to say about you. I am trusting that people will recognize the positive energy that we tried to give to people as Boney M. Maybe that energy will still be just as strong and uplifting 100 years from now!"

Fab Morvan

Milli Vanilli
"Girl You Know It's True" (1988)
Germany

"There are so many important details of the story that many people still do not know. But for me, the whole ordeal, the whole epic saga, taught me to follow my instincts, to believe in my dreams and to never ever stop moving forward," states Fab Morvan. He's speaking of his incredible trek through the international pop music universe in the late '80s and early '90s and the tremendously challenging circumstances that befell him during that time. Today, he is a singer, songwriter, painter and DJ. Nearly 25 years ago, he and musical partner Rob Pilatus were youthful, charasmatic performers who suddenly found themselves at the center of a scandal that rocked the music industry worldwide.

Fronting the dance-pop group known as Milli Vanilli, the creation of German record producer Frank Farian, the duo became megastars following a series of number one hits. Infectious songs like "Girl You Know It's True," "Blame It on the Rain," "Baby Don't Forget My Number" and "Girl I'm Gonna Miss You" topped the charts of North and South America, Asia and Europe. Their albums sold multi-millions across the globe. So impactful was their success that the pair won a Grammy award for Best New Group in 1990 and a Juno award for international album of the year. They were the recipients of three American Music Awards (favorite pop/rock single for "Girl You Know It's True," favorite pop/rock new artist and favorite soul/R&B artist). With exotic looks, skillful dance moves and sexy washboard abs, Milli Vanilli appeared to be unstoppable. There was just one fly in the ointment—Rob and Fab were not the true vocalists of their record hits.

When the news was revealed, a media backlash and storm of negative attention engulfed the two, whose careers suddenly vanished overnight. The severity of the aftermath appears to have been especially troubling for Rob, who faced brushes with the law and dismal work prospects. Following what some speculators believe may have been a prescription drug overdose, his life came to an end in 1998. Though the precise cause of his death remains undetermined, the Milli Vanilli saga ultimately became part of Pilatus' epitaph.

Morvan took a much different path. He managed to survive the drama and through perseverance found a life that he now describes as rich with creativity and positivity. In a clear, articulate and gentle voice, Fab relates his impressions of the challenging journey he has taken. He never becomes agitated during the discussion, and he never appears to be reluctant to speak his mind.

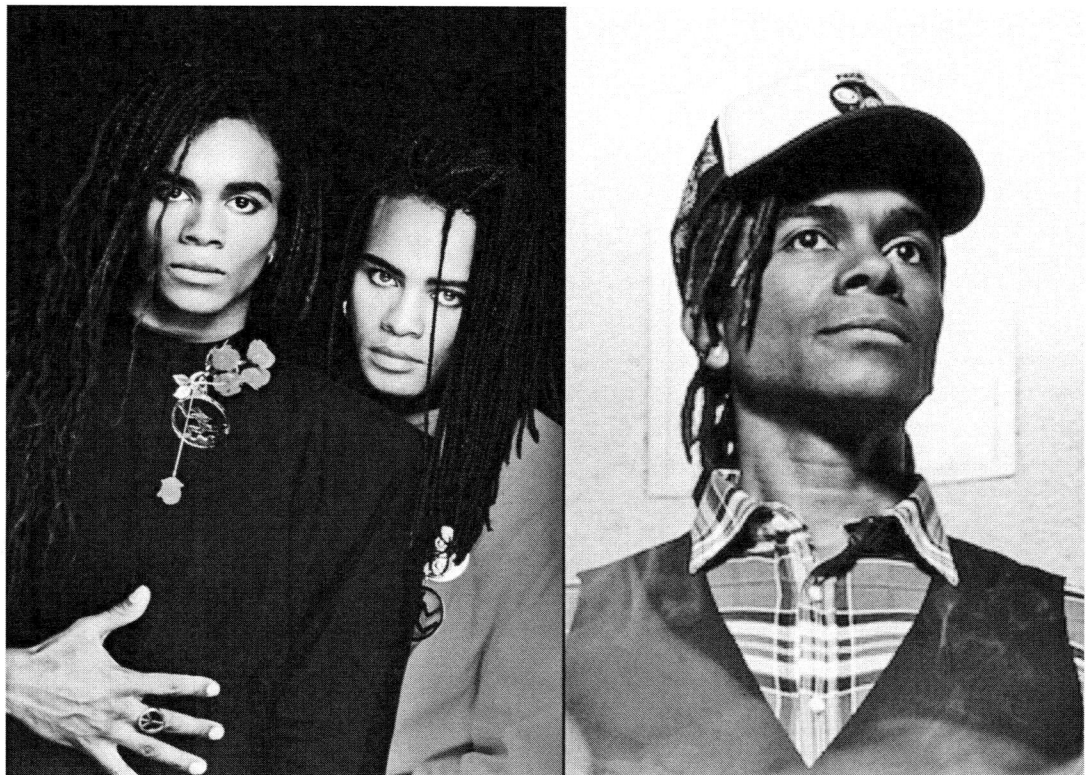

Left: **Milli Vanilli, fronted by Fab Morvan (left) and Rob Pilatus, as depicted by photographer Manfred Esser. The session was for the duo's *All or Nothing* debut album, released in Europe in 1988 (courtesy Manfred Esser).** *Right:* **Mr. Morvan in the twenty-first century.**

"When I was a young boy growing up in France, music always played a big part in my life," Morvan remembers. "Seeing the Jackson 5 and James Brown on TV, music was always something very seductive to me. My grandfather was a musician, though not professional, and I often saw him play on stage. When I watched him, a little light bulb went on in my head, and I thought, 'I would love to do that.' I noticed music made people happy, and it would change the way people behaved. I remember listening to Bob Marley (not really understanding English) and taking a dictionary to try and translate what he was saying. But the feeling I was getting from his music was amazing, even without understanding his words. I remember watching my parents listening to music, and I would see these two adults turn into kids, dancing and enjoying themselves. Music somehow made them look more human to me, rather than just seeing them as parents. It was something I really connected with, and the older I became, the more I realized what a universal language music is—what a positive effect it can have. I think that's where my love relationship with music started for me.

"In my late teens, I left France to try my luck in Germany, and I ended up in Munich, where I connected with Rob. We were singing, playing and performing with a band, and people started hearing about us, little by little. We didn't have any real success yet, but we were recording demos. We were trying to get on the map. Like every young artist, we always hoped we would connect with someone who would be able to open doors for us and maybe change our lives. Some record industry professionals eventually connected with us, and we were brought to producer Frank Farian."

Further back in time, Frank Farian may have had ambitions of becoming a successful solo singer in Germany. He detoured from this path when, instead, he created a highly successful group known as Boney M. Often utilizing his voice for the male vocal parts and incorporating those of other singers (such as Liz Mitchell) on many of Boney M.'s most popular records, the group became a tremendous international sensation. They scored numerous hits throughout the '70s and '80s, but encountered some public relations challenges when it was reported (years before the Milli Vanilli controversy) that Boney M. members Bobby Farrell and Maizie Williams weren't vocalists on the group's hit recordings. The news raised a few eyebrows, but Farian weathered the ruckus and enjoyed continued success with the group and other acts, including Eruption and Far Corporation.

"I didn't know who Mr. Farian was at all," Fab claims, recalling their first meeting. "Rob knew he was a big fish, and I was aware of Boney M. In France, of course Boney M. was big, but I was more into the music of [producer and artist] Cerrone. I was young when I met Frank, I guess about 22, and I didn't really fully get the connection between a producer and his artists or groups. I certainly didn't realize how a producer was often more important in the business than the artist out in front. I didn't understand how they pulled strings and controlled everything.

"When we actually got inside his music factory and saw all the gold records on his wall, of course you were going to believe anything the guy said. So when he told us (metaphorically) how high we had to jump, we were prepared to jump that high. As a young person, you felt the excitement and the power someone like Frank had, and you knew they were going to put you in the passenger seat. You would be part of an incredible ride. We wanted to take that ride. We knew our lives would change; we just weren't sure how, when or where. Or how high we would have to jump. But honestly, you have no clue what you're getting into when you are that young and inexperienced."

It appears as if the plan was to have Rob and Fab front the group Milli Vanilli for promotional and live performances, lip-synching songs the producer had recorded with other vocalists. Says Fab, "We fell into a trap that we just didn't see coming. I've told the story many times—we were young, trying to survive and this producer came along offering us a little advance money. The advance disappeared very quickly, and we came back and asked for more. He gave it to us. It was like pennies to them, but to us it was a lot. We signed a contract; we thought this money was ours—like a paycheck. We weren't thinking they would be demanding that money back. So then we found ourselves in the position of having them tell us we either pay that money back or we do what they were telling us to do. We were up against the wall and thought by doing what they asked of us, we were getting out of the situation. Instead, we were actually getting in deeper and deeper. But we just didn't know it. And no one knew how successful we would become."

The overwhelming public response to Milli Vanilli and the wave of success that overtook the pair was addictive, according to the artist. "Once you taste performing on stage, fans screaming, traveling, and even room service, you're in it," concedes Morvan. "You dial a couple of numbers, and the food comes up. You go out in the morning, leaving your room a mess, and when you come back, it looks like a palace again. You drive in limousines;

people carry your luggage; you're in first class on airplanes; you're a star in the clubs; you're on television. Everybody is a 'yes man.' They tell you what they think you want to hear—'You're the best; you're most beautiful person ever,' etc. Your room is suddenly party central. Once they get you with the lifestyle, they know you'll stay. When you taste life in the fast lane, it's almost impossible to resist it.

"And then there's the drinking. It was becoming difficult to deal with the whole situation; you wanted to numb yourself. And then you start doing drugs to cope with the fact that you know what you are doing isn't cool. You're bound by contracts; you're afraid if you don't do what they tell you to do, you think you'll never work in the industry again. You're caught between two things—stay in or get out. I felt like Dr. Jekyll and Mr. Hyde," he sighs.

Fab describes feeling increasingly stranded as their fame grew. "Rob was the one person who had seen it all with me, starting from the bottom. We did it together. He was the one person who knew how I felt, and I knew how he felt. The musicians who played with us were very cool, but you couldn't share much with them because everything was so hush-hush. It appeared like we were part of this big entourage, but in reality we were alone. If you wanted to confide in someone, you'd always have to think of the consequences. We began secluding and isolating ourselves more and more. We didn't even need to speak [with each other] that much about our situation. We just knew what it was. We knew each other for so long, we just had to look at each other and that was sufficient. We were like brothers and knew what the other was thinking. Instead of speaking, sometimes we actually just let out a sigh as things happened. We were our only support system. We knew we couldn't trust anybody else.

"We had about 75 people on our payroll when we were touring," he adds. "We were the youngest. Imagine—you have adults working for you, and everybody's kissing your butt because you're cutting the checks. And listen, we were young people in a position of power, at least within this group, and I admit sometimes we abused it."

Morvan pauses for a moment and then reflects further on the spiraling series of events that took place. "From the start, we were never cool with the idea [of being the front men]," he contends. "After every great thing or show we did, you'd go back to your room, and reality would set in. 'It's not me. I didn't record those tracks.' That's what I'd hear in my head. When we started achieving this huge success with the first single in Germany ["Girl You Know It's True"], we told them right away we wanted to start singing. But of course it was too late. Their plan was in motion, and there was no turning back. If we had been in Milli Vanilli the way *we* envisioned ourselves, I'm sure we would have been just as successful, but I'm also pretty sure, at that age, we would have gone through the same trials and tribulations. I'm certain we still would have fallen into the whole fast life thing anyway. So many new artists who find success fall into that trap.

"It came to a point where Rob and I decided what we were going to do, at least as far as our lifestyles were concerned," Fab continues. "We were living in America by this time (1990); we were huge and about to go on a world tour. When we finished the tour, we would clean up our act and start living healthier lives. We'd at least fix that much. We never made it to that point because the world tour was cancelled when the news came out. There were rumors circulating about us not being the singers, and there were continuous fights going on between Frank Farian and us. Frank finally decided to go to New York and tell the Associated Press that we didn't sing on the Milli Vanilli records. He then flew right back to Germany. That was it; he was done. How ironic, since he was the mastermind behind it all.

"What happened to us was unfortunate. I have no doubt that there are many other artists in this book with their own horror stories. And I am sure they would all agree that, back then, artists were not as savvy as they are today. We signed the recording contract without an attorney or manager. We had no experience whatsoever. [As the scandal broke,] the media didn't care about any of that. The media were like wolves—they smelled blood and went after us," he continues, exhaling with just a hint of frustration in his voice. "Where else were they going to go? Certainly not to the label. They held *us* responsible. Frank let the cat out of the bag and just walked away. And then there was the American label, Arista, headed by one of the major gatekeepers in the industry. Do you really think that anybody was going to go head-to-head with someone of his caliber back then? He was untouchable, so who was going to question him?

"I remember when we were at our peak, the executives at the label would say, 'Man, those records are flying off the shelves like hotcakes!' I'd never heard that expression before. They explained to me that it was just so easy to sell our records. All they had to do was put us out there. Other artists on the label had to work really hard to sell their records. It's amazing what I've heard over the years about the label. It was staggering to me how much money the label had made off the Milli Vanilli records, and now that they were done with us, they would invest in new ventures and give life to other projects. Life goes on for some.

"Where did everybody go during that time?" Morvan asks sternly. "It's like all the reporters in the country just shut their eyes because the gatekeepers were in control. Back then, you just couldn't go against them. I think if we had experienced this success and scandal today, I'm not sure whether we would have fared better or worse. But one thing that would have been different today would be that our voices *would* have been heard. In the '80s and early '90s, if you wanted to be heard, you had to go through those same media outlets. There were no other options. Today, at least you have Facebook, Twitter, social media—you can be heard and let people know what you are really thinking.

"When you are forced to use the traditional media, like television, they tell you, 'Okay, we'll interview you for an hour, and they end up editing you to two or three minutes— that's big in TV land—which you have no control over. With social media, you *can* tell the whole story—uncensored. Had we possessed that ability in the early '90s, it would have been a whole different ball game. So many people who contributed to the scandal were able to walk away free and clear, as if they did nothing wrong. That's the messed up part about it all. The smallest link in the chain, Rob and Fab, were the ones who got all the attention. To me, it was ludicrous to believe that two young kids out of Europe could orchestrate, control and mastermind the whole deal."

Over the years, Milli Vanilli's surrender of the Grammy award has remained a major focal point of the drama. "I think one additional and rather obvious reason we got hounded so much was because Rob and I were Grammy winners," Fab believes. "We decided to give the Grammy back because *we* thought it was the right thing to do. But it was always reported as the award was taken away from us. No, *we* gave it back. We were doing an interview with a journalist who worked for the *Los Angeles Times* that day and were planning to return the Grammy afterward. But by that afternoon, the Grammy committee jumped the gun and made the announcement that they wanted it back." The three American Music

Awards the duo received were never withdrawn, reportedly due to the fact that organizers felt the awards were bestowed upon Milli Vanilli by music consumers and were not subject to recall.

"I took it personally for many years," Fab admits. "In Los Angeles, I saw so many gossip magazines and newspapers on store shelves publicizing the so-called 'Milli Vanilli Scandal.' I thought to myself, 'Look how much money this story is generating for these people.' Scandals are a business. It generates money, whether it's true or not, and whether it's in a newspaper, magazine, on TV or on a website."

Morvan eases back in his chair, as he contemplates the 1998 death of his friend Rob (which followed a series of post-scandal public lawsuits levied against the pair and an unsuccessful attempt at a recording comeback). "Fame and success will gradually rise and disintegrate over the years," he reflects. "That's somewhat natural for most artists. In one day, Rob and Fab lost everything and had to deal with it right then and there. It was so bad that Rob [eventually] lost his life over it. That's how heavy it was. For me, to be standing here today, still believing in myself and to still have love for the music (not the music business), is something I can be proud of. I think once you have been infected by music and have a love for it, it never lets you go no matter what happens. It actually gave me the strength I needed to survive this crash. I knew it was going to be a long journey, and I knew I had to keep myself healthy.

"I've given this analogy in the past—when you're in a fight, you tense up; you flex. You know the punch is coming at you, and it's going to hurt, but it's not going to knock you out. But with Rob, he wasn't ready for it, and when he got punched with the realization, he got knocked out. He never expected the train to stop so abruptly; I always expected it would stop. And that's why I was able to take on the blow. To me, music was the light, the sparkle at the end of the long tunnel. I looked around and asked myself, 'What else is there for me in this life?' I couldn't live without music, and I wasn't going to give up on it. When I made the choice of staying with it, I immediately felt better. The more music I started to create, the more my confidence was restored. I started feeling worthy again. It was a process of learning how to love myself again. Music was my healing partner. My manager, Kim Marlowe, who was there early on, helped me put the pieces back together again. Other than her, there wasn't anybody. I just took it step-by-step, day-by-day, and eventually I healed. But I'll carry the scars within myself always. You can't forget something like that."

The conversation switches gears, with the focus now on the subject of maturity. Despite all he's been through, Fab looks decidedly youthful today and says he is comfortable with the aging process. "When you look at life and how short it is, you realize you have to surround yourself with the right people and the right things," he believes. "You'll only learn those lessons over time and with age. Yet, ironically, there is a belief in our society, especially in the western world, that when you age, you're not as cool any more. All they care to see is that you are older. But the fact is you have so much more to give and say because of your experiences. So when I sing or write today about love, friendship, disappointment, etc., I talk from experience—not from theory.

"It's true in the entertainment industry—it is to your advantage to try to maintain your body and face, in addition to your mind. It's important if you plan on moving with the times and to remain relevant. To me, health is all. You have to be aware about what you eat because everything you put in yourself can affect your mind and body. I stopped all the drugs and bad stuff long ago. I know by being careful, it will help me stay on top of my game. I'm not staging any comeback—I've been here all along. And I am still driven.

I want to write that one special song. I want to write and sing a song that *everyone* will want to sing because it makes them feel good—a song that means something. Most of my compositions are inspirational in tone. Of course you gotta have a good groove and an awesome melody, but once you get past that, you really want it to be emotionally charged."

Fab, who also DJs, has released numerous dance singles with independent labels over the past few years, as well as his first solo album in 2003, *Love Revolution* (using his full name, Fabrice Morvan), for which he co-produced and wrote almost all the tracks. In the summer of 2014, the singer provided vocals on the NightAir single "One of These Nights" (a hip dance reinterpretation of the Eagles' classic), and "Mind Over Matter," a collaboration with Dave Damelo in 2015. That same year, Fab performed a medley of Milli Vanilli hits with one of the group's actual singers, John Davis, live on the *Willkommen bei Carmen Nebel* show in Germany. Fab and Amass-T released the single "Calor" in 2017.

Morvan says he will never allow himself to be obscured by the shadows of his past. "I don't ever hide—not ever," he says firmly. "There's no doubt that a stigma is attached to me. I'll tell you this—that stigma, being the underdog and having some people not really expecting too much from me, is okay with me. I use it as motivation. Very few artists in this day and age can live up to the hype. I'll surprise [the doubters] and you will hear people say, 'Wow!' I believe it'll happen. Negativity won't get you anywhere—it's like an anchor pulling you down to the bottom of the ocean. You must be positive and believe in yourself. Anyone who ever achieved anything will tell you it's a positive mindset that's gotten them to a good place and lifted them out of the valley of darkness. Reading also helps open your mind and is a great thing to do, whether it's self-discovery books, positive philosophies or learning about a great human story, which can inspire you to make the necessary changes in your life.

"I feel blessed to be an artist and to have various outlets for expressing myself. When you don't have a way to tap into your soul, what do you do? It's easy then to turn to alcohol and anti-depressants, etc. You have to love what you are doing in life, or you're going to perish emotionally. Everyone doesn't have to be an artist or musician, no, but you have to find out what makes you happy. Grow and evolve—get better at being who you are. That's what life is for—to accomplish and excel. Keep moving forward. That's what I've been doing. You haven't seen the last of me; trust me. Maybe I'll be remembered for just those two words—Milli Vanilli, but I want those words to stand for a way of life—even though it's far from being easy. When you fall, you stand back up, and you move forward."

Romano Musumarra
Producer, Composer
Artists: Jeanne Mas, Elsa, Princess Stéphanie et al.
France

Not only is he a classically trained Italian composer with an ear for strikingly beautiful melodies, he is one of Europe's most distinguished and accomplished producers, composers and arrangers. His extraordinary handiwork can be heard on many of the greatest French pop and dance records of the '80s, from the stellar hits of Jeanne Mas and Princess Stéphanie of Monaco, to the works of durable luminaries like Sylvie Vartan and Véronique Jannot. In more recent years, his artistry and production skills have touched the careers of such notables as Celine Dion, Katherine Jenkins, and Alessandro Safina, as well as international opera stars like Vittorio Grigolo and the late Luciano Pavarotti. His name is known and respected worldwide—Romano Musumarra.

Today, this gentle, soft-spoken man continues to enjoy the balance he has achieved between his illustrious past and the musical triumphs he creates in the twenty-first century. "I am very happy that my work from the '80s is still remembered and appreciated," he says humbly, "and I also love working with so many great new artists and record companies today, which are keeping me very busy. To be very honest, I truly feel I have a lot more yet to compose."

Romano recalls his youth and coming of age in Italy from his modern day home in Canada. "When I was very young, about five years old, I lost my father. My mother wasn't a professional singer, but she used to sing opera in our home all the time. My mother had these very old records, and I still remember that I would start to cry when I would listen to them. It's a strong memory that I have—I guess I was very moved by the music. When I was seven, I started to play the organ in the church. I was almost too small to reach the pedal, but I was kind of a prodigy. In my heart, I still thank my mother for letting me study music when I was so young. By the time I was 10, she placed me in the Saint Cecilia Conservatory in Rome, and I had the chance to study classical music for about 10 years. At the age of 16, my mother passed away. I eventually left school and started playing rock music with some small bands in Italy. I was a bit lost at that time, but I guess I tried to find myself through music, and that was the beginning of my pop career. I formed a band called La Bottega dell'Arte (Boutique of Art), and we were very successful touring for a few years.

"I used to work with electronic keyboards at the very beginning, when this instrument

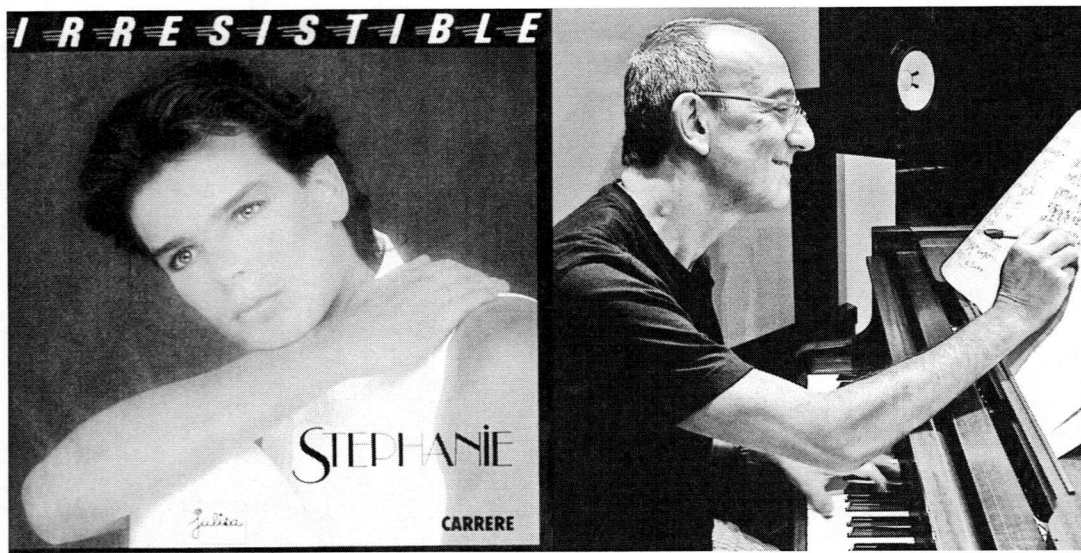

On the left, Carrere Records' 7-inch single version of "Irresistible," sung by Princess Stéphanie and arranged by Romano Musumarra. The song was reportedly the second biggest pop hit in France for the year 1986. On the right, Romano at work today (Stéphanie photography by Meylan/Sigma).

was first introduced—the Moog and equipment like that. I was very good at programming them. I made an album [with Mario Maggi and Claudio Gizzi] called *Automat* in 1978, before the invention of the polyphonic keyboard. We recorded with monophonic keyboards, one note at a time and without a sequencer. (I re-released the album on iTunes on my own label, Mube Records.) Later, I had the chance to collaborate with many musicians in Italy, one being Pierluigi Giombini. We worked in the same studio where I believe he recorded Gazebo's 'I Like Chopin' and 'Dolce Vita' with Ryan Paris.

"I tried to work in dance music in my early days, but I wasn't really successful with the genre. However, I did have a hit dance recording in Holland with the group Moses called 'We Just' in 1985. The dance genre wasn't really my cup of tea because I was, in those days, in two different worlds—the electronic world and the world of classical music. I was drawn more to what I would call the pop side of music, where I could incorporate strong melodies rather than just pure dance beats. I soon began composing, arranging and producing for other artists."

By the mid-'80s, Musumarra entered one of the most prolific periods of his career. His collaboration with an eclectic female singer sporting a punkish, new wave look and raven hair took France by storm. "I met this girl named Jeanne Mas," he remembers. "I was 23 or 24, and she was very young too. She had done a demo for a producer in France at EMI Records, and I heard it. I proposed a song to her that I had composed called 'Toute Première Fois' (though the lyrics were still in Italian at this time), along with two or three other songs. We recorded a demo together, and she got a deal with EMI almost immediately. The executives at the label really loved this music, this new sound. I mixed electronic and acoustic sounds in this song, which was very unusual at this time. We didn't have computers and big sequencers yet, so I used my electronic keyboard and a smaller sequencer to create the sound. I also recorded her [self-titled debut] album, and within three months, the single

'Toute Première Fois' reached number one in France. I think we stayed at the top of the chart for about five weeks and sold more than a million copies of the single."

Mixing engaging melodies with quirky hooks, lively choruses and irresistible beats, 'Toute Première Fois' (co-written by Roberto Zaneli) and the follow-up single, "Johnny, Johnny," remained pop chart and club hits for several months in France. According to Romano, Mas became a challenging artist to work with by the time preparations for her sophomore album, *Femmes d'Aujourd'hui,* were being made in 1986. "The second album with Jeanne was rather a natural next step for me, like a continuum," observes the producer. "I was very excited by our success, and I had so many ideas and new sounds in my head that it was quite easy and logical for me to make another album with her. In structure, it was very similar to the first one, and the style still sounded fresh. People didn't have time to get tired of the sound yet.

"To be honest, however, I don't really have fond memories of this second album because Jeanne's personality had started to change after our initial success. She became what you might call a real *artist*," he laughs. "Sort of—*a diva*. She became very nervous. I was obliged to work with her in what I must admit was a beautiful studio, but it was located far away in Denmark. I was lost in the snow way out there in the middle of nowhere. I was virtually alone most of the time for two months, working only with musicians (who were coming and going) and a sound engineer, who looked a bit like a Viking. Of course Jeanne would be there some of the time, but she was also very busy with promotions, and she was often away making appearances. I even ended up losing weight while I was there. I was very uncomfortable making that album, and it was difficult to finish it. But it did turn out quite good, and it was very successful."

Femmes d'Aujourd'hui helped establish Mas as one of France's premier dance-pop artists. The single "En Rouge et Noir," a commanding song that bridged new wave, pop and dance with a dramatic, almost anthemic urgency, was a colossal chart hit in the country. Two fiery remix versions, one by Claude Grillis and the other by Dominique Blanc-Francart, were popular in the clubs. The track was chased by a series of memorable and highly popular follow-up singles, including "Sauvez-Moi" and "L'enfant." "After reaching number one with multiple singles by Jeanne," he continues, "several other artists and producers started to call me. I started doing more and more work in France, and it was much more lucrative for me to be there. So I moved to France. I soon was working all day long, seven days a week for several years. I was very happy, but I don't think I really had the time to analyze it or ask myself how I felt about what was happening to me. It all came so fast, and the wave of success was quite substantial."

Demand for Musumarra's talents soared to a new level after he went into the studio with Monaco's Princess Stéphanie, the daughter of actress Grace Kelly. The princess had been in the spotlight for some time, and her youthful, sometimes controversial antics brought her copious amounts of media scrutiny by 1986. The time seemed ideal for Stéphanie to become a pop star. Her debut dance single, "Irresistible" (also known as "Ouragan"), took Europe by storm, and the artist was at the top of France and Germany's pop charts nearly overnight. "I had composed this song," recalls Romano, "and I originally proposed it to Jeanne Mas. She and I had a difficult relationship by then, and she refused to record it. I proposed the song to another singer, and she refused it as well. I don't know why, as this singer wasn't famous, and it might have boosted her career. I met a producer named Yves Roze, and he was looking for a song. He had an idea to turn Princess Stéphanie into a singer. At that time, she was living in Paris, all alone in a big apartment with her dog and chauffeur.

"She was fooling around a lot back then (she had not yet matured), and she had nothing to do but cause scandals. Her father (Prince Ranier III) was very upset with her, but she was who she was. Yves met with Stéphanie, and they became friends. He proposed my song to her, and she accepted the idea of recording it. Unfortunately, she wasn't what you would call a professional singer, so we had a few problems. We had to record and re-record many, many parts of the song with her, and we were editing them for what seemed like centuries. In the end, we got the finished composite of these tracks, and it sounded great. The promotion surrounding the record was the dream of every artist, with almost no work involved. It was as though every TV and radio station wanted to have the princess sing, and so promoting the record was extremely easy. Then we went back in the studio and recorded the English version [known as "Irresistible"]."

Stéphanie's debut album (titled *Besoin* in most of France and recorded and mixed at Marcadat Studios in Paris between May and August of 1986), was a dynamic mix of energized dance confections and pop tracks that seemed to captivate almost all of Europe. The set was particularly well-received in Germany, where the singles "Irresistible" and "One Love to Give" were Top 10 smashes. "I recorded three singles for her album, 'Ouragan/Irresistible,' 'One Love to Give/Flash' and 'Fleur(s) du Mal (à Paul)/I'm Waiting for You,'" says Romano. "I was too naïve, too young, and too busy—and as a result I didn't get involved in the rest of the album. They went with other producers and arrangers to handle those songs. I didn't have an agent at the time, and I wasn't offered the opportunity to produce the entire album. I arranged and composed the biggest hit, 'Ouragan,' but to be truthful, I didn't get a lot of money for doing the actual work on that production. There were a lot of people involved with the deal. I received royalties as the composer, but I wasn't the publisher. Still, the great success of the project was a very good thing for my career," he admits.

Musumarra also lent his talents to the world of motion pictures, where he was introduced to a young and promising actress and vocalist named Elsa Lunghini. Says Romano, "It was a very good experience working with Elsa and recording the hit 'T'en va pas.' In 1986, I was working on a soundtrack and composing music for the movie *La Femme de ma vie*, the story of a violinist who was an alcoholic. The director of the film was Régis Wargnier. It was my first time composing for a movie and his first time directing. He later won an Oscar for the film *Indochine*. We had this little girl in the film, Elsa, and Regis had a scene in the movie in which she was telling her father, who was leaving his wife, that she wanted him to stay. The director needed a melody for the scene, and so I wrote 'T'en va pas,' which basically means 'don't go away.' I composed the verse for the film, and the publisher (Georges Mary) suggested I add a chorus and release the song as a single to promote the film. So I wrote the chorus, and I went into the studio with Elsa to record it. She was a truly lovely little girl and a really good singer."

"T'en va pas," a soft but richly orchestrated, melodic and danceable pop gem, was a tremendous success throughout Europe. The song held the number one position in France for almost two months. The artist went on to release her 1988 debut album *Elsa*, which was highlighted by such tracks as the high-energy dance hit "Jour de neige" and a pop-flavored duet with Glenn Medeiros, "Un Roman d'amitié." Following his success with *La Femme de ma vie*, Romano went on to create scores for over 20 motion pictures. By the late '80s, Musumarra's regal position in the music business was undisputed, and the musician was regarded as a master craftsman of French pop. "After four or five years in France, I was, I admit, very big in the industry," he concedes. "The French government gave me a medal and made me a 'Chevalier de l'ordre des arts et des lettres'—what you might call a Minister of Culture. For a time, my work accounted for something like 15 percent of the entire French pop music market. I can't say my personality or ego really changed as a result of all that. I was simply too busy to concentrate on it. I was meeting so many new people, going to new studios and traveling all the time, but my attitude about life stayed the same. I don't think the success ever went to my head."

The producer and composer was able to create hit records that were often successful beyond the confines of France, something most French artists found extremely challenging.

"I think one of the reasons why French pop music had a difficult time being accepted in other countries was because the French had a different way of composing," Romano conjectures. "There are two ways to compose a song—the Anglo-Saxon way and a 'rest of the world' way," he laughs. "I think, to some degree, sometimes music in the French and Italian languages were too romantic for the overall European market. It's difficult to explain, but French and Italian sounds were unique. Very often in those days, we had a dilemma with our artists in that they had strong accents that sometimes just didn't work on the international market. There were very few artists who could break the international wall.

"I've had hits outside of France, such as the music I made with Alessandro Safina, an Italian tenor. I produced his first album, and the single 'Luna' was a tremendous hit (sung in Italian) in France, Italy and throughout Europe in 2000. But the surprise was that it became a big hit in the east—countries like the Ukraine and Russia. It became an enormously popular song there. Sometimes you don't know why a song catches on, but it just happens. Over time, the appeal of languages can change. Even within the last 10 years, I've seen the Italian language become much more popular internationally, even by those whose primary language is English. Today, I think people appreciate how good other languages sound—how exotic they can be—even trendy!"

Despite his remarkable achievements in Europe and so many other parts of the world, Musumarra's name and most of his works have yet to be recognized by the mainstream in the United States. "In 1991," he recollects, "I made an album in New York with Dana Dawson [1974–2010] called *Paris New-York and Me* for Sony. She asked me to sign a deal with Sony in New York, but under the condition that I'd move to the United States. I turned the deal down because I didn't want to move to New York, Nashville or Los Angeles. This was the only chance I ever had to work in a serious way in America. I worked with Celine Dion for her English records, but I knew if I really wanted to work with American artists, I'd have to live in that country. It simply wasn't my wish to do that." Dawson's dance-pop singles, "Romantic World" and "Tell Me Bonita" (lifted from her debut album with Musumarra) hit France's Top Five and were popular in Belgium and Sweden.

Romano concedes the European recording industry of the '80s, like its American counterpart, was filled with shady characters whose integrity was often, at best, suspect. "The music industry in Europe was difficult in terms of [questionable practices] by labels, producers, managers and in terms of how some artists were treated. You had to deal with it—

there was no way around it, and it was extremely challenging. At the time, we had several small labels and a few big ones in the market. A major one in France was Carrere. The label had its own distribution network and was a sizeable force in the record industry. However, it was a label that was, you might say, better to stay away from. Carrere used to sell records and never report those sales. They used many tricks in those days. I did 'T'en va pas' with that label, and we sold over a million singles. The real number was probably closer to two million. But what would happen is everyone would make enough money with the one million copies that were reported on paper. If you were okay with the money you made, you didn't inquire further. You didn't rock the boat.

"Producers in France had to pay the Société des auteurs, compositeurs et éditeurs de musique (SACEM) in advance for the number of records they would be pressing. SACEM was very good at protecting songwriters, but even they couldn't control things beyond a certain point. If a record company didn't declare some of the actual sales numbers, they really had no way to know what was really going on. Most of the unscrupulous people from those days are gone now."

Despite having composed, arranged and produced a countless number of enchanting melodies, hit songs and albums, Romano's well of creativity has yet to run dry. But his approach to music is less about external sources of inspiration than it is about tapping into the musical spirit that restlessly stirs within him. Observes the composer, "People often notice I live in these beautiful regions in Italy and Canada, and they assume I must be inspired by them," he says. "My answer is always the same. I am not inspired by places. The music is just inside of me. For example, I was in my car driving home when the chorus of 'T'en va pas' came to me. I had the music in my mind, and I just wrote it out when I got home. I will give you another example—last night I woke up in the middle of the night, and I had a melody in mind. I got up and just wrote it down—that's how these compositions come to be. It's just inside of me, and I have to find a way to bring it out. I do not need 'inspiration,' as they say. Sometimes the environment, the things people *think* inspire an artist, can actually block the process because you are distracted by your surroundings."

Today, Musumarra is focused on expressing his creativity relatively free of the business pressures he felt during the hectic days of decades past. He smiles, saying, "What I really prefer today is to compose music that I truly feel—without a deadline. When I can compose for an orchestra, I really enjoy it. I came from classical music, and so when I can compose for strings and brass, I am really happy. This is my favorite moment, my favorite time. My classical background has been a part of many of my pop hits. 'T'en va pas' has a classical orchestration, though it does not incorporate real strings—it was electronic. In the '80s, using real strings and instruments wasn't very trendy, but that's changed today. Today artists often ask me (if they have a big enough budget) to write for an orchestra, even if it's just a small string section. It's very hip today to go back to the way we used to do things.

"I love composing, and to me, it's the most beautiful hobby that a man can have. At the same time, I really enjoy life today apart from music. I love sports—I run or ski every day for one or two hours if I have the time. Whether it is 25 degrees below zero or a hot day—I enjoy seeing the natural side of life. This morning I was in the forest getting maple from a tree, and it was beautiful being out there in nature. It is a joy that I discovered almost too late. I remember when I turned 40, and I realized I had never looked at a tree—

really looked at it and thought of it as something that is alive. In the past, it was just an object. It's really too bad that I didn't appreciate these things sooner."

Romano insists he isn't very nostalgic about the '80s. "I understand that the '80s were my time, and I appreciate that people remember those hits. But at the same time, I have made some wonderful, very successful records in the last few years that I am very proud of. It's hard for me to think of a specific song from the '80s that would be my favorite or that I am most proud of. I actually prefer my recent productions more. But I think the highlight of the '80s for me was 'Ouragan' with Stéphanie. It was just so huge. For about six months, I felt like the king of France—it was just so crazy."

Musumarra's composition "On écrit sur les murs" was a Top 10 hit in Frace for an ensemble known as Kids United in 2016, one of the artist's many modern day accomplishments. "I still work in France and Italy on many big productions. I think of Garou, Pavarotti, Il Divo, Katherine Jenkins and many other artists I have been in the studio with over the last several years. I can say that I am very proud of 'Luna' by Alessandro Safina. But—I'm still the '80s guy, and I guess I always will be," he says, shrugging his shoulders and laughing acceptingly. "I think I'm a good melodist," he says with humility, seemingly hesitant to acknowledge his skill. "I hope people will like the melodies I have composed. Maybe somebody will be listening to my music 100 years from now. I don't know—it's not that important to me in some ways.

"We are all the same—we all have the same weight and importance in the universe. There's no difference between you and I. So, even if one man is a murderer and another man is a priest, in terms of the spirit, I believe they are all the same. I know that sounds crazy. But I don't think there are bad men and women—there are bad conditions, circumstances, situations and family settings. They create people who do bad things. But we are all part of a design in the universe. I can't say anything I've done is more important than what someone else has done. That's why I think the things we focus on aren't always that important. I think it's more important that we forgive and try to help each other. Whatever a person does in life, whatever I do in life, we are all here doing something together in the same time—the same lifetime. It can be very beautiful and powerful if we all make our marks in the world."

Taco Ockerse
aka Taco
"Puttin' on the Ritz" (1982)
Germany

Almost from the moment the song "Puttin' on the Ritz" was first written and published by Irving Berlin in 1929, numerous entertainers have attempted to make it their own—and why would they not? The clever and catchy tune slyly celebrated the lavish lifestyles and fashionable dress code of the elite and had all the earmarks of a hit. The popular expression mirrored in its title was inspired by the behaviors of the über wealthy taking up residence at the swanky Ritz Hotel, *the* place to be seen in the day. Fred Astaire, Benny Goodman and Ella Fitzgerald all took a stab at recording the song with varying degrees of commercial success. A few decades back, Gene Wilder and Peter Boyle performed the song in the 1974 Mel Brooks movie comedy *Young Frankenstein*. Neil Diamond gave it a shot in 1998, and both Robbie Williams and Herb Alpert added a version to their respective 2013 albums.

Yet nobody has been able to match the worldwide success that Taco Ockerse enjoyed with his rendition, released throughout most parts of the world in 1982. Going simply by the name Taco, the singer's pop-synth-new wave dance juggernaut capitalized on the dominant musical trends of the period and swept the planet, reaching the Top 10 of numerous countries and selling over a million copies in the United States alone. While such a monumental accomplishment might seem like a dream come true, the artist has never let the song or his success define his life. Over 30 years after reaching the heights of fame, today Taco is a warm, observant and articulate man with a great sense of humor. He refuses to take himself too seriously, and over time he's developed a remarkably grounded and steady approach for handling the rollercoaster ride that has most definitely been his life in show business.

"I was born in Indonesia and came from a musical family," says Taco, whose parents were of Dutch ancestry. "My grandfather on my mother's side was a professional musician, and he had an orchestra. On my father's side, his dad played the violin. My parents did some work in musical shows in our little Dutch colony. In my home, there was always swing and jazz music playing. American music came very naturally to me. Later, we moved from the Netherlands to Singapore, and my brother and I were placed in the International Schools of America. So I had to leave the Dutch culture behind and get into the American one. I had to learn English, and they kind of made a second-hand American out of me until I graduated in 1973.

Left: A concert brochure promoting a performance by Taco in 1984 shows the tuxedo-clad artist as he appeared during his "Puttin' on the Ritz" phase. *Right:* Taco continues to record and perform in the twenty-first century.

"My family eventually moved to Hamburg, Germany. I was getting a bit older, and I really didn't know what to do with myself, so my dad suggested I try acting school. It was an opportunity to learn German, which I didn't have a clue how to speak, and to make some money on the side. I worked as an extra at a repertory theater, and it was wonderful. I worked in many productions, making some money and taking acting and dancing classes. I was very naïve and ambitious, so I made the most of roles where I had nothing to say. I guess the directors kind of noticed me; they started to give me a line or two. They started doing musicals, and one of the first productions they did was *Sweet Charity*. I remember a friend of mine got a part in it as a dancer, and I thought if *this* guy could be a dancer, why couldn't I? I then pushed myself on the cast and crew there and said I'd make a great stand-in—and that I was, of course, a great dancer. I told them, 'I can do *everything*!' With all the productions, I learned a great deal."

Ockerse started hanging out at rock clubs, jamming with musician friends. He soon found work doing demo records. "Gradually, I got connected with recording studios and started working as a background singer. Hamburg was a very small artistic city, so I was able to get connections and referrals easily. Just by chance, my demos were heard, and I got my first record contract with Polydor and even got on a television show."

Taco began recording singles like "Träume Brauchen Zeit," a light, breezy ballad in the German language schlager vein. "It wasn't quite right—it wasn't what I wanted to do," he laments. "They wanted me to sing schlager songs, and that got very frustrating. I did manage to release a cover version of Elton John's 'Nobody Wins' [released in Germany as

"Keiner Gewinnt"], but nothing happened with that either. After doing the *Grand Prix d'Eurovision* music competition in 1981, I went to the big boss of the record label and asked to get out of my contract. He had a heart and let me go. I just didn't want to sing this type of music all my life. My other artist friends all said, 'Are you nuts? Giving up a contract?' I kind of retreated into myself for a while."

The disco era had come to an end, and dance music had started to expand in innovative directions by the early '80s. The dance genre encompassed a variety of sounds, and electronics became the name of the game. Melding rock and punk with the beat sensibilities of dance, new wave music was making headway. Germany and the UK became major hubs for this emerging style. "I started noticing that German new wave and dance music were gaining momentum with Kraftwerk and groups like that, and I began thinking about mixing old world elements with the new sounds happening," Taco says. "Nobody had done it yet. I tried to find people who might be interested in it, but nobody cared for the idea. It's the story of my life. Through hanging out in clubs, I met this guy who was friends with David Parker. David was a producer with a very straight English pop background, and he'd never done anything like what I was suggesting before. He agreed to give it a try. He contacted Werner Lang, who was with the Peer-Southern Publishing Company, and the three of us sat down and discussed the concept.

"In David's small home studio in his cellar, playing on a little Casio keyboard, we developed Irving Berlin's 'Puttin' on the Ritz.' The song has nothing to do with pudding or Ritz crackers," he laughs. "Back in the '20s, it was a common New York colloquialism referencing going out and having a classy time at an upscale location. The idea was to do a whole new technical arrangement with it. It was a day-to-day process, testing different sounds. The tap dancing portion of the song was a whole mix of things. It was a choreographer (a friend of mine from the opera house in Hamburg who taught me a whole routine for the song) and I dancing on the record, and we also manipulated some tap shoes on the floor.

"Then I had this idea for the end of the song where you have all the different melodies. At first I thought I wanted all these big Broadway musical bits in there—sort of homage to the great show tunes. Later, when we recorded the final version, we had to take it all out because the Irving Berlin copyright said you could never take any other composer's song and mix it with a Berlin tune. It helped us out in the end because we replaced our original medley with Irving Berlin tunes like 'White Christmas' and 'Alexander's Ragtime Band,' which worked quite well."

The project represented a new beginning for Ockerse. "I suppose I had big dreams about it at the time," he admits. "I was in my early 20s, and for me it felt like the last straw. I had tried so many things—I toured with disco bands, I had sung schlager, done shows—none of that had really worked out. Now I wanted to *really* change my image. That's where the whole look came from with the makeup on my face, gelled hair—kind of like the *Chicago* show style. That was very important to me—that people would not recognize me. I didn't want any association with the schlager days. My choreographer friend convinced me not to change my name. He said I should stick with Taco because I had a bit of a name established already. The make-up worked out great because when I took it all off, people didn't recognize me.

"Well, we finished the 'Ritz' track and shopped it around, and once again, nobody was interested in it. I laugh at it now because, as I said, it's sort of been the story of my life. It's like, 'Oh, fuck!' If you go into this business and take it seriously, forget it. There will always be someone who kicks you in the ass. But David had a deal with Peer-Southern, and we needed that connection. Back in those days, the publishing companies would go to the record companies and tell them they had such and such artists and that they'd like the label to produce them. Peer-Southern took the track to RCA Records, but they didn't want the track—no way. The story goes that at one point, an executive at Peer got the boss of RCA drunk and told him they'd give the label the artists they wanted, but they'd *have* to take Taco too," he laughs heartily. "That's how I got my deal. Not very glamorous."

"Puttin' on the Ritz" was absolutely *not* one of those songs that instantly broke onto the charts, the artist insists. It took a *very* long time. "It was released, just like hundreds of other songs back in the '80s," he states, "but if you don't have a record company that gives a fuck, it's just 'put out there' so they can say they released it. But that's it—they don't do anything with it. I got pretty frustrated very quickly because they didn't do a thing to promote it. I had one friend at RCA who said it was such a shame to see a good song like it going down the drain. I decided, at my own expense, to make a deal touring the locations of a huge German retail shop chain, Karstadt (something like Macy's in the U.S.). I had myself brought out like a puppet behind the main store window, with this computerized music playing. I'd do a performance of the song when enough people gathered in front of the window. People would buy the record, and I'd do an autograph session. That was really funny, and we had a lot fun going on the road with that. I really looked like Dracula or something with all the make-up.

"Even after that tour, still nothing happened with the record," claims Ockerse. "I was thinking, 'Well, that's the end of that!' At that time, my father, who was in the fashion business, had opened his own boutique. I thought I might as well help my dad with that since the music wasn't taking off at all. Then something very funny happened. I was selling clothes at the shop every day, which wasn't too exciting, and I got a phone call. I was asked to do some promotion for the record in Sweden. I said, 'Why not?' I flew there, and there was a limo waiting for me at the airport. I was like, 'Oh my God, what's going on?' I think they thought Liberace was going to come out of the plane, and here I come in my blue jeans suit looking like Paul Bunyan. I didn't really understand what was happening because I only had the one song—the A and the B- side. I didn't really understand that the song was taking off there. I was going to do a show at a disco, and I peeked through the curtain to see the crowd. The guys were all in tuxedos, and the girls were wearing gowns. I was kind of in shock. I quickly put on all my make-up and sang the song. I think they made me sing it about five times. I was told the song had hit number one, and the RCA rep from Sweden told me 'Puttin' on the Ritz' saved their label. The company was about to close down in Sweden, and my song saved their asses. Before I knew it, I was on Swedish TV and doing tons of interviews. Meanwhile, in Germany, the whole thing was still dead."

With a groundswell building, Taco soon began to experience the first pressures of show business success. The artist's voice quickens as he describes how the pace began to accelerate. "The Swedish reps told me they were going to need an LP because the song had reached gold status," Ockerse recalls. "Well, David Parker and I had about two weeks time to get the *After Eight* album done. On the plane trip back to Germany, I was already working on the lyrics and thinking of ideas we could use. We did the basics of the whole album back down in his cellar. It was totally crazy.

"He had a little shower in the basement; that's where the rain sound effect comes from in the song 'Singin' in the Rain.' We're talking early '80s—we had to work with what we had. We eventually got to the Peer-Southern studios and were able to get more musicians and arrangers involved. I had bookings to get back to in Sweden, and the orders for the LP were already piling up. RCA Germany finally put promoters on the job when they saw how big the song was in Scandinavia, and then the song started taking off in Germany, too.

"From that moment on, I had no time to enjoy this turnaround that had happened to me. It was now like, 'You have to function—now!' Before, I was more like the guy who just wants to have a good time. On the one side, it was a lot of fun because it's what I always wanted to do. But when you get down to the nitty gritty, you pay a high price. You have no free time. Back then, you *had* to be *everywhere*. I was living out of a suitcase, and I was constantly on the road, doing TV, radio and shows. It was actually stressful. I would tell myself, 'Don't get sick, keep functioning, stay with it and pray to God the producers and label will get it all on. All this over an artist they didn't even want," he says with a slightly sarcastic edge. "And then even *those* people were gone. The weird thing was the people at RCA no sooner signed me, and then they left the company. Or they were kicked out or fired—I don't know. So I always seemed to have people handling my career who weren't into my drift."

"Puttin' on the Ritz" was a multi-national sensation and managed to make the rare leap across the Atlantic to North America. Says Taco, "I had been on the road, touring all of Europe, and after two years of working, I really needed a break. I didn't even know what the word holiday meant any more. RCA in America wasn't interested in the song, but Canada was. Canada was really pushing the record, and it had reached platinum status there. Because they were exporting the record to the U.S., RCA in New York finally caught on and noticed they were losing money. So that's when the big boss at RCA in America started pushing the record. When I found that out, I knew I wasn't going to get any holidays. The song was already bubbling under the Hot 100, and then I started really freaking out. I panicked a little. For a little European guy, it was kind of scary.

"You have these visions of American show business when you are from Europe," he confesses. "You view it as another planet—so far away. In Europe, you can do your performance and pull it off, but in America—*what am I gonna do?* Here I come with a Fred Astaire hit, and they want to see little old me? You see the lavish sets of the TV shows; the level is so much bigger, and you just go, 'Oh my God!' It was very intimidating. The pace was quicker in the U.S. too. In Europe, you'd have a week to prepare for a show, but in the States it was *Solid Gold*, a Bob Hope special, *The Merv Griffin Show* and all these television programs, back-to-back. You'd get one day of rehearsal at best. I was always thrown into deep water. Thank God I had done some musicals and had a theater background. Most of the time I was alone, but I was often very glad when my wife was with me. She got thrown into a lot of situations with me and had to meet a lot of people, and it really helped to have her with me when she could be there. I had my father come over at one point, and fortunately I had some family and friends in the U.S."

By the summer of 1983, Taco's single had reached the Top Five on the *Billboard* pop chart and was a commercial, radio and club giant. But success in the States was a hollow victory for the singer. "Unfortunately, I got screwed in the U.S. by my management. To work there, you *had* to have management. I didn't have time to properly decide who would represent me. I had 24 hours before I was getting on a plane to America, and I signed off on a contract. I'm still owed money from that contract and revenue that was earned on the U.S. tour. I never saw a cent of it. It left a very bad taste in my mouth. That was very heavy; a bitter experience. I'm not the kind of guy who says, 'You want me to perform? Give me the money now!' I'm very European. If we do a deal and shake hands, it's all straight forward. If I wanted to have a good human connection with someone in Europe, you could do that. I found in the U.S., it was all on the surface. I had many people in America say to me, 'Taco, you get too deep.' Too deep? I was just being me," he says with frustration in his voice.

"At one point, I had a really great band with me—really wonderful musicians who I liked very much. My management would put me in a limo when we were touring, and the boys in the band would have to go in a really crummy bus. I would get big baskets of fruit, and the guys would be in another room with nothing. I don't like that kind of thing at all. Hey, we were all doing the same work. That was really weird for me. In the States, I guess you work your way up, and when you hit that status, you're on a different level. It was like you had to lose respect for those who weren't at your level. It should be more like a family. We've all been waiters or worked at tough jobs. But in the U.S., it felt like you became different from the guys in the band. I can't cope with that when I see it, and I still can't to this day."

The widespread use of drugs in the industry was also in constant view, according to the artist. "I was seeing drugs way back, even when I was still in school," he says almost matter-of-factly. "I'd see all these rich kids opening tin foil packets, rushing to the toilets. I was never into drugs. Like every good European, I'm a wino," he chuckles. "I grew up with wine at the table. I will say it was shocking to me in the United States to be at all these prominent parties, especially in Hollywood, and there'd be bowls of cocaine around. They'd give you a dirty look if all you wanted was a glass of wine. But honestly, I didn't need anything more. I had seen so many people who couldn't handle it. I remember one of our audio technicians was totally coked up during one of our shows, and he completely couldn't function. I saw things like that, and I would tell myself, 'Don't even get started with the stuff.' When I was touring, I was the up front guy—the one on stage. I couldn't get sick or messed up. If you get into drugs, you're going to screw up everything. I don't have anything against anyone who does it, but if you're halfway intelligent, you have to understand the consequences. To me, it doesn't mix with show business. So many singers or entertainers think they are more creative or 'with it' when they're on stuff, but they aren't—they usually just suck. And there's no way you can be on stage every night and recuperate when you're doing all that stuff."

Taco can still recall the lighter side of touring in America and recollects an especially memorable television appearance. "I think it was on *Good Morning America* or some show like that in Los Angeles. The gimmick was that they were having me try all these different flavored tacos. I'd have to say, 'Mmmm—yum, that's wonderful!' and things like that. But towards the end of the segment I said, 'Well, I guess I'm the only artist who can eat myself!' All of a sudden, somebody yells, 'Cut!' I'm like, 'What did I say wrong?' he laughs heartily. "It's so funny to me now. I was a European cat in America who wasn't hip to the slang of the day."

Born of a dire necessity to accommodate rapidly growing media demands and the need to promote Taco in multiple places at the same time, a video for "Puttin' on the Ritz" was hastily put into production. With the MTV video boom well under way, the clip was praised as one of the most memorable innovations of its day (and currently sits on YouTube with well over six million views). Its retro-meets-new wave flavor, darkly contrasting images of wealth and poverty, almost sinister tap dance sequence, and the clever use of a glowing walking stick kept the song and the artist's eclectic style in the spotlight. However, in more recent years, the video's use of background singers performing in blackface has caught the eye of some critics and stirred some controversy. Taco explains the genesis of the video and insists the concept was never intended to project racism, subtly or overtly.

"I was working such a crazy international schedule, and I couldn't be everywhere at the same time any more," he recalls. "So we needed a video urgently. It actually wasn't the first video for the song. Before the song was even a hit, we had done a quickie promotional video for it filmed in an old castle, with me standing on a mantelpiece. There were two assistants blowing cigarette smoke at me from down below. But we needed something better. They flew me to Brussels, where the label had found a new, up and coming video production company. It was a mad rush. It was like they had 24 hours to bring this baby into the world. The setting was actually an old warehouse that was just about to be demolished. There was debris everywhere; it was cold and dirty. So here I am in my tux, and I met with the team and the director, Jean-Pierre Berckmans. He was very talented and willing to work with any ideas anyone had. All he had at the start was a basic concept—I was to be the king of the beggars. He had oil barrels everywhere with fires burning in them—the type you see homeless people huddled around to stay warm on the streets. You can imagine how unpleasant the cold air was in this place, with the smell of smoke. I couldn't sit anywhere, and my clothes would slowly get covered with the soot in the air. The director also wanted white mice in a lot of the scenes, so there were these fucking creatures all over the place," he says, shaking his head disapprovingly.

"Then I met my background dancers. They were very nice, but—how shall I say this? Although they were very talented, they were not exactly as glamorous as the *Solid Gold* dancers. So, I came up with the idea of incorporating the Al Jolson look as a reference to the vaudeville/silent movie era—putting the dancers in blackface. Everything you see in the video, from the slow-motion Bob Fosse style of dancing, the blue lighting, to the blackface, was the result of a spur-of-the-moment decision. There was no time to think it through. The tap dancing routine shown in the clip was another example and something I had been doing for a while in shows. So I showed the dancers my routine, and they picked it up very fast. We were in the warehouse early in the morning, worked all through the night, and were out by early the next day. Then I was back on the road again. I can assure you there was no racism or hurtful intent in any of our minds making that video. The goal was to get in and get out." Taco worked with director Berckmans again on the video for a follow-up single, "Let's Face the Music," which featured the artist singing and dancing among exploding cocktail tables and in front of a stage engulfed by real flames.

"The criticisms only began to surface in recent years, when more people were able to see the clip on YouTube," the singer observes. "But most people really enjoy the video and always tell me I looked like Tim Curry. However, I was really inspired by Joel Grey, the conferencier from *Cabaret*," he laughs. "I'm always asked about the lighted walking stick, too. At the time, this was a relatively new innovation. A friend of mine took a long glass neon light that operated on batteries (because we didn't have wireless sabers in those days).

The handle contained the battery pack. He had to improvise a large case for it and used a long plastic water pipe. At every fucking airport in the world, the police would pull me aside and interrogate me. I think they thought it was some kind of a bazooka gun. I still have it—it's gathering dust somewhere in my attic."

Eventually, the media frenzy that had brewed over "Puttin' on the Ritz" settled down. RCA released a number of follow-up singles off the *After Eight* album, including "Cheek to Cheek," which fared well in some parts of Europe. However, with his spectacular debut largely viewed as a novelty, momentum was lost. Ockerse remembers the challenge of those days. "Because they released several singles from the LP, I worked the *After Eight* album for a very long time. 'Puttin' on the Ritz' and the crooner thing was really a gimmick for me in the beginning. I loved the camp aspect, but like the schlager music, it wasn't something I wanted to do all my life. *After Eight* was really, in my eyes, a concept LP. When it came time for a follow-up album, that's when the problems started happening. I wanted to move on and try other things, but RCA was very resistant. The second LP, *Let's Face the Music*, was pretty much the same thing again. We did try some other types of sounds and styles, like the stand-alone singles 'Superphysical Resurrection' and "Under My Tight Skin.' I wanted to get away from my voice sounding like it was being heard through a transistor radio. It was a struggle to get the records made with a straight sound, a dance-pop sound, especially when the labels didn't support me. That side of the business wasn't easy. It even got to the point where they told me if I wanted to do my own thing, I'd have to go to the United States and live there. It was a risk at the time I didn't want to take because I didn't have enough contacts there. To go to New York and get started all over again wasn't something I was prepared to do. I knew what it was like to live there. And I guess having been burned by my management in the States added to my anxiety. To be honest, the idea scared the fuck out of me, so I struggled in Germany to find new producers."

Taco released a number of singles and albums between 1984 and 1989, as he floated among a variety of recording labels. His *Swing Classics: In the Mood of Glenn Miller* LP for Polydor in 1985, featuring traditional arrangements of 1940s classics with a hint of pop, was well-received. The aptly titled album *Tell Me That You Like It* followed in 1986, which saw the artist move away from standards to more contemporary easy listening and pop songs like "You're My Answer to It All." The remainder of the decade and into the next was peppered with dance records in the style of Stock Aitken Waterman hits, including "Got to Be Your Lover" and "Love Touch." But the accolades bestowed upon his debut recording failed to carry over to the majority of his subsequent works.

Ockerse takes a sip of brandy and eases back in his chair. He thinks a moment about the realities of the music business back in the '80s. "You must understand the record companies," he explains. "There were very few creative people at the labels. They put the music out and just hoped it would work. If it didn't, you were out. In my case, they only got behind my record when they saw it was doing well somewhere else. It was never like the label would get behind me as an artist and try to build me into something big. A lot of artists became frustrated by that situation. That's why you had that big trend in the '90s—people like Prince starting their own companies and distributing their music by themselves.

"Today, it's not really any better. Now it's all about the producers. Artists come and go, for the most part, and have little value, unless they are like a Bruno Mars, who is a singer, songwriter and kind of the whole package. To be honest, that was never me—I *needed* a good producer, a pool of people and a team behind me. Now that's harder to find than it was even back in the '80s. I was lucky to have been a success in the era I was in. Though there are more channels of distribution available today, and technology makes it easier in a technical way, it's much harder to get a professional team behind you in the twenty-first century. And you can't sell as much today. I went gold for 'Puttin' on the Ritz' in the U.S. for selling over one million copies. Today, a gold record is given for maybe 500,000 copies. The music business has completely changed. At least I got paid—what I got, I got. At least I didn't have what the label was spending on marketing me deducted from my check.

"I am also proud to say that I was able to record most of my songs in one take," he continues. "My music wasn't a composite of various sessions, as so often occurs today. In current pop music, one take is out of the ordinary. Up until the '70s, singers like Gloria Gaynor and the stars of Motown all went into the studio and recorded without the benefit of Pro Tools, pitch tuning and radical editing. That's the old school. Nowadays, the industry is focused on choreography and the producers. The singer has become progressively less important. I think the shift really began in the '80s, when digital recordings and advances in technology took over.

"Had I been able to craft my career with more freedom following all the success, I'd have liked to have sung what I do now in my shows—a mix of swing, pop, and soul with modern arrangements. I would have liked to do more work like the *Tell Me That You Like It* LP. I guess I would like to have been the Michael Bublé of that time," he smiles. "But I don't want it to seem like I'm thinking negatively. I got to see the world, they paid for everything, and I experienced some amazing things. I look at my career and am both satisfied and dissatisfied with it. It was a big rollercoaster ride. I was on top, and I was down in the dumps. I've seen both sides of it. I look back and think it would have been great to have kept my career at such a high level, with big shows and nice orchestras. But if the support and the money are not there, you have to work with less and deal with reality. I'm happy the quality is still there in the shows I do today, and I still love performing. But the whole career thing—it's not that important. I had it; it was great, and I enjoyed it in that moment— but it's not everything. You walk down the street for a time, and then it's over, and you turn down a new street. It's time to move on. It's nothing sad; it's life."

Though Taco doesn't allow his mind to become absorbed with the past, the significance of his contributions to pop culture are not lost on the artist. "Every time I hear somebody is doing a cover of 'Ritz,' I kind of growl a little," he laughs. "But Herb Alpert did a really nice, hip jazz version of the song that I liked very much. But you know what makes me really proud of my version? I got to speak to Irving Berlin on the phone back when the song was at the top of the U.S. charts, and he was so excited. In the old Hollywood days, everyone recorded the song, from Astaire to Sinatra. But it was never a big hit for anyone. Mr. Berlin was 85 when I spoke to him, and he was so genuinely happy, saying, 'This is the first time it's a hit!' That was a very big thing in my life. A real legend, Mr. Songbook himself, and he's thanking *me* for making his song a hit. I still get goose bumps from that."

Taco continued to work in live musicals and on music productions for artists such as Kid Creole and the Coconuts (*The Conquest of You* LP) through the '90s. The artist recently released a new electro-swing version of his classic, "Puttin' on the Ritz 2017," which included a mix featuring vocal samples by Fred Astaire. Though Ockerse is often called upon to perform his primary hit at European retro-'80s concerts, a life balance remains his top priority.

"I think a lot of artists make the mistake of seeing their career as number one and forget that you must maintain a private life. I am grateful my career took off when I was in my mid-20s and not at 16 or 17, like some of these kids today. They don't have a fucking clue how to have private friends or people that ground you. I think that's the whole key to everything. It's very important to enjoy your work, but don't overrate it. It's not the whole world. It's so much more important to say no sometimes, take time off, spend time with friends and pursue hobbies. In the end, that's what you are left with. Sometimes being in the kitchen cooking is more gratifying than being out in some nightclub in the middle of nowhere. Heck, I have fun just looking for sales in the stores."

Taco pulls no punches when discussing the past, but he is less eager to analyze his legacy and the impact his uncommon, seemingly immortal version of "Puttin' on the Ritz" has had upon the world. After a long pause, he says, "It's so difficult in show business to make a name for yourself. But I guess I did it. It's mind-boggling to me how many people still look at the video for the song today on YouTube. Millions are still into it, and that's very exciting. It was a great accomplishment for me. And hell, they still ask me to perform it on TV shows—things like 'Where Are They Now?' or 'Are They Still Alive?,'" he laughs.

"But I don't live in the past. If you live in the now, you don't really think about your legacy. For me, it's been one hell of a trip. I guess I hope people will enjoy my music and will remember that we had a great moment together. I try to live that way. Live for today and enjoy life; live now, and live it up!" he cheers, raising his glass of brandy. "I think I even wrote something like that in my Class of '73 yearbook!"

Linda Jo Rizzo
"You're My First, You're My Last" (1986)
Germany

A former model and a native New Yorker, Linda Jo Rizzo combined sharp looks, a powerful voice and a go-getter personality to become one of the most exciting and memorable dance music stars of the '80s. Her accomplishments as a lead vocalist with The Flirts and as a solo star drew scores of dancers onto the floor throughout the world. Working with prolific producers like Bobby Orlando and Fancy, she became one of the key voices of a hybrid Italo-disco/Hi-NRG/new wave sound that swept Europe and the United States. It's been a long and thrilling ride for Rizzo, who often travels today between homes in New York and Germany. She takes some time to enthusiastically reflect upon a music career that has prospered on both sides of the Atlantic for decades.

"I never really thought about being a singer when I was younger," says Linda. "I wanted to be on stage, and I had a real a passion for that. I sang in the church on Sunday, I sang in school, and everyone always said I had a nice voice. But I never thought of taking it anywhere. I had gone to Italy when I was 18 to model and ended up being there in the summer when everyone goes on vacation. I had very little to do, and I wound up with a job singing for the season. Then I did some more gigs in Portugal. I came back to the United States after spending five years in Europe, and I went back to college.

"One evening, I was having dinner with some friends of mine from Milano, and Bobby Orlando, a music producer, was at the table. I didn't know who he was, but some people at the table told him I had a great voice, and they suggested he bring me down to his studio. He said okay and invited me to come down the next day. He was recording another artist, Nadia Cassini (Igor Cassini's ex-wife) I believe, and they took a lunch break. He asked me to go up to the mike and sing something for him. So, I had the song he was producing in my head, and I sang it. The next day, I had my contract with him. It was totally crazy, and it just happened without any plan at all.

Honestly, dance music was not my thing when I started recording with Bobby," Linda admits. "I loved disco music to dance to. I was in the discos during the '70s, dancing to all those great songs by George McCrae and Gloria Gaynor, but it was not the music I envisioned singing. I was into pop-rock. My biggest idol was Janis Joplin when I was a kid, which was far off from the disco scene."

Linda's big break came with the formation of a group called The Flirts, with whom she eventually became a full-time member. The Flirts were a revelation when they first broke onto the scene, though the group's history remains a bit muddled. Initially, three

Left: Linda Jo Rizzo strikes a pose with The Flirts, seen here in a mid–'80s label publicity shot. From left to right are Rebeka Storm, Pam and Linda. *Right:* Linda Jo Rizzo still delivers high-energy music today.

back-to-back hits by the female trio, "Passion," "Calling All Boys" and "Jukebox (Don't Put Another Dime)," stormed up the European and American dance charts with unparalleled speed in 1982. In Germany and Switzerland, "Passion" was a monster that swiftly climbed into the nations' Top Five. "Jukebox" was a smash in the U.S. and a sizeable video hit on MTV during the network's earliest days. Producer Bobby Orlando's electronic wizardry seamlessly combined a powerful beat with eccentric, new wave styled vocals. It was a new kind of girl-group sound that was well-timed to the Hi-NRG and alternative dance music trends sweeping both continents. The Flirts were often viewed in the same light as The Go Go's, but with a more pronounced disco beat. The group's debut album, *10 Cents a Dance* (on Bobby's "O" Records label in the U.S.), was a strong seller and featured the follow-up singles "Boy Crazy" and "We Just Want to Dance." The LP credited the "female Flirts" at the time as Andrea (Del Conte), Holly (Kerr) and Rebecca (Sullivan).

Orlando (also known as Bobby "O") was a proficient songwriter and producer who came into his own during the early part of the decade. Recording for his own label and countless other small indie record companies, he spearheaded Hi-NRG music, a sound he helped to fashion with heavy bass, synthesizers, piano, guitars and ringing cowbells. His production style became a call to arms in the clubs, sending such eclectic vocalists as drag star Divine ("Shoot Your Shot"), Roni Griffith ("[The Best Part of] Breaking Up") and some early work by the Pet Shop Boys ("West End Girls") to the top of the dance charts. Orlando also stepped out as a solo artist, garnering a massive club hit in 1982 with "She Has a Way." Recalls Rizzo, "The memories I have of Bobby Orlando—I can tell you he was always working. He was a very hard worker. He was very creative and nutty because he'd always have these ideas. You'd sit and talk to him, and he'd jump up and have this idea and run to the piano or his desk and write it down. That's why he was so successful—he had real talent in the realm of dance music. He whipped them out, one after the other."

The live performance and recording identities of The Flirts have been a source of some confusion for years, perhaps the result of Orlando's unique production methods. Linda's recollections of recording some of the early Flirts hits over 30 years ago have faded with time, but she is cognizant of the fact that few people realize the nature of the producer's creative process. "Bobby [was working on] another group called Waterfront Home that he was thinking of for me. I did a couple of demos and tracks, but then Bobby decided that I was going to be in The Flirts. I don't know how or why he came to that decision. I really wanted to be a solo artist. If you understand the theory behind how a girl or boy group works, there are usually only one or two members who do most of the singing. The rest do a lot of background vocals and provide visuals, etc. So, when Bobby recorded, I believe I was one of three girls that were the actual voices, who actually created the sound. It's funny; people ask me for a definitive list of which Flirts songs my voice is on. I honestly can't tell you for certain. Bobby would record the different voices with the same song and then edit the best sounds together in the studio. It was a sound you could not individualize because that was the idea of a group. 'The Flirts' was a project. I don't think he ever expected to have this big, big success where we would start to be identified by the public. I don't think he intended for us to have an identity—it was a blonde, a brunette and a redhead. That's it. You would see in later albums that the girls would change. I worked on The Flirts behind the scenes, so to speak, long before I had my face on the cover of a single or an album.

"I would like to mention Tony Marinello's name," adds Linda, "since he was Bobby's mixer for 12 years, and he was working at the time I sang with the Flirts. He was also Bobby's right hand man in the recording studio during the late '80s to mid-'90s and a dance music composer and writer. Once Tony finished [his work with] the tracks, they were then laid down to tape and Bobby headed off to mix the vocals and music. Voila! You had a record. Tony said Bobby used to call himself 'the Ronald McDonald of the music industry'—over a billion served."

The album *Born to Flirt* was released in 1983, and it clearly documented Rizzo's participation in the line-up. The LP featured the hit singles "Danger" and "Helpless (You Took My Love)," which placed high on the German and Swiss pop charts. "When I had been in Europe," recalls Linda, "I had done work with groups and then other things that I did alone—which I preferred. I'm a performer, and I like the freedom to be able to move around on stage and do what I do. When you were in a '80s group, especially The Flirts, you were totally choreographed. I can dance, but I'm not a 'dancer,' so to study a dance move was less spontaneous to me. I like to just give my heart. In a group, that's more difficult because everybody has a role to play and a move to make. The hands have to go up together, your foot's got to go out together with everyone else's, and frankly that's torture to me. When I joined the touring version of The Flirts, the other two girls that were in the group with me were much younger, so I felt kind of funny in the beginning. I was wearing these little leather mini skirts and was doing all these crazy dances. To be honest, I felt a little silly" she laughs.

"On the *Born to Flirt* tour," says Rizzo, "I was a front man. Since the other two girls in the group were not singers, we would lip synch to the tracks. I really wanted to get out there and sing and perform. I spoke with Bobby about going solo, and he asked me to be patient, saying he had plans for me. Unfortunately, nothing really happened. So when I got an offer to record as a solo artist, I decided the time was right to make a change. I resolved my contract with Bobby, and there was no problem. Bobby continued with the group using other girls. After 1985, I moved on and didn't have any more contact with the other girls in The Flirts. (I only recently got back in touch with two members of the group thanks to Facebook.)"

While The Flirts continued to release club hits, Linda strategized a new direction for her career in dance music. Her collaborations with the iconic German dance music producer and artist named Fancy (also known as Ric Tess Teiges, a publicly somewhat mysterious star who was enjoying tremendous success on the German charts with hits like "Slice Me Nice" and "Chinese Eyes") proved to be inspired. Fancy, like Orlando, had a signature sound that included hard beats, electronic keyboard hooks, synthesizers and simple, yet irresistible English lyrics. Says Linda, "I met Fancy while I was on tour with The Flirts. We had come to play dates in Europe for two weeks. The two weeks turned into five months, and I met him at a concert in West Germany. He saw me on the stage with The Flirts, and he must have picked up that I had something. He came to me after the show and gave me his card. He asked that if I ever left the group to please call him. He was looking to produce a girl. Well, I was living out of my suitcase for those five months, and I lost the number.

"This was the craziest thing. I went back to America to dissolve my contract with Bobby and came back to Germany three months later—this was in 1985. I had a record company lined up to record with, and they cancelled at the last minute. So I wound up in Germany with my daughter, who was only four years old at the time, and I thought, 'Oh my God, what am I gonna do now?' I took a job in a piano bar just to get by, and the second week I'm singing there—who walks in for dinner? Fancy! Of course, he had no make-up on and looked like an ordinary man. He calls me over and asks why I never called him. I said, 'Well, who are you?' I didn't recognize him of course. He identified himself, and I apologized for losing the number. He asked me to come by his studio, which was four doors away. He said, 'We're gonna make a record!' Linda lets out a big laugh. "I recorded my first solo record, which was 'Fly Me High' at one o'clock that night in his studio. That's how it all started. I get goose bumps when I tell the story because it really seemed like destiny to me. Of all the places in Germany, he walks into the one piano bar I happen to be singing in."

"Fly Me High" was released by EMI Records in Germany in 1985 and possessed all the musical trademark elements synonymous with her new producer. His musical style was the perfect match to Linda's commanding voice. The song caused a few ripples, but it was Rizzo's spectacular debut on an indie label based in Merenberg, Germany—ZYX Records—that placed the singer front and center. By then, ZYX was a well-established dance music purveyor and frequent visitor on the nation's Top 20 chart with artists like Scotch, Tullio de Piscopo and Valerie Dore. Linda's launch on the label, "You're My First, You're My Last," was produced by Fancy and proved to be a sensation in European clubs in 1986. The song packed dance floors with its pounding rhythm and catchy lyrics (which were written by Rizzo). For a time, the style became identified not only as German-made Italo-disco, but as "the Linda Jo Rizzo sound." "That was one of my favorite songs that I made with Fancy. I started writing lyrics when we worked together. As the producer, he would get someone to do the music, and then he handed it off to me, asking me to write the lyrics. 'Can you write?' he asked me. 'Well, I guess so. I was good in English in school,' I responded." Linda laughs.

"That was the first song I wrote. Fancy wasn't in the studio all the time. I spent the most time with Alfons Weindorf [also known as Elvine]; he was the musician and arranger. Fancy would approve the song and work with Alfons to create the music. I'd get the demo, the instrumental version, and then I'd put the text to it. I'd sing it to Fancy and see how he felt about it. But he wasn't always in the studio—he trusted us. The lovely thing about Fancy was he gave us room to grow. We were all young, and he wanted us to develop on our own. He wasn't interested in being the boss. He was very fair-minded.

"Fancy was very shy and had sort of a mysterious way about him," Linda adds. "You can compare him to someone like Freddie Mercury. Freddie was very wild on stage, but Tess (Fancy) was not. His 'Fancy' image is very collected and calculated, but he's a very low key and kind of shy person in regular life. He has a great heart, and all the people that worked with him, I believe, liked him very much. It was a great time in my life working with him."

Though professionally successful in Germany, living in the country was an acquired skill for a New York City girl, says Rizzo. "I loved my work, and I stayed in Germany to do that. In the beginning, I didn't speak German, but everyone in the music business here spoke English. So that was never a problem. I wanted to sing, and I didn't care where I did it. I would have done it in Iceland if they wanted me to go there. I'm an Italian American and grew up in a very Italian family. The culture of Germany was sometimes challenging for me coming from that background. I've been here [over 30] years, and it still is difficult. Italian families are always 'mangia, mangia!' The door is always open, you sit, you eat and you drink and have fun. The German culture can be more reserved and conservative. That was hard for me to adjust to. It's just a cultural difference. They enjoy their lives and might think Italians are kind of strange," she laughs, "we're so flippy and open."

Rizzo was no stranger to challenges, even as far back as her earliest days spent forging a career in the U.S. "In America, it was very hard to have a big, clean career without going down the side streets of sex, drugs and all of that," Linda says frankly. "That's just my viewpoint. I wanted to sing and work based on my talents and not because I had to sleep with somebody. Germany afforded me that opportunity, and I am very grateful for that. And I must say, in Germany, the music business is much more upfront and clean. It's really on the books. You are respected and paid properly. In America, there is so much shit to deal with, and I just didn't want that. Even when I was modeling in the U.S. in my early days, I'd be 18 and every other door you knocked on they'd want to pull you into the bedroom. Give me a break!"

In the years that followed her breakout solo success, Linda released a string of high-energy hits on ZYX, including "Heartflash (Tonight)," "Perfect Love," "Keep Trying" and a remake of the Flirts' hit, "Passion." "I worked so hard during those days; I don't think I knew what was really going on. I went to Europe with one goal, and that was to make it. I was a single parent with a young daughter, and so there was an extra push on my side because I *had* to have that success. I was supporting a family. I didn't realize I might be thought of as a star at the time. So many years ago, it didn't register in my head. I enjoyed being on stage, the traveling, the fans and all the wildness. That's all I took notice of. It's amazing because people today tell me that they heard my records played everywhere back then. I don't think I fully realized that at the time. I didn't even know my records were sold [as imports] in America." Linda shakes her head in disbelief.

By the '90s, the Italo-disco frenzy had ebbed, and Rizzo began singing on what was known in Germany as the gala scene—parties where people ate, drank and danced, accompanied by live entertainment. She worked the circuit well into the new millennium and then began singing for larger corporate events with sizeable bands. With the crash of major economies worldwide around 2008, those bookings dried up. "I always tried to adapt, and after the economic slowdown, I put my own band together and started doing small events. And my opportunities have grown from there. I've worked with a keyboardist all the way up to a full band, depending on the venue's budget. A small budget doesn't scare me off. I wouldn't be able to do my disco music, but I could do cool things like soul music and swing. I have to be very honest. Today I live two lives—the '80s concerts, and I have the live scene. I can sing practically anything except maybe jazz or opera. I've built a name as a reliable singer, and I am called to do a lot of different things."

Linda's determination and resilience were on full display early in her career, she says. "I'm a hard-headed Aries, and I just put on my blinders, and I just go. Probably the hardest time I ever went through was about 25 years ago. I had my first daughter with me here in Germany and was in a relationship with an Italian man. I had two more children. He was from Southern Italy and was very much against my music, which I discovered later in our relationship, of course. After the two children, I wanted to continue to be on stage—and that was *not* in his dimension. He eventually told me I had to choose between him and the music. I chose the music. That was probably the most difficult time in my life because I was raising my children, yet I just wasn't ready to become an Italian housewife. I literally had to start to build my career again and make sure I was able to support my family on my own. I did it, and I don't regret for one moment the choice I made."

The singer observes the personal changes that have come with maturity. "I think as an artist—and when I say artist it applies to singers, actors, musicians or whatever the talent may be—when you are in the limelight, you live a sort of non-reality. As you age, maybe marry and have a family, you try to find a balance between this fantasy world and the real world. I'm in my 50s now, and this year was the first year I started to feel that I was becoming 'older.' You know? My kids are all out of the house and living in New York. The work I do is wonderful, but it can't compare to those days in the '80s, those fantastic times where I was working every single weekend. That's the past.

"I've gone through some changes in the past year with my thinking. You start to notice that 25, 30 years have gone by. I'm still here, and that's wonderful, and I'm thankful, but I realize that those amazing times aren't coming back. That's something an artist has to wrap his or her head around, and I think you have to recreate a new balance for yourself. If you do that, you keep a younger mindset. If you don't and just lament the loss of those years, you get old. It's not as easy as it was back then—you *do* get tired. But you have to keep trying. Your audience and fans are also 25 years older, and they accept that you've aged, but they still want to see that you are alive and energized. Truthfully, the problem isn't usually with the fans—the problem is within us as artists. We have to accept ourselves and keep moving forward. There is a benefit of aging. You learn. I'm a stubborn, impulsive person and when I was young, like around the time of The Flirts and working with Fancy, I made hasty decisions. That's who I was. I had to learn through many, many mistakes to slow down a little bit and listen to what others say. I had to learn not to always jump into the fire—to be cool. It took me 40 years to learn that and to realize I could have done some things differently if I hadn't been so impulsive and hot-headed."

She still enjoys remembering the energized decade that brought her so much success. Of the many performance milestones Rizzo enjoyed, one stands out as exceptionally memorable. "I did this show where I toured with Fancy for a number of years. We had like 15,000 people in the audience, and I was shaking. I have the worst stage fright. I still have it after 30 years. I die a little before every show, and the bigger the show, the more I die. Heart palpitations and everything. But when I hear the crowd screaming for me, it's such a high!" Linda pauses for a moment, trying to come up with a better description of the euphoria she feels. "The orgasm I get on stage—no man could ever give that to me!" she laughs. "It's true. I could go through life without any partner, but don't take my music away!"

Linda recently recorded the pop single "Stronger Together," which featured a cameo by Fancy, and 2015 remixes by Michael Fall earned the track extensive club play. She indulged in a remake of the Eddy Huntington Italo–staple "USSR" and was featured on the single "Out of the Shadows" by '80s-style pop singer TQ. The singer performed with '80s icon Sandra and italo-disco star Savage in a rare New York City concert in 2017, while launching her album *Day of the Light (80s Reloaded)*.

"I think it's a good time for releasing new music like this," the singer observes. "Especially today—with people being under so much pressure. The economy, wars, the bad job situation—because of all these negative things in the world, music is so important. It gives you that evening or an hour of happiness. Or that three-minute song, like 'Day of the Light,' which takes you away from the shit!" she states. "I love to make people happy," she says after pausing for a moment. "I love being on stage, seeing people smile and having fun and feeling good. If I'm remembered by people as someone who made them feel good and gave them a feeling of warmth, then I did my job."

Jack Robinson

Songwriter

Artists: Gloria Gaynor, Princess Stéphanie,
David Christie, Grace Jones, et. al.
France

Jack Robinson knows how to write a catchy song lyric. He first made his mark in pop songwriting back in the early '70s. Robinson picked up speed during the classic disco era by writing the lyrics to Gloria Gaynor's 1975 evergreen "(If You Want It) Do It Yourself," "Do or Die" by Grace Jones in 1978, and "Strut Your Funky Stuff" by Frantique in 1979. Tina Charles' phenomenally successful 1976 hit, "I Love to Love (But My Baby Loves to Dance)" became one of his most popular creations from the glitter ball period. He scored more successful singles with singer and production partner David Christie ("Saddle Up") and hit the jackpot with the landmark international '80s dance smash by Monaco's Princess Stéphanie, "Irresistible." An American living in Paris, Jack is keen to talk about the era and the challenge of writing a song that has the power to endure for decades.

Born in Seattle, Washington, Robinson came from a musical family. His mother was a singer who wrote comical lyrics, song parodies and always had lots of records in the house. Jack humorously describes himself as "an untalented piano player—who played with a vengeance." After serving in the U.S. Marines, he became a news correspondent (first with Associated Press in America and then United Press International) and settled in France in 1962. "Every time I'd sit down to write something serious, I'd always have this mischievous side of me that would want to write the same story in a humorous or even horrible way. I guess I always had that creative streak," he admits. When he was 24 years old, he says he was lucky enough to secure a position as a disc jockey for Radio Luxembourg. He began meeting show business people from all around the world, which led him to become involved in music publishing as a professional manager. The position allowed him to serve as an agent, shopping songs to producers and artists. Eventually, he learned record production and became a lyricist. His first international hit as a producer was "Dancing in the Moonlight" by King Harvest.

"I spoke fluent French, but I never became part of the culture, so to speak," Jack remembers. "I never wrote lyrics in French. In the early '70s, I was approached to create lyrics for a French artist who wanted to sing in English, David Christie. I told David that I didn't want to write a French lyric in English. I didn't want to create something that would sound less than it would if it had been created in English. So I didn't make any concessions with regard to the difficulty a Frenchman or European might have to sing my songs. I always felt a lot of songs written for Europeans sounded like crap to be honest. The lyrics always seemed limited. Though David spoke some English, I virtually taught him to sing in the language.

"David had an eight-track studio at his house (at a time when people were still using four-track), and we'd work for hours at a time until a song phrase sounded as if an English-speaking person was singing it. David and I became a great songwriting team, and we started churning out demos. Then other singers would pick them up and cover the songs. We put together an album called *Napoleon Jones,* with David singing in English. That album had 'If You Want It (Do It Yourself)' and 'I Love to Love' on it. We marketed so many of our compositions using that album.

"Subsequently, Tina Charles covered 'I Love to Love,' and it sold something like 40 million copies worldwide," he says with pride. "I was married to my previous wife at the time, and I can recall very distinctly a Saturday afternoon when my kids weren't home, and I guess I was horny. I suggested to my wife we get it on, and she said no. She wanted to go shopping. I thought to myself, 'I want to make love, but my baby just wants to go shopping!' Well, that wouldn't make a good lyric, but I was so frustrated that I just started to write this song, which turned into 'I Love to Love (But My Baby Loves to Dance).' I called David and told him I had a great idea for a song and drove over to his house. I described the idea of the song, and he sat down at the piano and came up with the verse, the chorus—the whole song in just five minutes, right in front of me. I connected the words to his music, and the result was amazing. We started selling an enormous number of records by marketing these Christie recordings to other artists. We just wanted to build a catalog of good songs." The duo's single for Tina Charles hit the number one position in England and Ireland in 1976, and ten years later, thanks to a vibrant remix by Sanny X, it became a Top Five hit in France, Germany and the Netherlands.

"I wasn't really worried about promoting David as an artist (and neither was he) because we were selling so many records via others," Jack claims. "Late in the '70s, David said his mother had expressed concern that she never saw him on television. It got David to thinking we should hold back some songs, not give everything away, and see if we could get him a big hit to make his mother proud. I was kind of reluctant, but for 18 months we gathered songs for him. We wrote 'Saddle Up' in 1979, and it became a hit in 1982–83," says Jack. Christie's smash, a funky euro-disco jam with catchy lyrics, a punchy beat and plenty of horns, hit the number one position throughout Europe.

"Personal experiences were often the foundation of the lyrics I'd write," Robinson says. "'(If You Want It) Do It Yourself' was one of the first songs I wrote with David Christie, and it was inspired by my father. He always told me that if I wanted something in life, to work for it and go get it. The Gloria Gaynor version of 'Do It Yourself' was one of the only songs she sang in that period (1975) that made it onto the R&B charts. It didn't go that high, but it was a club hit. It did much better in Europe and stayed for a much longer time on their charts.

"I remember when I was a marine. We'd go on these long marches in the California desert. They'd let us stop for a minute to sit and light up a cigarette, and as soon as we did, the sergeant would suddenly shout, 'Saddle up!' That became the inspiration for David Christie's song of the same name. Some things stay with you all your life."

Jack's song lyrics blended well with European tastes, but he says he never wrote expressly for that market. "I wrote for English speaking people," he claims. "That said, when we were writing songs, our primary targets were always Great Britain and Germany. Germany was the heart of disco and dance music. If you had a hit in these countries, you pretty much knew the song would be a hit in France. If you wrote for France, your song usually had very little international value.

"Lyrics were less important in markets like France, where there is a lot of resistance to learning English. It almost didn't matter what the lyrics were because many people wouldn't understand them anyway. I think that's still true today. The French have a lot of difficulty with English, despite the fact that the two languages are very close. In Germany, Scandinavia, Holland, Spain and Belgium, English is a more common second language. I always tried to make sure that my lyrics would stand up in America or England. The English have no time for bad lyrics or imitation English lyrics. Today, many of the top European producers are very careful about ensuring their international artists have sharp English lyrics. A great example of this would be Daft Punk or David Guetta. I've found the French today to be extraordinarily hip at times, but those artists who are successful tend to be so outside of the country, not within it. Strange phenomenon."

Robinson is well aware that only a limited number of dance-pop hits made in France managed to make their mark beyond the country's borders during the '80s. "In the case of Jeanne Mas ('En Rouge Et Noir')," he observes, "she had an outstanding producer and composer named Romano Musumarra. He also wrote the melody for the hit we had with Princess Stéphanie of Monaco. He was actually an Italian, and Italians have an incredible talent for melody. They just have music in their blood. I knew Jean-Michel Rivat, who produced Desireless and the international star Joe Dassin here in France. So sometimes there were people in the French music industry who had some influence in the international market. But there were very few French language songs that would travel in the '80s. Though the French had memorable melodies, quite often the lyrics tended to be more poetic than musical. And if you don't understand French, you're probably not going to get off on it."

Jack says there were many changes in the music business as Europe entered the '80s. "The MIDEM (Marché International du Disque et de l'Edition Musicale) music convention was an extraordinary business trip I'd take annually to the south of France in the '70s. It was a great deal of fun. I met everybody; even Clive Davis from Arista Records in the U.S. would be there. It was a time of creative joy. I thought the industry became more—professional—in the '80s. The majors got more interested in dance music. It had been handled more by independents previously. The majors always told me in the '70s they didn't like dance music. They had to put some out, but they definitely didn't like it. That's when I was working with Grace Jones and Gloria Gaynor. To be honest, I didn't love the '80s. I felt the major labels took over the creative side of the business. Everything became more glitzy. Videos became essential, whereas before that we had live or filmed TV shows. A lot of money was spent in the '80s, and it didn't have the same feel as the previous decade. But I guess I was fortunate to have some big hits [during this period]."

Robinson's path eventually crossed with that of Stéphanie Grimaldi (also known as Princess Stéphanie of Monaco). Stéphanie was born in 1965, the youngest child of Rainier III, Prince of Monaco. A tragic car accident in 1982 killed her mother, the legendary actress Grace Kelly. Stéphanie was also injured in the accident and required several months to recover. She went on to work in fashion with Christian Dior and became one of Europe's most talked about young celebrities. In 1986, she recorded one of the most popular singles of the era, "Ouragan," which has also been reported to be one of France's best-selling songs ever. It was a powerful and addictive floor-filler laced with a pounding beat and the singer's modest (but effective) vocal work. The track was also released abroad in its original English language version, "Irresistible," whose lyrics were written by Jack Robinson. It narrowly missed hitting the number one position in Germany. Combined, the tracks were reported to have sold over two million copies worldwide and were highlights of Stéphanie's self-titled debut album (also known as *Besoin* in France).

Says Jack, "Stéphanie was a wild child and was living on the edge—way over the top at the time. She had a dual hit with the same song—my version in English and the French version 'Ouragan' by another lyricist. I think 'Irresistible' had my best lyrics ever. It took me three weeks to write it. Normally, if I know the title of a song, I can write it in two or three days. It took me three weeks to come up with the idea for this song because I knew I was writing it *for* somebody (which was unusual for me, and the only other exception was Grace Jones). In this case, it was a 20- or 21-year-old princess.

"I pictured her life—she's not supposed to be hanging out with this dude, but he's irresistible. I wrote the song based on the music composed by Musumarra, and writing a lyric to someone else's music is like doing a crossword puzzle. You are beholden to write syllables that fit the music. The melody was so strong, and it was very difficult for me. The producer, Yves Roze, kept calling me up asking where his lyrics were. After they were finally written, I submitted them to him, and he said that Stéphanie really liked them and that they would record it right away. I'm not sure whether the royal family had to give approval of the lyrics, but there was nothing that would have been a problem. It was a simple song about being in love with a bad boy."

One of the lyrics in Robinson's hit for the princess contained the alternative word "irregardless," which broke a bit from the lyricist's usual insistence upon the use of proper English. "I knew the word didn't exist," he laughs, "but who the hell would care? *Irre*.... *Irre*.... I just couldn't come up with another word that would fit in that context. So I said 'irregardless.' I can say in all this time that hardly anybody brought the word choice to my attention—just an English teacher once. It was the only time I ever cheated in a song.

"Stéphanie was just the hottest thing in France and Germany that year. She was having a crazy life, getting in trouble and always in the media. I think her father was pretty upset with her a lot of the time. Today, you don't see much about Stéphanie, and I think she leads a much quieter life now. My experience working on the song for her was a thrill. It was amazing to have scored such a big hit, but it involved a lot of agony," he claims.

Looking back at the industry, Robinson says the music business has always been something of a minefield. "One of my very early jobs in the music business was working for a great pioneer American publisher in Los Angeles, whose name was Michael Goldson," recalls the lyricist. "He formed a company called Criterion Music, one of the biggest independent music publishers in the country. He told me that the major labels all have the same attitude—their philosophy is, 'Sue me, and I'll pay you. If you can't afford to sue us, fuck you!' There were all kinds of thievery in America, and I had my share of problems with the music business. I produced 'Dancing in the Moonlight' for King Harvest [in the early '70s], and it was a huge hit in the U.S. But the label kept it lower on the charts so we wouldn't claim too many royalties. Neither the band nor the production team was paid. In France, I'd say the record labels were much more honest than those in America, even if they were offshoots of the U.S. companies. The French writers' society, Société des auteurs, compositeurs et éditeurs de musique (SACEM), really protects songwriters and publishers and were real watchdogs to ensure that sales figures were accurate. They were almost like a police force. But still, there was one French executive who was legendary for cheating, and I had to sue him several times. However, I've found that France is probably the safest place to be in the music business.

"The British companies—I'd say you had to keep your eye on them too, despite the so-called 'Englishman's word,' nobility and all that. I've had enough experience with them to know they will opt to avoid paying if they think they can get away with it. An international hit always complicates matters, and it was up to the producer to oversee the collections of royalties. I'm sure there were millions lost between France and, say, Germany, but what they did declare on a big hit was often so spectacular that all the people involved would just go 'oh wow' and accept it.

"I recall a German label executive who had an opportunity to pick up a big hit by a small independent U.S. label that didn't know better. What he did was release singles and albums by this new hit artist on the A-side, and the B-side would be his Joe Blow artist—and he'd keep the royalties. I'm talking about sales of possibly millions of records. I'm told the Japanese are extremely honest in their payments, but, unfortunately, I've never had any experience with them," he says with a shrug.

Jack is still busy in the music industry today. While developing plans for his own musical comedy play to be set in the disco era and working on a compilation album of his many compositions and those sung by David Christie, he continues to be actively involved in the music-publishing world. He says at the heart of everything, he is still a lyricist. "I don't know where the lyric writing talent in me comes from. With growing up in the radio atmosphere of the '40s and '50s, all the great musicals—I figure I must have at least 3,000 song lyrics in my head. It was like going to school for me, analyzing all these lyrics. I think the last lyricist I really studied was Hal David. I would think of all his wonderful songs with Burt Bacharach and wonder where they came up with all those ideas. I guess I accumulated all these lyrics in my head by others and tried to come up with something original myself.

"I would like people to say that they had a significant moment with my music," reflects Robinson. "I especially hope people will remember my songs with a laugh, recalling a good time they had when they first heard something I wrote. Maybe they'll say they just remember one of my songs—period. You know, that would be good, too. Someone asked me recently if I wrote 'I Love to Love.' I said that I did. They responded, 'You know Jack, that was my grandmother's favorite song.' I busted out laughing. At least I was able to touch people that I've never met, people of different generations. In my spare time, I still play songs by Harold Arlen and Johnny Mercer, Cole Porter, Rodgers and Hart and the Gershwins—people like that. I always think, 'My God, these guys will *never* die. They are eternal thanks to their music.' I think I'd like a little bit of that," he laughs.

Fabio Roscioli
aka Ryan Paris
"Dolce Vita" (1983)
Italy

"I am very proud of 'Dolce Vita,' absolutely. This song is a masterwork. I was very lucky to sing it, and I think my voice was a very good fit for the song," says Fabio Roscioli firmly with a rich Italian accent. He is better known as Ryan Paris, and he is speaking of his trend-setting international hit that brought the singer worldwide fame. The sanguine electronic dance track left music fans awash in a glow of euphoria in 1983, as Paris' haunting vocals and the song's irresistible melody cast a hypnotic spell over the populace of numerous countries. "Dolce Vita" (translation: 'Sweet Life') was truly a product of Italy, conceived by Italian composer and arranger Pierluigi Giombini and songwriter Paul Mazzolini (also known as Gazebo). It helped to fortify the Italo-disco revolution, itself a progression of the previous decade's disco sound. The strength of his smash single kept Ryan, the son of an accomplished painter, in the spotlight for years and established his masculine, yet soothing voice as one of the genre's most romantic and instantly recognizable. Paris resides in Germany today and happily shares his memories of living *la dolce vita*, always with a sense of humor. Immediately, one can feel his passion, humor and exuberance. He nearly always smiles throughout the conversation.

"I really started in music when I was about four years old," says Paris. "My grandfather was an opera singer in Toscana. He was singing with Maria Callas at the time. He had a big phonograph, and as a child, I knew all the songs he would play on it—all the operas. I would sing them. When I got a bit older, I started listening to pop records in the '60s. I remember my favorite song was 'Twist and Shout.' I listened to The Beatles, The Bee Gees, James Taylor. I loved this kind of music. The music always seemed to just kind of come to me. So I guess I was influenced by the old Italian music and the pop and rock I heard that was sung in English. When I was about 18, I started to study the guitar. I got so good at it that I started to teach it. I went to England and met some more music people in London, who also influenced me. I came back to Italy and joined two or three rock bands. One was called Berenice's Hair (derived from the name of a constellation)—it was the '70s, and bands had all these crazy, strong names," he laughs. "At that time, I didn't know the English language that well. For me, it wasn't a language; it was a sound. So I invented words when I sang. I would change the lyrics to a song like 'Yesterday' to something like, 'Yesterday, I was running just to run away.' I soon started to

Left: **Ryan Paris promotes his self-titled debut album on European radio in 1985.** *Right:* **Paris actively releases new songs today, including regular updates of his classic hit "Dolce Vita."**

think it might be a good idea if I started to sing songs in a good way!" Ryan laughs again, heartily.

"My first professional appearance, before 'Dolce Vita,' was at the age of 20. In Italy at the time, there was a rock singer named Rita Pavone, who was very popular. She was married to a big artist manager named Teddy Reno. I was doing background vocals for a friend of mine, Andrew Capizz, under the name Teddy Rhono, just for fun. We recorded for an Italian record company in Bologna that was having hits with [the synth-pop group] Gaznevada. Later, in Rome, I was about 26 years old and teaching Brazilian guitar at a music school. There, I met a great teacher and musician named Irio De Paula. He was a Brazilian who loved Rome—and I loved the music of Brazilians—Milton Nascimento, Jobim—*fantastico*. He invited me to his house where every Saturday there would be big jam sessions, and on this particular day he was playing a song that I knew. I asked if I could sing the song, and he let me. After I finished, another gentleman came up to me and said, 'It's incredible. You have a beautiful voice. You are able to communicate so well with it!' So I started playing Brazilian music with this man, and for a few months we played nightclubs and places like that.

"I really wanted to concentrate on my singing, so I went to New York and stayed with a friend to see what would happen there," Ryan continues. "I spent three months there, and it was fantastic. I loved New York—it is a beautiful city. I decided to come back to Italy, however, because I was determined to get a number one record, and I thought I had a better chance of succeeding in my home country. I connected with a producer and composer named Pierluigi Giombini and let him hear my music, which was rock-oriented. I was coming from more of a rock background at this point. He said he liked my voice and that I sounded a little like—*come si chiama*—uh, Stevie Winwood. He played some records for me that he had produced called 'Masterpiece' [by Gazebo] and 'You Are a Danger' [by Gary Low]. They were number two and number five on the charts at the time, I think. I really liked the sound—they sounded so new and incredible with all the synthesizers. He said, unfortunately, he could not work with me because I was singing in Italian. I said, 'No, No! I always sing in English.'" he laughs. "Not very well, but my singing was better than when I spoke the language."

Fabio's stage name came about as a result of some pillow talk he enjoyed with an English background singer named Fiona. "We were together, and we spent an afternoon in bed looking through an Italian-English dictionary to find a good name for me as a singer," he recalls. "I liked the name Ryan, thinking of the American actor Ryan O'Neal. She suggested 'Ryan Berlin.' I came up with Ryan Paris, and that was it. I then went to work with Pierluigi. He was a fantastic musician and producer, but a crazy person. I mean that in a nice way. He was like an artist expressing himself out in the universe, and he was kind of—what is the word—eccentric. I think that's the word. The first time I heard 'Dolce Vita,' I made a jump that almost destroyed the lamp on the ceiling. Well, we recorded the song, and it went to number one," says Paris, somewhat modestly.

"Dolce Vita," became one of the biggest recordings ever produced in Italy. According to Ryan, Belgium, Spain, the Netherlands, Ireland, Norway, Switzerland and Austria all sent the single to the number one position. In Germany, it reached number three, and the British embraced the hypnotic track as a Top Five smash. In his native Italy, the song reached the Top 10 and shared a position among the top songs of the year with artists like Culture Club, Irene Cara, The Police, and David Bowie. Contemporary estimates place the track's total sales around the five million units mark, according to the artist. Young, lean and handsome, Ryan was a sensation on Europe's top television shows, including the all-important *Top of the Pops* program in Britain. "Dolce Vita" was released in the United States as a 12-inch single via the American division of the Carrere label and was an underground club hit.

"It's interesting," the artist observes, "because in Italy, 'Dolce Vita' was not quite as powerful on the pop chart as it was in other countries, but it was a very big hit in the Italian discothèques. All the people of Europe would come down to Spain and Italy in the summer—men looking for girls, girls looking for men, and everything in between. They would remember the song from the parties and nightclubs, and when they returned to their countries, they would ask for the song. Carrere Records bought the song from [the publisher] Severo Lombardoni, and BBC1 filmed the video for the song in Paris [for the British release]. The song just went up, up, up. The record was an amazing success in Spain. I have heard that it is the biggest selling record in Spain—*ever*—750,000 maxi-singles sold.

"For me, music is one of the biggest expressions a human being can make. It is like God coming through a human being. It's true! A song can be very powerful in any genre, but this song really had something special. It was incredible because it was very commercial with the bass—bum-bum-bum-bum-bum from the beginning—the melody was very Italian, and the arrangement was very English. It had a real Mediterranean flavor and a sound that only Giombini could create. He was one of the greatest producers of the '80s. There were many parts of me in the song too. In the central part, there was a touch of South American music and a bit of a rock music influence, which reflected me. Just a beautiful song."

"Fall in Love" was Paris' highly anticipated follow-up to "Dolce Vita" (co-written by Gazebo with Pierluigi Giombini, who also produced the track under the name John Bini), and the song was released in Italy in 1984. Though a well-crafted track with many of the ethereal qualities of its predecessor, its somewhat darker and more melancholy mood failed to resonate as strongly with Europe's record-buyers, charting only modestly in England, France and Spain.

"I didn't feel any pressure on myself to follow 'Dolce Vita' with something just as big," claims Paris. "My father and my mother—*they* felt some pressure. I think they were worried about my future and wanted me to continue to have hits. 'Fall in Love' is a very nice song, but it was not created specifically for me. So things went downhill from there." Later in 1984, Paris signed with RCA Italiana for his next release, a maxi-single collaboration with Giombini called "Paris on My Mind." The electronic pop-dance singles "Harry's Bar" and "Besoin d'Amour" followed in subsequent years, but neither made significant dents in the charts. "I went over to BMG [the Bertelsmann Music Group, which eventually absorbed RCA] for a while, which was a very, very bad story. 'Dolce Vita' was done by the producer on a small label, but he was connected with the big companies too. [RCA] said, 'Give Ryan Paris to us, and everything will be okay.' The [self-titled] album that came from them was really bullshit. But it's okay. Yes, I went down, but I feel like I am in the Roberto Benigni movie, *The Tiger and the Snow*." Quoting the film, Paris exclaims, "'I am a poet! I am a poet!' I am a poet, too—and a musician."

Despite the gargantuan success of his signature hit and a long dance music-recording career that continued on into the '90s, Ryan says he didn't directly reap significant financial rewards. "They did not pay me very much to sing 'Dolce Vita.' I don't have any money from the many records they sold. Really—but I am very happy. I was always able to make a living with the music. I am still a singer and a producer today, and I have had many successful releases. I am very happy because the people still love my music. I also do shows and have a big tour planned—Poland, Mexico, Germany, France and China. I always live with the music. And it has helped me get through any bad moments.

"I eventually moved from Italy to Germany. I think you get more stability in Germany," claims Paris. "Creativity from Italy—stability from Germany. I wrote a song called 'I Wanna Love You Once Again,' which was very successful. Then the music from the '80s became popular again, and I started doing more shows. Little by little, all my music came out again, and people rediscovered it. A few years years ago, [a new version of] 'I Wanna Love You Once Again' spent nine weeks at number one in Poland and was a big radio hit. A new single I made, 'Sensation of Love' (sung by a young man named Miro, but composed and produced by me) was on the Bulgarian charts for nine weeks and reached the number 15 spot. And I'm working on a new album, which I think will be … *fantastico*!" the artist says as he gently brings the fingers and thumb of his right hand to his lips, kisses them and joyfully opens them in the air. That album, *You Are My Life*, was released in 2016 in a limited edition vinyl format. Paris' latest material has a contemporary, yet distinctly European edge and shows the singer to be in fine vocal form today. Meanwhile, "Dolce Vita" has continued to be remixed, re-recorded, and reinvented many times over the years (by Ryan and others), a further testament to its enduring qualities. In 2016, he released "Dolce Vita 2K16," recorded with Doctor Vintage, and the single "Buonasera Dolce Vita" in 2017.

"I am a very normal person," Paris says. "I don't have a big head about 'Dolce Vita,' and I don't say things like, 'Oh, I had a number one record!' It's okay—it's good and fantastic—but the song and success were not the only things in my life." Ryan takes a moment to focus on other blessings, notably his son, and expresses great pride over the young man's development as an artist in his own right. "My son is a great singer," he says with pride. "His name is Alexander Patrick Giacomo. He is 14 years old and has done seven concerts in Brazil and five concerts in America. Already! His voice is better than mine."

Ryan pauses when thinking about his philosophy for managing life today. He relates some personal anecdotes about challenging experiences in his private life (that he says he'd prefer to keep private), but then returns to his usual good cheer, remembering he's managed to get through all of it. He reveals he has a solid belief in reincarnation and that he enjoys studying older religions. "I think, really, life is a fantastic adventure and an opportunity to receive and give love. I think the secret of life is just to ask for what you want. I had so many opportunities in life. I was able to meet the wonderful musicians—Chick Corea, Al Jarreau, and so many others. I've had a beautiful life, and I have a great son. How can I explain this to you? This life is so nice, and it makes me laugh and smile so often. That's the thing. It's important to enjoy life. You must remember, paradise and hell are here on earth. They are not the things of the afterlife. I enjoy studying the mystical things of life, but in a normal way—nothing crazy. Through the music, you can really see and feel the heights, the sensations of life. I had a very big opportunity in life to see this clearly because I was on a stage. I was able to feel the very strong reaction of humanity to the music.

"I want to be remembered like Achilles at Troy," Fabio laughs once again. "Being remembered for thousands of years—no, I'm just joking! You know, I try to do my best every time. I try to make music that communicates something. I'm a very free-feeling person, and I always want my music to be good. I have always been this way, so I do not have any regrets. To be remembered? I would like it if people thought I was a good singer and that I wrote some good music. We artists—we are definitely influenced by the hand of God. I think—I don't know—I think I still have to make another number one record with a song of my own. And I hope that God, I hope that He is following me still!" Ryan emits one more exuberant chortle, not unlike the echoing laugh heard in "Dolce Vita."

Jennifer Rush
"The Power of Love" (1984)
Germany

She is widely and justifiably regarded as one of the premier international artists of the '80s. Jennifer Rush's intoxicating voice, with its sophistication, distinctively operatic quality and commanding power, helped to place her among the most respected and in-demand vocalists in all of Europe and Britain during the decade. The soaring and lushly orchestrated number one synth-ballad "The Power of Love" and a series of infectious dance hits, such as "Ring OF Ice" and "Flames of Paradise" (featuring Elton John), kept this extraordinary singer-songwriter at the top of the charts throughout her tenure with Germany's CBS Records. A New York native who continues to busily tour throughout the world today, Jennifer has much to say about her uncommon journey as a global ambassador of pop music.

Rush was born Heidi Stern in the early '60s, and her story began within the environs of Astoria, New York, a congested, ethnically diverse neighborhood in the borough of Queens. "My parents were divorced, and I remember living with my brothers and mother during my very early years," she says. "I was very happy, and I didn't know at the time that Astoria was considered by some to be a 'bad' neighborhood in those days. My parents were young—my mom, Barbara, was like 23, with three kids already—so she was overwhelmed. We moved into Manhattan when I was just a toddler to live with my father (Maurice Stern) and his soon-to-be second wife, Rita. My father lived on the Upper West Side then. It was a neighborhood where artists of all types lived—dancers, singers, painters, etc. The five of us lived in a small apartment (but perhaps not *that* small by Upper West Side New York standards) with no living room, as that had been cut up to make a bedroom for two children. The other rooms were an eat-in kitchen and the room where my stepmother and my father taught voice, the most important one to the grown-ups. That's where my dad learned his operatic roles. There was a baby grand piano in there, and my father also used the room to paint.

"In my youth, I never showed any interest in the music business or in practicing a musical instrument, although I studied violin at Juilliard and hated it. I was repeatedly told I had huge aptitude for the instrument – but it wasn't the right timing for me. Ditto for the piano, although knowing the basics was very helpful in songwriting and overall for working with musicians or on my own voice later in life. The instrument I chose to play was the guitar, and I always enjoyed it—always in private. The middle child in our family, my brother Stevie, is a few years older and a great guitarist, singer, painter. He was always very, very generous in lending me his guitars. All of my guitar-playing took place as my father

Left: Jennifer Rush poses for the camera of Manfred Esser in 1985. Photographs taken during this session were used to promote her smash single "The Power of Love" in the UK that year (courtesy Manfred Esser). *Right:* The artist today as photographed by Beowulf Sheehan.

was divorcing his second wife. He was also a Professor of Voice at the University of Washington, in Seattle [where we also lived for a time]."

As a teen, Jennifer experienced her first taste of life in the recording industry, though the venture was a less than successful one. "It was in Seattle where my dad met a producer, who had a studio and did loads of recording and writing jingles for radio stations," she says. "This guy made my first Heidi Stern demos and drove down to Los Angeles to get me a recording 'deal.' I found out later this deal included him being my producer. So my dad gave the rights to a record label—and it was released. Of course, it went nowhere—and to be honest I wasn't terribly upset. I do, however, remember calling a radio station asking them to play my song—too many times—and the DJ asked, 'Is *this* Heidi?' He was on to me," she laughs.

"At this point, I met a great, great man who made a huge difference in my life—a black singer, composer and producer named Gene McDaniels (1935–2011). I was seriously impressed with him, and he let me stay in his house in Beverly Hills while we worked on some songs for me. His house was absolutely gorgeous, but not swanky or obnoxious. He took me to the studio with him; we worked on some songs, and he sang a duet with me. I learned a lot from him. He told me stories about how so many of the singers-songwriters who were black had all their song rights stolen from them. He was around my dad's age, so I really listened to him. And I enjoyed his company.

"My dad was planning to go back to Germany to sing for the Düsseldorf Opera House. Eugene told me to go with him and meet with CBS Records there. I didn't want to go there and was happy with the day job I had. I know that sounds ridiculous, but it's true. I was making a great salary, and with the job I had, I would be able to go to college. I knew I could sing, but for me, security was really important. Moving around all the time and overhearing grown-ups worried about finances had left an impression on me. Gene told me if I were to lose 10 pounds before going, I would be 'fierce.' So I listened and lost the weight. Previously, I was always a happy, chubby kid, and no one ever mentioned weight in my house. But I knew I had to have the right look.

"My plan was that I would go over to Germany and be a songwriter, but I didn't tell my dad this," she recalls. "I had no clue how I'd do this. I went over for an extended summer, and nothing really happened for me. However, my dad was performing all the time at the Düsseldorf Opera House. So it was decided I would go back to Seattle. Another year passed, and then my father and brother persuaded me to come back to Germany. I didn't want to, but I guess I decided to follow their suggestion. I met with a guy who was in the publishing house of CBS Records. I took the train from Düsseldorf to Frankfurt and sang three songs in their studio. This guy immediately took me upstairs to the head of the company, but the president was not interested in me as a singer. So the publishing guy gave me a contract to be a songwriter instead. Eventually, I *did* start recording a bunch of singles (some were horrific), and he started to organize the producers for the first Jennifer Rush album."

Before her debut singles and album on CBS could be released, there was the matter of her name to tackle—Heidi Stern just wouldn't cut it, at least according to the executives at the label. Recalls the singer, "I was very, very angry when they wanted me to change my name, but I suppose I was reacting more like a young, naive person not wanting to 'sell out.' I was told the change was needed because my name sounded way too German and that I didn't 'look' like my real name. I came up with the Rush and the secretaries in the office at CBS came up with Jennifer, after they were asked what name they would choose. I wanted Samantha but was told by CBS that Germans would have a hard time pronouncing it. My father reminded me that loads of people have changed their names—as he had. He was at one time called Mauro Lampi. So I agreed to make the change.

"I must point out that without my dad, Maurice Stern, there would never have been a 'Jennifer Rush,'" she adds. "He was in total control of everything that was happening. However, when the actual songs were recorded with CBS and the first project got underway, he was performing in Düsseldorf on stage. He did not travel with me. I was allowed (and enjoyed) being thrown into the water, and I learned how to swim, so-to-speak."

A formidable production duo comprised of Candy de Rouge (Bonnie Bianco, Falco, Thomas Anders) and Gunther Mende (Tina Turner, Helen Schneider, Nena) took charge of Jennifer's self-titled debut album. Production on the project began in 1983. "Working with German producers was interesting—maybe because, of course, I had never been famous before," observes Jennifer. "It was in hindsight a very good mix for the situation. It was simply a combination that worked. The two gentlemen at the time didn't speak one word of English. Imagine. The producer responsible for the musical part and some of the guide lyrics could sing just enough English for me to get the idea. They had an old friend named Mary Susan Applegate, who they had worked with before, so she was able to contribute to the process. To be honest, during the recording of most of that first LP, we didn't know if it would ever be a *real* album."

The singles "Into My Dreams," "Witch Queen of New Orleans" and "Come Give Me Your Hand," were released, and their distinctive sound helped to slowly bring attention to Jennifer's name and voice. Her commanding vocals were well-suited to synth-pop tracks, and TV appearance offers began trickling in. Rush achieved more noteworthy attention in 1984, when the song "25 Lovers" became a Top 30 hit in Germany. The single "Ring of Ice" (a metaphor representing the hopelessness of a doomed relationship) was a powerhouse follow-up, released in an extended dance mix that attracted the favor of German radio and club DJs. Her voice rang true with emotion, her songs were lyrically savvy and her sound was unlike anything that had been heard before in the European pop market. Rush gained a strong following in Sweden and the northern countries of Europe, and she hit the number two position in Germany with her debut album. Though tracks like "Madonna's Eyes" continued to demonstrate her dance-floor prowess, it was an extraordinary power synth-ballad (written in part by the artist) that ultimately made Jennifer Rush a household name throughout Europe.

"'The Power of Love' was the last single we released from the first set," Rush remembers, "and I was already writing and recording songs for the second album. The trick here was I was going around to radio stations in Germany, sort of plugging 'Power' before it was actually released. I would play the tape of the song for the programmers, and somehow they loved it. I was surprised. Period—out. I was living by this time in a kind of very unrenovated apartment in Munich with [my daughter] Ariel's dad at the time. I had already received about 10 gold/platinum awards and was never home. I had a map in the kitchen on the wall, and one day I looked at it and thought, 'Hey, I need to go to the UK.' So, I called up CBS Frankfurt and got the telephone number of someone to call at the UK branch and asked if they had time to meet with me. The gall, right? [*She laughs.*] The German company did not organize that trip—I just paid for my own flights and hotels. To me, that was natural. I had never been in the UK and honestly was amazed it was such a short flight from Munich.

"When I went into the CBS building in London, it was a great experience. I finally heard English again!" she laughs heartily. "The food was also amazing—beef everywhere—gosh—food that was very similar to New York. Germany had good food, too, but seeing steak and all that was wonderful. My birth mother was a huge fan of BBC radio and would listen to tapes of their shows when I was a teenager. I guess that may have helped to make me feel very comfortable in England from the get-go. [The UK branch of] CBS simply decided to release 'The Power of Love' as a single. It was the label president who was relentless about the song, and he felt it could be a hit. It took months, for sure, to get to number one. It kept falling off the charts, and they kept re-releasing it. That is the truth. So, by the time my second LP was released in Germany, I finally reached number one in the UK. 'The Power of Love' did very, very well," she says, modestly. "I still love England to this day—and that includes other countries that were once perhaps considered England—Scotland and Ireland. Great, great people and very warm."

Eventually, "The Power of Love" became the UK's biggest selling single of 1985, with some reports indicating it was the last million-selling song of the decade in that country.

It also enjoyed the distinction of placing in the *Guinness Book of Records* as the bestselling single by a female solo artist in the history of the British music industry. (Rush's hit was displaced in 1992 by Whitney Houston's "I Will Always Love You.") "The Power of Love" was also a major hit in Spain under the title "Si Tu Eres Mi Hombre y Yo Tu Mujer." Says the artist, "When I was approached to sing the song in Spanish, I initially balked at the idea. I spoke no Spanish at the time, or very little, and felt bad that I didn't really understand the lyrics as well as I should. But it was a huge success in Spain—and that prompted me to learn Spanish. I did eventually—and then my Spanish singing was perfect. I have sung many of my hits in the language. Spain left a very big impression on me, as did so many wonderful countries, and I remain extremely fond of this nation."

Despite the international attention the single received and the singer's appearance on high profile television shows like *American Bandstand*, the song failed to make much of a dent in the U.S., where Rush remained relatively unknown. Air Supply gave "The Power of Love" a cover shot in 1985, as did popular songstress Laura Branigan ("Gloria") in 1987. But it was Celine Dion's rendition of the track that ultimately achieved major American pop chart success. Dion's 1993 version earned her a Grammy nomination and the lucrative number one position on the U.S. survey. "I have absolutely no problem with Celine singing the song," maintains Jennifer. "I was called up by her producer (who I was working with anyway) and the publisher—both telling me she was going to release it. I admit I thought it was kind of weird, but if I had been a bitter bitch over something like that, I would never have survived in this business."

An "international version" of Jennifer's debut album, incorporating tracks from her German follow-up LP *Movin'*, hit the record shop racks of numerous countries in late 1985. Meanwhile, the *Movin'* album reached the top spot in Germany and was the country's biggest selling LP of 1986. More power-synth singles were released in extended dance mixes, including "Destiny" and "If You're Ever Gonna Lose My Love," and though they failed to make an impression in the UK, the songs were colossal hits in Germany and popular throughout Europe. Tracks like the high-energy "Ave Maria (Survivors of a Different Kind)" further secured Rush's dance floor credibility. "I think I really began to appreciate that I was a successful recording artist by this time," she says. "I think for me, the moment came in Germany when I was staying in a hotel in Frankfurt when I was recording the *Movin'* album. Right outside my window—at night—was a group of biker guys and girls. They were playing my music full blast. I thought, wow!"

Jennifer decided to relocate back home to the United States to work on her third album, *Heart Over Mind*, released in 1987. Collaborating with a host of well-known pop songwriters, musicians, producers and fellow artists (Harold Faltermeyer, Desmond Child, Bruce Roberts, Richie Sambora, and Michael Bolton among them), the set was a feast of upbeat styles and energy, with more of an American flair. The "I Come Undone" single successfully launched the collection in Germany, but it was the rousing "Flames of Paradise" duet with Elton John that garnered the most attention. A fiery, high-energy dance floor stomper, the song saw Rush at last break into the U.S. Top 40. In Germany, the song was a Top 10 smash. The blistering synth-beat anthem "Heart Over Mind" bolted up the U.S. dance charts and scored high chart positions in Germany, Austria and France. Despite the set's success, Rush feels that her American launch could have had greater impact.

"*Heart Over Mind* was a great album to do—all in the U.S. and very exciting. It was a project full of firsts for me. And I was back living in my beloved New York City's Upper West Side again. I wanted success in America. And it was a thrill to work with so many great, great people. Desmond Child was such a wonderful person and songwriter. He had just written tracks with the band Bon Jovi, and Desmond told me that my record was the first time he was a producer. He and I wrote a great song together called 'Down to You,' and we maintained a close friendship for many years. He was actually the first of many producers here in the States I totally respected, and I remember him very fondly. He has spoken of it in the press, so I will allow myself to say that, for a gay man, he had it tough. Here he was writing all these songs for Aerosmith and major rock artists (and he was also a great singer), but he felt that being gay prevented him from getting the recognition he deserved. When you are young, this stuff *does* get annoying and can be hurtful."

Rush says the *Heart Over Mind* LP arrived at a time when she truly wanted to find recognition in her homeland. "Being successful meant that you sold loads of records, and as an artist, that's what I wanted to do—sell records and write songs. There are countless times we artists write and sing things with just the public in mind. After all, it's also for the public's enjoyment that we perform our music, not just for our own satisfaction. Satisfaction also comes from adding to the lives of others. I *wanted* to be a hit in America. I felt I was young enough to achieve it, but it just didn't work out. Very frustrating.

"I rented a house in Los Angeles and had signed with the William Morris Agency. For a multitude of reasons, it was difficult to get everyone on board with the international aspects of the *Heart Over Mind* project. I heard I created some huge friction at CBS in Frankfurt when I started working with other producers, rather than the ones from Germany from the beginning of my career. I was living in New York, and to me, it was natural to see and do something different. I thought it would add to my international appeal as well. The thing was, it was the timing that may have worked against me again—looking back. The president of CBS Records in the States was leaving his position, which isn't a great thing when you are releasing your first album in America. But when it was all said and done, I was extremely happy with the LP. When I heard Elton and me on the radio for the first time, it was thrilling. I think it *still* is—when you are in a car or somewhere and you hear yourself on the radio or on a big sound system. We tried to get things off the ground in the U.S. with that duet, but unfortunately it just wasn't enough. If it had gone to the top of the chart, things might have been different."

Rush recorded two more albums for CBS, *Passion* in 1988 (the last album of original material released in the U.S.) and *Wings of Desire* the following year. The sets continued her hot streak in loyal territories like Germany, Austria, France and Switzerland. The collections featured more compelling and splendidly orchestrated, synthesizer-fused tracks, such as "You're My One and Only," the infectiously jubilant "Love Get Ready" (featuring her brother Bobby Stern on sax), and the retro-style dance hit "Higher Ground." However, with a new decade upon her, the artist decided the time had come to shake things up.

"After *Passion*, I had one record left on my CBS contract," Jennifer recalls. "Many artists would have just delivered anything in order to get their agreed-upon guarantee money. And it was *a lot* of money. I struggled with that aspect of the situation. I felt I was still young enough to get another contract, but if I just delivered 'anything,' I would be done for. I thought (what turned out to be) my last LP with CBS, *Wings of Desire*, was good, but like most artists, I would have liked more time to work on it before releasing it.

"I decided not to do another one with CBS after that for another reason as well—and a very, very valid one. Since Germany was where I would be under contract (and that would be true no matter which label I signed with), it was obvious from past experiences that I was not going to get any support from CBS in other territories at all. The people working at CBS in Germany were great, but I had already been there a long time, and now I was living in the United States. I had seen how divisions of the label in different countries didn't always work together so well. So here was Heidi with her millions and gazillions in sales figures in Europe—and I just really had the feeling I wasn't going to continue to do well if I stayed on at CBS. So, I decided to bail and got a contract with EMI, which turned out to be great for me, especially from an artistic point of view," she says proudly.

Jennifer scored one additional hit with CBS, the 1989 Top 30 UK single featuring Placido Domingo, "Till I Loved You" (from the musical *Goya: A Life in Song*, and previously covered by Barbra Streisand and Don Johnson). "Working with Placido was so great," she says. "When I recorded that duet with him, he came over to the studio straight after having sung at the Met. He probably figured his voice was 'open' and that he should do the duet right away. He was a really nice man, and he came with his son—who probably suggested me for the project. My dad was to be Placido's replacement, in case he got sick. The most bizarre thing about this recording was that CBS Germany told me they wouldn't allow me to do this duet because I was too young to sing with Placido. I told them I would start to age and get fat again to make it work. How ridiculous to say I was too young for such a wonderful opportunity!"

The artist recorded three albums for EMI in the '90s, *Jennifer Rush, Out of My Hands* and *Credo*. Each showed the artist's ongoing creative evolution, while continuing to deliver the sumptuous dance and pop melodies that were her specialty. Tracks such as "Fortress," "I Can't Say No," "Vision of You," "Sweet Thing" and "Credo" were ambitious and adventurous highlights of the period that continued to win over fans. Sales of her albums remained strong, though they were not quite as impressive as they had been in the previous decade. She recorded *Classics* in 1998 with producer Leslie Mándoki, a critically acclaimed set that featured orchestral renditions of her biggest hits and breathtaking originals like "The End of a Journey." A three-disc collector's compilation called *Stronghold*, primarily composed of her vast CBS repertoire, became a major seller in 2007. The artist signed with Sony/BMG and unveiled an album of all new material in 2010, *Now Is the Hour*, which peaked just shy of Germany's Top 20. The set featured a blistering dance single, "Echoes Love."

Rush considers the many factors that led to her extraordinary success over the decades and identifies the obstacles that created stumbling blocks on her professional path. "Clear and simple—I believe that timing has been a major consideration throughout most of my career. I was very aware I would not keep having number ones on the charts all the time, and I knew it was in my best interests to let myself change and evolve over time. You take a few more chances, and you try new things, new sounds. Sometimes they click with people; sometimes they don't. One thing I can say is I think I've always had a great appreciation for different cultures and markets. Since I did come out of Europe as an artist—even though I am an American—I knew the value, the importance of recognizing different countries. I think that awareness has been very helpful in my career. Within Europe, there is a huge difference in mentalities, musical tastes, etc. from place to place, and I was able to deliver songs and albums that appealed to many of them. For instance, my album *Credo* had great

South African choirs on it. Having just toured through South Africa recently, it was amazing how many people were aware of those songs. That was extremely satisfying for me. I also knew from my upbringing that languages were important—so I loved learning Spanish. By doing that, I was able to enjoy great support in countries like Spain.

"Timing can be a good or bad thing, and I've certainly experienced both sides of it. Had 'The Power of Love' happened just a few years later, we would have totally had the MTV video thing down pat, and my version of the song might have reached number one in the U.S. It was also difficult to get the U.S. record company to agree with the German label's president. Friction like that can work against you. There was just so much I could do myself—even though I was living in Manhattan since 1985–86 and constantly flying over to Europe to work.

"Listen, you can have many wonderful things in place when you are working on a project. I had a contract with William Morris, strong managers, great, great producers throughout my career and loads of support from within the American record label (and also at the publishing houses as a songwriter). Even with all that behind me, the U.S. market remained hard to crack. In the '90s, I was singing and working with gem producers and getting some great songs (either writing them with colleagues or receiving them from them). I really enjoyed the work I did in that period, but the records weren't as successful in Europe as in the past. I did learn to accept this, and ultimately it did work out for the best, especially as far as raising my daughter was concerned. I had to try to find a balance between my music career and being a mother. By living here in New York, I could be just a plain mom (who also worked). My daughter really didn't know—and kids really don't care—what a parent does for a living," the singer says, shrugging her shoulders. "So, timing and life—it all balances out in the end."

After reviewing the details of her past, it seems to be momentarily startling for Jennifer to realize that her amazing history in music spans over 30 years. She says her life has changed considerably during that time, and the artist likes where she is today. "I am so very thankful for everything I have achieved," she says earnestly. "I have the support of thousands of fans in so many countries, and as an artist, that is really incredible. I know I am blessed to keep working as I do. I do not, however, have that kind of burning fight-to-the-finish mentality I did when I was younger. I really needed that to make it in the business back then. I think it all kind of hit me about seven years ago, actually—that I have had so much success and so many blessings in my life. I got to see and experience all of Europe—that alone was amazing. So, you know, I don't have to prove anything to myself now, if you know what I mean. At this point in my life, I am realizing it is okay *not* to be running around, going crazy. It's okay to take things slower—it's also smarter. Kind of a 'smelling the roses' kind of thing. Through so much of what I've done, it's really true that my daughter, who is doing so well today, was always my biggest concern. I'm just glad she wasn't blinded or affected in any negative way by any of what I was or did in my career.

"I am glad—and a bit awestruck and proud—that the songs I have sung, written or contributed to have given others such joy," she says softly. "And that is the absolute truth—it's been a great ride, one that I continue to enjoy to this very day. To ultimately realize how absolute and timeless music is—and to know that I was and am, in my own way, part of something that powerful—well, that *is* pretty cool."

Sabrina Salerno

aka Sabrina

"Boys (Summertime Love)" (1987)
Italy

The women of Italy, with their style, passion, love for life and show-stopping looks, have given the world much to adore. In the realm of entertainment, many would argue they are unparalleled. The cinema has certainly done its share to keep Italian women vividly in focus. The striking talents of Claudia Cardinale, Virna Lisi, Gina Lollobrigid, and Sophia Loren forged an indelible impression on the public, as their films brought the allure and beauty of Italian women to an international audience. In popular music, compelling twentieth-century vocalists like Ornella Vanoni, Mina, Anna Oxa and Gianna Nannini magnificently represented the far-reaching power and spirit of the Italian female voice.

In the mid–'80s, a young girl from Genoa added her name to the list of celebrated and accomplished Italian women who have captured the world's attention. All eyes were on Sabrina Salerno, more commonly known simply as Sabrina, whose sexy looks and vivacious vocal style caused a sensation. She was one of the most instantly recognizable women in contemporary pop music culture at the time, scoring multiple dance hits that sold millions across Europe. The World Music Award winner's signature classic, "Boys (Summertime Love)," a rambunctious plunge into the joys of uninhibited fun in the sun, and lively, chart-topping follow-ups like "Hot Girl," "All of Me" and "Gringo" kept Sabrina a fixture on the radio, MTV, and in the clubs. Her dazzlingly curvaceous figure and seductive beauty guaranteed the singer a wealth of paparazzi attention right from the start of her rise to fame. However, it was her determination over the years to expand the scope of her career that ensured Sabrina's longevity in the business.

Three decades after turning the dance-pop world upside down, this sharp, expressive, unpretentious and still stunningly beautiful woman remains a hugely popular and energized artist who never hesitates to say what's on her mind.

"I never really wanted to be a singer or to do television—it was never my plan when I was young," Salerno insists. "When I was thinking of my future as a teenager, I believed I would be a doctor or a psychologist. I don't really know what happened. I won a beauty competition, and then when I was about 16 years old, I went on a casting call for a TV show called *Premiatissima*. They immediately chose me from the thousands of girls auditioning. At that age, you would do these things just to see where you could go and what you could do. I wasn't really convinced it was the right path for me to follow, but I told myself to just

Left: **Catapulting to the top of the international pop charts with her smash single "Boys (Summertime Love)," the dynamic and alluring Sabrina, seen here in 1988 promoting her "My Chico" hit, became a European sensation.** *Right:* **The artist remains a striking beauty today.**

try this road and see what happens. I knew I could decide later if I wanted to come back to my studies. I looked at these things as an opportunity. I could earn a lot of money because, in the '80s, the economy was very prosperous. So imagine being 17 years old and earning a lot of money every month, working for one of the most popular TV shows in the country and performing with very famous actors. I thought, 'This is crazy!' I was able to act, sing, dance and be a host. I felt confident in my potential, but I was a little afraid because I never really did it before and wasn't even sure if I even really *wanted* to do this kind of thing.

"The next thing that happened was I found myself in a recording studio at the age of 17, which was another thing I could never have expected. Claudio Cecchetto was a big producer and a radio DJ at a station that was the best in Italy in those days. He started to produce a few singers just as I started to do the television work. Italian dance-pop music was beginning to have a bigger international impact. The music of Italy was becoming very popular in Spain, France and Germany. When I met Claudio and he offered to have me record a dance song, I thought it could be something important in my life. Again, I thought it was a path I should try following. To be honest, I wanted to be more of a rock star at that point. I loved dancing, and dance music was very popular then, but I really hoped I would be able to do rock music. But life is funny, and sometimes you have to compromise."

Sabrina's first single was released in 1986 and sung in English, the language she prefers when it comes to performing. "Sexy Girl" (though oddly packaged in Germany by ZYX Records in a plain white 12-inch record sleeve that failed to capitalize on the artist's sensuality) was a sizeable hit. The song reached the upper regions of the Italian, German, Austrian and Finnish pop charts. About six months later, Cecchetto and Salerno returned to the studio to record the tracks that would comprise her first album, *Sabrina,* released in 1987. With its release, Sabrina became a star. The set's lead single "Boys (Summertime Love)" created excitement across the continent. An effervescent, high-energy dance party firmly packed into nearly six minutes of addictive beats, anonymous male rapping and irresistible Italo-style hooks, the track blasted its way to the Top 10 in nearly every European market. The song was especially popular in France, where it held the number one spot for several weeks. "Boys" peaked at number three on the British charts, a decidedly rare feat by an Italian artist.

The relentlessly catchy follow-up single, another electrifying, hook-laden dance jam called "Hot Girl," fared well in most of the same territories. Both songs were remixed numerous times, including a ferocious treatment of "Hot Girl" by the UK's resident production wizard at PWL Studios, Phil Harding. His version of the song featured erotic vocal gasps and whipping sound effects set to a thunderous beat. Going forward, almost without exception, the artist's singles featured racy cover photographs. Sabrina's self-titled debut album on Five Records out of Milano was a sizeable hit and contained remakes of such disco nuggets as Labelle's "Lady Marmalade" and rock staples like The Knack's "My Sharona" and Rod Stewart's "Da Ya Think I'm Sexy." Sabrina had arrived.

"I reached a point in my life where I hit number one all over the world," the artist recalls. "So by that time, whenever I asked myself what I wanted to do with my life, of course I said, 'I'm a singer!' I kept going with it. Claudio's songs all had that sexy theme. I didn't think of the songs as a personal reflection of who I was; I think it was all about creating an image for me. Having a recognizable image started to be very important in the '80s, and today I think it's become even more important. I really think Blondie (Debbie Harry) got that started, then Cyndi Lauper and Madonna. Creating a look back then was crucial, and it often had to be very exaggerated. The colors of the fashions and the extreme styles, the heavy make-up—it was all kind of shocking. For sure, for me to be sexy required I have an extreme look as well. I played with my image because I understood everything about me was relevant—my clothes, my body, the music. If I was going to have a sex symbol type of style, I needed people to see strong visuals. I think at the time, Samantha Fox and I were probably the most powerful girls in music with that kind of image. And it worked for us. It was all part of that period."

Salerno's sex goddess image was cemented in place by a video that was widely circulated for the "Boys" single. Though an otherwise standard clip with no plot, the video became the talk of Europe thanks to what was probably the first official pop music "wardrobe malfunction." In portions of the video, Sabrina, her ample bosom bouncing among the guests in a crowded swimming pool, is forced to tug her bikini top back into place. The effect was amusing, as well as titillating, rallying thousands of young males to become Sabrina fans.

"If you remember, the 'Boys' video was censored by MTV in the UK. It was crazy. If you look at me in that video and compare it to what is in today's videos, I look like a nun. Yeah, but that look I had in the clip projected an image that got people's attention. I can't deny it. You know, even if a look was considered cheap or vulgar, those images led the way for everything we have today. Really, what happened in that video was an accident—*truly*. And that video was created for the television show called *Festivalbar*. It wasn't filmed like a real video for a song—it was meant to be like a short film segment that they played while announcing who was going to be performing on the TV show. I think we filmed those shots in 10 minutes—*10 minutes*. But the host of the show was Claudio Cecchetto, and realizing that the video was powerful, he thought it would be great to release it as an official song video, without censoring those scenes. I saw the clip and saw myself tugging my bikini top, and I was like, 'Oh shit! They didn't tell me *that* was going to be in it.' I was so fucking angry! I called Claudio and said, 'I don't want to know you any more. You crazy man—what have you done to me?' He told me I would sell millions of records because of it. It turns out—he was right," she chuckles.

"The same type of thing happened to me on another very important TV program sometime later. I always had problems with my body and what I was wearing," she laughs again, appreciating the humor of her exploits. "I was dancing and singing and—bang—something came off. [*Author's note: Sabrina is no doubt referring to a televised segment where she loses her scant wrap-around mini skirt while singing her hit "Gringo" in 1989.*] Some people think these things were deliberate, but they weren't. I was actually furious about it after the show. The director of the show wrote a book and talked about how angry I was. I remember asking if it looked bad on TV, and he said, 'No baby, it was cool. Don't worry about it.' I was still so young—I was stupid, and I trusted everybody. [Now that I am in my late 40s], I can look back on all that and say, yes, those crazy things *did* play a part in my success. It would be foolish of me to now say something like, 'I shouldn't have done that.' It happened, and it was a long time ago," the singer says with a carefree smile.

With the artist's newfound front and center position came the pressures of stardom and fame. "I did experience a lot of pressure to duplicate the success of 'Boys,'" she admits. "But there was that moment that came where I had to say, 'Okay, I just don't care.' Otherwise you would go crazy. It's impossible to live your life worrying about whether your next song will be a big hit.

The first time I realized I was famous was at an airport in Spain. The record company people told me how well my records were doing in Europe and how so many people wanted to see me perform, particularly in Spain. I arrived at the airport there with my road manager, and I saw all these photographers and lots of people gathering. I said to my manager, 'Hey, there must be someone very famous here.' I didn't realize they were there for *me*, and when I finally understood that, I was in shock. To tell you the truth, I wasn't happy about it. They were so crazy taking pictures, and there were so many people and police officers everywhere. From that moment, it was a nightmare being in Spain. I was very popular there, and for about two years, I was living in Spain and leading this crazy life. I always had to be dressed a certain way and posing, and that wasn't freedom. That was actually killing me. It was too much. Success in those days was good; I realize this. It was good for popularity and good for money. But my life was often like a nightmare," the artist sighs.

Sabrina's success was, indeed, formidable throughout Europe. However, despite the efforts of Sire Records (a division of Warner Bros. in the U.S.), who picked up the "Boys" single for distribution and promoted the artist on American TV shows like *Entertainment Tonight*, the singer's charms failed to catch on in the States. "Truthfully, I never worried about being successful in the United States," she assures. "My life was a mess because I was running around, going from country to country. I don't know if I would have been able to take on more work promoting my records in America. I never worried too much about the UK, either. It was good to make it there, but I didn't stress about it. I think Ivana Spagna and myself are the only Italian women who reached the top of the charts in England in those days."

Samantha Fox, the blonde British siren who, like Sabrina, had caused a sensation with her provocative appearance and such suggestive '80s dance hits as "Touch Me (I Want Your Body)," was often reported to be in a rivalry with her Italian counterpart. "It was a funny situation," Sabrina says, tossing her long, dark hair back as she addresses the subject. "I was so fed up with everyone asking me, 'What do you think of Samantha Fox?' Listen, in the '80s we knew it was a great marketing gimmick to sell more records if we appeared to be enemies. The people liked the idea of us being against each other, sexy blonde vs. sexy brunette, and the newspapers found it catchy. So we went along with it. But when we finally met in 2010, I suggested to Sam we do a recording together that will finally stop everyone from asking those stupid, silly questions about us. We recorded a new version of Blondie's 'Call Me.'"

The ladies' high-octane duet generated a great deal of media attention and was a top hit in the clubs. The song's video caused a stir with its final scene depicting the two singers affectionately kissing. "Sam is like a sister to me. She and I had very similar careers in that we were sex symbols in dance music. I think I understand her, and I can look at her, and I often think I know what she's thinking. She's a very nice girl, and I think she is very courageous. Her coming out was very brave, and I appreciate her attitude and courage. I don't think in the music or entertainment business there have been too many sex symbols that have come out and said they were gay or lesbian voluntarily."

With the frenzy of her debut hits behind her, Sabrina parted ways with Cecchetto. "Claudio didn't really want to work with women in general," she claims. "I believe he felt women were too complicated, and he preferred to work with men. He worked with Tracy Spencer ["Run to Me"], Taffy ["I Love My Radio"] and me. Then he was finished with women." Sabrina shrugs her shoulders and dismisses Cecchetto's decision, adding, "We are very close friends to this day, but he just didn't like working with women, so we never did a follow-up album. So, what can you do?" Perhaps second only to Sabrina, one of Cecchetto's biggest success stories around the same period was, in fact, with a male vocalist. Sandy Marton teamed with the producer for a series of Italo-disco hits, among them "People from Ibiza" and "Camel by Camel."

Despite disconnecting from hitmaker Cecchetto, Salerno lost no momentum, and she quickly teamed up with the dominant British producers of the day, Stock Aitken Waterman, for her next big single. "All of Me (Boy Oh Boy)" was released in 1988 and was extremely popular in the UK. The track reached the Top 20 in France, Switzerland and Germany. The artist took a hand in writing her next hit, "My Chico," which reached the number one position in Italy. In October of 1988, both "All of Me" and "My Chico" held strong positions in Italy's Top 20, according to a *Musica & Dischi* chart. Having two top hits at the same time was a decidedly extraordinary accomplishment for any artist. In 1989, she released the

Giorgio Moroder-penned single "Like a Yo Yo" (which reached the top of the Finnish chart) and "Gringo," a slice of revved-up Euro-disco with a western theme (co-written by the artist) that enjoyed Top 10 status in Italy and was a sizeable success in Germany. Two more albums were released in Europe between 1988 and 1990, which were essentially collections of her hits of the period packaged mostly in extended and remixed versions.

"I worked with many producers after Claudio," recalls Salerno. "Some were fine, others were *not* such a good experience. It was also a challenge to find the right material. Giorgio Moroder wrote 'Like A Yo Yo.' I liked the song and the demo, but I didn't care for the production. When I first heard the song, it was more like a rock song—it wasn't a dance song. But by the time they released it, the track had a dance sound. But again, that was the era. I was supposed to do dance music—that's what people wanted from me. Even now, they still want me to do dance, dance, dance!" she laughs.

As the '90s unfolded, Sabrina continued to release dance singles that were well-received. "Yeah Yeah," released in 1990, was recorded for the Casablanca label, and the following year's "Shadows of the Night," was a production completely helmed by Moroder. The 1991 album *Over The Pop* was a strong seller in several European territories. Sabrina later teamed with singer Jo Squillo for the hit "Siamo Donne," her first commercial recording sung in Italian. The track was a popular entry at the *San Remo Festival* that same year. The "Cover Model," "Rockawillie" and "Angel Boy" singles marked the artist's final excursions into the dance music market during this period and were followed by Sabrina's decision to seek a change of direction.

"The problem was that I was totally alone during all this success," Salerno concedes. "I didn't have anyone with me to guide me or to help me make decisions. When I was in my mid–20s, I decided I couldn't keep going on with it and that this was not the kind of music and lifestyle I wanted to keep pursuing. I had to stop working like a crazy girl. I lost interest in it because I became very disillusioned with the music business and my management. It's the same story a lot of singers have, especially when they are in the business at a very young age. I wanted to work with Nile Rodgers—there was some discussion of doing that—but my producer at the time didn't want it. So I gave up. I gave up my contract; I gave up everything."

After cutting ties for a time, Sabrina reinvented herself for 1995's LP, *Maschio Dove Sei*, her first album sung entirely in Italian and produced by Massimo Riva. The artist steered clear of dance music with this project. The rock-oriented LP was favorably reviewed, but many fans found it difficult to embrace her new sound. She continued to hone her acting skills, appearing in television programs like *Cocco di Mamma* for Rai 1. A sophisticated album called *A Flower's Broken*, produced by her husband, Enrico Monti, gave the artist a very contemporary and welcome re-entry into the electronic dance music market in 1999. However, RTI Music, the label releasing the project, was in the process of being sold, and promotional efforts for the album ground to a halt, stifling any hope of commercial success. As the twenty-first century got under way, Salerno, undaunted, hosted a TV show called *Matricole & Meteore*, starred in the independent film *Colori,* and continued to tour, singing her '80s hits to gargantuan crowds in Poland, France, and numerous other countries. She released an album of new material and remakes of her biggest hits called *Erase/Rewind* in 2008 (at the encouragement of her brother, according to the CD liner notes), which was accompanied by a hip and stylishly photographed video of the title track. Sabrina took part in the television show *La Pista*, which also featured singer Amii Stewart, and has toured in concerts featuring Samantha Fox, David Hasselhoff, Jean-Pierre Morgand of Les Avions and many others from the era.

The artist says that as a female, she has always found life in the entertainment business challenging. "I was treated with respect in the record industry, but it's true that it was a man's world," Sabrina states. "It's still a man's world, not only in music, but also in cinema, the medical industry, politics—everything. In Italy, we call it 'Tetto di cristallo,' the glass ceiling, where women can only rise to a certain level regardless of their abilities. Men have most of the power. As far as my look in the '80s and how men treated me, I must tell the truth. In my experience, usually men were very afraid of a sexy, strong-looking woman. When they are face to face with a beautiful woman and realize she is not stupid, they are afraid. A clever, intelligent man would never judge a woman based only on her appearance. You have to get to know a woman. You can't say she's stupid because she's blonde and beautiful or smart because she is less attractive. There are beautiful women who are very intelligent and some who are very stupid. You can't make generalizations in life. I was never treated badly because I have a very aggressive character. So it was quite hard for anyone to treat me improperly. I always say what I am thinking—there is no gray area. I tend to be very black and white.

"It's a different world for me now. Unlike in the '80s, I can work independently now. Of course when you do your own thing, it's another point of view, and it's very satisfying. But you have to understand, if you get it wrong, if the project doesn't work out, it's all on you. If a record I make doesn't become a hit, I get it wrong, and it's produced by me, that's okay. At least I tried it, and it was what I wanted to do.

"[A few years ago], I had written a song, and I couldn't find the right producer. I made contact with a songwriter and producer named Rick Nowels, and he thought my song was great. I worked with him, and he and I produced it. It was called 'Colour Me.' I've did a wonderful video for it, and I'm very proud of it. It's not a pure dance song; it's also a pop-rock song. I think my voice sounds much better on rock songs, even though nobody recognizes me when I sing them. It was my decision, my thought, my investment and I put my name on it. And that is something I am very proud of. Life is strange. We will see what happens, but I still say that I'm more afraid of having success today than of having a single that doesn't work out."

Sabrina is the mother of a young son today and facing, like her peers, the typical hurdles presented by the process of maturation. However, she seems unbothered by most of it. "I think I am blessed with good DNA," she laughs. "My father, for example, is [over] 70 years old, and if you saw him, you would think he was 50. And he has a very young fiancée. So I think I inherited some of his DNA, and that's where I guess my energy comes from. But still, I do not like being out all the time and going to this party and that party. You know, even though I had this sexy, party girl image, I'm actually a very private person. I don't like to go to discos and parties—I don't like the confusion. Today, I am often asked to go to events where there are very important people—and I rarely go. My friends say I'm crazy not to go because of the work I do, but I'm just not interested in doing things like that. This is just how I am.

"I think my way to be sane and healthy has been to say what I think—and I don't keep things inside me. Allowing myself to be this way is a way to be free for me. We are not completely free in our society, but in my little world, I am who I am. I'm not afraid to say what I think. It's a luxury to be able to say what you feel, and I admit I am not a very diplomatic person. I have had a lot of problems during my career with that. Whether I had the biggest and best director or music producer in front of me, I would not hesitate to say I didn't like this or that. That created a lot of problems for me. I refused a lot of work when I didn't like something about it. My husband and friends probably think I'm crazy for turning offers down. Maybe I am. But again, being crazy, doing what you want, and even saying no to a lot of money is a *very* big luxury that I am lucky to have."

After over 30 years of being a world famous entertainer and having one of the 1980's biggest dance-pop hits, Sabrina remains very relaxed about her choices and her longevity in the business. "It's funny," she smiles, "because I wouldn't even think of doing anything else today. Singing is what I do, and I'm happy with it. It's true; sometimes I wonder what would have happened if I had become a doctor or if I had done something else that I really loved. But I *am* doing what I really love today. I love to sing, to dance and to act. You know, sometimes it is like I have two different personalities—I'm doing one thing, but sometimes I think about doing something else.

The artists of the '80s who made dance music were sometimes considered somewhat disposable. I'm one of the very few from Italy who keeps going and is still working. Many of the other artists from my period are doing other types of work today. I am still recognized on the street, and my popularity is still very high. If I go to France or Spain, it's the same there. I think it's partly because I've done a lot of television, theater, and movies—I think that has helped me stay in the spotlight. They know I've sold 20 million records in the '80s; they saw me at the *San Remo Festival* in '91; they saw me host prime-time TV shows and act in movies. This has helped me to maintain a higher profile. I'm not sure that would have happened if I had been just the singer of 'Boys.'

"I learned something in my life—to live day by day," she observes. "I don't want to plan for the future. I think we have to live more for right now. Sometimes we lose days and weeks because we spend them worrying too much about the future. I admit I do worry about the future in a bigger way—beyond work and my career. That may come from my having a son who is [young]. I don't like the world we are living in these days. I don't care for the politics, and it seems like everyone is stressed and ill. It's not so easy to live in the world today—I think it's one of the tougher periods in our global history. There are still millions of people with nothing to eat, no clean water to drink. And wars—as long as we have demand for petrol, I think we will always have wars. We have the technology to change that, but still we keep the world running on petrol. There's no respect for other people, for animals, for the environment. It seems like everybody I know is getting divorced. I have 10 friends with children the same age as my son, and seven of them are getting divorced.

"Shouldn't things be better by now in the twenty-first century?" the singer suggests. "It's still money and power driving everything. To me, it seems like everything started to change with the attack on September 11th at the Twin Towers. From that moment, it seems like things went into a decline. Maybe I'm too negative, but I do feel that way. In the '80s, life seemed a little easier, a little better. Maybe there were the same problems going on, but we didn't see them as much. Today we have the technology to see what's happening in Africa, the Mid-East, Russia and all over the world the minute it happens. We can see all the images. Before, we couldn't see so much."

Sabrina Salerno epitomized the euphoric, youthful energy that defined so much of Europe's dance-pop music scene in the '80s, and though she is fully aware of the contribution she has made to the decade's pop culture history, she has no desire to trip on it. "I will probably always be associated with 'Boys' and dance music," she says with a big smile. Her eyes sparkle as she speaks. "It's not a bad thing. I know I've been very lucky. When I think of how many beautiful voices, how many talents are in the world who will never have even a little piece of the success I had, I thank God. I know I have been very lucky, very blessed. But you know what would make me happy? If I would just be remembered simply as an *Italian woman*—and as everyone knows, that's a *real* woman!"

Ivana Spagna
aka Spagna
"Call Me" (1987)
Italy

"The tone, the sound, all the lyrics and rhymes I created were so important. I wanted them to be made in such a way that the song would be easy to sing and would cause a true feeling of happiness. You know? That was so important to me," reveals Ivana Spagna. It would be difficult to find a European artist from the '80s who was more successful at achieving her goals. Known throughout most of the world as simply Spagna, the artist wrote and sang a nearly uncountable number of joyful, chart-topping dance-pop hits that consistently filled club floors and sent spirits soaring. From her early success as a songwriter and singer with the studio group Fun Fun ("Happy Station," "Colour My Love"), to triumphant solo hits like "Easy Lady" and "Call Me," Spagna remains one of the most important and highly regarded personalities of the era. She is an artist whose drive to make people rejoice has never diminished.

"I came from a very normal family," Ivana recalls of her early life. "We were very ordinary, but without much money. When I was young, my dream was to be a dancer. I thought about dancing to classical music. I never thought about singing. I would dance in front of the big mirror in my parents' bedroom, imagining a grand orchestra playing the music. But my parents didn't have the resources to send me to a good school where I could become a professional dancer. I never had the feeling in my early life that I was destined to become a successful entertainer—never, never.

When I was 18 years old, I formed my first band. We would perform in small clubs in Italy, and people would dance to our music. I was the lead singer, and I would play the piano. My brother, Theo Spagna, was the bass player, and Larry Pignagnoli [also known as Alfredo Pignagnoli and sometime later listed as I. Abacab in production credits] was the guitarist. We'd sing songs by Kool and The Gang, Donna Summer and many others. We started together, playing in these dance clubs for almost 12 years, and that's how we began composing together. I was always singing in English, and that's why I started composing in the language from the beginning. It came very easily to me, even though I may not always speak it so well. When I was in school, I loved the language so much because of its musicality."

Spagna (who recorded a handful of soft rock singles in the early '70s for the Ricordi label) began contributing more and more to a distinctive Italian dance sound that emerged

Left: **Spagna contributed her powerful voice and songwriting talents to countless Italo-disco records before emerging as a hugely popular solo singer in the mid–'80s.** *Right:* **The artist continues to release hit dance songs in the twenty-first century (courtesy Ugo Cerutti/Ivana Spagna).**

in the early '80s. These records, often categorized as Italo-disco, became major radio hits and increasingly commercially successful in Italy and throughout Europe. "There were many bands like ours in the early '80s, and many were playing dance music," she observes. "We all started in the same way. Then, as we moved on from playing the clubs, we all got into our own studios and started working and composing this type of Italian dance-pop music that we used to perform every night. I'm not sure why there was such an explosion of Italian dance music at the time. Perhaps at some point, myself, Larry and Theo set a good example for many of these musicians. There was a trend to compose more material in English. They may have seen my success, an Italian singer and composer having hits in English, and they may have wanted to emulate that."

In the early '80s, Ivana wrote or co-wrote innumerable hit records for other artists of the day and often contributed vocals on several studio concept projects. Among the endeavors she had a hand in were Baby's Gang ("Happy Song," later covered by Boney M.), Carol Kane's "I Don't Believe," "Rise Up (For My Love)" by Yvonne K (also known as Yvonne Kay), and Hot Cold's "Love Is Like a Game" (also covered by Tracy Spencer). She describes the origins of yet another of these voice and/or writer-for-hire ventures called Fun Fun, which became one of her most popular enterprises. "We decided to stop playing the clubs, and Theo, Larry and I created our first small studio. I was living with Larry at that time; he was my man. Dario Raimondi and Alvaro Ugolini were DJs, and we became friends. I had started writing, and we were making some records for artists in other countries. I was doing so many things. So Dario and Alvaro came to us and wanted us to do a project with them. We agreed, and I remember we did all the work in our home studio in the house—not a big studio as many people might think.

"I had to create the lyrics, create the melodies—and I had to cook for everybody," she laughs. "We didn't have the money to go to restaurants every night. You see, although we had some success with a few previous productions, you would sometimes have to wait one year or more before you would see any money come in [from royalties] as the writer of the song. We invested all the money we had into our little studio, so we really didn't have anything else left. To be creative with the music and cook for everybody at the same time—well, I can tell you that was a very tough period. I like to remember those days, though. Not many people know that's how it was for us, and it shows how humble our beginnings really were.

"When it came time to sing the first songs for the Fun Fun project and start recording them, I called a friend of mine named Antonella Pepe. We had often worked together, and people used to call us all the time to be vocalists and background singers on various records. So she came in, and we sang as 'Fun Fun.' We altered the voices a bit on each of the songs, and that was it."

Fun Fun hit the ground running in 1983. "Happy Station," the entity's first single, was a bouncy concoction with an infectiously energized steam engine rhythm. The song was a top pop chart hit in Italy, Germany, the Netherlands and as far away as South Africa. The track enjoyed a long life in the clubs thanks to several extended remixes (the "Scratch Version" being particularly popular). The follow-up release, "Colour My Love," ensured the Fun Fun concept wasn't just a flash in the pan. This blithesomely upbeat exploration of the high-energy Italo-disco sound became the group's signature hit, and a Top 20 smash in Germany, Holland and Sweden. The song managed to cross the Atlantic thanks to a licensing deal with America's TSR Records and reached the Top 10 of the U.S. dance chart. An album was released internationally in 1984 called *Have Fun!*, from which singles like "Give Me Your Love" and "Tell Me" were major successes. Angela Parisi contributed additional vocals to the project, and the group used different performers for live onstage appearances. Fun Fun went on to have more hits in subsequent years (without the participation of Spagna), including the singles "Baila Bolero" and "Give Me Love."

"We tried so many melodies and tunes to develop the original Fun Fun songs," says Ivana, recalling the success of the project and briefly singing snippets of "Happy Station" and "Colour My Love." "I was always looking for a very special sound. I never wrote a song in my life thinking about it being a hit—I swear. I always created music from my heart because I always thought that other people, since they have hearts too, might be able to feel that and enjoy it. If you only write a song thinking about success or reaching the Top 10, to me, it's not a good idea. You are going to lose that connection and that natural process of developing something from the heart.

"It was something beautiful—actually much more than just beautiful—when Fun Fun became successful in so many countries. It was wonderful to see the concept do so well.

As a result of the success, I started thinking about doing more for myself as a solo singer. I was a writer and vocalist and thought I should probably be doing some of this work for me, not just other artists or studio concepts. By this time, I had really done so much of that for others—it was really amazing how many songs I had written or sung. I had even written some material for the group Change, which originally featured Luther Vandross, and sang on one of their albums. I was a little nervous about that project because Change was an American group, but they told me I had the right 'musicality' to do it. So I closed myself off in a room with my English dictionary, and I came up with some of their songs. That's how I did most of my work," she reminisces.

In 1986, the artist teamed with her partners Theo and Larry to release her first major solo record, "Easy Lady," distributed by CBS throughout most European territories. A melodic, beat and horn-fused celebration that made excellent use of the electronic and synth-pop styles so popular at the time, the song brought the name Spagna firmly into focus. The track was part of her debut album, *Dedicated to the Moon.* Says the artist, "Larry prepared the arrangement for 'Easy Lady.' It was like any other production we worked on—we always wanted to find the right tune, at least according to us. The song wasn't originally written the way you know it, with the chorus and just the title words. I had written a slightly more complicated lyric using the phrase 'clinging with affection.' My brother suggested changing it so that we would just keep repeating the word 'lady.' He wanted to make it simpler, but I thought that was *too* simple. But he asked me to trust him because he felt it would flow much better that way. Eventually, I felt he was right. So we finished the arrangement, and the end result was the song you hear today. We had to *feel* it. You know, when you write a song, one day you can like it so much. Then the next day you say, 'God, I don't like it any more!' It was like that for us during those days. One day we'd say, 'Oh, this is beautiful—wonderful!' When we'd go back to work the next day, we'd say, 'No, that doesn't work. Let's start over from the beginning.' I can't begin to tell you how many times that happened."

Now gaining significant momentum as a solo star, Ivana says she needed to create a distinct personal image in a pop landscape that was filled with the unique looks of new wave, rock and dance luminaries. "If I tell the truth about my style, you will laugh for about half an hour," she says with amusement. "When I first had success as a solo artist, a lot of people must have thought that I spent a lot of time creating an image for myself. Since the time I was doing Fun Fun, I used to cut my hair myself and dye it red and black and whatever I wanted. I did it myself because I didn't have money to go to a hairstylist. I remember when the time came to prepare the cover of the 'Easy Lady' single, Theo told me I would be going for a photo session. I certainly didn't have money to go out and buy clothes for it. I didn't have money to do anything. So I cut my hair myself. I did end up going to a stylist to get the coloring done. My hair was red and black at the time so they had to dye my hair like six or seven times to make it blonde for the picture they used on the single sleeve. Then I had to find some clothes without spending any money. I went to a place where they rented clothes, and I was able to borrow a few things. I put my outfit together in two days. I always loved painting, writing and inventing. I guess this time I needed to invent *myself.*

"Later, when I had success in England, the people there were used to seeing every kind of person with thousands of different types of looks. When I came out with 'Call Me' and it became a success in the UK, I actually saw mannequins in London shops dressed identically to the way I looked. I thought to myself, 'I guess they *do* like my image!' But they had no idea I put those looks together in a day or two. I think Madonna was really the best as far as style goes, though. I never met her, but I always thought she was very clever. I never wanted to be another Madonna, even though some people compared me to her. Madonna is Madonna, and nobody else could be like that. If I had tried, it would have been impossible. I really believe you have to try to be number one in your own way. If you try to be like someone else, you will always be number two. You need to be yourself—and sometimes when you are, good things can happen."

With demand high for a follow-up to "Easy Lady," Spagna surpassed most everyone's expectations. "Call Me" began making its mark early in 1987 and was a swift-sell throughout Europe. The high-energy song proved unstoppable in several European territories, reaching the Top 10 in France, Switzerland, Italy, Sweden, Norway and Germany. A number of muscled-up remixes kept the track on the charts for many weeks, and the alternate versions even managed, several months later, to bring the song to a Top 20 position on the U.S. dance chart. The only country that appeared to be immune to Spagna's charms was the United Kingdom—temporarily.

"After 'Easy Lady' was a big success in Europe," recollects the singer, "we decided to release 'Call Me' as the next single. All the countries were very interested in promoting it—except for England. We couldn't get any interest from the CBS label or any DJs in the UK. Well, the song went to number one in so many countries, and it was especially popular in the clubs in Spain. Many people from Europe and the UK would visit Spain for the summer holidays, and they were hearing my song on the radio and in the discos. So, after the three-month season there ended, the English people returned to the UK and were hitting the record shops trying to find 'Call Me.' The shops didn't have it, and the people started demanding it from the record company. Within two weeks, the song climbed the British charts all the way to number two. I remember it was the number because Michael Jackson released a song that same week. I could've been number one, but I had to settle for second. What can you do?" she laughs.

No less impactful was Spagna's 1988 sophomore album, *You Are My Energy*. Considered a dance-pop masterpiece by many, the artist scored a Top Five hit in Italy with the single "I Wanna Be Your Wife" and returned to the British hit parade with the jubilant "Every Girl & Boy," which, in its "Bang Bang" remix, was an riveting dance-floor smash. A third single, "This Generation," was widely regarded not only as a stimulating dance journey, but as a thought-provoking commentary on the times. As a result of her diverse repertoire, Spagna's fan base was as broad as any singer could hope to have during this period.

"I had a very diverse audience," she says proudly. "In any country, I can tell you pretty much *everybody* was buying my records. In the '80s, my audience included children, young people, the middle aged, older people—truly, everybody. I guess maybe that's a bit strange because I might have looked a bit like a weird person because of my hair or my dresses, but all types of people came to my shows. I remember the first concert I gave in Italy, there were so many young children in the audience, and they were shouting, 'Spagna! Spagna! Spagna!' It was like they were calling me to come and play. I guess to them I looked like a crazy doll. I have also always had a strong gay following, too, and I can tell you in particular, I always love performing in gay clubs. Gay people *always* want to have fun. They dance like crazy."

The sordid realities and darker side of life in the '80s music industry, including sexism, were apparent to Spagna, but she says she never personally experienced problems related to them. "When I was young and working with Theo and Larry, I can tell you I used to work—*like a man*. So I was in many ways treated like just another man. We needed to physically prepare our stage, and I used to help the other musicians set up. It was a lot of work. Then we would play a five-hour gig. Then we'd have to take everything apart, carry the instruments back to our truck, and go back home at eight or nine in the morning—and all for almost no money. We just worked for the passion of it all. So from the very beginning, I was working like a man. I didn't experience what you would call sexism. I always felt a kind of respect from people in the music industry. I was very respectful to others, and I believe if you give respect, most of the time you will receive it back—maybe not all of the time, but most of it. The same is true of the audience—if you respect them, they will respect you. I didn't feel it was a man's world—I just did my job; I was never a diva—just a singer. And I didn't have any trouble being a woman.

"In the '80s, I think everyone experienced the same social problems in all parts of the world. I think perhaps we *still* have all those same problems today. Wars, AIDS, poverty, everything. But as far as drug abuse was concerned, for me the 'drug' was to be on the stage. When I was singing, that was like being in another dimension. I never used drugs and was never involved with them. I didn't need them because I had everything I needed with singing, composing and performing. My world was full. I used to drink wine, yes, especially when I was with good company. I like red wine—this was my drug then, and it still is today."

Though she had already made a respectable impact on the American dance chart, the United States was still largely unaware of Spagna's formidable ranking in the international pop music scene. It was a dilemma faced by many European artists. "I would have liked to have had bigger success in the U.S.," Ivana observes. "I will tell you what happened. It was around 1990, and I was still in Italy. I broke up with Larry—by then we had lived together, and I loved him like a brother, and he felt the same way about me. So we agreed to split as a romantic couple. I no longer got along with the manager I had during that period, and I felt he wasn't helping me move my career ahead. I thought I needed a break from everything—to go away. I remember it was the 16th of December, my birthday, and I was having a little party. I told my guests that by March I would be living in Los Angeles. Nobody believed I would actually do it. In February, I did a TV show in London, and after the show, I told my manager I was going to Los Angeles to look for a house to rent. He told me I was crazy. I didn't care—I went anyway, and I started living in California. I really just felt it was time to change everything in my life.

"When I first lived there, I didn't do anything involving music. But I knew a very important person in the music industry there, Bobby Colomby. He had been a drummer with Blood, Sweat & Tears and he was [Senior VP of Creative Development] of Sony Music in California. After I had settled into the California scene, I rented a piano for my home, and I started making songs again. I would send the demo tapes to Larry and Theo in Italy and work with them on the music. They started developing the arrangements and we'd send each other everything on cassette by mail. I sent some of this new music to Mr. Colomby, and eventually, he called me. We met, and he told me he wanted to handle my third album, *No Way Out*. I started working with American musicians and putting the album together. Bobby put me in the studio with great musicians like [violinist] Jerry Goodman, and we did a lot of work on the project.

"At one point, I was invited to be interviewed by *The Wall Street Journal*," Spagna continues. "I did the interview in New York City. The journalist who wrote the article was a woman, and for some reason she wrote so many bad things about me. There was no problem during the interview. I was answering all of her questions, and I thought everything was fine. When the article came out, it caused quite a bit of [negative] publicity, and it resulted in some calls by the media to Sony to find out what was going on with this reporter and me. For two days, my face was on all the entertainment gossip shows, CNN, things like that. The American press was calling me 'the new Madonna,' even though my album hadn't even been released in the U.S. yet." She chuckles at the odd situation and the level of attention she was receiving.

"But once the album did come out," Ivana says, her voice taking on a more serious tone, "I was a bit disappointed because Sony never did a good job of pushing it. I never did any other American television, no radio interviews, nothing. However, my old manager from Italy must have seen me on one of the U.S. news shows, and he contacted Sony Italy. He told them that he still had a contract with me, and if they didn't bring me back to Italy, he was going to sue for—I don't know—two million dollars at the time or something like that. I guess he saw me on TV and thought, 'Okay she's going to be famous once again.' So I had to return to Italy and throw away all the work I had done in America. Bobby was very upset and said angrily, 'That's Italy!' It was a phrase I won't forget."

Though the single from her American project, "Love at First Sight" (remixed by Black Box) was a top hit in Italy and the *No Way Out* LP a moderate success in 1991, subsequent single releases like "I Always Dream About You" (from the LP *Matter of Time*) and "Lady Madonna," though popular in her native land, failed to find as sizeable an international audience as her previous efforts. By 1994, the artist was ready to begin yet another phase in her career, and the timing was perfect. "Elton John was looking for an Italian voice for the song 'Circle of Life' for the Italian soundtrack to *The Lion King*," she says. "They would choose the voice they preferred to sing the song in each country that the film was released in. They offered me the opportunity, and I thought, 'Oh God, I definitely want to try this!' I think it was about 48 hours after I did the demo that the Walt Disney Company got in touch with me. When Elton heard my voice, he decided I had to be the one to sing the track. I sang it in Italian, and I suppose that it was destiny that it got me into singing in the language. Before, I never wanted to sing in Italian and always preferred singing in English. But at that time, singing in Italian was something new for me—a challenge. I remember that I was then called for the *San Remo Festival* in Italy, and that inspired me to write my first Italian language composition, 'Gente Come Noi,' a ballad. I was able to sell a half a million copies of that song, so it was a very good beginning."

Spagna released a series of Italian language albums through the remainder of the '90s and well into the 2000s, including *Lupi Solitari* in 1996 and *La Nostra Canzone* in 2001. Despite the new adult contemporary style she honed on these sets, the artist was never all that far from the dance floor as the twenty-first century got under way. A sharp-edged retake of "Easy Lady" (under the moniker of Ice & Cream vs. Spagna) garnered interest in 2004, and sophisticated updates of "Call Me" by Nicola Fasano and Steve Forest, along with a multitude of other remixers, caused a major club stir in 2010. "I was happy with my Italian music, but of course I would prefer to go to other countries and have my music heard beyond Italy," she says. In 2016, the release of her single "D.A.N.C.E." (ft. Joser) inspired throngs to hit the floor—it was a smash in Europe that brought the singer back to the continent's pop charts.

The artist also has very definite modern-day humanitarian priorities in mind for the future. "I have taken care of many stray cats here in my home, and my next big project—but I will surely need some help from God—is to build a big facility to help care for these animals. I'd like to see if I can get as many stray cats and dogs off the streets as possible, help keep them healthy and find good homes for them. This is very important to me—perhaps bigger than even my music. Of course I must continue to sing and do my music, or I will be able to do nothing for them," she smiles.

According to Ivana, life today isn't that much different from her days in the '80s spotlight, at least not as far as creativity is concerned. "When I am doing something new, I have the same feeling of excitement and passion I did 20 or 30 years ago. Can you believe that? This is really a gift. Can I tell you—I always thank God. He really gave me something incredible—my enthusiasm, if that's the right word. I can be many things when I am at work, but I am never boring. I can be tired or happy; I can even be desperate. But I am *never* boring. When I work on new music, it is often difficult to sleep because my brain is always going, and I am always thinking. 'Should I change this? What if I went back and did this? How would it sound if I tried it this way?' That's how I am, and I am always excited. When I perform today, whether by myself or on a tour with other singers, sometimes—at the end of a song—I realize I *do* have to end the song at some point," she laughs. "I am sometimes in another dimension, and I am enjoying the moment so much, it feels like it could go on and on. It's like a dream—a fantastic dream. I love that contact I have with people through my music. I've always been that way.

"Each song I wrote—whether it was successful or not—was a part of me. There was one song that really affected me, and when I hear it today, I still feel something inside. It is 'Matter Of Time.' When I lost my mother, after having lost my father, I went into a long and difficult period of sadness. I wrote that song when that happened, and maybe it was God's way of helping me get through that time. It is very hard to get through a time like that when you lose the people you love. It feels like you have lost everything, really.

"I just have one very uncomplicated wish," she says in a soft voice, thinking about her legacy in dance-pop. "It would be nice if people would say, 'Singing and songwriting was Ivana Spagna's passion and her life.' And I would like people to know that I was always grateful to God for this gift."

Amii Stewart
"Friends" (1984)
Italy

Vocalists who achieved a number one dance song at the height of the '70s disco era had no guarantee of future prosperity, at least in America. That icy conclusion became abundantly clear to many singers who enjoyed the mirror ball spotlight, only to find themselves hopelessly outcast after the so-called death of disco. Amii Stewart was a very distinct exception. She was among a select few artists in dance music who successfully transitioned from the '70s to the '80s with stellar results. Her singing career first shifted into high gear when her thundering powerhouse single "Knock on Wood" (an all-time classic of the disco genre) created a worldwide sensation in 1979. When disco took a nosedive in the U.S., the vocalist continued her recording career, focusing her attention on Europe. Relocating to Italy, she became one of that country's most sophisticated and respected entertainers, enjoying a string of tremendously popular international hits throughout the '80s and '90s. She continues to be a celebrated artist across the continent in the twenty-first century. From her home in Rome, Stewart thoughtfully shares her perspective on what it takes to win the elusive prize of longevity in the music business. The artist begins by reflecting on the days of her youth, which were spent in America's capital, Washington, D.C.

"I was born into a big, fun loving, country style family. The adjective 'big' is a bit of an understatement, as my mom was one of 13 children. Either my grandparents just loved each other to death or didn't own a TV set!" she laughs. "I am number five in a line of six children that my mom and dad (Mary and Joseph—I kid you not) brought into the world. I was named after my mother's sister Amy—a gentle, sweet and very proper lady whom I never heard raise her voice or say one curse word. Years later, when I moved to New York and joined Actors Equity, there was already an Amy Stewart listed. There could only be one of each name for obvious accounting reasons. I remember thinking to myself, 'If I change my name and then become famous one day, how would my family know it's me?' So, instead of changing my name, I altered the spelling from Amy to Amii.

"Our family is devout Catholic, and we also happened to live right across the street from a monastery. Almost every Sunday, the priests were invited to our traditional country-style, 'eat till you pop' afternoon dinners. The tables stretched from the dining to the living room to accommodate our extended family and friends. After dinner, the plates would be cleaned away, and the playing cards would come out. So, although we were God fearing, it never got in the way of a loud, talkin' trash, play-to-the-death card game for nickels, dimes and—dare I say—50 cents!" she smiles brightly. "Sometimes the grown-ups, egged on by

Left: Singer and dancer Amii Stewart's scintillating costumes complemented her athletic figure, powerhouse voice and striking beauty, captured in this promotional shot from her 1979 album release *Paradise Bird*. **Right: Today, Amii continues to perform, record and work in musical theater.**

us kids, would have a jitterbug contest ('So the young bloods can see how it's really done!') They called it 'cuttin' the rug.' Everybody in my family could and sometimes would 'dance till the cows came home.' My dad, especially, could really throw down. Thus, music was a fundamental ingredient of my youth. My dad, an army veteran, worked at the U.S. Printing Office, but he also played reed instruments (mostly clarinet) for the military marching bands. He probably would have been a serious musician had he not met my mom and started a family. He would often go down into the basement on weekends and practice. I'd sit on the steps and listen, just adoring him. His mom Geneva was an accomplished pianist and played for the silent movies. My oldest sister is named after her."

Amii is able to recall hearing the voice of Billie Holiday, her mother's favorite vocalist, as a young child. "I must have been about three years old, because I have a memory of being in the crib holding on to the bars to keep myself erect," she recollects. "My mother is ironing and singin' to Lady Day. My mom sang and smiled, hugged and kissed all of us, all the time. I see it as if it were yesterday. During my youth, I became accustomed to hearing the greats—Dinah Washington, Louis Armstrong, Ray Charles, Mahalia Jackson,

Nat King Cole. As I got older, I'd lock myself in my brother Joe's room on hot summer afternoons and sing for hours to Nancy Wilson (my all-time favorite) and imitate Ray Charles. Then I'd hop over to Ella and Sarah for the 'variations of a theme.' Let me explain: I'd take, for example, the song 'I Loves You, Porgy,' sung by Ella. Then I'd study the same song by Billie, then by Satchmo, and so on. That would go on all afternoon. The breathing, the phrasing, the cadence, the emotion—I learned back then there are no wrong notes when you sing from the womb.

"Then one day, along came the group Rufus with Chaka Khan singing 'Feel Good,' and I almost lost my mind and my voice. The funk jumped off the turntable. Stevie Wonder and the Temptations took me to the verge of being thrown out of the house. I drove everybody crazy. To make matters worse, I knew every jingle and opening song to every TV show and sang them every single time they appeared. It got so bad they put an industrial roll of brown scotch tape on top of the TV—a threatening last resort. Didn't work."

Stewart started dancing by the age of nine, following in her older sister Brenda's footsteps. It became her passion and main focus for the next 15 years. Because of her skill in dance, she was accepted into the Workshop for Careers in the Arts, founded by Peggy Cooper Cafritz and Mike Malone. In later years, it became known as the renowned Duke Ellington School of the Arts, and remains a highly regarded learning institution today. Says Amii, "At the workshops, I honed my natural talents for dancing, singing and acting. What a glorious time that was for me and for all those who were lucky enough to be in the right place at the right time. My teachers were of the caliber that even today is awe-inspiring: Mike Malone, Louis Johnson, Debbie Allen, Glenda Dickerson and Charles Augins to name just a few. I knew early on that I was born to be an artist. I had no idea if I had the stuff to become 'famous.' I just knew I was hell bent on being one of the best in whatever I did. If it didn't happen, it wouldn't be because I didn't give it my all. I was insecure as a child (maybe most kids are at that age), but my mentors at the Workshop were rigorous in teaching me the tools of the trade. They instilled in me that indispensable necessity—self-esteem—which gave me the assurance that I, too, could shine. I possessed an inner light and could become whatever I chose, and no one could extinguish that light. The stage would become the barrier between me and the dark monster of uncertainty. Onstage, *I* ruled. Fiercely, yes, but always with humility. What you learn at an early age you never forget."

By 1975–76, Amii moved to New York and became an understudy for the role of Ella and a pit singer in the cast of the musical *Bubbling Brown Sugar*. "I'd made an audition as a chorus dancer/singer six months previously in the Miami company and was chosen by the producer to come to New York," she says. "The score was all Duke Ellington material—glorious. By that time, I was a seasoned but untried professional dancer/singer/actress. Musicals were my world. My old ballet teacher/mentor Charles Augins then chose me for the London's West End production, but this time I was hired as his assistant director/choreographer and was given the lead role of Ella. You see, I was so hungry to prove my worth that while I was on Broadway, I sat in the wings every performance and literally learned the whole show by heart. I could play everybody's role (choreography, songs and blocking included) with my eyes closed."

Disco fever had a tight grip on the United States and Europe by the late '70s, and the pop charts of virtually every country were crowded with dance music singles. "Singing disco was the furthest thing from my mind," claims Stewart. "I was 22, living in London, renting my very first house and making great money doing what I'd always dreamed of. I thought I'd died and gone to heaven in a Bentley. (I used to rent one to pick up family and friends at the airport when they came to visit from the States.) [Music producer] Barry Leng came to see the show one night and came backstage to introduce himself. Barry had these sparkly eyes and a happy-go-lucky manner. He was like a mad scientist with a mop of curly blond hair and a quick wit. He asked me if I would like to go into the studio and sing a demo. I asked him, 'What's a demo?' I'd only ever sung live, so I didn't have a clue. He explained and we made an appointment to get together on a Monday when the theatre was dark. Well, when the day rolled around, I had a really bad cold and went to the studio with a box of tissues under my arm. (The studio was a dump. It was just plain ol' filthy, but it had the acoustics of life, and the engineer was a wizard.) There I met Simon May, a very kind and considerate person and a great songwriter. The first track we cut was 'You Really Touched My Heart.'

"I remember I had to stand back from the mike because the arrow was permanently in the red if I didn't. In the theatre, you're taught to project your voice all the way to the 'exit' sign over the door in the back of the stalls. Their eyes popped when they heard my voice, the range and control. Barry and Simon were easy to work with. We were in total sync from the jump because they just put on the track and let me fly. Theatre and dance gives you fierce discipline, so I didn't just show up—I came prepared to nail it. I got the song in the pocket in a couple of hours, chorus included. Spontaneity is everything, so the first takes are always the best takes. When I needed guidance, they were there—Simon for the melody and lyrics, Barry for the rhythm and arrangement ideas. We laughed a lot, but we also worked like Trojans. The project was commissioned by Hansa Records, a company based in Germany owned by Trudy and Peter Meisel, who then took 'You Really Touched My Heart' to Ariola Records for the licensing deal in 1978. The song was released and was received well."

The next track the artist recorded, "Knock on Wood," was a remake of Eddie Floyd's 1966 laidback soul nugget. Amii's version was anything but easygoing. Says the vocalist, "We went back in and did 'Knock on Wood' some weeks later. I remember the first time I heard the track, I thought Barry must have gotten hold of some exceptionally good weed the night before. The track was pumping like a freight train—unbelievable. In those days, there were at least three versions made of every single, so I'd do the long one (six minutes or so), and they'd do the edits afterwards.

"It was one of the hardest sessions vocally, but also the funniest because I felt like Dorothy caught in the tornado. They'd pump the track, and with a devilish grin from the other side of the glass, wait to see what I'd come up with. The long version just went on *forever*. They invented the 'ooh-oh-oh-oh-oh-oh' at the end of the key line. For the rest, well, it's an incredible feeling when you enter 'the zone,' and you surrender yourself completely to the music. When it's over and you hear what you've done, it's as if you've had an out of body experience. Leaving the studio, I was dog tired but euphoric and probably still a little in shock!" Amii laughs.

"In the theatre the next day, the cast was so excited. They asked, 'How'd it go?' I told them, 'It's definitely different, but I don't think it'll go far.' I just continued doing the show. The cast bought *Billboard* magazine every week to keep me informed on 'Knock on Wood''s progress. I still didn't believe it. Looking back now, I was a little afraid to leave my comfort zone. The cast had become another nurturing family for me; I felt safe. When the song got to the Top 50 in the States, Trudy called me into the Hansa office and told me it was time to leave the show. 'What? Give up my day job?' I gasped. She said, 'Amii, I don't know if you are aware of it, but 'Knock' may be on its way to being number one in the States and probably all over the world. It's time to get serious. You'll have to travel, do photo shoots, videos, interviews. 'Go home and pack.' The rest is history, as they say."

"Knock on Wood," released in 1978, was like disco on steroids. From its super-charged, pounding syndrum intro, to Stewart's commanding vocal rendition, the track ventured into previously unexplored, ultra-high-energy musical territory. The song reached the top spot on *Billboard*'s pop chart and was a staple on the U.S. club chart for almost six months. The single, which earned Stewart a Grammy nomination, narrowly missed the summit of the Italian and French singles charts and was a mammoth Top 10 hit throughout Europe. The *Knock on Wood* album was a huge seller in the U.S. and abroad, and the follow-up single, an equally robust remake of The Doors' "Light My Fire," was a sizeable hit.

"After I left *Bubbling*, it was like a whirlwind," Stewart says, almost breathlessly. "Trudy was true to her word. The controlled madness began in a big way. I would go to the office, and the reporters would arrive for the interviews every 30 minutes. It started off with a couple of hours of interviewing. But relatively quickly, there were days I'd be going four to five hours doing back-to-back phone and live interviews and brief photo shoots. You see, with 'Knock' in most of the Top 50 charts worldwide simultaneously, I couldn't be everywhere at the same time. So the interviews were crucial for promotion. I remember doing interviews for six hours straight (I kid you not). By the end I felt like a broken record. My success happened so fast that it seemed like I'd come out of nowhere. They wanted to know the story of the girl behind that fierce disco image. I think they were a bit let down to find I was neither a rebel nor a bad girl. There was no surprise behind door number three. I was just a naive, young artist who got lucky her first time out. The trick is to stay there!

"Barry, Simon and I really worked as a well-oiled machine in the beginning," Amii recalls of her spectacular debut. "They believed totally in my ability and creativity as a vocalist, so you could say I had total vocal control. We would always choose together which takes would be the final ones. Sometimes we'd choose a take that wasn't picture perfect vocally, but that expressed the perfect emotion. Very often they'd have to convince me to stop singing. I am never fully satisfied with my vocals, so sometimes they'd just come in and drag me away from the mike. The music perspective from behind the console is usually more objective than the one from behind the mike. I absolutely loved some of the other tracks on the album, like 'Closest Thing to Heaven' and 'Get Your Love Back.' 'Light My Fire' was challenging because of the nose bleeding high notes I wanted to hit. I can remember my diaphragm working like an accordion. They always had my supply of honey, herbal teas, etc. on hand for energy because I can't eat when I sing."

Part of Stewart's instant mass appeal was no doubt linked to the widely distributed official video of "Knock on Wood," a promotional device that was well ahead of its time. Laced with crude (by today's standards) yet engaging visual effects, Amii moved and danced with grace, power and speed through the roughly three and a half minute clip. Dressed in an exotic, almost Egyptian-style costume (including a head dress that resembled multi-colored ram's horns), the singer made a dazzling impression. "I truly must thank Trudy

Meisel, who commissioned Miranda Holland to create my image and design those fabulous, groundbreaking costumes, all handmade creations. She lived in the English countryside and would hire senior ladies of the village to do the beading and double stitching, while watching the soaps and gossiping over cups of tea and biscuits. She was a creative wizard. The head dress for 'Knock' used to drive me crazy. Wearing it was like performing a circus act because it was so top heavy. It's true that the costume was out of this world, but you really had to be careful not to get your feet tangled up in it.

"I'll never forget my first time on American TV. I was in Vegas doing the *Dinah Shore Show*. I'd sent the costume to the cleaners on my arrival at the hotel. The next day (the day of the show), after makeup, etc., and with 20 minutes till show time, I started to get dressed for the number. I discovered that the costume had stretched at least 10–12 inches longer and was dragging on the floor between my legs. The set had a long staircase for the grand entrance. I held the skirt coming down, but my heel got caught when I let it drop, and I couldn't get it out. I lindy-hopped and fought with that damn dress the whole three minutes of 'Knock' on primetime TV. *A disaster!* Needless to say, I got it altered afterwards (a little too late), but I never trusted that costume again. Since then, I have never ever waited until the last minute to check my costumes before going onstage," laughs the singer.

"I had some fierce costumes back then that really put my anatomy on show because I was a singer with a dancer's body. There were almost always dancers behind me, and I handled all the choreography—not just a little here an' a little there. I had stamina for days, so singing and dancing was no big deal for me. I was still intensely shy, so I wore a long robe, which I threw in the wings when I hit the stage. I was always cold and half naked and never quite got used to it. Making the videos for 'Knock on Wood,' and especially 'Light My Fire' and 'Jealousy' [from the follow-up album *Paradise Bird*] were grueling 10 to 12 hour affairs. In those days, there was no such thing as digital, so we taped a thousand times from different angles, changing light designs, dry ice for smoke effect, etc. I loved doing makeup and did my own for 'Jealousy,' with a rainbow effect for the close-up of my eyes.

"There were scores of music shows all over Europe in the late '70s and early '80s, and I did them all. Not to mention the live disco gigs. It was almost always the same line-up, more or less—Boney M., Precious Wilson and Eruption, Dschinghis Khan, Village People, Sylvester and so many others. It was a wonderful but hectic time. When the single hit big in the States, Trudy flew with me to New York, where the record company held a big showcase for the critics and press. From there, we went to Los Angeles, and I will never forget it. We were in a limo on the way to the Beverly Hills Hotel. Coming down Sunset Boulevard, I looked up, and there was a *huge* cutout poster of me in the 'Knock' costume dominating the skyline. That was the moment for me when I realized I'd made it. It was exhilarating but also a little scary. The expectation was through the roof, and it's so easy to disappoint."

Following Stewart's breathtaking success, the very musical genre she'd found fame in came under siege. By the end of 1979 in the United States, thanks largely to an over-saturated record market and (some degree of) public and media burnout with the phenomenon, disco was declared dead. Europe continued to embrace the style, but the musical landscape was clearly changing. Amii's producers were faced with the daunting challenge of figuring out what would come next.

"Barry, Simon, and the record company were under tremendous pressure to come up with new material after a monster hit like 'Knock,'" observes the singer. "When you get to the top of Mount Everest, you'd like to stay there a minute and enjoy the view. How do you top that song? Almost impossible. My job was the easiest. All I had to do was get in the studio and make a slammin' vocal."

The *Paradise Bird* LP was served up just as the decade came to a close. U.S. audiences largely ignored the set, but the singles "Jealousy" and "The Letter" (both retreads of "Knock on Wood" to some degree) fared well in Italy, the Netherlands and Britain."I loved the song 'Paradise Bird' because it was a beautiful ballad, and to be honest, I've always considered myself more of a torch singer," Amii says. "The video was also lovely. When I'm in the studio, my only concern is the music in the earphones. You have to be focused on that and only that. I'd heard about the disco record burning fiasco in the States. It was a sorry sight to see, but I wasn't worried about my career per se. Coming from the theatre, I'd been talking to the guys about changing styles slowly, so as not to get caught in the shuffle. We were still going strong in Europe, so neither they nor the record company felt the urge to change too quickly. I could feel the itch because of my melodic music background."

Stewart's next album arrived in 1981, released under two different names and with slightly different track listings in the U.S. and Europe. American indie label Handshake Records released *I'm Gonna Get Your Love* in the U.S., emphasizing a trendy, high-energy remake of the Supremes' "Where Did Our Love Go" (a Narada Michael Walden production) and funkier soul tracks created by Raymond Reid and William Anderson of the R&B group Crown Heights Affair. Europe received the LP *Images*, which featured some alternate tracks created by the Leng/May team. "Trudy was a savvy business woman," says Amii, "and we had great respect and affection for one another. She could see the writing on the wall, and we flew to New York to collaborate with Handshake Records. I loved that period in New York. I'd left in '77 expecting to be away for only six months, and here it was four years later. I've always had great respect for composers and try to be true to their concepts. Today, I realize I could have been ballsier. But I was young and felt a bit intimidated working with such icons, and that hindered me a bit. I remember listening to demos for hours with the head of Handshake, looking for the right track. I honestly can't say I heard it. But being that I was dead wrong about 'Knock,' I decided to lay low. Everyone was wonderful to me, but I could feel the underlying tension in the air at Handshake. I would discover the company was on the verge of closure while in the middle of producing the project. The balloon was slowly losing helium and settling to earth. I continued on to San Francisco to work with Narada Michael Walden. That was something. Narada is special. He has an aura that sets the creative tone. His studios are beautiful and simply appointed, the atmosphere peaceful. It's like singing in an ashram. I loved working with him, but 'Where Did Our Love Go' did not inspire me. I didn't want another remake. I wanted to do melodic music with strings. I wanted to become a serious interpreter of song. In those days, a sister was supposed to sing R&B or soul. Well, I am not an R&B/soul singer. I'm a crossover melodic pop singer."

The album contained the first of many duets Stewart would perform throughout her recording career. The Smokey Robinson/Ronald White evergreen "My Guy/My Girl" paired Amii with R&B veteran Johnny Bristol. (The song was later revamped in 1985 as a duet with Deon Estus.)

"Johnny was a trip. He had a fabulous voice and knew it. He was also used to getting any lady he wanted. When he turned on the charm, I didn't bite. Instead, I would get on his case, which he wasn't used to. When he finally accepted that 'My Girl/My Guy' was just the name of the song and not reality, we got on great. We laughed a lot. He loved to recount his trysts, the women he'd had, sometimes in explicit detail trying to shock me. He was like a bad little boy. I remember one night we were in Amsterdam, I think doing a promotion. He fell asleep while talking to his girlfriend in L.A. When he woke the next morning, the phone was still off the hook. At checkout time the promo manager and Trudy went to pay the bill and had a shit fit. Johnny turned red as a beet; I howled. Needless to say they couldn't wait to get his butt back on that plane to L.A.

"Here is where the plot thickens," says Amii, describing her parting of the ways with the Simon May-Barry Leng team. "My last years in London were not rosy artistically. The songs just weren't coming any more, and Barry was becoming more and more self-absorbed and at odds with Simon and me," she recalls. "Barry was insisting on doing a duet with me. (I think he used to sing and play guitar in a band in the past.) Needless to say, I flatly refused. The inability to find another mega-hit took its toll. My contract was with them, and they were signed to the record company, who was also unhappy. The royalties became shaky, and I was no businesswoman. In the end, I made the two most difficult (but inevitable) decisions I'd ever made in my life. I broke with Simon and Barry and decided to stop singing to let the disco image die down. It was like holding my breath. My break with Barry was stormy, with Simon sad."

By 1983, Amii was back in the studio. With her return came a critically acclaimed, self-titled LP produced by Simon Boswell, released by the Italian division of RCA. The set was punctuated by the upbeat arrangements of tracks like "Working Late Tonight" and "Beginning of the End," but gone was the heavy disco sound with which the artist had been associated. It also marked the beginning of the singer's close connection to Italy, one that flourishes to this day. "I'd been going back and forth to Rome for years doing promotion and loved it," she says. "When RCA Italy found out I didn't have a contract, they offered me a deal I couldn't refuse. 'Sign with us and we'll give you complete artistic control. We'll put our recording studios at your disposal.' It was what I'd been longing to hear. That's how it all started. Italy is the motherland of music—melodic, classic or otherwise. In Italy, being black was an asset, not a label for the kind of music I was supposed to be singing. RCA were true to their word. They put me in a lovely residence and a recording studio with engineer on call, songwriters and a promo team.

"Now, I've always worked and studied hard. But that can also be said about a lot of artists. What I've got in my favor is that I'm *lucky*. Even when things go badly, I am resilient and keep on the positive path. You're bound to meet up with lady luck again, but you betta be ready, or she'll pass you by. RCA immediately put me with Simon Boswell, a hip songwriter of the time, and we started working on the first album. It was a glorious time for me. In those days, RCA was *the* major company with a stable of top artists, Italian and foreign. So even though I was recording in Italy, they could call sister companies abroad and have English material sent over. 'Working Late Tonight' was the lead single for the album, and I performed it at the *San Remo Festival* as a special guest. I remember that during the live performance the music went out for about five seconds. I kept on going nonetheless, and when the music came back, the dancers and I were still in sync. The audience loved it."

1984 was a *very* good year for Amii Stewart, and Italy continued to provide a musical environment brimming with creative possibilities. It began in earnest with a stunning duet ballad Stewart recorded with veteran Italian crooner Gianni Morandi called "Grazie Perché," a reinterpretation of the Kenny Rogers U.S. hit "We've Got Tonight." "The song took Gianni and me to the stratosphere of popularity in Italy," she recalls. "Gianni had been hugely famous since the early '60s, but when I arrived in the '80s, the company was looking for something to renew his image and jumpstart mine. The song was perfect for us both and went to number one in no time. I sang without understanding a word of Italian. There's only one way to sing a love song, so the intensity was easy. I've a good ear for accents, and that really helped. Gianni was very patient and always there. He is a lovely man, old school, shy and respectful. Today, he still sells out 30,000 capacity arenas after over 40 years in the business. He defies age groups and is admired by all," Stewart says affectionately.

Crossing paths with successful singer/songwriter Francesco Puccioni, better known as Mike Francis (1961–2009), Stewart entered a musical phase that saw the release of several of her most engaging works. Francis' lightly danceable productions made for easy listening in a landscape that had become filled with high-spirited Italo-disco stompers. It was the perfect fit for Stewart's vocal charm. The two artists joined forces with producer Paul Micioni for the landmark single "Friends," a delightfully uncomplicated and irresistibly breezy pop song with a sweet, gentle beat. The endeavor, remixed numerous times since its initial release, went to top the Italian pop charts and was a Top 20 UK smash. The song also returned Stewart to the U.S. R&B charts. The *Try Love* LP followed, which highlighted a sophisticated mix of soft ballads and sharp dance material, including the song "Fever Line." "Francesco was one of the first people I met at RCA, which has since become Sony," Amii remembers. "When I arrived on the scene, he was riding on a mega-hit called 'Survivor,' which I loved. He was also one of maybe three people at RCA who spoke English. We hit it off immediately. Francesco was one of the sweetest, most sensitive and elegant men and songwriters whom I've ever or will ever meet. God made *one* Francesco. There will be no more. Francesco was passionate about all things, beautiful and generous to a fault. He was passionate about his music and all things pertaining to art. Friendships were very important to him, and he had many. He loved beautiful women (of which he also had many), food, good wine, cooking, dancing, fishing, travel. And Francesco loved to laugh. We could and would laugh about anything and everything. Francesco was never cruel. He was my brother, and he shared his feelings with me like a sister.

"When I first heard 'Friends,' I fell in love with the sensuality and simplicity, which would become the trademark of Mike Francis and Paul Micioni productions. Back then, Paul was a producer and the top dance club DJ in Italy. He was a wonderful character who prided himself on his encyclopedic memory and owning the largest vinyl dance collection in Italy. They made a great duo because one had what the other lacked. The album *Try Love* with Francesco and Paul is one of my favorites. I loved being in the studio with them; it was so easy. The song 'That Loving Feeling' was like floating on air. 'I Gotta Have You Back' was also one of my favorites. I was at home with the elegant, sensual ambience Francesco created in his music. When 'Friends' was released in England and hit the charts, I was ecstatic. I couldn't believe I was going back to London on a high. Francesco's music was more conducive to my personality and reflected where I wanted to go melodically. It was a wonderful moment for us both."

The *Try Love* album's stunning jacket photograph was as visually sophisticated as the music it represented, with Stewart elegantly posed on a silver chaise longue, draped sensuously in nothing but a piece of red silk fabric. "The album cover was done by Alberta Tiburzi; a crazy but genius photographer of the time. The shoot took 12 hours; I kid you not. She would rant and rave at her assistants, who took it all without a whimper. I held that position on that lounge chair for forever. I'll never forget she looked at my breasts as they were draping the red silk fabric over my body and said, 'Beautiful breasts—how old are you?' I told her, and then she said, 'They won't be like that for long. Just wait a while.' I was speechless!"

Inspired by their success with "Friends," Stewart and Francis released the single "Together" in 1985, a lean and punchy dance duet that bubbled with its stars' irresistible chemistry. The song vaulted into Italy's Top 10. Observes Amii, "When we cut 'Together,' we were like two peas in a pod. We did it in a couple of takes because we were in perfect sync. I remember on one TV show we did together where we laughed like fools. The stage was all Plexiglas, and they had this smoke effect going on (smoke was big in the day). The only problem was that the smoke effect was oil-based, so it made the stage extremely slippery. Well, we bounced out on the stage, and before too long, I fell flat on my butt. Thankfully, the camera was on Francesco at the time. His eyes got as big as marbles. Then the Steadicam operator slipped and fell. Well, after that there was no containing either of us. We laughed our way through the whole song."

The singer says Italy was an extremely welcoming land for people of color. "In the '70s and '80s, luckily for me, Italy was the place to be if you were black American. They loved our work ethic, diversity, and vocal quality. (The whole truth be told it wasn't just about the art. It was also about our 'side B.' They went ballistic for the Brazilians too. You could serve tea and crumpets, their backsides were so fierce!) We were considered exotic. I was one of many black women who graced the Italian stage and fashion runways of Milan. Italy's love affair with black Americans started with World War II. The soldiers came and brought jazz in their backpacks. Blacks are open, generous, fun lovin', food lovin' and family-orientated, just like Italians. They fell in love with Louis Armstrong, Sarah, Ella. In the '60s, Lola Falana had her own TV show. By the time I arrived, it was like slipping under a feather comforter. Italians are wonderful people. They made everything so easy for me. Perfect strangers would take me by the hand if I was lost on the street and spend time to decipher what I was trying to say.

"The only challenge was gaining respect in the work place from the men. Italians are macho at work because the women usually run the roost with an iron fist. I remember a particular meeting with RCA. I'd been there for a while, and they were trying to persuade me to do a song that didn't convince me. I'd been taking Italian lessons with a private tutor at home, and my vocabulary was limited for speaking, but I understood what was being said. At one point, they were talking amongst themselves, thinking I didn't understand what they were saying. 'She doesn't get it. After all, she's just a woman.' Well, I excused myself without a word, feigning going to the restroom, called a cab and went home. About an hour later, I get a call asking where I was. I told them I was at home. They asked me why I'd left without say anything. Was I sick or something? I told them I was fine, but since I was just a woman and didn't know shit, I might as well go home. Silence. That was the game changer, and I won the respect of the execs at RCA."

Around the same period, Amii starred in an Italian TV show called *Tasto Matto*, further broadening the range of her appeal. She had also managed to make substantial progress in her quest to break free of the "disco queen" image. But while enjoying her new direction in Italy during 1985, Amii's signature glitter ball hit "Knock on Wood" suddenly resurfaced in Britain. This time, the spin was in the form of a heavily pumped-up revamp (as if the original version had room for any more power), remixed by Barry Leng and Alan Coulthard. The single, released on the Sedition label as "Knock on Wood Ash 48" (at least on the record jacket cover), leapt up the British pop chart and nearly duplicated the success of the '79 version. A megamix 12-inch single was quickly issued merging the remix of "Knock on Wood" with a fuel-injected retake of "Light My Fire," and an Amii Stewart greatest "remixed" hits album (called *The Hits*) came hot on its heels. Though the project returned Stewart's name to the upper regions of the British pop charts, she remains unenthused about Leng's endeavor.

Amii says she attempted (with little success) to sort out the royalty tangles that arose following her departure from Leng's production camp years before and other complications stirred up by the producer's reinvention of her trademark hit. She was eventually advised to let the matter go. The artist concludes, "…there's only one 'Knock on Wood' diva, and that's *me*! I was naive and paid the price. I have since produced my own versions of 'Knock' with my own publishing company, and I do quite well off of them. I've got my God-given talent and a music catalogue that extends well beyond disco music and Barry Leng. But most of all, my integrity is intact. I'm not for sale, and you can't touch that!" the singer says firmly.

In 1986, Stewart detoured from the gentler dance-pop sound she had honed with Mike Francis and teamed with legendary producer Giorgio Moroder (of Donna Summer fame) and Rob and Ferdi Bolland, a duo that had scored offbeat pop hits like "In the Army Now" by Status Quo and "Jeanny" by Falco in Germany and Austria. The set, called *Amii,* released by Teldec Records in Germany, featured the electro-dance singles "Time Is Tight" and "Break These Chains." However, the tracks failed to spark much interest. "I was not happy with the Moroder/Bolland brothers album," admits the vocalist. "I always felt that the songs were lackluster. The production was cold and didn't reflect my personality. My disappointment was palpable. When you think of the Donna Summer material Giorgio was responsible for, well, that's an impossible act to follow. I felt their hearts just weren't in it, and I'm sure the album proves that theory. They were cordial, but there was no camaraderie in the studio. No joy or excitement."

The *Time for Fantasy* LP arrived in 1988 via RCA Italia and reconnected the singer with Mike Francis, who co-wrote its popular single "Dusty Road." "The album was recorded in London with Greg Walsh. I enjoyed doing that album. I felt we recorded some good tracks. By that time, I realized something important. In those days, before everybody an' their mamma was singing in English, an Italian record company could only do so much to promote an in-house American artist. I'd had some great successes with 'Friends' and 'Together,' but slowly, slowly, BMG [the parent company of RCA Italia] didn't know what else to do. Either you did albums for the Italian market, or you ended up with a mishmash that was neither Italian nor European. There were some great tunes on that album—'I Still Believe,' 'It's You and Me,' 'Sometimes a Stranger,' 'Heartache to Heartache.' But I think I was in the wrong country for such an album. I should have been with BMG in London. I think it would have been a different story. The credibility of the promotion is everything."

Amii continued recording albums in the adult contemporary and rhythmic pop vein during the 90s and later formed the Perle Nere Edizioni Musicali Sas publishing company with her husband Giampiero, whom she met in 1985 and describes as "the most important person in my life." In 2010, she released the digital version of the popular 2004 LP *Lady Day*, a cast album based on a Billie Holiday musical. The following year, Amii supported a campaign to aid the women of Africa with the single "Walking Africa." The year 2012 saw the debut of her critically acclaimed CD *Intense* (with Amii serving as executive producer and co-writer of several tracks). The set featured the popular single "Ordinary People." Late in 2013, she teamed up with Gabry Ponte for the dance hit "Sunshine Girl." In 2017, she released a compilation of her twenty-first century recordings called *A Time to Love*. "I've been independent ever since I left BMG," says Stewart, "collaborating and producing CDs, expanding my lyric writing, performing in live concerts of every genre, musical theatre productions and developing television concepts. I'm happiest when I'm working. I love cooking, playing cards, nights out with friends and things like that. But nothing tops my work. It's an unjust word—work—because when I'm on, it's effortless. I was born hungry, and I'll probably die hungry. Not for money, but for the rush and then the acceptance (the applause). I crave the risk of doing something new and unusual. It's a love-hate relationship with the butterflies in the stomach feeling, the fear of failure. Defy the predictable and sing the shit out of a song no one expects you to sing. I don't know, I guess I really am just a Trojan at heart. If someone says 'don't,' that's my cue!" she chuckles.

Though Amii Stewart's career in dance-pop music has been extraordinary, even by the most stringent of measures, she firmly believes the future holds even more opportunities. "After more than 35 years in music, by the grace of God, I'm still going strong," she says proudly. "I still get butterflies, and I'm still hungry for the next project. There's always going to be something I want to do that will put the proverbial cherry on the cake. Hunger is truly a wonderful thing. It keeps your mind, body and spirit limber. As James Taylor says, the secret of life is to just enjoy the passage of time."

Ric Tess Teiges
aka Fancy
"Slice Me Nice" (1984)
Germany

The year 1984 was a landmark moment in time for Ric Tess Teiges (a.k.a. Ric Tess, Tess Teiges and Manfred Alois Segieth), the European pop star better known as Fancy. After recording folk tunes for years, the 38-year-old singer, songwriter and producer finally hit it big—really big—with high-energy dance music. Thanks to two ferociously foot-stomping club and pop hits, "Slice Me Nice" and "Chinese Eyes," Fancy was recognized as a musical innovator in Germany and a star of the Eurobeat scene worldwide. He is one of the most identifiable figures from the era. His electrifying recordings and sold-out shows in every corner of the globe have been among the most successful ever for a German artist. There has always been an air of mystery surrounding Fancy, and the man hidden behind the dark glasses continues to intrigue his huge fan base to this very day. He looks back on his incredible journey, offering some rare insights into the life he has spent amongst the strobe lights.

Fancy began his early school years studying in a monastery setting, but by the time he'd entered his teens, he had discovered the joys of schlager music, a generally upbeat brand of German pop-folk music unique to the region's culture (which later incorporated elements of the disco sound). Living in Munich, he learned to play guitar. "I had a rock 'n' roll band at one point called 'Tess & The Mountain Shadows,'" he remembers. "I was the singer and the bass player in the early days of this group. I eventually went to work for a publishing company and started working as a composer and demo-tape singer. I also tried taking my first steps as a producer. Step by step, I worked with more artists and started producing music for different record companies." Recording as Tess Teiges, he released a number of German language singles on the Ariola label.

The artist used a number of signatures back in the '70s and early '80s, among them Tess Ric and Manfred Perilano. They were each connected with a variety of functions, including songwriter, artist and producer. "I primarily envisioned myself as a producer," he says. "I was filled with enthusiasm for the disco and dance music of the era. I was really influenced by Giorgio Moroder and the early work of Bobby Orlando. I must say the Tamla-Motown hits were very inspiring to me as well. I was a big fan of Creedence Clearwater Revival, Donna Summer, Barry White, Cliff Richard, Jimi Hendrix—the list goes on and on. I knew some of these artists personally."

In the spring of 1983, Hansa International released a hit single in Germany by an entity

"Slice Me Nice," seen on the left in its 7-inch single version on Metronome Records, was a mammoth pop hit in Germany for Fancy in 1984. On the right, Fancy (Ric Tess Teiges) today. The artist continues to tour with '80s stars such as C.C. Catch and Bad Boys Blue.

known as Slip, produced by Fancy, using the name Tess Teiges. It placed Teiges firmly on the dance-pop map. The song was a fired-up electro-version of the Motown gem "Don't Leave Me This Way," and the track roared up the German pop charts into the country's Top 10. The production had the same energized sound that the Italians were successfully cultivating roughly 1500 km away. Fancy became forever linked to the Italo-disco genre (albeit with a German flair). Says the artist, "I was [Slip vocalist] Claudia Field's producer and a fan of this song, originally sung by Thelma Houston and Harold Melvin & The Blue Notes. I felt this song worked very well with the voice of Claudia, and when we came out of the studio with the final mix, she and I were very happy. We used the pseudonym Slip, and it turned out to be a big hit."

The best was still to come for the innovator. Fancy began working on a melody for a record he planned to make using his own voice, and by the spring of 1984, he began collaborating with musician, songwriter and vocalist Todd Canedy. "Todd heard my demo tape of 'Slice Me Nice,'" Fancy recalls. "The tape had the whole melody (intro, verses, bridge and chorus), the bass line, and the instrumental riff as well. I asked him to play all my melody tracks on a four-track tape, and I said to him, 'Write me a funny, crazy, power-disco-nonsense story!' He brought me the words 'slice-me-nice.' Very crazy indeed. Todd's wife had just had a baby. I gave my composition as a gift to Todd—he worked fast for me on the lyrics, and he did a very good job. I was not thinking of the money; it wasn't all about the money for me. Well, we went to Arco Studios in Munich, and we listened to the playback with all my melody riffs and my base line. Then I sang his lyrics. The final mix was played one week later in Hamburg for Intersong (Warner/Chappell) Publishing. The executives there said, 'Give us the tape, and in 24 hours we will bring you a deal.' The next day, I received the confirmation—Metronome Records would release 'Slice Me Nice,'" he says with pride.

Catchy (if somewhat outlandish) English lyrics, a relentlessly driving beat and Fancy's slippery and exotic vocals melted into a slick, sensational dance record. Reaching the number two spot in neighboring Austria, "Slice" flirted with Germany's Top 10 and held top positions in Sweden, Switzerland and territories throughout Europe and Asia. "By the summer of 1984, the song was an international 'disco-hammer-hit,' and 'Slice Me Nice' made me known worldwide with the artist name Fancy," he adds.

Wasting no time, Fancy continued to ride the wave of success that had suddenly swelled. Teiges unleashed the equally enticing and dramatic follow-up single "Chinese Eyes." A pounding floor-filler, the song's hard-edged beat and sexy S&M flavored lyrics once again fused divinely with Fancy's enigmatic vocal delivery. The single scored Top 10 positions in his native Germany and Switzerland, and the track proved to be an unstoppable force in numerous other territories. "Chinese Eyes" and its companion track "Come Inside" also reached the number two position on the *Billboard* club chart in the U.S. (The artist performed numerous live shows in the U.S. and returned to the American music magazine's dance chart Top 20 with a single called "Check It Out" six months later.) Fancy doesn't recall that much about the making of "Chinese Eyes" some 30 years later, but says the project started off, once again, with humor. "The only thing I remember is that I was lying on the floor when Todd was playing out the story as sort of a comedy song. I remember at the time I thought it was really funny and that it was a good fit for my new 'Fancy' identity. All the other work on this song was very serious though because we were under pressure to bring in another hit after 'Slice Me Nice.' We easily sold millions of copies of those records around the world. I don't know the exact number, but in the middle of the '80s, selling records was going very well. These hits and all the success came like a flash. There was no place and time to really enjoy it. The success kept you on a rollercoaster ride. When 'Chinese Eyes' was Top 10 in Germany and charting in different countries, I was thinking of taking a short break, just to relax a bit. This was totally impossible.

"The machine was working, and I really felt the pressure from different sides of the business. But I was proud of this success, and this feeling of accomplishment I had was almost like a little medicine, a buffer against all the pressure coming from the business side. On the one side, the record company wants the next release fast, and they want it to be your next big hit. On the other side, you have to think about the team that you have working with and for you. You begin to feel like you are in a mill, going non-stop, round and round. It really can be like an assembly line feeling," the singer admits.

Anthony Monn, the producer behind the early disco hits of model and vocalist Amanda Lear ("Follow Me"), was Fancy's co-producer (working with the artist's production company, Fancy Music Ltd.) for the debut album *Get Your Kicks*. The set was released by Metronome in 1985 and featured another hit, "Get Lost Tonight." Late that year, demand for new material by the artist was high, and the next single release didn't disappoint Fancy's growing legion of international fans. "Bolero (Hold Me in Your Arms Again)," though garnering modest attention in Germany, was a monster abroad. Spain and Portugal responded to the track by sending it to the Top 10 of their countries' pop charts. The song was also a sizeable smash in Sweden and the Netherlands. "'Bolero' is very special and has many different, yet very strong elements as part of its magic," the artist observes. "I think the 'chorus-lift' is 20 percent of what made it a hit; the deep voice I used to whisper the lyrical command to play me the bolero is 30 percent, and the very folklore-based melody-riff is 50 percent. Combined, I believe these elements gave the song its hit power."

Following this success, Fancy's *Contact* LP yielded more club and radio successes with "Lady of Ice" and the hard-edged "Latin Fire." Once again, Fancy co-produced the set with Anthony Monn. The formula of heavy beats, catchy, offbeat English lyrical hooks and Fancy's distinctive vocal delivery proved to be a winning formula. As the new year began, the artist became well-known as an international hit-maker, and he fashioned for himself a rather inscrutable identity for live performances, videos and TV. With dark glasses and austere, yet hip, uniform-style fashions, Fancy projected a rather aloof and mysterious appearance standing among flashing lasers and lighted dance floors. "I wanted to customize my artist name visually, and so I had a lot of costumes made and created a masquerade visage for my face. I was always a very private person. I was always kept hidden behind makeup and costumes," he admits.

The *Flames of Love* LP was developed and released in 1988, with Fancy taking more control of the creative process and producing several tracks (Monn handled the others). The title track was produced by Fancy at the Weryton Studios in Munich, and keyboardswere programmed by Alfons Weindorf, co-author of the song. "I think the reason the song 'Flames of Love' was such a success," Fancy conjectures, "was because the chorus became like an anthem. Combined with the drive of the disco-fox melody and my vocal performance, I believe the song just had a timeless feel that many people from many different regions could relate to. In Hong Kong, an artist did a cover version of the song in the Cantonese language. When you have your song covered in another country's native language, you know you've really achieved an international hit."

Fancy's production team expanded to include the writing skills of Alfons Weindorf and Sabrina Lorenz. "Since Alfons was already in the same studio working with singer Grant Miller (a protégé of mine, who had scored well in the clubs with 'Doctor for My Heart'), we were able to collaborate on 'Flames of Love.' Alfons is the younger brother of Hermann Weindorf, who worked with me on the playback of my songs 'Check It Out' and 'Come Inside,' recorded at Arco. Sabrina is a good friend of mine. She came out of drama school, acted in several films and then discovered she preferred to write lyrics. In the words my writers used, there's always plenty of beautiful poetry to be found. The time I spent working with both of these people was always very cheerful and creative," says the artist.

"Fools Cry" sent the singer back into Germany, Spain and Finland's Top 20. Fancy also took the then unusual step of remixing the track as a separate 12-inch maxi-single release, which kept the song in heavy rotation for additional months. The composition was the result of a teaming between Fancy and writers Charlie Glass and Sabrina Lorenz. Says Teiges, "Charlie, at that time, was a very young and creative musician. He played me a raw demo and half-melody of 'Fools Cry' without any text. I was thrilled by the melody part he had already developed, which he created in his small home studio. At Jupiter Studios in Munich, we then produced the title in its fully finished version. I was not satisfied with my singing, as usual, and I made infinite overdubs. A man named Klaus was the manager of the studio (we called him 'Cerberus Hellhound' because he was always very naughty), and he said to me, 'Fancy, you gotta have faith that you know how to make a hit after singing and mixing for so long!' Well, he was right. And 'Fools Cry' turned out to be a very big success!"

Reflecting on his huge popularity, the artist remembers, "I was backstage at an 8,000-person concert venue and needed to use the restroom. Unfortunately, the facility for the artists was out of order, so I had to be taken to the nearby ground floor public men's bathroom. Police and special guards unlocked the toilet and secured the area for me. On the way there, I felt like I was on the red carpet running to a premiere. I thanked the chief of security, and he said, 'We had to do the same thing for the Pope!' That's when I really knew I had reached a very significant level of fame," he laughs.

Stardom came with its share of rewards and problems, according to the artist. "There have always been small and big challenges in my career and also in my private life. Success can be lonely and difficult at times. For example, I had to quickly learn that I couldn't have a normal phone number. I could also tell you endless stories of stalking. There were times I felt seriously threatened, and these problems could possibly manifest themselves at any time. But there was always a counterweight to all that negativity. I have been blessed to have the affection and enthusiasm of many fans over the years, which is a rare and wonderful gift."

The 1990s saw many changes in the music industry, and the powerful influence of American hip-hop began to keenly affect the sounds coming out of Europe. Fancy gave Metronome Records one final LP, *All My Loving* in 1989, and one more single, "When Guardian Angels Cry," a lush composition that harkened back to the rich tapestries of his original hits. He emerged in the new decade with a somewhat updated style. The signature Fancy sound remained intact, but the element of rap was added to the mix. The artist signed to Germany's ZYX Records and released the album *Six—Deep in My Heart*, which contained updated versions of his hits. Steve D5 (also known as Stephen Aldo Dockery) handled the rhymes on the hip-house singles "Fools Cry Rap" and "When Guardian Angels…. Rap," which billed Fancy as Grandmaster Tess. Fancy had no fear of blending hip-hop vocals into his dance records. "Steve D5 was from Seattle, and at the time, he lived in our studio-home," the singer says. "He added those refined rap-lyrics to my hits, and I was very excited. We built the full LP around that. Steve's rap verses were the starting point, and then my chorus was added. When everything was finished, I presented the product to Metronome Records. Although they were very interested, they had new staff handling their products. They were strangers to me, and I was uncomfortable with this. Instead, I took the project to ZYX Records, and I still work with this company today!"

Though Fancy's endeavors in rap-dance met with mixed reviews, the artist continued to release numerous LPs and tracks for a wide variety of record labels during the '90s. The decade culminated with the release of "Slice Me Nice '98" and a hit mix medley sponsored by the popular Fetenhits brand, a single that returned the artist to Germany's Top 20. Two LP's released at the same time, *Best of Fancy* and *Hit Party*, reached the Top 20 of the Media-Control charts. Later, via Universal Germany, the artist released an album containing newly recorded versions of his hits and dance music standards sung in the German language (*Die Hits auf Deutsch*). The well-received set *Forever Magic* (released initially in Russia, Kazakhstan and the Baltics) came out in 2008. Early in 2015 he released the single "Follow Me (Have a Celebration Mix)," lifted off his 30th anniversary album, *Shock And Show*. Throughout, Fancy's fan base has remained sizeable and loyal, and he contends he is the German pop solo artist with the greatest number of worldwide concert events to date. The year 2016 saw the release of the single "Stronger Together" with singer Nea! on ZYX Records.

The artist says his personal goals, interests and priorities continue to change and evolve. "Life and the spirit of the times change a person," he says softly. "So one's wants and needs change over the course of life, too. Today, my needs and goals are different, and I adapt to them. For example, I support a territory that protects Siberian tigers." Fancy also has a great love of art, and he is a skilled and accomplished painter. He's been taking brush to canvass for years, expressing himself with unusual, abstract and expressionistic visions that reflect his depth. His exploration of art and music are among the many facets of a man whose philosophy today centers around finding balance, staying engaged and enjoying his freedom. He says, "I think it keeps me fit in the head and body when I am with young people or young-minded people, whether socially or at work. I am a bit relieved that I am not facing the world today as a newcomer. The times we live in now are very different, and it has become much more complicated to build a career."

Fancy, who cites the *Flames of Love* LP, "A Voice in the Dark," "I Love You" (from the *Forever Magic* album) and "Fools Cry Rap" as among his personal favorite recordings, is proud of his contributions but reluctant to acknowledge the breadth of his musical estate. Says the artist, "There is still a lot to do."

Harriette Weels
MaiTai
"History" (1984)
Netherlands

If you walked into the busy Virgin Megastore housed on Oxford Street in London during the summer of 1985, you stood an excellent chance of hearing the pounding beats and powerful harmonies of the exotic female trio known as MaiTai (alternately spelled as Mai Tai and Mai-Tai over the years) blasting from the record retailer's audio system. Originally comprised of Carolien de Windt, Mildred Douglas and Harriette (Jetty) Weels, the group's most popular hit single, "History," raced up the British charts that year and became a smash throughout Europe. The track was also a significant hit on the American dance survey. Their success brought worldwide attention to the Netherlands, a country that was a hotbed of energized pop and dance music ingenuity at the time and the base where the ladies of MaiTai forged their careers. Harriette speaks of Holland with great affection, and though her journey has had its share of challenging setbacks, she warmly remembers her experience in one Europe's most popular female ensembles.

"I was very interested in sports when I was young," Harriette cheerfully recalls. "I was participating in a lot of running and jumping events, and that was my thing. In high school, a teacher pointed out to me that I had talent in music. Later, I met John Seine, owner of the Europop Booking Agency, and Eric Boom, who had been a guitarist with the group The Lords. They encouraged me to join the Dutch soul band The Free in the late '60s. The Free had a few hits in those days and were a supporting act for Aretha Franklin. I also did some solo recording work under the name Jetty Weels and jammed in some bands for a while. John later introduced me to the funk group American Gypsy. My best friend Mildred Douglas was dating a member of American Gypsy and was in the band Rockaway Boulevard, a group I also sang with. My friend Carolien de Windt was also doing some singing work.

"In this tight, creative Dutch community, we were all connected with each other. Many musicians and artists were working at clubs like The Citadel in Holland, and you'd find Rockaway Boulevard and American Gypsy often playing their music there. I eventually got a gig with another band called Street Life. The guitar player of the group was ill one night, and a gentleman named Jochem Fluitsma came in to take his place. We met, and he really liked my voice. He told me he had a small studio and said he would get in touch with me to do some work.

Left: **Performing as MaiTai, (left to right) Carolien de Windt, Mildred Douglas and Harriette Weels burned up the British charts in 1985 with the smash hit "History."** *Right:* **The MaiTai line-up is today comprised of (left to right) Harriette, Eve Luhukay and Carolien.**

"Well, I didn't hear from him," she continues, "and so about six months later, I started singing Dutch songs with yet another group called Braak. We were booked to do a television show, and there at the studio I once again met Jochem, who was playing guitar for a Dutch singer on the show. We got to talking again after the show, and we discovered we lived very close to each other. He said he was going to call me to do some work together—for sure this time. Carolien had been working with singer Precious Wilson at this point, and Mildred was working with an artist and musician in Holland named Daniel Sahuleka. I bumped into Carolien, and she asked me to think of her if any singing gigs came up. The next day, my phone rang, and it was Jochem asking me if I could do some backing vocals that night for an artist he was working with. He told me to bring a singer with me if I knew of anyone. Of course, I phoned Carolien, and we did the session. Jochem was very impressed with us and said, 'I think I'm going to write a song for you girls!' Within a day, he phoned me to say the song was ready!" the singer says, smiling brightly.

"Carolien and I went to the studio and met with Eric van Tijn, a producer, and Jochem. They asked us if we knew a third singer who could join us. Mildred lived close to the studio, so we phoned her and told her we needed a singer. On that same afternoon back in 1983, we recorded our first single, 'Keep on Dancin'.' By Monday morning, the producers took the tape to CNR Records in Holland and sold the single to them. Our working name was Blue Night in the studio, but the label decided that wasn't going to work. A person at the record company said he browsed through a cocktail book and saw the drink called 'mai tai.' They felt that was a good fit for us because it was a tropical drink, and we were all from the Caribbean. Well, we started getting a little airplay and did some radio interviews and singing spots. People seemed to like us because we were always happy, and we were extremely good at singing live. From there, MaiTai was launched. Working with the boys was a joy, and it was a great experience because it opened a totally new view of the world for us!"

The ladies recorded additional disco-friendly songs that became the impetus for a self-titled album released in Holland in 1984. The group's distinctively assured and soulful harmonies were a departure from the sweeter sounds of other girl groups from recent years, and van Tijn and Fluitsma's funky, infectious music was well-synched to the dance music trends popular in the clubs. Observes Harriette, "Believe it or not, sometimes we would finish recording the vocals in just one day. Twelve hours—with breaks of course. Most of the time, we got the songs in advance and were able to rehearse them at home. The typical MaiTai sound featured all three of us singing the first, second and third parts of the song, with our voices building up.

"There was an underground scene in Amsterdam, and pirate radio stations played our music a lot. One of the stations was Radio Decibel. Two of the DJs from that station, Adam Curry and Jeroen van Inkel, became part of a much bigger national station called Radio Veronica, and they played our songs. Then a popular music television show invited us to perform, and that was it—from then on, we were red hot in Holland. We recorded some great songs, like 'What Goes On' and 'Am I Losing You Forever,' and we were appearing on a lot of shows. Still, despite the momentum we had, for some reason it was very hard to reach the top of the charts in Holland.

We did a tour in 1985 in Suriname, which is a mostly Dutch-speaking country on the northeastern coast of South America where Mildred and I were born (Carolien was born in Curaçao). On the last day of our tour there, we received a telex (that was how we got long distance communications back then) that something big was starting to happen for us in England. We were told that when we got to the airport in Amsterdam, we would be going straight on to London."

MaiTai jumped the all-important British hurdle when one of their records started to create a buzz in England. "Our newest recording, 'History,' apparently had broken out of the underground clubs, and Richard Branson of Virgin Records heard us and liked us a lot. He signed the group to his record label. By the time we arrived in London, the song had jumped from something like 48 on the UK pop chart to number 16. Everybody thought we were from the States. We were proud that everyone thought we were American, but we really wanted everyone to know we were from Holland, just a one-hour flight away. 'History' was huge in Britain, but again, oddly, not as big a hit in our homeland," she says, still seemingly perplexed by the fact.

However, "History," with its lyrical testament to the defiant acceptance of lost love, rang true with music fans throughout the rest of Europe and resounded with equal strength on American dance floors. It was a Top 10 hit in the UK and several other countries, scored a Top 20 position in Germany and reached the Top 30 in Switzerland. Weels examines the song's far-reaching appeal. "In my early days as a singer, I was very shy. I was sort of living in a cocoon in a way. This is *not* true any more," she laughs. "If you listen to the music of MaiTai, I played a very strong role in the harmonies. But I didn't do a lot of solos or lead vocals. I let the other girls take the lead, and I was fine with that. But when I was introduced to the song 'History,' I thought to myself, 'This is good. I think I need to sing the lead on this. I can do it!' I sang it, and somehow it really seemed to fit my voice. When it was finished, everyone seemed to like the way I handled it, and they seemed to really enjoy hearing me in the spotlight. I was extremely happy that it became MaiTai's biggest hit ever, all over Europe. I think the reason it was such a smash was because our vocals were strong, the message was cool and people liked our style on it. I also think it was the guitar licks. The song sounded a bit like something Nile Rodgers would have done with Chic."

Irma Koningferander (who passed away early in 2014) and Lydia Weltevreden, former owners of the famous Adirly Dance Center in Amsterdam, orchestrated MaiTai's onstage moves. "We had great choreography, which I think added to our appeal in live performances and on television," the singer adds. "You could meet all kinds of artists at Adirly, and half of Holland's show business stars went there to learn their dance moves!"

The hot streak continued as Mai Tai enjoyed more international success, notably with the racy "Female Intuition" in 1986 (another funk-fused hit favoring the style of "History"), with lead vocals by Mildred. The pop-flavored jam "Body and Soul" also scored well, cementing the group as a formidable act of the period. Harriette believes the era gave talent from the Netherlands a great opportunity to shine. "I never felt I had to be in Germany or England to do music—I felt Holland was an exciting place to be in the industry in its own right. One way or another, the European disco and dance music scene was influenced by the Netherlands. We had a very distinct sound when you think of the music of Vanessa ('Upside Down'), the Dolly Dots ('She's a Liar'), and even the sounds created by our producers, Eric and Jochem. I can hear the influence of our producers in many of the songs that came from other Dutch artists, and I think many people started to realize there was something really good happening in Holland. Our artists had a fresh and unique quality, and if Mai Tai hadn't hit the scene so big, I think another Dutch group surely would have."

Weels says the excitement that punctuated this period of her career was extraordinary. "I'd have to say the highlight of our success for me was performing on *Top of the Pops* in the UK," she says enthusiastically. "It was such a *big* show to be seen on, and it was the type of event that made you realize you had reached the big time. We also did *Soul Train* in the U.S. This sort of thing rarely ever happened to Dutch singers. There was 'Venus' by Shocking Blue and the Stars on 45—and Golden Earring had some hits—but there were very few Dutch artists who were known worldwide. I felt like we opened a few doors. We once did a gig for Johan Martin Schröder of Martinair. He organized a huge celebration for the Dutch Royal Family, and he chose MaiTai to perform. Everybody was there, and it was extremely impressive. We enjoyed so many big and wonderful events in so many different countries. I was incredibly blessed to visit places that I would never have been to if I had been, say, a secretary in an office. And I knew that. I'm being very honest—it meant a lot to me."

In the years that followed their breakout success, MaiTai enjoyed continued popularity. Their music remained in-demand in Europe's biggest clubs, and the group even managed to place highly respectable positions on the charts of their homeland (with songs like the upbeat "Turn Your Love Around" and "Bet That's What You Say"). The group's third album, *Cool Is the Rule*, was issued in 1987, but the project was less impactful than previous efforts. A greatest hits collection followed. By the end of the decade and following a financial setback similar to those experienced by many artists of the era, Weels says it was time for the members of MaiTai to look for a new direction.

"Before all the success of MaiTai," she insists, "the other ladies and I were all very close. Because of our backgrounds in Suriname and the Caribbean and the small community we were part of in Holland, I think we had a bond. We really felt like sisters in our souls—and we still do. We never had a single negative statement printed about our relationship, and we never had a scandal in the media. However, we did have some problems during our time together, but they had *nothing* to do with our friendship. We were doing really well; we were getting pretty famous and singing everywhere. But we weren't paying close enough attention to things like watching over our finances, keeping our international presence on track, and having a good lawyer. Our attention was completely focused on performing. Our Dutch manager often kept us in Holland, where he could quickly earn his commissions. As a result, we lost many opportunities to perform in countries like the United States, where there was rising demand for us. I think we might have been able to build an even bigger fan base had we been able to do that.

"We also had a British manager, who handled a great deal of money for us that was part of our Virgin Records deal. We had no issue with the Virgin deal—Virgin was completely upfront with their end. We were paid some advance money based on the Virgin-CNR agreement, but a significant amount of the remaining money from the arrangement that was due us (a very large sum) disappeared under his watch—and then he filed for bankruptcy. When we realized what had happened, we obtained an attorney through CNR and were advised *not* to sue him because it would supposedly take too long to ever collect. Using a record label attorney was clearly another mistake we made. They made it seem like it was impossible for us to collect what was rightfully ours. I guess I'm over it now, and I think Carolien and Mildred are too. It happened to a lot of people back then. It was kind of like a disease in the music industry."

Harriette pauses a moment, clearly agitated by the memory. "When it happened, we never came out about it," she admits. "It wasn't until years later that we began to tell a few people. I remember friends asking me why I was still working so hard and wondering how come I didn't live in a big villa with a swimming pool, after being so successful in the '80s. I would say, 'Our blood, sweat and tears are filling the pools of our former managers. They are the ones with the pools. You know—fortunately, I am a very positive person, and I think if I hadn't had that type of personality, I don't think I ever would have survived some of the difficulties of life—like those deceptions.

"We didn't split at the end of the '80s because of any argument," Weels says of the group's break-up at the time. "No way. Mildred wanted to go her own way and see how it felt to be a solo singer. Most of the time, when people in music groups have an argument, it's because of nothing—really small, unimportant things. I've come to realize that life is so short—I know everyone says that, but it's true. In a split second, anything can change or perhaps even be fatal. This is life. Of course, we had our differences, but I think it's more important to be happy and peaceful, and that's what we always tried to project. MaiTai never really stopped; we have been performing throughout every decade. The group is currently comprised of Carolien and I, as Mildred doesn't sing any more. She's very happy as a painter now. Eve Luhukay (also known as Eve L'Kay) also sings with us today. We are rebuilding ourselves, and I think we may even have more success in the future than we had in the '80s. We have appeared with U.S. R&B singer Karyn White and recently released the singles called 'Baby I Want You Back' and 'One Nite Man,' including some very cool remixes, which have done very well. The music industry today is a very hard business—personally, I think it's a thousand times harder now than it was in the '80s. But we are working hard, and the feedback we are getting today is very positive. I can tell you I feel very optimistic about our future, our rebirth.

"I'm never bored singing our hits today," assures Harriette. "I'm grateful and happy that I am still on the stage, doing my thing and making people happy. Isn't that great? I love when I meet young people who know the songs of MaiTai because they have heard the albums that their parents still own. That just fills me with happiness. I am grateful for every second I wake up and can enjoy the life I have. On stage, I am working at full speed, and it is all from my heart. I think MaiTai will be remembered for a long time. We weren't as big as ABBA or Michael Jackson, but I think we made some great music that people will be listening to far into the future. I guess you could say, 'History' made history!"

Appendix: The Record Shop— Noteworthy Tracks

The following is a small sampling of some noteworthy '80s dance-pop tracks by artists who found success in Europe and Britain and are not profiled elsewhere in this book. Some are well-known classics, some are a bit more obscure, and some may have been completely missed by aficionados when these recordings first hit music store shelves decades ago. However, all are significant products of the era by important artists who contributed great energy, excitement and a lot of fun to the period.

ABBA "Super Trouper"/"Lay All Your Love on Me"/"On and On and On"/"When All Is Said and Done"/"The Visitors"
Adele Bertei "Build Me a Bridge"/"When It's Over"
A-ha "Take on Me"
Amanda Lear "Diamonds"/"Hollywood Is Just a Dream When You're Seventeen"/"Red Tape"/"Darkness and Light"/"Love Your Body"/"No Regrets"/"Tam-Tam"/"Stato d'Allarme"/"Assassino"/"No Credit Card"/"Les Femmes (She Wolf)"/"Wild Thing"/"Ragazzino"/"Ripassi Domani"
Amazulu "Too Good to Be Forgotten"
Andrea "I'm a Lover"
Andrea Jürgens "Japanese Boy"/"Mama Lorraine"/"Playa Blanca"
Aneka "Japanese Boy"/"Little Lady"
Angie St. John "Hot Nights in Ibiza"/"Letter from My Heart"
Les Avions "Nuit Sauvage"
Azul y Negro "La Noche"/"The Night"/"Me Estoy Volviendo Loco"
Baby's Gang "Challenger"
Bad Boys Blue "You're a Woman"/"Pretty Young Girl"/"I Wanna Hear Your Heartbeat (Sunday Girl)"/"Kiss You All Over, Baby"/"Love Really Hurts Without You"/"A World Without You (Michelle)"/"Lady in Black"/"A Train to Nowhere"
Baltimora "Tarzan Boy"/"Woody Boogie"/"Living in the Background"
Bananarama "Cruel Summer"/"Robert DeNiro's Waiting"/"Venus"/"I Heard a Rumour"/"Love in the First Degree"
B.B. Band "All Night Long"
Bee Gees "E*S*P"/"You Win Again"
Bel Canto "Dreaming Girl"
The Belle Stars "Iko Iko"/"Sign of the Times"
Belouis Some "Some People"/"Imagination"/"Target Practice"/"Animal Magic"
Bill Withers "Lovely Day" (Ben Liebrand Sunshine Mix 1988)
Bizzy & Co. "Take a Chance"
Black Box "Ride on Time"
Blancmange "Don't Tell Me"/"Living on the Ceiling"/"Blind Vision"
Blind Date "Your Heart Keeps Burning"/"How Did You Get to Me"/"Hit the Road Jack"
Blue System "My Bed Is Too Big"/"Under My Skin"/"Sorry Little Sarah"/"Magic Symphony"/"Love Me on the Rocks"/"Love Suite" (Remix '89)
Bomb the Bass "Beat Dis"

Bonnie Bianco "Stay" (with Pierre Cosso)/"It's Goodbye"/"The Heart Is a Lonely Hunter"/"When the Price Is Your Love"

Boris Gardner "I Want to Wake Up with You"

Boy George "Everything I Own"

Brian Ice "Talking to the Night"/"Tokyo"/"Night Girl"

Bronski Beat "Smalltown Boy"/"Why?"/"Hit That Perfect Beat"

Brother Beyond "The Harder I Try"/"He Ain't No Competition"

Bruce & Bongo "Geil"

Buzy "Body Physical"/"Baby Boum"

Carlos Pérez "Poco a Poco"

Carol Kane "I Don't Believe"

Carrara "Shine on Dance"/"Disco King"/"Welcome to the Sunshine"/"S.O.S. Bandito"

The Catch "25 Years"

C.C. Catch "Strangers by Night"/"I Can Lose My Heart Tonight"/"You Shot a Hole in My Soul"/"Heartbreak Hotel"/"Heaven and Hell"/"V.I.P. (They're Callin' Me Tonight)"/"Nothing But a Heartache"/"Cause You Are Young"/"House of Mystic Lights"/"Soul Survivor"/"Good Guys Only Win In Movies"/"Backseat of Your Cadillac"/"Are You Man Enough"

Charlene Tilton "C'est la Vie"

Christophe Jenac "Nous N'Avons Pas Choii Ce Monde"

Ciao Fellini "Noche a Bahia"/"Rockaliente"

The Clash "This Is Radio Clash"/"Rock The Casbah"

Claudia Mori "Non Succederà Più"

Club House "Do It Again (Billie Jean)"/"Superstition Medley with Good Times"

Cognac "Don't Bother to Knock"

Cora "Amsterdam"

Curtie And The Boom Box "Let's Talk It Over in the Ladies' Room"/"Shocking"/"Black Kisses (Never Make You Blue)"

David Lyme "Bambina"/"Let's Go to Sitges"/"Bye, Bye Mi Amor"/"I Don't Wanna Lose You"/"Playboy"

Debut De Soiree "La Vie La Nuit"/"Nuit de Folie"

Divine "You Think You're a Man"/"Walk Like a Man"/"I'm So Beautiful"/"Hard Magic"/"Hey You!"

Dolly Dots "P.S."/"Do Wah Diddy Diddy"/"Money Lover (Bite the Dust)"/"She's a Liar"/"Love Me Just a Little Bit More (Totally Hooked on You)"/"Trick of the Eye"/"What a Night"

Eddy Grant "Electric Avenue"/"Gimme Hope Jo'anna"

Eddy Huntington "U.S.S.R."/"Up & Down"/"Meet My Friend"/"Physical Attraction"

Edelweiss "Bring Me Edelweiss"/"I Can't Get No.... Edelweiss"

Eighth Wonder "I'm Not Scared"/"Cross My Heart"

Elsa "T'en va pas"/"Mon cadeau"/"Jour de neige"/"Jamais nous"/"Quelque chose dans mon coeur"

Engelbert Humperdinck "The Spanish Night Is Over"/"Torero"/"L'Amour"/"Sometimes"/"Chains of Love"/"It Doesn't Have to Be"/"A Little Respect"/"Drama!"/"Stop!"/"Radio Dancing"

Erasure "Oh L'Amour"/"Sometimes"/"Chains of Love"/"It Doesn't Have to Be"/"A Little Respect"/"Drama!"/"Stop!"

Eros Ramazzotti "Terra Promessa"/"Ma Che Bello Questo Amore"

Eurythmics "Sweet Dreams"/"Sexcrime (Nineteen Eighty Four)"/"Here Comes the Rain Again"/"I Need a Man"/"Beethoven"

Fake "Brick"/"Frogs in Spain"

Falco "Der Kommissar"/"Maschine Brennt"/"Junge Roemer"/"Vienna Calling"/"The Sound of Musik"

Five Star "System Addict"/"All Fall Down"/"Love Take Over"/"Let Me Be the One"/"Can't Wait Another Minute"/"Rain or Shine"

Finzy Kontini "Cha Cha Cha"/"O La La"/"Mister Gringo"

A Flock of Seagulls "I Ran"/"Space Age Love Song"

France Gall "Babacar"/"Ella elle L'a"

Francesco Napoli "Stai con Me"/"Ma Quale Idea"/"Balla.... Balla!"/"Balla.... Balla Volume 2"/"Piano, Piano"/"Mondo Magico"

Frankie Goes to Hollywood "Relax"/"Welcome to the Pleasure Dome"/"Two Tribes"

Fun Fun "Happy Station"/"Colour My Love"/"Give Me Your Love"/"Could This Be Love"/"Living In Japan"/"Baila Bolero"/"Give Me Love"

Gianna Nannini "Hey Bionda"/"I Maschi"

Gipsy Kings "Bamboleo"

Gold "Capitaine Abandonne"

Gloria Gaynor "My Love Is Music"/"Don't You Dare Call It Love"/"Be Soft with Me Tonight"

Goombay Dance Band "Sun of Jamaica"

Guesch Patti "Etienne"/"Let Be Must the Queen"/"Cul Cul Clan"

Guillermo Marchena "My Love Is a Tango"/"Signs of Time"/"Time for Lovers"

Hannes Kröger "Der Blonde Hans"/"Es Wird

The Record Shop

Nacht auf St. Pauli—Der Blonde Hans Part II"
Haysi Fantayzee "John Wayne Is Big Leggy"/"Shiny Shiny"
Haywoode "I Can't Let You Go"/"Roses"/"Getting Closer"
Heather Parisi "Cicale"/"Ciao, Ciao"/"Crilù"
Heaven 17 "Play to Win"/"(We Don't Need This) Fascist Groove Thang"/"Penthouse and Pavement"
Hithouse "Jack to the Sound of the Underground"
Hong Kong Syndikat "Too Much"/"Concret + Clay"/"No More Sorrow"
Hot Cold "Love Is Like a Game"
Images "Corps a Corps"/"Quand la Musique Tourne"/"Love Emotion"/"Les Démons De Minuit/La Coeur en Exil"
Italian Boys "Forever Lovers"/"Midnight Girl"
Ivan "Fotonovela"/"Baila"
ixi "Der Knutschfleck"
Jakie Quartz "Vivre Ailleurs"/"À la vie à l'amour"/"Emotion"
Jason Donovan "Too Many Broken Hearts"/"Nothing Can Divide Us"
Jayne Collins "Madonna's Eyes"
Jessica "Like a Burning Star"
Jive Bunny & The Mastermixers "Swing the Mood"
José Hoebee "I Will Follow Him"
Joy "Touch by Touch"
Judy Cheeks "I Still Love You"/"Just Another Lie"
Jules Tropicana "Come On"/"Jane Remembers"/"Welcome"
Julie Pietri "Éve Lève Toi"
Kano "Queen of Witches"/"It's a War"/"Another Life"/"Carry On" (with Sahara)
Ken Laszlo "Hey Hey Guy"/"Don't Cry"/"Tonight"/"Glasses Man"/"1.2.3.4.5.6.7.8"
Klein & M.B.O. "Dirty Talk"/"Keep in Touch"/"The MBO Theme"
Koto "Jabdah"/"Dragon's Legend"/"Chinese Revenge"/"Visitors"
Kristian Conde "Dolce Vita"
Kylie Minogue "Locomotion"/"I Should Be So Lucky"/"Je ne sais pas pourquoi"/"Got to Be Certain"/"Wouldn't Change a Thing"/"Never Too Late"
Lady Lily "Patrik Pacard"/"Alice in Wonderland"/"Non e Vero"/"Cash Machine"
Laid Back "Sunshine Reggae"/"White Horse"/"High Society Girl"/"Baker Man"

La Compagnie Créole "A.I.É. (Amoun'La)"
Latin Lover "Casanova Action"
Lee Marrow "Sayonara"/"Shanghai"
Leinemann "Mein Tuut Tuut"
Lian Ross "Fantasy"/"Saturday Night"/"It's Up to You"/"Neverending Love"/"Oh Won't You Tell Me"/Do You Wanna Funk"/"Say Say Say"
Limahl "The NeverEnding Story"
Lio "Sage comme une image"/"Les Brunes comptent pas pour des prunes"/"Fallait pas commencer"/"Je casse tout ce que je touche"
Lova Moor "Et je danse"
Lucia "La Isla Bonita"
Lune de Miel "Paradise Mi Amor"/"Feeling of the Night"

Lian Ross (aka Josephine Hiebel) of "Fantasy" (1985) fame says, "We started to produce the song in 1984, but it had taken us over one year to finish this track because [producer Luis Luis Rodriguez of Modern Talking fame, using the name of Bobby To] was never satisfied with the mix. So he did another and another and another, until he was finally happy" (photography by Humphrey van Esch, courtesy Lian Ross/Krystian Faarben).

Man 2 Man Meets Man Parrish "Male Stripper"
Mandy (Smith) "I Just Can't Wait"/"Victim Of Pleasure"/"Positive Reaction"/"Boys and Girls"
Manuel de Leo "Let's Go Tango"/"Hasta la Vista"/"Never Forever Away"
Mari Wilson "Wonderful [Wonderful to Be With]"/"Just What I Always Wanted"/"Beat the Beat"/"Let's Make This Last"
Marianne Rosenberg "Er Gehört Zu Mir" (Remake '88)/"I Need Your Love Tonight"/"Ich Denk an Dich"
Markus "Ich Will Spaß"
M/A/R/R/S "Pump Up the Volume"
Martinelli "Cenerentola"/"Voice (In the Night)"
Masquerade "Guardian Angel"
Matia Bazar "Ti Sento"/"Noi"
Max Him "Lady Fantasy"/"Danger-Danger"/"Japanese Girl"/"Melanie"/"Just a Love Affair"
M.C. Miker "G" & Deejay Sven "Celebration Rap"/"Holiday Rap"/"And the Bite Goes On"
MC2 "Xtasy"
Mel & Kim "Showing Out"/"F.L.M."/"That's the Way It Is"/"Respectable"
Melissa "We All Live Together–So Bad"
Mica Paris "My One Temptation"
Michael Cretu "Samurai (Did You Ever Dream)"/"Gambit"/"Carte Blanche"
Mike Francis "Survivor"/"Let Me In"/"Times Out of Time"/"Lovely Day"/"Suddenly Back to Me"/"Dreams of a Lifetime"/"Dusty Road"/"Still I'm Runnin' Back to You"
Mike Mareen "Love Spy"/"Cecilia"/"Agent of Liberty"
Miko Mission "How Old Are You?"/"The World Is You"/"Two for Love"
Mory Kante "Yé Ké Yé Ké"
Moti Special "Cold Days Hot Nights"
Murray Head "One Night in Bangkok"
My Mine "Hypnotic Tango"/"Zorro"
Mylène Farmer "Libertine"/"Sans contrefaçon"/"Ainsi soit je…"/"Pourvu qu'elles soient douces"/"A quoi je sers…"/"Sans logique"
Mysterious Art "Das Omen (Teil 1)"
Nada "Amore Disperato"
Nathalie "Don't Look"
New Baccara "Fantasy Boy"
Nina Hagen "New York New York"
O'Chi Brown "Whenever You Need Somebody"/"Two Hearts Beating as One"/"100% Pure Pain"
Off "Electric Salsa"/"Time Operator"
Ofra Haza "Im Nin Alu"
O.K. "Okay!"/"E-D-U-C-A-T-I-O-N"/"The Wild, Wild Western"/"1.2.3.4. Une Grande Affaire"
Opus "Live Is Life"
Orchestral Manoeuvres In The Dark "Maid of Orleans"/"Locomotion"/"Enola Gay"/"Secret"/"We Love You"
P. Lion "Happy Children"/"Dream"
P4F "P.Machinery Medley with Relax"
Paco (Ibáñez) "Amor de mis amores"
Patricia Kaas "Mademoiselle Chante Le Blues"
Patty Ryan "(You're) My Love (You're) My Life"/"I Don't Wanna Lose You Tonight"/"Stay with Me Tonight"/"Don't Tell Me Lies"
Paul Hardcastle "19"/"Don't Waste My Time"/"Rain Forest"
Paul King "I Know"/"Follow My Heart"
Pedro Marín "Dos Enamorados"
Pet Shop Boys "West End Girls"/"Always on My Mind"/"What Have I Done to Deserve This?"/"Left to My Own Devices"/"It's a Sin"/"Opportunities (Let's Make Lots of Money)"/"Domino Dancing"
Pete Shelley "Homosapien"/"Telephone Operator"/"Witness the Change"/"I Don't Know What It Is"
Peter Kent & Luisa Fernandez "Solo Por Ti"/"Con Esperanza"
Petula Clark "Downtown" (Peter Slaghuis Remix 1988)
Philippe Cataldo "Les Divas du Dancing"/"Ne t'en fais pas"
Pia Zadora "When the Rain Begins to Fall" (with Jermaine Jackson)/"Rock It Out"/"Let's Dance Tonight"/"Little Bit of Heaven"/"Real Love"
Pink Project "Pink Project"/"Scratchin' Superstition"/"Smoke Like a Man"/"B.Project"/"Hypnotized"
Pleasure Discipline "For Hours Now"
Precious Wilson "Cry to Me"/"I Don't Know"/"Red Light"/"Only the Strong Survive"
Princess "Say I'm Your Number One"/"In the Heat of a Passionate Moment"/"Tell Me Tomorrow"
Radiorama "Chance to Desire"/"Yeti"/"Bad Girls"
Raff "Self Control"/"Change Your Mind"/"I Don't Want to Lose You"/"Hard"/"Ti Pretendo"
Raffaella Carrà "Ballo, Ballo"/"Tele-Telefonarti"/"Amico"/"Rumore"/"Far l'amore/Fatalità"/"Cuando calienta el sol"
Raggio de Luna (Moon Ray) "Comanchero"/"Viva"

Rah Band "Clouds Across the Moon"
Rainhard Fendrich "Macho Macho"
The Real Thing "Can't Get By Without You" (The Decade Remix 1986)
Rebel MC/Double Trouble "Street Tuff"
Los Reyes "Bamboleo"
The Reynolds Girls "I'd Rather Jack"
Ricchi e Poveri "Mamma Maria"/"Made in Italy"/"Voulez Vous Danser"/"Pubblicità"/"Hasta la Vista"/"Magnifica Serata"/"Azzurro"/"Sarà Perchè Ti Amo"/"Se M'Innamoro"
Rick Astley "It Would Take a Strong Man"/"Whenever You Need Somebody"/"My Arms Keep Missing You"/"She Wants to Dance with Me"/"Together Forever"/"Take Me to Your Heart"
Rick Fellini "Welcome to Rimini"
Rob 'n' Raz featuring Leila K "Got to Get"
Rocky M "Disco Lady"/"Fly with Me to Wonderland"/"Look in My Heart"
Rondò Veneziano "La Serenissima"
Samantha Fox "Touch Me (I Want Your Body)"/"Hold on Tight"/"Do Ya Do Ya (Wanna Please Me)"/"I'm All You Need"/"I Surrender (To the Spirit of the Night)"/"I Only Wanna Be with You"/"Nothing's Gonna Stop Me Now"/"I Promise You (Get Ready)"/"Love House"/"I Wanna Have Some Fun"/"Naughty Girls (Need Love Too)"
Samantha Gilles "Let Me Feel It"/"Music Is My Thing"
Sandy Marton "OK Run" [M-Basic]/"People from Ibiza"/"Camel by Camel"/"Merry Merry Christmas and a Happy New Year"/"Exotic and Erotic"/"White Storm in the Jungle"/"Modern Lovers"/"Love Synchronicity"/"La Paloma Blanca"
Savage "Don't Cry Tonight"
S.B.B.L. "Purple Mix"
Scotch "Disco Band"/"Mirage"/"Delirio Mind"/"Take Me Up"/"Money Runner"/"Pictures"
Secret Service "Flash in the Night"/"Dancing in Madness"/"Let Us Dance Just a Little Bit More"/"Don't You Know Don't You Know"
S-Express "Theme from S-Express"/"Superfly Guy"
Sheree "Ronnie Talk to Russia"
Silent Circle "Touch in the Night"/"Stop the Rain"
Silver Pozzoli "Around My Dream"/"Step By Step"/"Chica Boom"/"Pretty Baby"
Sinitta "Feels Like the First Time"/"Cruising"/"So Macho"/"Toy Boy"/"Cross My Broken Heart"/"Hitchin' a Ride"/"Love on a Mountain Top"/"I Don't Believe in Miracles"/"Right Back Where We Started From"
16 Bit "Changing Minds"/"Where Are You?"/"Too Fast to Live"/"(Ina) Gadda-Da-Vida"
Sonia "Listen to Your Heart"/"Can't Forget You"/"You'll Never Stop Me from Loving You"
Soulsister "Like a Mountain"
Squash Gang "I Want an Illusion"/"Moving Your Hips"
The Star Sisters "Stars On 45 Presents the Star Sisters"/"He's the 1 (I Love)"/"The Duke of Dance"/"Danger"/"Are You Ready for My Love"
Stars on 45 "Stars on 45"/"Stars on 45 II"
Stephan Remmler "Keine Sterne in Athen (3–4–5 × In 1 Monat)"
Taffy "White & Black"/"Walking into the Daylight"/"I Love My Radio (Midnight Radio)"/"I Love My Radio" (U.K. Mix)/"Once More"/"Step by Step"/"If You Feel It"
Talk Talk "Talk Talk"/"Such a Shame"/"It's My Life"
Tantra "Hills of Katmandu"
Terence Trent D'Arby "Sign Your Name"/"Dance Little Sister"

Sexy English singer and model Samantha Fox scored a Top Five U.S. hit in 1986 on the *Billboard* pop chart with the provactive "Touch Me (I Want Your Body)." She is seen here during a photo shoot with Manfred Esser a little over a decade later (photography by and courtesy Manfred Esser).

Germany's The Twins, (left) Sven Dohrow and Ronny Schreinzer, as photographed at the height of their '80s fame by Manfred Esser (courtesy Manfred Esser).

The Three Degrees "Jump the Gun"/"Set Me Free"/"Gimme, Gimme, Gimme"/"This Is the House"/"The Heaven I Need"
The Twins "Face to Face—Heart to Heart"/"Ballet Dancer"/"Not the Loving Kind"/"Love in The Dark"/"Time Will Tell"
Thereza Bazzar "The Big Kiss"
Time Bandits "I'm Specialized in You"/"I'm Only Shooting Love"
Tony Esposito "Kalimba De Luna"/"Papa Chico"/"As Tu Às"
Toto (Total) Coelo "I Eat Cannibals"/"Dracula's Tango"
Tracy Spencer "Run to Me"/"Love Is Like a Game"
Trio "Da Da Da Ich Lieb Dich Nicht Du Liebst Mich Nicht Aha Aha Aha"/"Anna—Laßmichrein Laßmichraus"/"Boom Boom"
Trio Rio "New York-Rio-Tokyo"
Tullio de Piscopo "Stop Bajon (Primavera)"/"'E Fatto 'E Sorde! E? (Money Money)"/"Radio Africa"
Two of Us "Blue Night Shadow"

Valerie Dore "The Night"/"Get Closer"/"It's So Easy"/"Lancelot"/"King Arthur"
Vanessa "Be My Lady"
Vanessa "Upside Down (Dizzy Does It Make Me)"/"Dynamite"/"Cheerio"/"In the Heat of the Night"
Vanilla "Paradise Mi Amor"/"In the Year 2525"
Various Artists "Italo Boot Mix"—Vol. 1–14/"Italo Dance Power Vol. 1"
Via Verdi "Diamond"/"Sometimes"
Vivien Vee "Give Me a Break" (Ben Liebrand Remixes 1988)/"Higher"/"Pick Up"/"Let Him Go"/"Americano"/"Eve of Destruction"/"Heartbeat""/Everybody (Respect to Me)"/"Cross My Heart"
Wang Chung "Dance Hall Days"
Wax "Bridge to Your Heart"/"American English"
Wee Papa Girl Rappers "Wee Rule"
William Pitt "City Lights"/"Funny Girl"
Yazoo/Yaz "Situation"/"Too Pieces"/"Don't Go"/"Nobody's Diary"
Yello "Bostich"/"I Love You"/"You Gotta Say Yes to Another Excess"/"Oh Yeah"/"The Race"

Index

ABBA 4, 19, 45, 223, 225
Anders, Thomas 4, 9–17, 93, 177
Ariola Records (Germany) 4, 105, 111, 203, 212
ARS Records 21
Astley, Rick 32, 36, 38, 66, 72, 82, 85, 87, 88, 229
Les Avions 189, 225

Baby Records 98–100, 122, 125, 126
Bad Boys Blue 47, 213, 225
Bananarama 37, 82, 85, 86, 225
Barrett, Marcia 129
The Beatmasters 60
Berlin, Irving 148, 150, 156
Bianco, Bonnie 4, 177, 226
Big Fun 36–41
Black Box 21, 198, 225, 226
Blue System 13, 50, 225, 226
BMG (Bertelsmann Music Group) 4, 25, 173, 181, 210, 211
Bogaert, Jo (Technotronic) 18–23
Bohlen, Dieter 9–12, 15, 50
Bolland (Rob & Ferdi Bolland) 210
Boney M. 128–133, 136
Boswell, Simon 207
Boy George (Culture Club) 28, 226
Bramble, Derek 76, 78, 79
Branigan, Laura 4, 45, 179
Branson, Richard 94, 220
Brilliant 86
Bristol, Johnny 206
Brooks, Mel 1–3, 148
Burns, Pete (Dead or Alive) 24–35, 37, 44, 72, 82, 84, 85

Canedy, Todd 213
Carrere Records 142, 146, 172
Carter, Bob 69–71
Catch, C.C. 12, 213, 226
CBS Records 10, 28, 65, 67, 175, 177, 178, 180, 182, 195, 196
Cecchetto, Claudio 100, 184, 185–187
Change 195
Chany, Philippe 116–119
Charles, Tina 88, 165, 166
Chieregato, Miki 98, 99, 101
Child, Desmond 179, 180
Christie, David 165, 166, 169

Clarke, Vince (Erasure) 38
CNR Records 219, 222
Coldcut 55–57
Colomby, Bobby 197
Copeland, Stewart 21
Cornelius, Don 107
Coulthard, Alan 132, 210
Creswick, Phil (Big Fun) 36–41
Cretu, Michael 91, 93, 94, 228
Crocker, Frankie 70, 107
Curnow, Ian 82, 83, 85, 87, 88

Dawson, Dana 145
D.D. Sound 110, 112
Dead or Alive 24–35, 37, 44, 72, 82, 84, 85
Dean, Hazell 28, 32, 42–46, 66, 84
de Piscopo, Tullio 161, 230
de Rouge, Candy 177
Desireless (Claudie Fritsch) 64–67, 167
de Walden, Christian 4
de Windt, Carolien (MaiTai) 218–219
Dion, Celine 141, 145, 179
Divine 28, 44, 82, 84, 85, 160, 214, 226
Dohrow, Sven (The Twins) 230
Dolly Dots 221, 226
Domingo, Placido 181
Douglas, Mildred (MaiTai) 218–222

EMI Records 20, 43, 47, 78, 79, 105, 142, 161
Esposito, Tony 131, 132, 230
Estus, Deon 206
Evangeli, Barry 43, 44, 84
Evans, Yasmin (Yazz) 53–63

Falco 114, 177, 210, 226
Fancy (Ric Tess Teiges) 51, 158, 161, 162, 164, 212–217
Farian, Frank 50, 128–134, 136, 137
Farrell, Bobby 129, 131, 133, 136
The Flirts 158–161, 163, 164
Fluitsma, Jochem 218, 220
Ford, Dave 87
Fox, Samantha 37, 47, 51, 82, 177, 185, 187, 189, 229
Francis, Mike 208, 210, 228

Fritsch, Claudie (Desireless) 64–67, 167
Fun Fun 192–195, 226

Gasparini, Roberto 98
Gaye, Marvin 107
Gaynor, Gloria 42, 58, 156, 158, 165–167, 226
Gazebo (Paul Mazzolini) 121–127, 142, 170, 172, 173
Gillespie, Mark (Big Fun) 36–37
Giombini, Pierluigi 122–124, 126, 142, 170–173
Giscombe, Junior (Junior) 68–75, 108
Gonzalez 105
Graham, Jaki 76–81

Hammond, Pete 66, 87, 132
Hansa Records (Hansa International, Germany) 10, 15, 129, 203, 204, 212
Harding, Phil 82–89, 185
Harrow, Den 96–102, 126
Harry, Debbie 82, 185
Hasselhoff, David 6, 189
Hirschburger, Klaus 90–95
Houston, Whitney 179
Hubert Kah 90–94
Humperdinck, Engelbert 4, 14, 226
Huntington, Eddy 100, 164, 226

Imagination 104–109
Ingram, Ashley 105, 108
Inner City 20, 37

Jackson, Michael 55, 108, 196, 223, 228
James, Rick 71
John, Elton 149, 175, 179, 180, 198
John, Jason (Big Fun) 36, 40
John, Leee (Imagination) 104–109
Johnson, Alan 2
Junior (Junior Giscombe) 68–75, 108

Kamosi, Manuela (Ya Kid K) 19, 20, 22
Kemmler, Hubert (Hubert Kah) 90–92
Kennedy, Errol 105, 108

Index

La Bionda 110–115
La Bionda, Carmelo 110–115
La Bionda, Michelangelo 110–115
Landers, Audrey 4–6
Lear, Amanda 4, 111, 112, 214, 225
Lekakis, Paul 100
Leng, Barry 203–205, 207, 210
Les Avions 189, 225
Levan, Larry 107
Levine, Ian 36, 37
Liebrand, Ben 225, 230
Loeb, Caroline 116–120
Löhr, Markus (Hubert Kah) 90
Lombardoni, Severo 97, 123, 172
Lunghini, Elsa 141, 144, 226

Madonna 22, 30, 31, 33, 95, 119, 185, 196, 198
MaiTai 218–223
Mándoki, Leslie 181
Marinello, Tony 160
Mas, Jeanne 141–143, 167
May, Simon 203, 204, 207
Mazzolini, Paul (Gazebo) 121–127, 170
MC Eric 19, 22
McDaniels, Gene 176
Medeiros, Glenn 144
Mende, Gunther 177
Mercury, Freddie 107, 162
Metronome Records 213, 214, 216
Micioni, Paul 123, 208
Milli Vanilli 21, 47, 48, 50, 53, 131, 134–140
Minogue, Kylie 36–38, 66, 72, 82, 87, 88, 227
Mitchell, Liz (Boney M.) 128–133
Modern Talking 9–17, 47, 50, 51, 93
Monn, Anthony 111, 214, 215
Morandi, Gianni 208
Morgand, Jean-Pierre 189
Moroder, Giorgio 55, 87, 111, 188, 210, 212
Morvan, Fab 48, 134–140
Musumarra, Romano 141–147, 167, 168

Naggiar, Freddy 98, 99, 122, 124, 125
Napoli, Francesco 50, 226

Ockerse, Taco (Taco) 47, 148–157

Orlando, Bobby 28, 124, 158–161, 212

Paris, Ryan (Fabio Roscioli) 123, 124, 142, 170–174
Parisi, Angela 194
Parker, David 150, 151
Pepe, Antonella 194
Pet Shop Boys 29, 39, 85, 124, 160, 228
Pignagnoli, Larry 192–195, 197
Pilatus, Rob 48, 134–139
Pozzoli, Silvio (Silver Pozzoli)) 98, 229
Princess 86
Princess Stéphanie (Grimaldi, of Monaco) 141–144, 147, 165, 167, 168
PWL (Pete Waterman Limited, PWL Empire, The Hit Factory, SAW) 36–41, 44–46, 66, 82–89, 132, 185

Raimondi, Dario 194
RCA Records (various) 10, 151, 152, 155, 173, 207–210
Ricchi E Poveri 52, 596
Righeira 110–114, 124
Rivat, Jean-Michel 167, 174, 175
Rizzo, Linda Jo 158–164
Robinson, Jack 165–169
Rodriguez, Luis 111, 227
Ross, Lian 227
Roze, Yves 144, 168
Rush, Jennifer 47, 50, 175–182

Sabrina (Sabrina Salerno) 82, 183–191
Safina, Alessandro 141, 145, 147
Salerno, Sabrina (Sabrina) 82, 183–191
Sandra (Sandra Lauer, Sandra Cretu) 16, 90–91, 93, 94
Savage (Roberto Zanetti) 164, 229
Schreinzer, Ronny (The Twins) 230
Scott, Tee 70
Seventh Avenue 36–38
Sigue Sigue Sputnik 78
Slip 213
Sony Music (various) 16, 25, 28, 30, 32, 67, 145, 181, 197, 198, 208
Soul Train 107, 221

Spagna (Ivana Spagna) 131, 187, 192–199
Stewart, Amii 74, 83, 189, 200–211
Stock Aitken Waterman (SAW, PWL) 29, 32, 36, 37, 38, 40, 42, 44, 45, 72, 73, 82, 84–88, 155, 187
Summer, Donna 4, 27, 55, 82, 87, 111, 128, 192, 210, 212
Summers, Jazz 55
Sylvester 28, 205

Taco (Taco Ockerse) 47, 148–157
Technotronic 18–23
Teiges, Ric Tess (Fancy) 51, 158, 161, 162, 164, 212–217
The Three Degrees 82, 230
Top of the Pops 5, 28, 39, 78, 96, 106, 172, 221
Trani, Marco 123
Tsiboe, Reggie (Boney M.) 132
Turatti, Roberto 98, 99, 101
The Twins 230

Ugolini, Alvaro 194

Valerie Dore 98, 162, 230
van Tijn, Eric 219–221
Vanessa 221, 230
Virgin Records (various) 91, 93, 94, 218, 220, 222

Walden, Narada Michael 206
Warner Bros. Records (WEA, various) 4, 119, 186, 213
Waterman, Pete 28, 29, 32, 37, 44–46, 66, 73, 82–89; *see also* PWL; Stock Aitken Waterman
Weels, Harriette (MaiTai) 218–223
Weindorf, Alfons 162, 215
White, Jack 4, 6, 45, 55
Wilde, Kim 72, 80
Williams, Maizie (Boney M.) 129, 131–133, 136
Wingfield, Pete 2

Yazz (Yasmin Evans) 53–63

Zandri, Stefano 98, 100
ZYX Records 161, 162, 185, 216